THE SHEEP INDUSTRY OF
TERRITORIAL NEW MEXICO

THE SHEEP INDUSTRY OF TERRITORIAL NEW MEXICO

LIVESTOCK, LAND, AND DOLLARS

Jon M. Wallace

UNIVERSITY PRESS OF COLORADO
Denver

© 2024 by University Press of Colorado

Published by University Press of Colorado
1580 North Logan Street, Suite 660
PMB 39883
Denver, Colorado 80203-1942

All rights reserved
Printed in the United States of America

 The University Press of Colorado is a proud member of the Association of University Presses.

The University Press of Colorado is a cooperative publishing enterprise supported, in part, by Adams State University, Colorado State University, Fort Lewis College, Metropolitan State University of Denver, University of Alaska Fairbanks, University of Colorado, University of Denver, University of Northern Colorado, University of Wyoming, Utah State University, and Western Colorado University.

∞ This paper meets the requirements of the ANSI/NISO Z39.48-1992 (Permanence of Paper).

ISBN: 978-1-64642-546-4 (hardcover)
ISBN: 978-1-64642-547-1 (ebook)
https://doi.org/10.5876/9781646425471

Library of Congress Cataloging-in-Publication Data

Names: Wallace, Jon M., author.
Title: The sheep industry of territorial New Mexico : livestock, land, and dollars / Jon M. Wallace.
Description: Denver : University Press of Colorado, [2023] | Includes bibliographical references and index.
Identifiers: LCCN 2023033217 (print) | LCCN 2023033218 (ebook) | ISBN 9781646425464 (hardcover) | ISBN 9781646425471 (ebook)
Subjects: LCSH: Sheep industry—New Mexico—History. | Sheep ranches—New Mexico—History. | Sheep ranchers—New Mexico—History. | Rangelands—New Mexico—History. | Range management—New Mexico—History.
Classification: LCC HD9436.U5 W355 2023 (print) | LCC HD9436.U5 (ebook) | DDC 338.1/76309789—dc23/eng/20230911
LC record available at https://lccn.loc.gov/2023033217
LC ebook record available at https://lccn.loc.gov/2023033218

Cover photo by Henry A. Schmidt, 1900–1919[?], Henry A. Schmidt Pictorial Collection, Pict 000-179-0718, Center for Southwest Research, University Libraries, University of New Mexico, Albuquerque

CONTENTS

List of Illustrations   *vii*

Preface   *ix*

1. Sheep Come to New Mexico   3

2. Sheep and the Market Economy   25

3. The Industry Matures   82

4. Frank Bond's Sheep Empire   132

5. Montague Stevens, Great Promise and Harsh Reality   153

6. Thomas Catron and Financing a Western Sheep Ranch   175

7. The End of the Open Range   204

Epilogue   224

Notes   229

Bibliography   269

Index   283

ILLUSTRATIONS

FIGURES

1.1. Population of New Mexico   10
1.2. New Mexico livestock populations   11
2.1. New Mexico wool production   48
2.2. Total value of woolen and cotton manufactures   52
2.3. Annual earnings for live sheep and wool, cattle, and farm crops   77
3.1. Lieutenant Colonel Jose Francisco Chaves, New Mexico, 1903?   89
4.1. Sheepman Frank Bond and his son   134
6.1. United States Senator and attorney Thomas B. Catron, Santa Fe, New
    Mexico, 1915?   177
6.2. Politician and sheep rancher Solomon Luna, New Mexico, 1896?   193

TABLES

2.1. Sheep ownership, 1858 California drive   45
2.2. Wool production, fall 1899 and spring 1900   57

PREFACE

The story of sheep in territorial New Mexico is the story of how a rudimentary, if important, industry on the remote northern frontier of Mexico developed and expanded to play a role in America's industrialization. It is a story of rapid technological, organizational, and financial advances and the men who brought them about following the US annexation of the region. It is also a story of evolving and, almost certainly, improving living conditions in the territory as the sheep industry expanded to encompass innumerable families of modest means. The transformation ultimately touched many, perhaps most, New Mexican lives and helped establish the territory as a productive part of America. There was a cost, however, in widespread ecological changes in the lands brought about, in large part, by heavy grazing.

When Anglo-Americans began traveling to New Mexico over the Santa Fe Trail, the first sign of life they saw upon approaching the settlements was often a herd of sheep on a hillside, usually watched over

https://doi.org/10.5876/9781646425471.c000

x PREFACE

by a lone flock master. This was hardly surprising since sheep played an important role in village life. As *The New Mexico Blue Book* succinctly stated later in 1913, "The backbone of industrial husbandry in New Mexico for at least 200 years has been sheep raising, and it is still chief among the income producing occupations of the people."[1]

But there was more to it. Sheep growing was also a source of pride and fulfillment for many of those involved, even as the herds of domestic animals imposed an unprecedented burden on the environment. Reminiscing in the late twentieth century about his Hispanic sheep-growing community, seventy-year-old Abe (Abelicio M.) Pena, whose family had raised sheep in the San Mateo–Mount Taylor area for generations, stated, "there's something went out of our lives when we had to give up sheep [for cattle]." For the Navajos, whose lands straddle today's New Mexico–Arizona border and who had been raising sheep since the eighteenth century, the federal stock reduction program that seriously decreased their sheep and goat holdings in the 1930s was, aside from its serious economic consequences, an attack on their pastoral identity and, for some, their deepest spiritual beliefs, with which sheep had become associated.[2]

Sheep growing had indeed been a leading commercial activity, as well as an important part of village life, from the Spanish colonial period onward. A small cohort of Hispanic mercantile families, over a period of decades, built the industry and by the time of the US military occupation in 1846 were exporting their stock to Mexican markets in massive annual drives down the Camino Real. After the American annexation of New Mexico, large new markets for mutton and an entirely new market for wool opened up in the United States. Well connected, well financed Anglo merchants and growers, recently arrived in the territory, joined their Hispanic counterparts in expanding, modernizing, and adapting the sheep industry to take advantage of the new opportunities. Their numbers and influence grew steadily through the territorial years. While the human population of the territory expanded considerably, tripling at most, over the half century following the annexation, the sheep industry grew more than fortyfold, as measured

Preface   xi

by annual revenues. As a continuing mainstay of the New Mexico economy, the industry brought to the region a degree of prosperity that it might not otherwise have enjoyed while providing employment for the significant sector of the population.[3]

Any broad historical account of New Mexico must at least touch on its sheep industry, and a considerable body of work discussing various aspects of the industry is available. The existing work is fragmented and largely descriptive and, with few exceptions, reveals little about the industry's driving economic underpinnings. This void is perhaps surprising, considering not only the considerable influence of the industry on life in the territory but also its important role in the integration of New Mexico into America's expanding national economy and American life in general. The present work provides a rigorous, comprehensive account of the New Mexico sheep industry, as well as the men who built it, in the territorial period. The account will focus on the extraordinary industrial transformation, how and why it transpired as it did, incorporating its important social and ecological ramifications. Through the early decades of the territorial period, Hispanic sheepmen dominated the industry, a holdover from the Spanish-Mexican period. Their long experience raising *churro* sheep and trail driving them to distant markets served them well. However, Anglo-Americans, drawing on their financial resources, information networks, and market connections, gained dominance by the later decades of the territorial period while Hispanic sheepmen continued to fill important leadership roles.

The work will consider stock ownership, trade, financing, transportation advances, and the role of mercantile capitalism. It will also address the on-site matters of labor, grazing practices, breeding, feeding, the widespread distribution of New Mexico stock, and Navajo stock growing.

Sheep have always taken a back seat to cattle, and cowboys, in popular visions of the nineteenth-century West, and fine works dedicated to the western cattle industry and how it actually functioned are available, notably Gene M. Gressley's *Bankers and Cattlemen* and John Clay's *xii* PREFACE

classic, *My Life on the Range*. New Mexico's sheep industry prior to the Civil War is covered in John O. Baxter's fine treatment, *Las Carneradas, Sheep Trade in New Mexico, 1700–1860*. No rigorous investigative work, however, has been dedicated to New Mexico's all-important sheep industry for the duration of the territorial period when it was central to New Mexico's economy and, by extension, life in the territory. Hopefully, the general reader will find the following story of sheep in New Mexico interesting and informative and the dedicated investigators will discover useful material, broadening, if only slightly, their knowledge and understanding of New Mexico's territorial period and the nineteenth-century West.[4]

This account draws on statistical data—livestock counts, shipping records, and the like—dating in a few cases back even before the territorial period. These data may not be terribly accurate (by today's standards), unintentionally or otherwise. Throughout this work, an attempt has been made to employ seemingly reasonable data to the extent possible. Nevertheless, absolute numbers cited, individually or within data sets, but particularly pertaining to the earlier territorial years, may be questionable. They are employed to provide a degree of quantitative support for the matters under discussion in the text. More significant are the trends over time exhibited by the data. The overall trends over a period of decades can be regarded as more reliable than the individual points from which the data sets are constituted.

A few words about terminology are appropriate here. All peoples of New Mexico not American Indian, truly Spanish, or of Spanish-Indian mixed race were, and still are, commonly called *Anglos* or *Anglo-Americans* and will be identified as such in the text. The term *Hispanic* is used in the text to designate the Spanish-Indian mixed-race population of New Mexico, the predominant demographic group during the territorial period. Anglos of the territorial era usually called these people *Mexicans*, as they often called themselves, an accurate designation before the annexation but not after.

A work of this kind does not emerge from a vacuum. The author is deeply indebted to Samuel Truett for his insight, continuing support,

Preface xiii

and encouragement for this project. Durwood Ball and Jason Smith also offered welcome guidance. Clark Whitehorn provided helpful advice for preparing the work for publication. Ramona Caplin and Bryan Turo generously shared their knowledge of New Mexico history and contributed to my understanding of the territorial period. The staff of the University of New Mexico Center for Southwest Research, Albuquerque, particularly Nancy Brown-Martinez and the late Ann Massmann, were most helpful in making me aware of and providing critical primary-source material. The staff at the New Mexico State Records Center and Archives, Santa Fe, helped considerably in providing material in the state collection. Dennis Daily and the staff at the Archives and Special Collections at the New Mexico State University Library, Las Cruces, were likewise helpful in pointing me toward useful, uniquely available material. And, finally, I wish to express my debt to the late Dr. Ferenc Szasz, with whom I had encouraging discussions early on in this project.

THE SHEEP INDUSTRY OF
TERRITORIAL NEW MEXICO

1

SHEEP COME TO NEW MEXICO

The sheep industry of territorial New Mexico grew up from a foundation laid by Hispanic ranchers and merchants during Spanish and, later, Mexican sovereignty. The sheepmen followed traditional old-world husbandry practices, characterized particularly by open-range grazing. Sheep were well adapted to the land and usually provided a reliable, even essential, food source. Accounts of colonial New Mexico have attributed its survival largely or entirely to its sheep herds. In the words of Charles F. Lummis, sheep "rendered the Territory possible for three centuries . . . [and] made its customs, if not its laws." Over time, the flocks grew, surplus production developed, and sheep growing became commercialized. Sheep, along with some cattle and goats, became the principal basis for New Mexico's limited wealth and commerce until well into the territorial era. Sheepmen undertook large, months-long sheep drives south down the Camino Real to Mexican markets, which in time became part of the annual cycle of colonial life.

https://doi.org/10.5876/9781646425471.c001

4 · SHEEP COME TO NEW MEXICO

The increasing livestock count, however, began to bring about notable changes in the New Mexico environment. The influence of sheep pervaded every corner of society.[1]

THE CHURRO

From the Spanish colony's founding in the late sixteenth century until well into the territorial period, sheep growing in New Mexico was based on the *churro*. *Churros* had been the common sedentary sheep of southern Spain; their lineage extends back to Roman times. They thrived in Spain, which has a climate and natural environment similar to that of New Mexico, and they were a good choice for the northern colony. Unimpressive in appearance—*churro* means "coarse" in Spanish—they were small, modest wool producers, but easy to feed and easily managed because of their strong herding instinct. Anglos referred to them as the common "Mexican" sheep. They could forage for themselves and withstand hunger and harsh climatic conditions. Most important in the semi-arid environment of New Mexico, they were drought resistant, needing to drink from a stream or pond only every few days. They could survive the rest of the time on succulent plants and the morning dew. The ewes were good mothers, and *churro* mutton was well regarded for its good taste. The *churro's* hardiness, drought resistance, and herding instinct made it well adapted to long trail drives, so it arrived at its final destination in good condition.[2]

Churro wool production was more than adequate for the needs of the *pobladores* (settlers). Because of its low grease content, the *churro* wool could be cleaned by beating, by the wind, or by hand without a great quantity of water, often a scarce commodity. The long, coarse, straight strands of its fleece were readily spun and woven by hand into cloth for clothing. *Churro* fleece was also useful for weaving blankets and carpets, although not for fine wool applications. Until the late nineteenth century, the *churro* flourished and multiplied in New Mexico.[3]

The Navajos came to appreciate the utility of *churro* wool at an early date. Having acquired the sheep by raiding the *pobladores'* flocks, and possibly also by trade, they had become highly skilled weavers by the late eighteenth century. Writing in 1830 or 1831, mountain man and trader James O. Pattie noted that the Navajos were producing wool products markedly superior to the Hispanic output. Rightfully famous for their wool blankets and rugs, they preserved the *churro* breed and employed, and continue to employ, its fleece for those applications.[4]

THE SHEEP HERDER OF THE OPEN RANGE

While great changes came to the New Mexico sheep industry during the territorial years, the herder's life and work changed little during the entire period of open-range grazing. The herder's life during the Spanish-Mexican period and beyond was hard and dangerous. The herders generally came from the more impoverished rungs of society; in the early years many were captive Indian slaves or peones. A *pastor* had to be robust in body, since his life was, minimally, one prolonged hiking and camping trip. A skilled outdoorsman, he slept under the stars or in a small tent year around—rain, snow, high winds, or oppressive heat notwithstanding—usually trailing his herd several miles every day. He cooked himself two meals a day, at dawn and at nightfall. His small supply of provisions, a frying pan, a coffee pot and coffee, a sack of flour, some salt, a bag of red pepper, were packed on his burro. Herding was most difficult—"very, very hard," according to Abe Sena—during times of drought when the sheep had to be driven long distances to grass and water. Catron County rancher Earnesto Carrejo, who herded sheep with his father before World War II, estimated, from a long lifetime of experience, that a sheepherder's life expectancy was only forty-five to fifty years.[5]

Indian raiding parties were an ever-present danger both to the herder's sheep and to his own life, as he was often alone or in a small group, poorly armed and poorly mounted, far from any village. Occasionally villagers went out in search of a missing herder only to discover he had been murdered and his herd was under the sole care of his dogs. As late as about 1870, Juan Luna of the prominent sheep-growing family was

6   SHEEP COME TO NEW MEXICO

one of several men killed in an Indian raid on the San Clemente Land Grant. Teenaged herders were sometimes taken into captivity and, in the case of the Navajo, forced to herd sheep. Too poor to own a firearm, generally, the *pastor* defended himself and his herd with a bow and arrows he made himself.[6]

Sheep owners charged their herders with keeping their stock watered and fed, of course, but also with protecting the animals, which have no survival instincts, from predators, poisonous plants, accidents, freezing winter storms, disease (notably scab in later years), and prairie fire, as well as Indian raiders. After the annexation, Anglo thieves and murderous cowboys were added threats.[7] A successful herder had to be able to sense in advance the full array of dangers and take appropriate action when needed, and he had to deal with field conditions that were changing from day to day. Isolated as it was, his life was not monotonous. As South Dakota herder Archer B. Gilfillan described the life, "the sheep rarely act the same two days in a succession. . . . No one herding day is exactly like any other day."[8]

Herders learned their profession from their forebears, the children of sheep-growing families often taken out to the sheep camps from an early age. Abe Sena recalled that in his family, during the summer months when school was out, the children were put to work as "assistant herders" in charge of about ten sheep with new lambs, starting at the age of about twelve. Ninety-two-year-old Thomas Cabeza DeBaca remembered herding with his older brother on the Baca Ranch during the early twentieth century, at age six. And on the Navajo Reservation in the early twentieth century, where raising sheep was the purview of women, Mary Chischillie presented a flock of thirty lambs to her nine-year-old daughter, who became a successful flock mistress at a very early age.[9]

The herder's financial responsibility was large. Prior to the annexation, a 1,000-head flock under his care might be worth $500–$1,000, four or more years of his usual compensation, possibly $10–$20 per month at most. A single unfortunate incident could be devastating and turn an ambitious *partidario* into a peon if he was unable to cover

Sheep Come to New Mexico   7

his patron's losses.[10] The best strategy in the face of an Indian raid was often for the herder to quickly flee but to send his dog to scatter the flock so as to render the theft of more than a few head difficult. Sheep rustling was otherwise easy and involved minimal risk.

Another shortcoming of the herder's life were the hardships endured by his family in his absence. His wife and daughters might have to assume, in addition to their traditional tasks, all the family responsibilities ordinarily performed by the man of the house, including fending off Indian attacks. Furthermore, they would be unduly subject to assault, rape, or seduction while their men were away, according to Gutierrez, a threat whenever men spent extended periods away from home, the case with soldiers, muleteers, and hunters as well as sheepherders.[11]

The profession of sheepherder in the West demanded more than physical stamina, skills and knowledge, and a sense of financial responsibility. A specific mental disposition, including but not restricted to stoicism, was required. The ability to work hard and responsibly in isolation was essential. In the words of Towne and Wentworth, who devoted years to the study of the western sheep industry, the successful sheepherder needed "the unique temperament which sends a man forth to live alone for weeks on end, devoid of human contact, but weighted with full responsibility." The herder's only companions, besides his sheep, might be his dog and burro. In the words of one Texas *pastor,* "*pastores* have very lonely lives. Sometimes they go for weeks with nothing to talk to during the day but sheep and goats . . . the voice of the coyote is company in the night's stillness."[12]

The sheep herder was not always completely solitary, since he sometimes worked together with a boy, possibly his son, or with another adult herder if the flock was large. And his *vaquero* would visit every few weeks. But his human contact was indeed minimal. Ranchwoman Agnes Morley Cleaveland might as well have been describing sheepherders when she noted of her cattle-ranching community in the Datil area, "We were all uncompromisingly self-contained."[13] Considering the array of requirements, it appears that the best herders must

8   SHEEP COME TO NEW MEXICO

have been men of a sort of mental acuity, although they were largely illiterate.

The Navajo followed a somewhat different practice from the Hispanic herders in the post–Civil War period. After the Navajo returned to their sparsely settled homeland following their wartime imprisonment at Bosque Redondo (Hweeldi), the women came to own family herds and assumed a central role in sheep growing on what became the Navajo Reservation, as described below. Although they had been raising sheep since the early eighteenth century, little is known about the extent of their ownership or their herding practices at this time. Living in extended family groups on the reservation, the women herders drove their sheep out from their semipermanent homes to nearby forage for the day, heading out in a different direction each morning to best preserve the grass. They sometimes drove the animals back home at noon and returned them to the grazing area later in the afternoon; they always drove them home at the end of the day. Under this system it was safe for unarmed women and children to manage the flocks. When the forage nearby was exhausted, the families relocated, in a systematic circuit, to a fresh, distant area determined by the season to reoccupy previously constructed hogans and to allow the forage land they had just left to regenerate. Instead of grazing their sheep on long treks far from home, following the availability of forage, they grazed their sheep close to home and periodically moved their homes as the nearby forage was consumed.[14]

Hispanic herders, as described by Abe Pena, took "pride in the profession." The men who "had the fattest lambs, who had the less losses" earned good reputations.[15] The herding profession could provide a decent life for those possessing the required attributes.

THE SPANISH PERIOD, 1540–1821

Domestic livestock were first brought to the land that became New Mexico in the sixteenth century by the first European explorers, the Spanish conquistadores. The earliest and most ambitious of their explorations, the Coronado Expedition, 1540–1542, a search for gold and silver numbering over 1,000 individuals, included herds of cattle and sheep in the line of march, forming a traveling commissary. The conquistadores successfully drove some of the livestock all the way to central Kansas and back again to the Rio Grande Valley of New Mexico, proving the animals' robustness and utility under the semiarid southwestern conditions. In the ensuing years *conquistadores* mounted additional expeditions, important for the information they gathered about the Southwest and for their extending the Camino Real north into New Mexico. Hernán Gallegos, an astute observer on one early exploration, described the Galisteo–Pecos River area as "suitable for sheep, the best for that purpose ever discovered in New Spain."[16]

The Spanish established their first permanent settlement in New Mexico in 1598 under Governor Don Juan de Oñate at the confluence of the Rio Grande and the Rio Chama. The soldier-colonists, accompanying friars, and their retinues brought with them large herds of livestock. The colonists established a subsistence economy based on stock raising and farming, and they soon discovered, perhaps not unexpectedly, that their newly claimed lands were well suited for sheep. In the small villages, which grew up over the following years, sheep provided not only meat but also wool for clothing as well as milk and tallow.[17]

The prominent role of sheep in village life is perhaps not surprising since many of the Spanish emigrants to New Spain in the sixteenth century could trace their roots back to the Sevilla area, which was notable for livestock production, sheep being the favored stock. And many of these New World settlers had a background in farming and stock growing; some of them or their descendants became the leaders of the New Mexico colony.[18]

The colonists favored sheep over cattle because of their superior adaptability to the land. Sheep were also more difficult for Indian raiders to steal than cattle and horses, which could be stampeded and readily driven away. Sheep move slowly and cannot be stampeded like cattle. A quick raid often only scattered them, enabling the herders to recover the animals, or most of them, after the raiders were gone. Additionally,

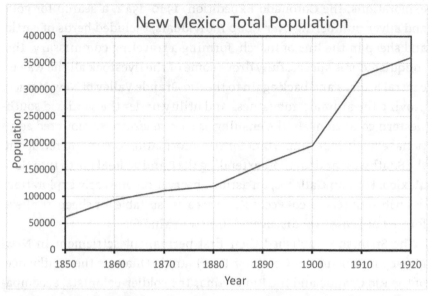

FIGURE 1.1. Total population of New Mexico versus year by decade, 1850–1920. The population increased at an accelerated rate after 1880 and the arrival of the railroads. The increase was even more rapid after 1900 due to the arrival of homesteaders from the East. Data are taken from US census reports, 1850–1920.

New Mexicans preferred their *churro* mutton to the beef produced by the cattle of the day, for which they substituted buffalo meat, obtained in organized hunts.[19] From the colony's founding onward through the US territorial era, New Mexico's sheep population greatly exceeded both its cattle and human populations (figures 1.1 and 1.2).

The church was a major factor in sheep growing prior to the Pueblo Revolt of 1680. The friars established missions taking up large tracts of land near several of the Pueblo villages, land that they devoted to agriculture and grazing, exploiting Pueblo labor. They were supported by the encomienda system in which leading colonists, the *encomendaros*, were awarded grants of tribute imposed on Pueblo households, payable in maize, cotton cloth, animal hides, and sometimes labor. The *encomendaros* provided the missions with military protection from nomadic raiders and assistance in converting the Pueblos

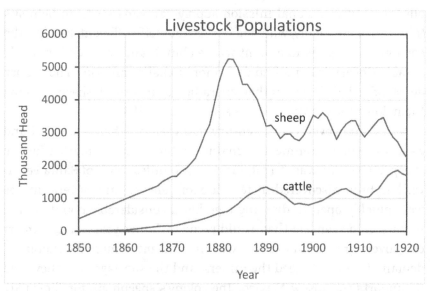

FIGURE 1.2. New Mexico livestock populations versus year by decade, 1850–1920. Series 1: Sheep. Series 2: Cattle. The sheep population reached a maximum peak of over 5 million head in the early 1880s, largely churros, and decreased thereafter to around 3 million as smaller herds of bred-up stock became favored. The sheep population always substantially exceeded the cattle population. Data for 1850 are taken from *Seventh Census, 1850*, which is not considered particularly reliable. Data for 1860 are taken from *Twelfth Census, 1900*, which revised the data from the 1860 census. This is probably reasonably reliable. Data for 1867–1920 are taken from New Mexico Department of agriculture, *New Mexico Agricultural Statistics 44*. This report contains the most reliable data now available.

to Christianity. The friars reported having fed many Pueblo Indians and Spanish colonists from their livestock reserves in times of famine, using this as a justification for the arrangement. The growing mission sheep herds proved the viability of large-scale, open-range sheep raising in New Mexico employing peasant or slave labor.[20]

The colony grew slowly but steadily, numerous small settlements and haciendas being established along the Rio Grande and its tributaries, mostly in the lower Rio Abajo, the lower-river stretch. The colonists located their capital at the site of Santa Fe around 1610. Mexican

12   SHEEP COME TO NEW MEXICO

officials sent occasional mission-supply caravans north to help sustain the fragile colony, which never became self-sufficient. In time, the colony's herds grew to a point where church and some civil officials, notably Governor Francisco de la Mora Ceballos and Governor López de Mendizábal, began rather sporadically to export sheep, driving them down the Camino Real for sale in Mexico.[21]

By the mid-seventeenth century, the caravans had expanded and assumed a more commercial character. The principal market for the sheep at the time was Parral, Mexico, 700 miles south of Santa Fe. Silver had been discovered in 1631, a boom ensued, and several mines were quickly opened, drawing together a considerable population of miners. In a scenario that would recur in future years under American sovereignty, local produce was insufficient to meet the increased demand for meat to feed the miners, and the shortage was alleviated by imports from New Mexico. The colony's sheepmen, for their part, found that large-scale, long-distance sheep drives across harsh, dry expanses to distant markets were commercially viable. The drives would multiply in importance in later years. The livestock population of the colony increased considerably in the years 1620–1670, as indicated by the magnitude of this trade. Large trail drives remained a fixture of the territory's sheep industry until the arrival of the railroads in the late nineteenth century.[22]

The Pueblo Revolt of 1680 caused only a temporary setback for the Spanish colonization initiative. The survivors fled south to the small Spanish outpost of El Paso, where they remained in exile for twelve years until the Reconquest. Thereafter, the Spanish under Don Diego de Vargas, now governor, reoccupied Santa Fe, the haciendas, and several outlying villages in both the Rio Arriba and Rio Abajo regions. They established the villages of Santa Cruz and Albuquerque at this time. And by the year 1700, the population of the colony is believed to have been about 3,000 individuals. The colony assumed a more secular character, missions were abandoned, and church leaders' authority was reduced. The settlers repopulating the colony were largely private subsistence farmers and stock growers rather than soldiers. Government authorities replaced the abusive encomienda system, a major cause of the Pueblo Revolt, with the less onerous repartimiento, in which tribute labor was imposed on individuals, rather than households, on a weekly basis.[23]

In the aftermath of the Reconquest, many Pueblos fled west to the Navajo lands, bringing along sheep abandoned by Spanish colonists fleeing the revolt. In a poorly understood cultural exchange, the Pueblos may have passed on sheep to the Navajos by some mutual arrangements. In any case, the Navajos took up sheep husbandry and wool weaving with alacrity around this time, along with Pueblo ceremonies and farming methods. By the mid-eighteenth century, they had developed considerable herds, although they had had little peaceful contact with the colonists. In fact, the Navajos continued raiding Spanish and Pueblo herds.[24]

From this time on, the colonists began to address their labor needs by the acquisition of captive Indian slaves acquired through a slave market that long predated their arrival in the Southwest and was conducted by the nomadic tribes of the region. The captives offered up for sale to the colonists had been taken forcibly from enemy tribes by nomadic war parties. After the arrival of the Spanish, the tribes at times extended their slave raids to the colonial villages. The *poblador* families generally absorbed the Indian slaves they obtained into their extended families, baptized them, and brought them up as Christians. They held the captives until they had worked off their cost of acquisition or longer, often many years. The captives intermarried among themselves or into the lower rungs of Spanish society, and, unable to return to their birth tribes, they and their descendants formed what became the large *genizaro* class in New Mexico society.

Later in the eighteenth century a system of peonage was introduced to address a continuing need for laborers. The more prosperous families contracted with desperate *pobladores* for their labor in exchange for taking on their debts. Such arrangements could lead to a lifetime of servitude for a debt of only a few hundred dollars in today's money when the patron arranged for a continuous succession of loans to the peon that could never be paid off.

14   SHEEP COME TO NEW MEXICO

The bound women and children were generally put to work as domestic servants or sometimes as weavers, captive Navajo women being valued for their weaving skills. The men were generally assigned to field work, including herding sheep, making them a factor in the sheep industry that extended until well into the territorial period. When offered their release, some captives and peones chose to remain with their masters. Southwestern peonage and captive servitude would persist for over two centuries.[25]

Sheep growing resumed quickly in the Spanish colony. The invading army confiscated some 900 head from Cochiti Pueblo as spoils of war, and the church imported an additional 1,500 sheep and some cattle to reestablish mission herds. The governor recruited additional colonists. The Spanish government provided in 1697 a large consignment of livestock from Mexico, which the colonial officials allotted to the settlers on the basis of need, most families receiving from ten to twenty-five ewes and two or three cows. Captain Fernando Duran y Chaves received thirty-eight ewes, which he drove to Bernalillo, where his family had settled before the revolt. This herd was the seed for a considerable family fortune. Chaves's descendants would distinguish themselves as soldiers, political leaders, merchants, and sheepmen through the territorial period.[26]

Besides livestock allotments, secular authorities adopted a land policy with long-term repercussions. Several officers in de Vargas's force received large tracts of land in compensation for their military service, while every family received a land allocation of some size. In later years many additional land grants were awarded to prominent, well-connected individuals for services to the state and also to communities.[27]

By 1715 the new social structure, headed by a small, emergent class of wealthy, patriarchal, land-owning families, was well defined. Several New Mexican families destined to be influential in later years, besides the Chaves family, began their rise at this time. The large land grants some families received provided the wherewithal for raising livestock on a commercial basis. The elite intermarried almost exclusively among themselves, maintaining their pure "Spanish" identity, true or fictional, while building a tight, closed web of mutually beneficial commercial alliances. Never constituting more than a small percentage of the population, they came to possess most of the colony's wealth, which was largely in the form of livestock. These *rico* families thus dominated the sheep industry while the overwhelming majority of the populace, mixed-race *mestizos*, filled out the lower socioeconomic rungs of society, although many owned or had access to land and possessed a few head of sheep. At the very bottom of the social order were the *genizaros*; these detribalized, Christianized Indian slaves—largely Apache, Ute, and Navajo, forcibly removed from nomadic tribes—were estimated to constitute one third of the colony's population by the late eighteenth century.[28]

A new allocation of labor took place, with most of the colony's physical work falling to *mestizos* and *genizaros* living under the protection of a wealthy patriarch. They were engaged largely in subsistence farming, working irrigated fields along the river bottoms. Some were occupied tending the growing sheep herds of the *rico* families, which within a few decades surpassed the size of the pre-revolt mission herds.[29]

The colony stabilized and grew during the eighteenth century. The census of 1757 gave a population of over 5,000 individuals and nearly 50,000 sheep and goats.[30] Over half the population congregated in and around the towns of Santa Fe, Albuquerque, Santa Cruz, and El Paso; the remainder lived at the river haciendas, now grown to settlements of more or less interrelated families and usually dominated by one or two comparatively wealthy, sheep-growing *patrones*. The *ricos* lived predominantly in the Rio Abajo, ever the more prosperous part of New Mexico, where many of the private grants were located. In contrast, community grants, smaller land holdings, and comparatively dense populations of small farmers characterized the Rio Arriba. Political authorities viewed these grants as buffers against nomadic raiders.

By the mid-1730s, New Mexico's flocks had multiplied significantly, and the new class of sheep-growing *ricos* began, at least sporadically, to export sheep and wool to Mexico. The trade caravans resumed.

16 SHEEP COME TO NEW MEXICO

Chihuahua, settled around 1707 and now the metropolis of New Spain's northern frontier, was the principal trading destination, important silver deposits having been discovered in the area. Again a relatively concentrated population of miners materialized quickly, and local produce was insufficient to feed it. New Mexico mutton helped reduce the shortfall. The size of the colony's sheep exports apparently rose more or less steadily, and by the late eighteenth century a sheep trade with Mexico was firmly reestablished.[31]

Living conditions in New Mexico seem to have improved somewhat by the late eighteenth century. A measure of economic advancement in the colony during the eighteenth century is provided by the 1785 probate records for Don Clemente Gutierrez, known as the King of the Chihuahua Traders. His estate included 7,000 yearlings and two-year-olds being held for sale, 6,600 more sheep purchased from neighboring ranchers for fall delivery, and another 13,000 ewes held under *partido* contracts with twenty-four Rio Abajo citizens. The population of the colony in 1802 was reported to be 35,751, mostly farmers in the Rio Grande Valley. Sheep exports increased markedly after about 1785. Some sheep were driven as far as Mexico City, where the price doubled between 1794 and 1809. Markets in the towns of Sonora, Coahuila, and Durango opened.[32]

Governor Fernando de la Concha estimated that 15,000 New Mexico sheep were sold in Chihuahua in 1788 for about 30,000 pesos ($650,000 in 2020 dollars). Fifteen years later, in his economic report of 1803, Governor Fernando de Chacón stated that 25,000–26,000 sheep were being exported annually. Long of major importance to New Mexico's internal economy, sheep had yet to dominate the trade with Mexico, textiles and hides still being more important. This soon changed.[33]

By the early nineteenth century the trade caravans had become well-organized annual affairs. The New Mexico *commerciantes* congregated with their livestock and other trade goods loaded on *carretas* and pack mules at La Joya de Sevilleta, the last Spanish settlement north of Jornada del Muerto, for departure in November. The caravans now incorporated typically 500 men, later to expand to as many as 1,000,

Sheep Come to New Mexico 17

including a military escort. Sheep and wool blankets were now the predominant export goods. The sheep, however, were owned by a small handful of merchants.[34]

The Chihuahua market could be treacherous because of large, unpredictable price fluctuations that could wipe out a New Mexican's profit margin or worse. Some colonial traders became deeply indebted to Mexican merchants. Additional problems included misunderstandings of business agreements, sharp business practices, and outright theft, all reflected in eighteenth-century litigation described in surviving documents. The New Mexicans, continually buffeted by difficult market conditions, operated as best they could under the prevailing system. Fortunately for them, the demand for sheep increased in the late eighteenth century and into the early nineteenth century. A small group of New Mexico traders, the smartest or luckiest, managed not only to stay out of debt but to realize substantial profits.[35]

By the early nineteenth century, sheep had become an external trade item of considerable importance. About twenty elite families dominated the colonial economy, several being engaged in the Mexican trade. They traded imported goods with the Pueblos and the general colonial population in exchange for their produce. They extended credit to the cash-poor *pobres* against future deliveries of their crops and livestock, which were sometimes pledged several seasons in advance, reducing some of those struggling growers to peonage. The *ricos'* ascent was expedited by the recognition of sheep as a medium of exchange, capital on the hoof, as little hard currency was in circulation. Items of merchandise in the colony took on a value according to the number of sheep for which they would trade. Dowries often took the form of livestock, entirely or in part.[36]

Conditions changed slowly for the remainder of the Spanish period. New Mexico society was conservative, closed to outside influences, and largely ignored by an overextended, declining Spanish Empire. The sharp *rico-pobre* class distinction, believed more extreme than it had been before the Pueblo Revolt, became a defining feature of life in New Mexico from the latter eighteenth century on through the nineteenth

18 SHEEP COME TO NEW MEXICO

century. Ultimately, against a backdrop of social and economic changes, the colonists of the Spanish period established a substantial livestock population and a strong tradition of sheep husbandry, one of the most important legacies of the period.

THE MEXICAN PERIOD, 1821–1846

Mexico won its independence from Spain in 1821 after a decade of instability and armed conflict. Little is known about New Mexico commerce during this period. The Camino Real trade did decrease overall, and the Chihuahua sheep market collapsed. Without the outlet provided by the Mexican market, New Mexico's sheep population increased dramatically and seems to have reached unprecedented levels later in the Mexican period. A livestock census conducted in 1827 gave a total of 240,000 sheep and goats in the colony. The Rio Abajo became firmly established as the colony's dominant sheep-growing region.[37]

Under the new central government in Mexico City, the colony, never accorded much government support, experienced even greater neglect than in the past. Political, economic, and military unrest were endemic throughout the Mexican period. Mexican authorities reduced the already inadequate colonial military force to the detriment of public safety. Peace with the Navajos, which had persisted since 1805, came to an end in 1818, a particular blow to sheepmen whose flocks they raided with regularity thereafter. Indian raids intensified generally after 1821 when the impoverished Mexican government discontinued annual annuities to the nomadic tribes.[38]

After Mexican independence New Mexico sheepmen faced the same, or even greater, challenges. On the large drives to Mexico, trail expenses for the herders' food and compensation were significant, as in the past. And losses of stock from poisonous weeds and bad water along the way were likewise expensive. For a period of years starting in 1832, the Mexican government imposed onerous taxes on imported livestock, making matters even more difficult for New Mexico sheepmen. Furthermore, the government exacerbated the business climate

Sheep Come to New Mexico 19

by introducing high import duties on merchandise and a complicated system of internal passports and shipping manifests. Also, large, unpredictable price fluctuations in the Mexican sheep markets remained a serious problem. In bad years the markets might be glutted so that there was no demand at all for New Mexico's sheep.[39]

Remarkably, the sheep industry not only survived but flourished during much of the republican period. By the early 1830s, New Mexico sheepmen were delivering 15,000 head annually to Durango alone, selling them at nine reales per head. Mariano Chaves (y Castillo), whose ancestor, Captain Fernando Duran y Chaves, had received a substantial sheep allotment from de Vargas, set a pre-annexation record for a single grower when he drove a reportedly 30,000 head to Durango in 1832. The trade expanded so quickly that in 1835 alone, the colonists exported some 80,000 sheep to Mexico, almost half belonging to the Chaves family. Despite unstable markets during the last decade of Mexican sovereignty, New Mexicans requested *guias* (permits) to export at least 204,000 head to Mexico between 1835 and 1840. And into the early 1840s they appear to have been exporting 30,000–50,000 head in the better years.[40]

The *rico* sheep-growing families were the predominant benefactors from this market. Further class consolidation ensued. About two thirds of the exported sheep belonged to members of the Chaves, Otero, and Sandoval families, while most of the rest belonged to four other prominent families—Ortiz, Pino, Perea, and Armijo. In total, only twenty-eight sheep owners from sixteen families delivered substantial herds during the Mexican period. *Partidarios* and other small producers might on occasion sell a few head of their own to their patron to be driven south. Santa Fe trader Josiah Gregg reported that the patrones paid these men between fifty and seventy-five cents per head and sold the stock in Mexico at 100–200 percent profit.[41]

At the time of the annexation, the Hispanic population was reported to be 50,000 but may have been much larger.[42] No real middle class existed. Since a single skilled herder and his dog could readily tend 1,000 head, year-around employment of only a few percent of the

20   SHEEP COME TO NEW MEXICO

Hispanic population, likely *partidarios*, peones, or *genizaros*, would have been sufficient. And existing land issues were restricting the further growth of the sheep industry.

Open-range sheep growing was a land-intensive activity. And the grazing lands were owned or controlled in large part by the *rico* families. On the average, about five acres of New Mexico grassland were required to raise a single sheep, although conditions varied considerably throughout the territory and considerably over time. During extended periods of drought, which might last as long as three or four years, the land could support considerably significantly fewer sheep and might suffer degradation if the grazing burden was not reduced. With Individual flocks often numbering about 1,000 head, land was a major consideration for every sheepman.

After the Spanish repopulation following the Pueblo Revolt, most of the populated areas fell within land grants awarded by the state, some of which encompassed hundreds of thousands of acres.[43] Grantees, in collaboration with political authorities, situated their lands along rivers or streams, which served for domestic water needs, irrigating crops, and, critical for sheep, watering livestock. They employed the bulk of the grant areas, the uplands extending away from the water courses and irrigated fields, for grazing. The grants remained intact well into the territorial period and in a few cases into the twentieth century. Sheep growers sometimes also used the unclaimed lands beyond the grant boundaries, public domain under the Spanish and Mexican governments, for grazing.[44]

Sheep raising on grant lands or adjoining public domain persisted after the annexation until the 1870s or later. The narrow ownership base during the Mexican period was a result of government favoritism in the awarding of private land grants to the well-connected elite, while even community grants were often dominated by one or more influential *rico* families. This land policy surely limited more widespread sheep ownership than would otherwise have been the case.[45] This was particularly true in the late Mexican period when Governor Armijo awarded a few immense private grants to a handful of influential citizens.

If the government land distribution policy discouraged more widespread participation in sheep ownership, the all too frequent Indian raids stood in the way of further expansion of the industry under any conditions. Licenciado Don Antonio Barriero saw a solution in government intervention when he wrote in 1832, "It may be said that, if New Mexico can establish a permanent peace with the wild Indians, and if it will provide its people with knowledge of the most advantageous methods of trading in sheep, the province will prosper from the income of this branch of industry alone as much as Chihuahua has profited from that of her mines. Happy the day when the government will extend its protecting hand to this territory; then these fields, at present uninhabited and desolate, will be converted into rich and happy sheep ranches!"[46]

The Mexican government, lacking in revenues and in a more or less continuous state of chaos, never acted on Barriero's suggestions. Later under American sovereignty his conditions were met with the help of the comparatively well-funded, well-equipped US Army, and the sheep industry flourished unprecedentedly.

As New Mexico's sheepmen contended with an array of difficulties, a new consideration materialized, likely a minor annoyance at first for a frontier society that lived with considerable hardship. The first Americans that arrived in New Mexico noted that grass tracts in the immediate vicinity of some villages had been significantly degraded. Climatic factors may have been an issue here. More pertinent, however, the diminished vegetation on these tracts can be seen as an early manifestation of the environmental costs of grazing, the lands nearest the villages having been heavily employed for that purpose. Nevertheless, immense tracts of high-quality rangeland remained in more outlying areas.[47]

Despite its problems, the sheep industry grew, but otherwise evolved slowly, if at all, during the Mexican period and was seemingly destined to persist indefinitely into the future with minimal change. Through the entire quarter century when they controlled New Mexico, distracted Mexican leaders, overwhelmed by serious internal problems, made no attempt to promote the sheep industry. If anything,

22 SHEEP COME TO NEW MEXICO

the opposite was the case. Onerous trade regulations and restrictions, inadequate military protection, and restrictive land distribution all conspired to suppress the full potential of the industry.

SHEEP AND NEW MEXICAN LIVES

Sheep impacted New Mexican lives in other ways besides providing sustenance and clothing. An immediate problem the colonists faced was the fact that their livestock were a magnet for Indian raiders. In an early repercussion of sheep ownership, according to Southwest borderlands historian James F. Brooks, Governor Pedro de Peralta relocated the initial settlement in 1610 to the more defensible site of Santa Fe, in part, because of continuing Navajo sheep and horse raids at the original location.

In another early development that affected many Indian lives, New Mexico governors Juan de Eulatel (1618) and Luis de Rosas (1637–1641) employed coerced labor, Pueblos as well as Apaches, Navajos, and Utes taken as captives, in their Santa Fe *obrajes* (workshops) to weave woolen goods to be sold.[48]

Later, on yet another front, as the colonial population increased, the availability of irrigable farmland for agricultural production in the Rio Grande Valley became inadequate, and sheep, providing a viable food source, took on increased importance. Ever more men became herders and consequently spent extended periods away from home. The larger growers, owning thousands of head by the late eighteenth century, became entrepreneurs of a sort, employing dozens of herders to manage their stock. The *ricos'* wealth and political influence increased with the size of their herds. The *partido* system expanded, and peonage grew when *partidarios* were unable to meet their obligations. The *rico-pobre* divide became more pronounced.[49]

In a somewhat related development, sheep played an important but indirect role in the nineteenth-century expansion of the Hispanic homeland outward from the Rio Grande Valley. The expansion was driven by a steadily increasing population and the concomitant need

Sheep Come to New Mexico 23

to open new areas of settlement. It began after peace was established with the Apache and Comanche in 1790 and continued for the next hundred years. Sheepmen led the expansion and established new villages throughout much of today's New Mexico and in border areas of four neighboring states.

The expansion proceeded in phases. As the human population increased, the sheep population, of necessity, also had to increase. In the first phase, sheepmen from the larger established towns, parent villages Santa Fe, Santa Cruz, and Albuquerque, managing larger numbers of stock and in search of new grazing tracts, began driving their herds seasonally to summer pasture in more outlying areas. In time, the sheepmen, sometimes traveling in family groups, built more or less permanent dwellings to live in for extended periods in these new areas. They sometime irrigated patches of land for growing crops. Eventually, numerous offspring villages with year-around residents, including San Miguel, Las Vegas, Mora, and Taos, grew up at these sites. These villages in turn gave rise to a larger number of even smaller offspring settlements. Some families relocated from the larger, increasingly crowded towns to these newer villages to claim the larger cropland allotments that became available, inevitably following the paths opened up by the herders. Range degradation near the older, established villages does not seem to have been an issue in the expansion. It was driven predominantly, perhaps entirely, by population growth.[50]

Sheep had a considerable impact on the lives of the sedentary Pueblos. Although the Pueblos were an agricultural people, their crops, dependent on the uncertain, variable New Mexico weather, were insufficient to completely sustain life. Theirs was a hybrid economy. They augmented their agricultural production by hunting and gathering. The introduction of domestic sheep into their society by the Spanish changed Pueblo lives irreversibly. By the 1630s, the friars had established the sheep herds connected with their missions, reportedly as large as 1,000 to 2,000 head, far larger than the herds of most of the colonists. The comparative abundance of mutton that followed provided a significantly enhanced level of food security for the Pueblos. Moreover,

24   SHEEP COME TO NEW MEXICO

sheep stolen from both Spanish settlers and the Pueblos provided an addition to the diet of the region's nomadic tribes.[51]

By 1640, the friars had established many *estancias* (working livestock ranches) near their missions, employing Pueblo labor. Even earlier, perhaps as early as 1609, the Pueblos had acquired flocks of their own. As the sheep multiplied, the church undertook the export of surplus stock down to Mexican markets with the caravans and exchanged the stock for tools, hardware, weapons, and other badly needed items. The animals were also traded for mission furnishings, including vestments and organs. Sheep also funded religious activities.[52]

Under the influence of the missions and their sheep herds, the Pueblos, who had been growing cotton and weaving it into cloth, the purview of men, into cloth for nearly 1300 years, started converting their looms from cotton to wool. By the 1620s, the wool was apparently clothing the Pueblos as well as the friars. The conversion to wool was almost total by 1680.[53]

The Navajos were arguably more deeply affected by the newly imported livestock than any other group. By the late eighteenth century, sheep had become important to their subsistence also. And sheep ownership brought about important changes in their social structure. In a complex process sheep became unevenly distributed. A network of entrepreneurial headmen, leading groups of as many as a dozen extended families, built up large herds to the detriment of the poorer, dependent families under their protection.[54]

The arrival of the US "Army of the West" in 1846 under Colonel Stephen Watts Kearny ushered in a new political and economic order that, among other things, removed the Mexican government policies hampering the sheep industry. The industry would subsequently be turned on its head by American growers and mercantile capitalists who had begun arriving in New Mexico following Mexican independence from Spain. These men would now expedite an expansion and modernization of the industry at an unprecedented rate as they integrated New Mexico's sheep and wool into a burgeoning American market economy. This is the subject of the following chapter.

2

SHEEP AND THE MARKET ECONOMY

THE AMERICANS ARRIVE

The arrival of Americans brought great changes to New Mexico, which manifested themselves slowly at first. American fur trappers and traders, merchants, and later stockmen began arriving with the relaxation of trade restrictions following Mexican independence from Spain, their numbers and influence increasing steadily throughout the Mexican period.[1] A handful of Americans saw and began to appreciate the grazing potential of New Mexico. The stockmen took up the traditional range practices, employing Hispanic herders, even as they sought out new American markets for New Mexico's mutton and wool. Foreign trade routes began to shift from north-south to east-west. In the ensuing years, under American sovereignty sheepmen trail drove New Mexico's *churros* to California to feed the gold seekers. And they shipped New Mexico wool to the textile mills of the Northeast, helping to establish a vital American woolen industry. Later they drove their

https://doi.org/10.5876/9781646425471.c002

26 SHEEP AND THE MARKET ECONOMY

churros throughout the Great Plains–Rocky Mountain region to serve as seed stock for establishing herds beyond the territory. The nation's sheep industry shifted significantly from eastern and midwestern farms, where it started, to ranches in the trans-Mississippi West.

Pike, Beaubien, and Maxwell

The American experience in New Mexico dates back to the time of Spanish sovereignty when, in 1807, a small US military reconnaissance mission under Lieutenant Zebulon Montgomery Pike, tasked with finding the headwaters of the Arkansas River and learning something of the Spanish presence in the region, was discovered by a Spanish militia detachment. The Spanish soldiers took the Americans into captivity and marched them to Santa Fe and then on to Chihuahua for interrogation. Except for a few obscure lone adventurers, Pike and his men were the first Americans to see New Mexico and report what they saw. Along the way south on the Camino Real, Pike observed a trade caravan destined for Mexico which included 15,000 sheep. He conveyed this information back to Washington in a comprehensive report that noted the importance of sheep in New Mexico's economy and estimated—accurately, as it turned out—that some 30,000 animals valued at $1 per head were being exported annually to Mexico.[2]

The first "foreigners" to find their way into New Mexico after the region was opened to US trade were a small, mixed group of Americans, French Canadians, and other Anglo adventurer-entrepreneurs. Largely fur trappers, or "mountain men," who had been operating in the northern Rockies since days of Lewis and Clark, they began expanding their operations to exploit the untapped fur resources of the southern Rockies. While native New Mexicans had not previously developed a fur trade for lack of a satisfactory market to the south, the Americans had connections with St. Louis merchant-investors, who in turn had connections with European markets. Many trappers established their headquarters in the northern gateway town of Taos. And within a few

Sheep and the Market Economy 27

years Santa Fe became an important base for traders dealing in an ever-broadening range of wares, including captive Indian slaves. By 1840 a few hundred American men are believed to have been living in New Mexico. Some of these men took out Mexican citizenship, converted to Catholicism, married into prominent Hispanic families, and became influential in public affairs. With their access to American markets, their influence far exceeded their numbers.[3]

Some of the more enterprising Americans took advantage of a new land policy that allowed foreigners who had obtained Mexican citizenship to partner with a native New Mexican and apply for a private land grant. Several such private grants, some very large, were awarded during the final years of Mexican sovereignty under Governor Manuel Armijo.[4] A few of the Anglo newcomers thus became landowners and entered the livestock business.

The colonial government awarded the first of these grants in 1841 to Guadalupe Miranda, Governor Armijo's collector of customs and provincial secretary of state, and French-Canadian Charles (Carlos) Beaubien, a prominent Taos merchant and onetime mountain man. The immense Beaubien-Miranda (Maxwell) Land Grant came to encompass some 1.7 million acres northeast of Taos, straddling today's New Mexico–Colorado border. The grantees populated the grant with a combination of sharecroppers, day laborers, and peones. From the outset they seem to have used the area for grazing, as it had been used even before the grant existed. The grantees introduced large permanent herds of sheep and cattle. The exact nature of Beaubien's participation in these grazing operations is unclear; for his part, Miranda was never more than a passive partner. However, Beaubien's son-in-law, Lucian B. Maxwell, acting as his majordomo, managed the agricultural and grazing resources of the grant. He, with the support of his father-in-law, built a considerable frontier empire as the economy of the region expanded after the annexation. After his father-in-law's death in 1864, Maxwell acquired the entire grant, now under American sovereignty, which thereafter became known as the Maxwell Land Grant. It was one of the largest estates, perhaps *the largest*, in the United States at the

28 SHEEP AND THE MARKET ECONOMY

time. Eventually the grant grew in population, by some estimates, to 500 *pobladores*. Maxwell came to possess some 50,000 sheep, 10,000 cattle, 1,000 horses and mules, and farmed 5,000 acres. He employed hundreds of captive Indian and peon laborers. By 1868 he had an annual income of $50,000 ($900,000 in 2020 dollars), making him one of the wealthiest men in New Mexico Territory.[5]

Maxwell assumed the role of patron, more or less indistinguishable from his Hispanic, grant-holding cohorts. The key to his rise in wealth, social status, and influence was his 1844 marriage to Carlos Beaubien's mixed-race, teenage daughter Luz. American social influence was minimal at the time. In the business world, family connections were all important, and such intermarriages between Anglo men and Hispanic women could, from a purely commercial standpoint, be quite beneficial to everyone concerned. The Anglo provided his Hispanic relatives needed business know-how and access to American markets while they, in turn, provided him a bridge to the local agricultural and livestock supply network. Spanish customs were well adapted to the isolated lands, the people, the cash-scarce economy, and livestock production on the grants. Like his Hispanic cohorts, Maxwell employed the *partido* system, mediated by a web of personal relationships, to raise his livestock. He conducted his livestock operations on a barter and cash basis, without recourse to bank loans, credit, or outside investors.[6]

Besides the Maxwell Grant, a few other similarly large grants were awarded in 1843. Maxwell and his cohorts were the first Anglo stock growers in New Mexico.[7]

The Santa Fe Trade

At the same time that American fur traders were establishing outposts in New Mexico, Americans on another front opened a general merchandise trade that would impact the sheep industry even more directly.[8] Their development of a trade route between Santa Fe and St. Louis, the Santa Fe Trail, was important for the expansion of New

Sheep and the Market Economy 29

Mexico's sheep industry. It became the principal conduit for transporting the territory's wool to eastern mills and remained so until the arrival of the railroads in the 1880s.

The Santa Fe trade, as it became known, started in 1821 when a pack train under William Becknell, out from Missouri and laden with goods intended for the Plains Indian trade, ended up by chance in New Mexico. The Americans sold their merchandise for a handsome profit and returned to Missouri with news of a lucrative new market for American manufactured goods. Mercantile floodgates between New Mexico and the United States cracked open, and caravans of heavy, Pennsylvania-built freight wagons were soon traversing the relatively easy, 800-mile trail. Well positioned and well prepared to assume an important role in New Mexico's commerce, the Santa Fe traders had access to a broad range of American markets through their business connections in Missouri.[9]

The Americans exchanged textiles, hardware, and liquor for New Mexico's traditional *efectos del pais* (woolen goods), but also livestock (oxen, horses, and mules from California, as described below) and Mexican silver and gold.[10] During the early years of the trade, merchants began experimenting with wool as a backhaul, providing the first western wool to northeastern woolen mills and giving birth to an industry that would grow to major proportions in the Rocky Mountain–Great Plains region.

New Mexican *ricos* who had participated in the Mexican trade expanded their operations as the Santa Fe Trail opened up new opportunities. Susan Calafate Boyle has described in considerable detail Hispanic participation in the Santa Fe trade. By the late 1830s, a substantial number were involved, sometimes dealing directly with wholesale suppliers on the East Coast, an initiative due in part to the decline in Mexican sheep prices after 1836. A few men who had prospered driving sheep to Chihuahua made even larger fortunes in the Santa Fe trade. Native New Mexican participation was, however, narrow in the sense that five families (Armijo, Chaves [sometimes spelled Chávez], Otero, Perea, and Yrizarri) conducted 80 percent of the Hispanic mercantile trade.[11]

30   SHEEP AND THE MARKET ECONOMY

The Santa Fe trade grew steadily for most of the Mexican period, a time of transition when New Mexico was importing goods from both the United States and Mexico but exporting sheep only to Mexico. For a brief period, St. Louis and Chihuahua merchants were in close competition, the Missouri traders gradually breaking the Mexican monopoly.[12]

Significantly, during this same period New Mexico's *rico* families began sending their sons east to American Catholic schools rather than south to Durango to complete their education.[13] This was critical for future success in business, law, and politics. Fluency in English, the ability to move freely and easily in American society, a thorough understanding of fee-simple land tenure and modern banking practices were all facilitated by an American education. Such skills would be essential for successful large-scale sheep ranching during the territorial period.

Military Occupation

Long before the arrival of Kearny's army, the *pobladores*, to their credit, had built a cohesive, functioning society under exceedingly difficult conditions. The growth of the sheep industry during the Spanish and Mexican periods is testament to the extraordinary sheep-growing resources, both natural and human, of the northern settlements. After twenty-five years of political chaos, inadequate military protection, onerous trade restrictions, and general neglect, most New Mexicans had lost any sense of allegiance to the Mexican government. Under the circumstances, it was an easy victory for the American forces. Some, perhaps many, of New Mexico's political leaders favored US annexation as a path to several benefits, including a broader electorate for popular elections, a more efficient court system, and faster economic development. They visualized, in particular, a significantly expanded sheep industry. Initiating a five-year military occupation, Kearny imposed civil order. He also established a provisional, if largely powerless, civil government and a legal system based on Anglo-American common law.[14]

Sheep and the Market Economy 31

This is not to say that life in New Mexico changed much in the early years of American sovereignty. It did not, although the Santa Fe trade continued to expand, particularly as the Mexican import taxes disappeared. The annexation of New Mexico and the large area that became the American Southwest, under the Treaty of Guadalupe-Hidalgo of 1848, was critical for the opening of large American markets for New Mexican produce, sheep and wool in particular, although this development advanced slowly. More immediately, the presence of the US Army and the numerous outposts it established benefited native New Mexicans by providing markets for their produce. It also suppressed hostage taking by the nomadic tribes. In time, New Mexico's captive Indian slavery and peonage came under increasing opposition from abolition interests in the Northeast and Washington along with diminishing support within the new territory. The integration of New Mexico into the US economy that the Santa Fe trade had begun in a small way received an added impetus in the interwar years with the arrival of an emergent class of professional mercantile capitalists who would deal in sheep and wool on a considerably larger scale than in the past. Otherwise, except for a handful of stockmen, the territory attracted few new immigrants due to its lack of gold and silver, its well-deserved reputation for Indian raids, and its scarcity of arable land, the most desirable tracts having been long since taken up by the *pobladores.*[15]

Americans who did come to New Mexico were quick to recognize the importance of sheep in the local economy, the sheep industry having grown considerably between its seventeenth-century inception and the time of the annexation. And with its large sheep population, the new territory became, by default, an important center of America's western sheep industry, to be joined by California a decade or more later. In his military reconnaissance report on General Kearny's traversal of New Mexico, Lieutenant W. H. Emory, Kearny's chief engineer officer, noted the importance of sheep and stated his belief that fine sheep-growing conditions existed throughout New Mexico. Ten thousand copies of Emory's report were printed by the Government

32   SHEEP AND THE MARKET ECONOMY

Printing Office. Secretary of War William L. Marcy employed the report to argue for, and secure, the inclusion of New Mexico in the southwestern lands that were annexed by the United States.[16]

The Americans found an extremely unsettled situation in New Mexico. The nomadic tribes, desperate to retain control of their traditional hunting grounds, were severely harassing the Hispanic and Pueblo settlements, threatening both public safety and livestock. During the Spanish and Mexican periods, Indians had killed or taken captive many *pastores* and their families and driven off innumerable sheep. At the time of the annexation, sheep herding seems to have been more dangerous than ever. As described in Emory's report, when the US Army marched through Las Vegas in 1846, the villagers reported to the officers that "120 sheep and other stock" had been stolen a few days earlier, either by Utes or Navajos. A few days after that, Indians murdered a villager. Some weeks later, by which time the army was near Isleta Pueblo, Navajos attacked a nearby village and "killed one man, crippled another, and carried off a large supply of sheep and cattle." In an altercation shortly thereafter, the Indians killed six *pobleadores* and wounded two. A few days later and farther south, the army passed through a town where Apaches had stolen "all the horses and cattle" the day before. A few weeks before that, the same band was said to have attacked a village farther north, stealing horses and taking fifteen or sixteen women into captivity.[17]

The nomadic raiders were not the only threat to the well-being of New Mexico. A more subtle development with long-term consequences was already underway. Army personnel traversing New Mexico encountered poor range conditions near several of the villages. The *pobladores*' sheep seem to have already exacted a toll on the land. Forage for the army's numerous horses and mules was often scarce. Lieutenant Emory reported that in the Las Vegas area "the grass was indifferent, being clipped short by the cattle." Lieutenant W. G. Peck reported that from a point fifteen miles southwest of Taos all the way south to Santa Fe "there is no grass." Upon the army's arrival in Santa Fe, J. T. Hughs reported that the men relocated all the horses to the "neighborhood of

Galisteo, twenty-seven miles southeasterly from the capital, for the purpose of grazing them, forage being scarce and extremely difficult to be procured near town." English traveler George F. Ruxton reported that the area between Santa Fe and Galisteo was "clothed with cedars but destitute of grass or other vegetation." Captain A. R. Johnston reported, "The grass was well eaten out before [meaning 'previously'] about camp and the country about Santa Fe, and today is thinly covered with grama grass and occasional cedar shrubs, betokening the greatest sterility."[18]

In contrast, the Galisteo Valley was, at that time, an area of productive farms, and the army found the grass and water to be "abundant and of good quality." This was, and continued to be, a popular site for travelers to stop and allow their exhausted livestock to recover and regain their strength on the fine grass. In later years army personnel from Fort Marcy in Santa Fe grazed their stock here. As late as 1879, the Galisteo Valley had no arroyos and was supporting large areas of sacaton. Subjected to continuing heavy grazing, the area is today deeply cut by arroyos, and the Rio Galisteo is dry most of the time.[19]

Continuing south, Kearny's army found no grazing for the horses within twelve miles of Santo Domingo Pueblo. At Santa Ana Pueblo, Lieutenant Abert reported, "We had much trouble to get wood for our fires and fodder for our mules; there was no grass to be seen anywhere in the vicinity." Summarizing the official reports, Leopold characterizes the middle Rio Grande region in 1846–1855: "the good grass in the woodland belt was, even originally, restricted to the well-watered bottoms."[20]

Despite the tone of these reports, New Mexico's grazing resources remained considerable and would continue to be so into the twentieth century. Emory reported "excellent grass on the Rio Pecos, abreast of the ruins where the modern village of Pecos is situated." Johnston reported that "the country from the Rio Grande to Tucson is covered with grama grass, on which animals modestly worked, will fatten in winter." Environmental conditions in New Mexico were uneven and would continue to vary greatly across the territory.[21]

34 SHEEP AND THE MARKET ECONOMY

In the years immediately following the annexation, the Americans established a small US occupying military force, which was accompanied by an even smaller political contingent, augmenting the Anglo community of traders and merchants. And a long period of pacification of the nomadic Indian tribes began. In 1851–1861 the average military force in New Mexico was about 1,700 men at an annual cost of $3 million in Washington dollars, a considerable increase in both men and funding over the small Mexican garrison stationed in the colony before the annexation. By the late 1850s, American troops were stationed at twelve widely dispersed forts and other outposts. From the standpoint of the Anglo and Hispanic citizens, the superior US force was badly needed, but even after it was in place, public safety remained elusive. The army, yet inexperienced in western Indian warfare, was ineffective in suppressing Indian raids at first.[22]

During the military occupation, Indians are reported to have run off 154,915 sheep from Bernalillo and Santa Ana Counties, 16,260 from Santa Fe County, 17,080 from Taos County, 43,580 from Rio Arriba County, 50,000 from San Miguel, and 171,558 from Valencia, for a total of 453,393 head in little over four years. This was a horrendous loss for the impoverished territory. For their part, the Indians were said to have systematically avoided stealing an entire flock so as to leave behind some breeding stock to replenish the herd for a future raid. With the financial backing of the US government, the relatively well-armed and well-trained army eventually imposed considerable public safety measures.[23]

Trade Grows

Under the military occupation and continuing for many years thereafter, the garrisons provided new markets for New Mexico produce. By 1850, Anglos constituted nearly 16 percent of the population of Santa Fe and at least 10 percent in the towns of Las Vegas, Albuquerque, Cebolleta, and Socorro, about half of these Anglos being directly attached to the military. Grain, hay, and other farm products needed for both food and forage commanded high prices at the forts. Lucian Maxwell became a prominent army contractor during the interwar period.[24]

Though many of New Mexico's farmers and ranchers, like Maxwell, benefited from the expanding domestic markets, they generally did not sell their produce directly to the army but rather dealt with fort sutlers, middlemen-expediters who linked numerous small producers to a single army fort, launching an emergent cash economy in the process. The sutlers were some of the first sedentary Anglo mercantile capitalists in New Mexico. The merchants would soon be dealing extensively in live sheep and wool.

By the late 1850s, *churro* wool, despite its shortcomings, had become a profitable return commodity over the Santa Fe Trail, the prohibitive shipping expenses of earlier years to the East Coast woolen mills having been overcome. In fact, the increased wool shipments enabled the Santa Fe trade to continue unabated after the territory's hard currency had been depleted from decades of unbalanced trade with the United States. New Mexico wool thus displaced hard currency on the backhaul.[25]

Some New Mexico merchants were now purchasing all or most of their westbound supplies on the East Coast, shipping them by rail to Pittsburgh and then by steamboat down the Ohio River and up the Mississippi and Missouri Rivers to Kansas City, Missouri, rivermen having learned to navigate the treacherous Missouri River. The freight wagons now departed for New Mexico from Kansas City, eliminating the expensive transport across Missouri. Wool traversed the same route in reverse. Hispanic merchants were shipping about half the merchandise over the trail by 1860, the most prominent still largely from the handful of *rico* families that had long dominated New Mexico's economy, although a few new families became involved.[26]

Hispanic Sheep Growers

The annexation and the arrival of a small but growing number of Anglo Americans brought no immediate change to the lives of sheepmen and herders or to most New Mexicans. Sheep remained an important

36 SHEEP AND THE MARKET ECONOMY

basis of wealth and a determinant for social and political leadership. The more prominent Hispanic sheep-growing families retained their standing during the interwar years and beyond. The families that had profited from the Chihuahua and Santa Fe trades held on to their sheep herds and the large ranches they had operated for decades. Indeed, they dominated sheep growing in New Mexico until long after the annexation. Some comments about a few large-scale, sheep-growing *rico* families are in order and are presented here.

Pedro Bautista Pino, arguably the leading citizen of New Mexico when his peers selected him to represent New Mexico at the Spanish Cortez around 1810, was described years later by Colonel Francisco Perea as "probably the wealthiest man in Santa Fe, being the owner of vast flocks of sheep and goats."[27] Pino's sons, Miguel, Facundo, and Nicolas, sustained by large land and sheep holdings like their father, carried on the family tradition of political, social, and, in their case, also military leadership until well into the territorial era.

The Chaves family is notable for, among other things, its long-running prominence in the sheep industry. At the time of the annexation, family patriarch Mariano Chaves was said to possess the largest hacienda on the Rio Grande south of Albuquerque. His son, J. Francisco Chaves, drove large herds of sheep to California in the 1850s and later had a distinguished military and political career. Manuel Antonio Chaves, Mariano's equally illustrious nephew, established a substantial livestock business around 1848. In the early 1850s he and his brother-in-law, Lorenzo Labadie, acquired lands along the Rio Pecos extending south from San Miguel through Puerto de Luna to Bosque Redondo and stocked them with sheep. However, their operation was plagued by Indian raids, and preoccupied with other activities, they turned their stock over to majordomos. Later, around 1864, Roman A. Baca, Manuel Antonio's half-brother, acquired land, including the Bartolome Fernandes Grant, for the family near the San Mateo Peaks in today's Valencia County. He established a 40,000-head herd on the grant and sent large wool shipments to St. Louis by ox team over the Santa Fe Trail. Manuel Antonio joined Baca around 1876.[28]

Manuel Antonio's son, Amado Chaves, had an illustrious career in law and New Mexico politics. Educated at San Miguel College, Santa Fe, and National University, Washington, DC, where he earned a law degree, Amado established a successful law practice, served in the territorial legislature, and was appointed New Mexico's first superintendent of public instruction. Despite his success in the Anglo world of law and politics, he returned every year to San Miguel Ranch to supervise the lambing and shearing of the family flocks, and he undertook selective breeding experiments aimed at improved wool production.[29]

From one of New Mexico's oldest *rico* families, Solomon Luna took over his family's considerable sheep operations when still a young man. Starting from his family's ancestral grant, the San Clemente Grant in Valencia County, which extended from the Rio Grande to the Rio Puerco, Solomon Luna grazed his herds on public lands extending west across the Plains of St. Augustine to the tiny village of Luna near the Arizona border. In the late nineteenth century he was made president of the New Mexico Sheep Sanitary Board and a few years later was elected president of the newly formed New Mexico Wool Growers Association. He later earned an important place in New Mexico history when he assumed a leadership role in the successful campaign for statehood and the writing of the state constitution.[30] But for him sheep growing took precedence over political advancement, which was well within his reach. At the turn of the twentieth century, his sheep holdings were believed to be the largest in New Mexico. In 1912 at the peak of his political career, he died in a freak accident at Montague Stevens's remote Horse Springs sheep-dipping facility.

Several other *rico* families remained prominent in sheep growing in the 1850–1880 period. The Armijos of Bernalillo County were reported at one time to own 500,000 head. In the same period the Otero and Perea families together are believed to have owned another 500,000 head. Don Jose Leandro Perea let thousands of sheep out on *partido* contracts in Bernalillo County and on the Ojo del Espiritu Grant on the Rio Puerco in Sandoval County, land that, incidentally, was seriously damaged with overgrazing, as described below.[31]

38 SHEEP AND THE MARKET ECONOMY

Staying active in sheep growing after the annexation, *rico* families faced challenging, evolving economic conditions. But they were generally conservative in their business initiatives. When writer Cleofas Jaramillo questioned her wealthy, politically active husband, Venceslao Jaramillo, concerning his acquisition of a large ranch, he replied, "We Mexicans can only make money with sheep, and land is getting scarce." Many ranchers were reluctant to adopt new, more efficient methods of sheep husbandry when they were introduced and soon after became necessary. And although some members of the old sheep-growing families remained prominent late into the territorial period, their numbers were limited and their influence gradually eroded.[32]

THE CALIFORNIA SHEEP TRADE

If sheep growing and the families involved remained largely unchanged in the aftermath of the annexation, significant changes in how sheep were marketed and financed did occur. They came almost immediately after the annexation in a dramatic way. Soon after the United States–Mexico War ended the Camino Real sheep trade with Mexico, a new, even more profitable market opened up in California, an unusually serendipitous development for New Mexico sheepmen.[33] And that market absorbed all New Mexico's sheep exports for the next decade.

The discovery of gold in California in 1848 and the gold rush it engendered brought a massive influx of miners to the region and a concomitant demand for food far exceeding local production capabilities. And it unleashed a frenzy of speculative activity in the New Mexico sheep industry, the likes of which the sheepmen had never seen. Whatever livestock existed in California at the beginning of the gold rush was quickly consumed by the forty-niners. Severe shortages of food, along with other shortages, quickly developed and prices rose astronomically. The food shortage was exacerbated because the once-great cattle and sheep herds of the California missions, which might have helped feed the miners, had been decimated by the secularization of the missions in the 1830s. Rumors of the high food prices filtered back to New

Mexico, and it wasn't long before massive sheep drives were departing the territory for California. Once again, New Mexico mutton would feed a quickly growing population of miners when local food production proved inadequate.[34]

Trade between New Mexico and California was not a completely new development. Despite the long distances and poor trail conditions, it had been sputtering along for a number of years. As early as 1829, New Mexico traders were traversing the Old Spanish Trail and, on a small scale, exchanging woolen goods (*efectos del país*) for California horses and mules. Later, an 1841–1842 expedition led by Francisco Estevan Vigil drove some 4,000 head of "stock," almost certainly sheep, over the same route, proving that such a drive was possible.[35]

The California trade differed in important ways from the Mexican trade. It was true that the task of driving sheep to California, always an arduous undertaking, was similar to driving them south into Mexico, although the trails were less developed, dryer in places, and plagued by greater Indian dangers than the Camino Real. However, the business arrangements were new. In the opening years the trade did not involve Hispanic livestock producers directly but was undertaken by Anglo-American speculators who amassed capital and purchased sheep from New Mexico growers, whose flocks had been expanding since the close of the Camino Real trade. The Anglos employed borrowed funds also to purchase the needed supplies and to hire armed guards and Hispanic herders. They then supervised the drives themselves or employed experienced majordomos in that capacity. These initiatives bore some resemblance to the operating procedures that Anglo sheep and wool merchants would take up in the post–Civil War period. In the first years of the trade the speculators sold their stock in California for large profits and returned to New Mexico with the proceeds from the sales, profiting entirely from the westward leg of their expeditions, the opportunities for return trade being paltry in comparison.[36]

The trade started almost by accident in August 1849, when a wagon train of gold seekers heading west over the southern route to Los Angeles happened to stop in Galisteo, New Mexico, for a week to rest their

40   SHEEP AND THE MARKET ECONOMY

teams and visit Santa Fe. One member of the train, remembered only as "Old Roberts," purchased 500 sheep for $250 (four reales per head) and hired two men and a boy to assist his Black slave in driving them to Los Angeles when the train resumed its course. Sometime in early 1850, Roberts sold his sheep, including lambs born on the trail, for $15–$16 per head, for a return of over $8,000 on his $250 investment, a considerable amount of money at the time ($280,000 in 2020 dollars).[37] This amounted to about thirty times what the sheep were selling for in Mexico.

Hearing rumors of high California food prices but probably unaware of Old Roberts's good fortune, a consortium of Anglo businessmen, led by Santa Fe attorney William Z. Angney and including Spanish business and political leader Manuel Alvarez, combined forces in 1850. Angney purchased 6,000 sheep from New Mexico ranchers and drove them to Los Angeles over the Old Spanish Trail. The drive was not without some adventure: it was attended early on by the theft of about 1,000 head by rogue herders and later had an unpleasant encounter with a Ute party. Upon his arrival, Angney turned down offers of $8 per head and drove his flock north to San Francisco, expecting even higher prices, but instead discovered a dearth of cash buyers. He declined proffered payments in bank drafts of dubious value, that is, checks drawn on banks in New York and St. Louis. But after some delay Angney sold his flock in 1851 and, having settled in California in the meantime, reinvested his profits in northern California real estate.[38]

Entrepreneurs were soon driving additional herds to the gold fields. Manuel Alvarez organized another drive on his own in 1851, purchasing 4,600 head from the Gallinas area near Las Vegas and from the Perea family near Bernalillo at prices of about $1.25 per head, over twice the Durango market price before the United States–Mexico War. He went into partnership with an experienced Spanish trader who was to serve as his majordomo. Unfortunately, the man died along the way. The sheep were eventually delivered to San Diego, where they were sold at auction for about $20,000 ($700,000 in 2020 dollars), making for a considerable profit. Angney and Alvarez were fortunate. In the same period, Joseph White, with a large herd from Chihuahua also bound for

Sheep and the Market Economy   41

California, lost a substantial part of his herd to desert heat and Yuma Indians. Other inexperienced Anglo speculators lost entire flocks on the dry stretch across the Mojave Desert.[39]

The speculative sheep drives continued through 1852, when three more departed New Mexico for California. Sketchy documentation indicates that Manuel Antonio Chaves participated in one of these drives, making him one of the first Hispanic sheepmen involved. Perhaps the most audacious and dramatic of the early drives was that led by fur trapper, frontier entrepreneur, and storyteller Richens Lacy (Uncle Dick) Wootton. Wootton joined forces with Taos businessman Jesse B. Turley in 1852, raising $9,275, with which the men purchased 9,000 head and the necessary outfit for the twenty-one-man party. They took a more northern route than Angney, going through Colorado, Utah, Nevada, and over the infamous Donner Pass into California. Their trek was, to say the least, one of high adventure highlighted by an encounter with a band of angry Utes near today's Montrose, Colorado, at which point Wootton fought the Ute chief in hand-to-hand combat for passage rights through Ute territory. Wootton won the contest and eventually got his herd to Sacramento, where he sold most of his stock at $8.75 per head for a handsome profit. He took one-third payment in gold and the balance in St. Louis bank drafts, taking a chance Angney had refused the year before. Over the next few years speculators profited handsomely from the California trade.[40]

Ambitious Hispanic sheepmen soon entered the trade. The first to undertake a drive to California were Antonio Jose Luna, his brother Rafael, brother-in-law Miguel Antonio Otero Jr., about to embark on a notable political career, and associate Ambrosio Armijo, all experienced sheepmen who in 1852 oversaw the drive of 25,000 head from their homes in the Los Lunas area through Apache country—the Gila River route—to Los Angeles. This was the largest drive to California up to this time. The leaders were owner-merchants. They unfortunately lost 11,000 head to quicksand but sold the surviving sheep in Los Angeles for $5.50 per head and still ended up with a massive profit. The New Mexicans returned home with $70,000 in coin and gold dust (over $2 million

42 SHEEP AND THE MARKET ECONOMY

in 2020 dollars). According to tradition, Armijo received his share of the profits in fifty-dollar gold pieces minted in San Francisco, some of which he had sewn into his leather vest for safekeeping on the journey home.[41]

In the early years of the California trade, no consensus on the best route having developed, several different trails were followed until the southern Gila route, dipping into Sonora, Mexico, came to be favored. In the winter of 1852–1853, flamboyant French-Canadian pathfinder and Santa Fe trader Francis X. Aubry assembled a fifty- to sixty-man crew, probably including Hispanic herders, and drove 5,000 sheep he had purchased in the Santa Fe–Albuquerque area, along with 140–150 mules and ten big freight wagons over the Gila route to Los Angeles. True to his reputation, Aubry found a 150-mile shortcut near Tucson, Arizona. The publicity-conscious trader left the drive well documented. He sold 1,000 head of sheep, some of his mules, and wool shorn from the sheep in the Mormon colony in San Bernardino for $12,000 and sent the rest on toward San Francisco, where they were sold, probably at $12 per head. After also selling his wagons and more of his mules, Aubry returned to New Mexico with nearly $60,000 ($2 million in 2020 dollars), another financial killing considering that he probably paid no more than $2 to $3 per head, and possibly much less, for his stock.[42]

In the meantime, another consortium, this time made up of former mountain men and led by Lucian Maxwell, Kit Carson, and John L. Hatcher, assembled a total of 13,000 sheep, constituted a thirty-three-man party, and headed out in early 1853 along Wootton's northern route but detoured even farther north to Fort Laramie to avoid the Utes that had so plagued Wootton. Each of the three principals apparently had acquired his own herd; on the trail they broke up into three widely spaced sections. Carson, in financial partnership with Henry Mercure and John Bernavette, had purchased 6,500 *churros* in the Rio Abajo, reportedly for less than fifty cents per head. After six months on the trail, they arrived in northern California and sold their sheep in Sacramento, getting only $5.50 per head.[43] This lower price still made for a handsome profit but signaled the abatement of the California meat shortage.

Sheep and the Market Economy   43

Francis Aubry arrived back in New Mexico in the fall of 1853, about the time Maxwell and Carson were selling their stock in California. He was very satisfied with the profits he had just realized and optimistic about the future of the California trade. With Alvarez's help, he quickly assembled another herd, 16,000 head this season, and by early October was on his way back to California. According to Bergman, all of Aubry's herders from his first California drive signed up again. He speculates that Aubry probably paid them as much for the nine- or ten-month period of the drive as they could earn in four to five years herding sheep for a New Mexico patron. This time, Aubry joined forces with several large-scale Hispanic sheepmen to form a drive of some 50,000 head. Some of the other participants were Francisco Perea (Bernalillo), with 10,000 head; Judge Antonio Jose Otero (Los Lunas), 8,000 head; and twenty-year-old J. Francisco Chaves, with a substantial herd. During this same season, somewhat ahead of Aubry's group on the trail to Los Angeles, Nicholas Pino, Peter Bautista Pino's son, conducted a 15,000-head drive, while another 35,000 sheep in three separate herds from Chihuahua made for an additional 50,000 head delivered to California.[44]

The size of the California drives had been growing steadily, and the 1853 shipment would have been the largest up to that time. But as Maxwell and Carson had discovered some months earlier, the California prices had weakened. Demand had decreased due to the import of the flood of sheep that had come not just from the Southwest borderlands but also from as far away as Ohio and Illinois. Some of the New Mexico ewes were used in reestablishing the California herds, which eventually were sufficient to meet the demand for mutton in the gold fields and reduced the need for continuing imports. Under rapidly evolving conditions, profits were smaller this season. Aubry's party took several months to sell all their stock. They returned together to New Mexico in the summer of 1854, Aubry soon to be killed in a Santa Fe barroom altercation.[45]

The character of the California trade changed at this point. California sheep prices decreased as rapidly as they had risen. In the

44   SHEEP AND THE MARKET ECONOMY

meantime New Mexico growers, experiencing an increased demand for their produce from the speculators, jacked up their prices.[46] Profits were squeezed at both ends of the trade. After 1854, the California trade was no longer a profitable arena for speculation but nevertheless remained reasonably profitable for growers. It was taken over entirely by Hispanic rancher-merchants.

The Perea, Otero, Luna, and Armijo families were all active in this continuing trade. After returning home, J. Francisco Chaves turned around immediately for a return drive. He assembled 18,000 head in late 1854 and drove them from the Rio Abajo via Los Angeles to San Francisco, just as the Panic of 1853 was fully setting in. This was an inopportune time to be marketing sheep, as the entire country was plagued with bank failures and bankruptcies, discouraging large business transactions. Unable to immediately sell his herd at a good profit, Chaves remained in California for the next three years, dealing in livestock of various kinds, gradually selling off his own sheep, and marrying Mary Bowie, a Montreal native living in Monterey, California, before he finally returned to New Mexico. Even in the face of Indian raids and desert losses, New Mexico sheep growers profited in the weakened market, if more modestly than the speculators, by trail driving and selling their own produce, as they had done in the Mexican trade.[47]

By 1856 conditions had apparently improved. That year members of the Luna and Armijo families trailed 19,000 sheep to California, Luna conducting another successful drive in 1857. Even later, in 1858, one of the largest drives up to that time, 100,000 head, departed New Mexico for California. The ownership breakdown of the herds from Valencia and Bernalillo Counties, driven in two distinct groups, as provided by sheepman "Santiago" (James Lawrence) Hubbell, is given in table 2.1. The sheep may have sold for about $4 per head. It will be noted that this stock was owned almost entirely by a few wealthy Hispanic merchant-sheepmen from the same families that had dominated the Mexican trade.[48]

The last large California drive, which included 50,000 *churros* under the direction of Francisco Perea and Jesus Luna, arrived in San

Sheep and the Market Economy 45

TABLE 2.1. Sheep ownership,1858 California drive

Sheep Owner*	Number of Sheep
Joaquin Perea	22,000
Antonio Jose Luna	17,000
Senor [Jose] Jaramillo of Los Lunas	17,000
Antonio Jose Otero	11,000
Rafael Luna	10,000
Toribio Romero	9,000
Ramon Luna	7,000
Miscellaneous persons	10,000
Total (ewes and wethers)	103,000
Ewes	20,000

* From Valencia and Bernalillo Counties. Hubbell provided these data for an article in the *Santa Fe Weekly Gazette* on October 9, 1858, which was quoted in Lee, *Bartolome Fernandez*, 35.

Francisco in November of 1860, just as Lincoln was elected to the presidency. California's sheep population had by now reached 1 million, and prices had dropped to $3–$4 per head. Trade with New Mexico ceased to be essential for California. The situation for New Mexico sheepmen was exacerbated by the onset of the Civil War when the US Army troops that had suppressed Indian raids in the 1850s along the heavily used Gila route to California, and other areas farther north, were withdrawn to eastern battlefields, giving the nomadic tribes a freer hand to attack the herds. Low prices and the increased Indian raiding shut down the trade that had been so profitable. The drives to California were no longer worth the risk for New Mexicans.[49]

The California trade flourished for over ten years. According to the US Census of 1880, some 550,000 sheep were trailed from New Mexico to California before 1858. And as indicated above, another 150,000 head were exported from New Mexico in 1858–1860 for a total in the range of 700,000. This exceeded the entire 1850 New Mexico sheep population, estimated to be 377,000, discounting Navajo holdings. The entire trade over the ten-year period added up to $4 million ($130 million in 2020 dollars) and brought to New Mexico a return of $500,000 in gold and

SHEEP AND THE MARKET ECONOMY

convertible paper ($16 million in 2020 dollars), increasing the short supply of hard currency in the territory. During the 1850s the annual sheep exports to California generally exceeded, perhaps by a factor of two or more, the annual exports down the Camino Real during the final twenty years of Mexican sovereignty. The drives undertaken by Hispanic merchant-ranchers from the early 1850s through the remainder of the decade accounted for considerably more of the exported livestock than the early speculative efforts of Wootton, Aubry, Carson, Maxwell, and their cohorts.[50]

On the negative side, the California trade broadened the *rico-pobre* divide in New Mexico. While sheep prices remained comparatively high and volume was large, the *rico* sheepmen made more money than ever. New Mexico's *pobres* gained little. The ownership base was narrow, just as it had been during the Camino Real trade. A large fraction of the exported stock belonged to the same handful of growers active in the past. At the opposite end of the economic scale, the hired herders generally came from the lower classes and were compensated poorly.[51]

As the California trade fell off, new opportunities appeared. An important sheep market opened in the Colorado mining camps, gold having been discovered in the Pikes Peak region in 1858. As had happened a decade earlier in California, another flood of men, the fifty-niners, pursuing dreams of instant wealth, poured into Colorado. And once again New Mexico *churros* fed a rapidly amassed population of nonfood producers, another uncharacteristically serendipitous development for New Mexico growers. For the next ten years and beyond, New Mexico sheepmen drove their herds to market over the relatively short distances to Pikes Peak, Denver, and Boulder. An even more momentous new opportunity came to New Mexico sheep growers with the development of the western wool industry.[52]

WOOL

Prior to the opening of the Santa Fe Trail, New Mexico wool had garnered little attention from sheepmen. This changed dramatically, although interest in wool developed slowly. Writing in 1857, W. W. H. Davis, former US attorney for New Mexico, commented on the state of wool production in the territory: "Notwithstanding the great number of sheep in the country, wool has never yet become a staple item of trade. . . . When New Mexico shall have become connected with the States by rail-road, the woolen manufacturers will find it to be in their interest to raise their own wool there instead of importing so much from abroad."[53] The wool industry indeed grew over the following decades, although not quite as Davis may have envisaged.

Sheep had proved particularly valuable in the frontier society of the colonial and republican eras because they provided both food and clothing. And, as described above, a cohort of landed *rico* families had built up very large herds and established a considerable export trade in live sheep by the time of the annexation. In contrast, wool production was undeveloped in New Mexico as well as nationally. Prior to the Civil War domestic wool production, then centered on small farms in the East and Midwest, and woolen manufacture, which was developing in the Northeast, were of secondary, if growing, commercial importance.[54] That situation changed precipitously. The woolen industry expanded greatly in response to wartime cotton shortages and continued to grow rapidly in the post–Civil War years. Under the impetus of opening markets in the eastern United States, the territory's wool production grew dramatically for the remainder of the nineteenth century, and wool took on major importance in New Mexico's export economy. It provided a welcome new source of income for ranchers. The amount of wool produced in New Mexico is plotted by decade between 1850 and 1920 in figure 2.1. A correspondingly rapid expansion of mercantile capitalism in the territory, with which wool became strongly linked, occurred in the same period. Ongoing financial relations between growers and the merchants, particularly as they pertained to debt, became a fact of life. And the territory became more strongly connected to the eastern US economy.

The Camino Real traders shipped *churro* wool sporadically to Mexico, but it never constituted a major portion of the trade. Hand-

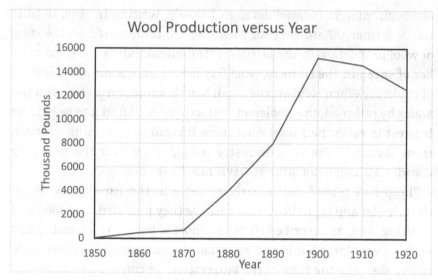

FIGURE 2.1. New Mexico wool production versus year by decade, 1850–1920. Production is seen to have developed quite slowly until 1870, when it grew rapidly for the remainder of the century, the western wool industry having been launched by the Civil War. Production fell off modestly in the early twentieth century. Data are taken from US census reports, 1850–1920.

manufactured woolen products, Hispanic and Indian, were on the short list of items, *efectos del pais*, shipped south in the caravans. But this woolen production was, and remains, a labor-intensive, modestly profitable cottage industry.

Opportunities Appear

Long before Davis, Santa Fe trader Josiah Gregg, who first came to New Mexico in the 1830s, saw a potential for commercial wool production. Struck by the paradox of fine grazing land and lackluster wool production, he was deeply critical of New Mexican sheepmen for their failure to breed quality wool-bearing sheep, describing their flocks as "wretchedly degenerate." At this time, the traders usually returned to Missouri with their wagons lightly laden, carrying only the hard currency generated by their trade and marginally profitable New Mexico

Sheep and the Market Economy   49

produce including wool, then, as Davis noted, regarded as inferior in quality. As it was, wool could be purchased for three or four cents per pound in New Mexico and sold in St. Louis for as much as fifteen cents per pound. Describing conditions of the 1830s, Gregg noted, however, that a wool backhaul "barely pays a return freight for the wagons that would otherwise be empty." He believed that a higher-quality product would be far more profitable and benefit New Mexico. Reporting on conditions in 1844, Santa Fe trader James Josiah Webb corroborated Gregg's assessment, also remarking on the poor quality of New Mexico wool. Concerning the backhaul, he went on to say, "The only products, beyond the immediate needs of the people, were wool (which would not pay transportation), a few furs, a very few deerskins, and the products of the gold mines."[55]

The Americans were not the first to criticize New Mexican productivity in any case. As early as 1803, Governor Fernando de Chacón wrote in his report on the state of the colony's economy that New Mexico's "natural decadence and backwardness is traceable to the lack of development and want of formal knowledge in agriculture, commerce, and the manual arts."[56] The governor understood, largely, the detrimental conditions that were retarding New Mexico's economic development. His concerns, which would remain essentially valid for decades, were pertinent to the sheep industry and would be eventually addressed in the post–Civil War period.

The wool trade grew slowly at first but soon eclipsed the California trade in woolens, which ended in 1848. Some New Mexico wool was shipped to Kansas City during the United States–Mexico War. After the annexation, the new territory's annual wool clip grew steadily. It increased from 33,000 pounds in 1850, when wool production was a barely profitable sideline for traders, to 493,000 pounds in 1860, a fifteenfold increase over the decade (see figure 2.1).

As it turned out, New Mexico, with its large herds, was well positioned to take advantage of a growing demand for wool. But the slow, expensive transport over the Santa Fe Trail still constrained the commerce in wool. Federal government agricultural experts took an interest; an 1869 government report accurately described the transport problem faced by the industry and advocated, as the solution, the construction of railroads into the territory. It stated, "This industry is crippled, however, by the difficulty of getting it [wool] to market, transportation costing as much as the original value of the wool." Indeed, the wool industry would not begin to truly flourish until the arrival of the railroads, as Davis had suggested.[57]

The Civil War Impetus

The Civil War gave birth to western wool production on a much greater scale than in the past, while a confluence of economic developments, starting before the war, resulted in a shift of the US sheep industry, in large part, from the small farms of the East and Midwest, where it had been centered, to the ranges of the trans-Mississippi West. The war revolutionized the sheep industry of New Mexico and contributed to the expansion of sheep growing elsewhere in the West in the post-war years.

Up to this time America's textile mills relied largely on the cotton plantations of the South for their raw material, cotton fabric being the favored output. At the outset of the Civil War, the South dominated the world cotton market, producing 85 percent of the raw cotton consumed in the United States, Britain, and Continental Europe in 1851. In contrast, domestic production supplied only about half the wool employed by the nation's woolen mills, which constituted a smaller industry in any case; the other half was imported. When the war started, the North effectively blockaded the Southern ports, severely curtailing cotton exports from the South. This reduced the supply and drove up the price of cotton, pricing it out of the market. New York prices quadrupled between 1861 and 1864. The Northern textile mills responded by converting their looms from cotton to wool, launching a new demand for wool. This was, in fact, a worldwide phenomenon: mills everywhere were converted from cotton to other fabrics, including both wool and linen. The US Army's need to supply its soldiers with wool uniforms

Sheep and the Market Economy 51

and blankets, which were manufactured in the northeastern mills, enhanced the demand for wool. Wool consumption in the United States more than doubled during the war from 85 million pounds per year to over 200 million pounds per year, while cotton consumption in the northern mills decreased to less than half the prewar level.[58]

With the onset of the war, Rocky Mountain wool prices rose dramatically from between twenty-one and twenty-three cents per pound in 1860 to between thirty-five and forty-five cents per pound in 1865, rendering the sale of western wool truly profitable for the first time. Western sheepmen started shifting their focus toward wool and away from mutton, an effort that would play out over a period of years. In New Mexico both sheep and wool production continued their prewar increasing upward trend. In the 1860s the New Mexico range sheep population reached about 1.7 million, mostly *churros*.[59]

During the same decade, the total value of woolen products produced in the US textile mills surpassed the total value of cotton products for the first time and would remain dominant for the next twenty years. The overall value of US cotton and woolen manufactures versus time is plotted by decades in figure 2.2. Traders were soon transporting larger wool shipments than ever over the Santa Fe Trail to Missouri commission merchants, who forwarded them to the northeastern textile mills. According to US census reports, New Mexico annual wool production continued to increase, going from 493,000 pounds in 1860 to 685,000 pounds in 1870 and then undergoing a sharp rise to 4 million pounds in 1880 (figure 2.1). Far more of New Mexico's sheep were being retained as wool producers rather than sent to slaughter. The sheep population and the number of growers increased. And range degradation accelerated, although few seem to have noticed or been overly concerned.[60]

The Long Walk

Since the sixteenth-century introduction of sheep into New Mexico, the herds and herders had been plagued by raiding parties from nomadic tribes. The situation had not abated since the 1832 comments

52 SHEEP AND THE MARKET ECONOMY

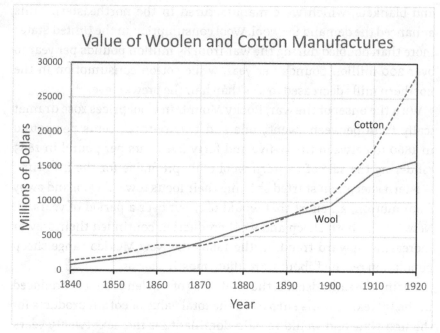

FIGURE 2.2. Total value of woolen and cotton products manufactured annually in the United States, 1840–1920. In 1860 the total value of woolen goods produced in US textile mills was about 60 percent of the value of cotton goods produced. When the Civil War curtailed the cotton supply, northern mills switched from cotton to wool. Woolen goods then surpassed cotton goods, increasing by 70 percent in value between 1860 and 1870, and dominated until about 1890. Thereafter, cotton products again exceeded woolen products in value, with the values of both quantities rising sharply in the early twentieth century. All data are from US census reports, 1840–1920, and have been converted to 2020 dollars using the annual Consumer Price Index for the United States.

of Licenciado Don Antonio Barriero. In fact, since the annexation, the security of the grazing lands had deteriorated. And the Navajos, their homeland comparatively close to the New Mexican settlements along the Rio Grande, had long dominated the raiding. New Mexicans claimed that the Navajos had stolen some 7,000 sheep in the last years of Spanish sovereignty, 1800–1823, to be followed by 50,000 head taken during the Mexican period, 1821–1846. It was claimed that 50,000 head had been recovered from the Navajos in retribution by Mexican militia forces. Thereafter, it was reported that from the time of the annexation through February 1851, 150,000 head were stolen from Santa Ana and Bernalillo Counties alone by Indian raiders, mostly Navajo, although 8,500 Navajo sheep were eventually recovered. Later 200,000 head were reported stolen before 1859, along with occasional murders of herders protecting their charges, and another 103,000 head were taken by 1864. For their part, the Navajo were estimated to have possessed over 500,000 sheep and goats by the mid-nineteenth century.[61]

Neither the Hispanic settlers nor the Anglo immigrants felt much sympathy for the nomadic tribes. An 1865 article in the *Santa Fe New Mexican* expressed a widely held sentiment: "With a country unsurpassed for stock and grazing purposes, we are yet almost unknown in the great marts of the east and why? Because numerous bands of Indians roam at will over our territory, plunder our farmers, murder our herders, and crush out that spirit of enterprise which would otherwise give us a remunerative competition with the rest of the nation in the production and sale of such articles as our land could well produce." The report of the US Department of Agriculture for 1869 presented an even harsher assessment: "The Indians infesting these regions [New Mexico], especially the Apaches, Navajos, Comanches, and their kindred tribes are the most formidable foes of civilization on the American continent."[62]

The devastating losses for the territory's sheepmen and, by extension, the entire population persisted until the advent of the Civil War when, in 1862, a Confederate force invaded eastern New Mexico. The Confederates were soon driven out of the territory by Union forces, but in response an enhanced military presence, tasked with fighting for the Union cause, was established. In New Mexico two volunteer infantry regiments were formed, one under the command of Kit Carson, now a lieutenant colonel in the Union Army. These units were constituted largely of peones offered freedom from bondage in exchange for their military service. In 1863, with an overwhelming military force, Carson's First New Mexico Volunteers entered the Navajo lands

54   SHEEP AND THE MARKET ECONOMY

and began rounding up men, women, and children for relocation to Fort Sumner on the Pecos River in eastern New Mexico. The army confiscated or destroyed at least 100,000 Navajo sheep, robbing the tribe of what had become an important food source. In a series of forced marches, later remembered as the Long Walk, thousands of Navajos— pregnant women, the sick, the elderly, and young children included— were driven the 300 miles across the territory to Bosque Redondo near the fort. The purpose was twofold: to punish the Navajo for their continuing livestock raids and to secure the region for the duration of the war. The walk was a brutal, hellish affair. Hundreds died along the way. Ute auxiliary forces attached to the army took into captivity a considerable number of women and children on the trail. A few Navajos were able to evade the army, retain their livestock, and remain out of sight for the next four years. For the great majority, the nightmare had just begun. There was some controversy over the action expressed in the New Mexico press, but generally the action enjoyed strong local support, particularly among the large-scale sheepmen.[63]

The first wave brought some 6,000 to incarceration at Bosque Redondo by July 1864, and 7,800 were on site by year's end. Eventually there would be 9,000 Navajo, who would be held four years until 1868, well after the war ended. The Navajo were instructed to farm the area to support themselves. But the land was poor, crop-eating insects were unmanageable, and the military presence was inadequate for protecting the Navajo prisoners from nomadic, slave-hunting parties. The experiment was altogether unsuccessful. Over the four years of incarceration US government provisions were inadequate or even unusable. Hundreds more died of hunger, exposure, disease, or simply broken hearts. The prisoners never adjusted to what had been a hostile land far from home.[64]

Finally, in 1868, the Navajo were allowed to return to their homeland on today's Arizona–New Mexico border, but within the confines of the newly established reservation, a much smaller area than what they had previously ranged over. They brought along 4,200 sheep and goats and 560 horses at that time. And they subsequently received from the US government successive allocations of 14,000 sheep followed by 9,450 and finally 7,500 together with 1,000 goats through 1878. These and continuing annuities made the tribe a ward of the US government. The livestock would become a valuable food source. The women assumed ownership of innumerable family flocks of sheep and goats, and employing their traditional weaving skills, they undertook commercial production of the fine wool rugs and blankets for which they became more widely known. Inequality grew with a few elite families controlling the best agricultural lands, an inordinate number of livestock, and government annuities distribution. In the last decades of the territorial period a few families began, for the first time, raising large commercial sheep herds. By 1915, 10 percent of the people owned 50 percent of the livestock.[65]

Navajo raiding persisted after the return west, as it had through the Civil War, but on a much-reduced scale. There is evidence that Indian raiders escaped with over 6,000 head in 1868. But now, returned to their homeland and wary of the army, the Navajo, once known as fearsome, wide-ranging raiders, albeit active in agriculture and herding, assumed a new identity as a quiet, pastoral society.[66]

The grazing industry, expanding into newly pacified areas in New Mexico and throughout the West, benefited immensely from the military campaigns. Sheepmen would no longer need to concern themselves with Indian raids and could concentrate on adapting their operations to the new demands developing in their industry. The pacification contributed to a confluence of additional favorable developments for the industry, including new eastern markets, improved transport and communication facilities, and commercial financing opportunities that took hold in the latter decades of the nineteenth century.

Slavery under Duress

As early as the 1850s, with growing abolition forces in the Northeast and Washington, legislative measures to regulate southwestern slavery emerged from Washington and Santa Fe. Prior to the Civil War,

56 SHEEP AND THE MARKET ECONOMY

proslavery sentiment pervaded territorial politics. The Master-Servant Act of 1851, an early attempt by the territorial legislature to regulate peonage, strongly favored the master and granted few rights to peones. This was followed by the Slave Codes of 1857 and 1859, eventually repealed, which likewise favored slave owners. Then, during the Civil War, Congress passed a series of laws intended to end southwestern slavery. But they lacked the essential specificity to be effective. In any case, the legislation was unenforceable in the West and, in large part, ignored by the territory's slaveholders. The Thirteenth Amendment to the US Constitution, banning chattel slavery in the South, had no effect in the Southwest. Finally, the Peon Law of 1867 clearly outlawed all forms of involuntary servitude in America, including Indian captivity and peonage. In the same general period, many New Mexico political leaders took on an antislavery stance, mirroring to an extent a growing territory-wide opposition to slavery. Southwestern slavery was now clearly under attack.[67]

Western Wool Flourishes

After the war, ranch profits came from a combination of live sheep sales and wool, although for a time New Mexico sheepmen still profited primarily from mutton production, for which their herds were best suited. In his annual report to the Territorial Assembly in 1867, Governor Robert B. Mitchell noted: "A very respectable number of our most enterprising citizens, I am happy to say, are already engaged in the laudable business of sheep growing, and are undoubtedly making it a profitable business, not so much from the sale of wool produced from these flocks, as their sales of mutton to the government for the subsistence of the soldiers, and Indians being furnished subsistence by the government." Nevertheless, commercial wool growing was becoming a permanent, even a dominant, feature of the territory's and the West's sheep industry.[68]

It was not all clear sailing for wool growers in the aftermath of the war. Postwar market imbalances created a challenge. The demand for wool quickly fell as cotton production resumed in the South, which soon reestablished itself as the leading world supplier of raw cotton. The demand for wool at the nation's textile mills decreased accordingly. To make matters worse for sheepmen, an influx of cheap imported foreign wool flooded the US market. And the military market for wool disappeared overnight, while the federal government placed large surplus stocks of army woolen goods on the open market, producing a temporary glut of such merchandise. Wool prices fell correspondingly. After the war Rocky Mountain wool prices collapsed from thirty-five to forty-five cents per pound in 1865 to eighteen to twenty cents per pound in 1868.[69]

TABLE 2.2. Wool production, fall 1899 and spring 1900*

State/Territory	Wool (lbs.)
Arizona	3,353,000
California	13,680,000
Colorado	8,543,000
Idaho	15,474,000
Montana	30,437,000
New Mexico	15,209,000
Oregon	18,350,000
Utah	17,050,000
Wyoming	27,758,000
Western Division Total	159,968,000
US Total	276,992,000

* *Twelfth Census, 1900*, Vol. 5, *Agriculture*, pt. 1, table 48, p. 673.

Worldwide production decreased in response to the glut and the concomitant depressed prices, and the postwar surplus of wool and woolens dissipated. By about 1870, the national wool market began to improve. In the West, if not elsewhere, wool growing remained profitable because of the low production costs of open-range ranching. The reawakened wool market led to an unprecedented expansion of the western flocks. As New Mexico's wool production began sharply increasing, commercial sheep ranching was just getting underway in northern Colorado and Wyoming. Other parts of the West soon followed.[70] Wool production of the western states and territories for 1900 is given in table 2.2.

Landed Hispanic families were the major producers in New Mexico's expanded wool trade through at least the mid-1880s. Jose Leandro Perea, one of the wealthiest men in New Mexico with an assessed wealth of $800,000 in 1875 ($19 million in 2020 dollars), was an important grower. He owned 75,000 sheep at this time, his estate having

58   SHEEP AND THE MARKET ECONOMY

increased steadily since the 1850s. Perea became involved in the wool trade early on. He is known to have outfitted a large train in 1867 carrying wool to Kansas City, which he exchanged for merchandise to be sold in New Mexico, establishing a routine he followed annually for many years.[71] Government livestock expert Clarence W. Gordon reported in 1880, near the time when the territory's sheep population reached its maximum, that three quarters of New Mexico's sheep were being raised by some twenty-one families, about 80 percent of which were "Old Mexican families," employing "inherited pastoral traditions" and, with their large herds, benefiting from economies of scale. According to his estimates, 72 percent of the territory's sheep were *churros*, so the sheep industry was still dominated by very large-scale family operations, running sheep that had not been upgraded for increased wool production. This situation would soon change. Wool was, nevertheless, a major product by this time.

Selective Breeding

Selective breeding of sheep for heavier fleeces was required to fully exploit the growing wool market. A breeding program had been ongoing in the East for many years, utilizing, among several breeds, Merinos. Prolific wool producers, full-blooded Merino sheep were, it is believed, first imported to the United States from France in 1801 and brought to a farm on the Hudson River for breeding. The Merinos were notable for the desirable fineness of their wool as well as their high fleece weight. Reasonably adaptable to western conditions, they became, in time, the basis for innumerable western herds.[72]

New Mexico was not totally unprepared for the new marketing opportunity since wool production had always been an adjunct to sheep growing. Well-capitalized Anglo sheepmen, many recently arrived in the territory, initiated selective breeding on a large scale. It became a permanent part of sheep ranching. In the early territorial years a number of Anglo sheepmen established herds in northeastern New Mexico. As early as 1859 George Giddings trailed the first purebred Merinos into the territory from Kentucky. Later, in 1864, 130 Merinos from Vermont, then a prime breeding area, were imported to Colfax County, an area of predominantly Anglo growers. A few years later M. M. Chase and John B. Davison brought in 200 Merino rams from Vermont to be bred with New Mexican *churro* ewes. Merchant-sheepman Felipe Chaves imported Cotswold rams from Canada. Others imported rams from Pennsylvania and Ohio. Between 1876 and 1880, on a much larger scale sheepmen drove herds east to New Mexico from California, where the flocks had been upgraded with midwestern stock during the California sheep trade of the 1850s. This imported stock significantly increased the number of graded animals in New Mexico. George W. Stoneroad, one of the largest importers, drove 10,000 Merinos from the Merced River in California to Puerto de Luna, New Mexico, in 1876. He purchased the sheep for $2.00 per head in California, and they were valued at $3.50 in New Mexico. A half dozen other Anglos imported large Merino flocks.[73] Altogether ranchers imported some 40,000 graded Merinos from California, although 13,000 head were subsequently driven on to Colorado. Trail losses were reportedly quite high, 36 percent, reflecting the inferior trailing abilities of the Merinos. Sheepmen also drove a few wool-producing sheep into the territory from Texas.[74]

New Mexico's large-scale Hispanic producers seem to have continued to specialize in *churro* wool, although a large herd was required to produce a profitable quantity. According to government livestock experts, Hispanic sheepmen took up breeding when they saw the Anglo Americans with improved flocks making more money from their wool and wether sales.[75] Wool growing became increasingly competitive, and efficient operations became a necessity.

The fact that Hispanic sheepmen did not attempt to develop quality wool in their flocks as soon as the wool market opened may seem perplexing. Some authors have attributed this to the shortcomings of the *partido* system, which shifted all the risk and little of the reward of sheep growing from the owner onto the *partidario*.[76] There may be some truth to this assessment.

An additional factor that would have affected smaller-scale sheepmen was the expense of breeding, both in time and money. Graded rams were expensive, as were the necessary shipping costs. And the returns on the investment would not be realized immediately but might in practice be delayed for a period of years. In the interest of economy, Montague Stevens and Solomon Luna shared a delivery of 150 Shropshire rams to Magdalena. Progress in breeding and wool production was thus retarded because top-quality breeding rams were beyond the means of many of the territory's sheepmen.

An additional, more concrete consideration is the high risk inherent in New Mexico sheep growing. As late as 1902, government livestock expert E. V. Wilcox, reporting on the western sheep industry, noted growers' common complaint about the risks: "One frequently hears the statement from sheep raisers that their business is in the nature of a lottery venture—when all goes well the profits are very good, but losses of an extremely serious nature may occur when least expected." The continuing detriments of periodic droughts and harsh winters as well as Indian raids, diseases, poisonous plants, and predators made any breeding program risky. Because of the trial-and-error character of breeding, any deviation from established practices compounded the known risks. Breeding for improved wool production may have remained a low priority in the minds of many established growers. Anglos immigrating to New Mexico after the annexation brought with them a knowledge of breeding that had been practiced in the United States for decades. That knowledge, when applied, substantially reduced the risks and served all the territory's sheepmen well.[77]

The cross breeding of heavy-fleeced select rams with *churro* ewes became widespread in the territory. And it would be practiced, to a greater or lesser extent, throughout the Rockies and Great Plains as sheep ranching developed in those regions. Once breeders gained some experience under southwestern conditions, they soon concluded that ewe bands had to be developed from Merino stock. The *churro* blood provided the offspring with the robustness, flocking instinct, and ease of handling needed on the western ranges, while the Merino blood provided heavier fleeces of commercially desirable wool, an important consideration since wool was sold by the pound. Favorable results came relatively quickly, although multiple generations of breeding were needed to obtain the most desirable crosses. The first cross of Merino bucks with *churro* ewes produced what were called "improved Mexican" sheep, which gave fleeces of about three to four pounds, essentially doubling the *churro* fleece weight. After the fourth generation of employing the Merino rams, the offspring produced "a fleece of about eight pounds of unwashed wool, tolerably fine, yolky and of a fair medium staple." At the same time, the animals retained the desirable churro characteristics. A considerable number of sheepmen employed, as a matter of necessity, the less desirable "improved Mexican" rams instead of expensive purebred Merino rams.[78]

Sheep breeding involved considerable challenges. Successful breeding was not to be accomplished casually; for the best results it required years of steady commitment and a degree of experimentation, as sheep grow differently in every environment. Breeding was thus a continuing process, and hands-on management was required. As government livestock experts Carman and colleagues noted in 1892, "It has been demonstrated by the experience of practical flock masters that the best methods for profitably conducting sheep husbandry, in the Territory [New Mexico], is for the owner to have personal supervision of his flocks, or if the management of the flocks must be left to hired help, to be sure they are capable, honest, and faithful." A well-founded choice of rams and breeding procedures adapted to the relevant range area was essential in a newly competitive wool market.[79]

While the Civil War had expedited New Mexico's and the West's entrance into the national wool market in a big way, the results of breeding for heavier fleeces did not fully materialize until some years afterward. Raton sheepman Daniel Troy identified the fifteen-year period 1877–1892 as a time of steady, widespread "improvement" in New Mexico flocks.[80] The crossing system employed in the West not only required considerable time and effort but was never wholly satisfactory.

62   SHEEP AND THE MARKET ECONOMY

A recent report estimates that by 1880 nearly 40 percent of New Mexico's sheep were of improved breeds, Merino-*churro* crosses. A decreasing but still substantial fraction of the wool continued to be *churro* produced. Changes were coming rapidly. By the early 1890s about 75 percent of the wool came from "improved Mexican" breeds, which had finally become widely available only a few years earlier. These were largely California Merino-*churro* crosses or their descendants. Beyond that, about 15 percent of the produce was fine-quality wool obtained from more carefully bred stock. Thus, only about 10 percent of New Mexico's output was still of the coarse variety produced by *churros*. Governor Miguel A. Otero Jr.'s 1905 report to the secretary of the interior asserted that 6 million sheep of improved grades were grazing in the territory. Although this figure is now believed to be an overestimate, the boast indicates the importance ascribed to sheep breeding by New Mexico government officials. By 1900 the average New Mexico fleece weight had risen to 4.25 pounds, not a spectacular result but still a significant increase.[81]

Two-Component Operations

The Santa Fe Trail had, after a slow start, made commercial wool growing in New Mexico viable. The Civil War made it profitable. As the national wool market expanded, the territory's sheep industry took on a two-component structure in which both live sheep and wool were major factors. Ranchers supplied raw wool to the textile mills of the Northeast, even as cotton rebounded after the war, while continuing to produce mutton. The 1879 arrival of the Atchison, Topeka and Santa Fe Railway (AT&SF) in Las Vegas, New Mexico, made it profitable to transport sheep east for the first time. From that time on, the territory's *churros* provided meat for an influx of immigrant factory workers in the industrializing East and Midwest. And Las Vegas, soon to be joined by Albuquerque, grew into a thriving shipping and commercial center for sheep and wool.[82]

The emergence of two-component operations gave New Mexico sheepmen a degree of stability they had not previously enjoyed. While the difficulties of open-range grazing would not be eliminated, the effects of market volatility were mitigated somewhat by wool production. The reason for this is that meat and wool prices did not necessarily rise and fall together; sometimes mutton and lamb prices rose to a relatively high level while wool prices were lackluster, as happened after 1890. Other factors could enter also. New Mexico governor L. Bradford Prince reported in 1889 that large flock losses over the winters of 1887–1888 and 1888–1889 were offset by an increase in wool prices. In his assessment, "no industry in New Mexico is more prosperous at this time than that of sheep raising."[83]

Through the 1870s and early 1880s, western sheepmen concentrated predominantly on wool, which remained sufficiently profitable under western growing conditions to sustain the industry, while meat prices remained low. They bred for heavier fleeces. However, by the late 1880s, wool prices had softened significantly, while sheep prices were on the rise. Chicago wether prices rose from $3.50 per hundred weight in 1884 to $6.00–$6.50 in 1891, and lambs were $7.00 per hundred weight, an attractive price. By 1888 Rocky Mountain sheepmen had concluded that wool production had become too unreliable to assure continued profits and redoubled their efforts to produce mutton, to which they had been giving low priority. To that end, they crossed mutton rams with the wool-producing ewes that had been so carefully developed since the Civil War. However, the growers took care not to breed away the wool-bearing capabilities of the offspring. Breeding as the markets demanded, New Mexico sheepmen never foreclosed either the wool or the mutton option. They could generally profit from both.[84]

Even before the establishment of a western rail system, the market for *churros* was growing broader. With the railroad's arrival, new markets for live sheep in Denver, Omaha, Kansas City, and Chicago began serving New Mexico growers, and meat prices assumed a degree of uniformity throughout the country, even though they might fluctuate significantly from week to week. Likewise, wool prices in the major markets of Philadelphia and Boston differed only moderately

64   SHEEP AND THE MARKET ECONOMY

but likewise fluctuated, a significant fraction of America's increasing wool needs being met with imports. Both cities were home to numerous wool brokers who purchased wool from all over the country and sold it to the woolen mills in their regions.[85]

The broadened markets together with two-component production not only stabilized the New Mexico sheep industry to an extent but drew New Mexico further into the national economy. By the late nineteenth century, business conditions for ranchers had improved significantly from a few decades earlier when they sold only live sheep in volatile, highly localized markets.

As variable as mutton and wool prices might be, they combined to provide a decent return over an extended period for many New Mexico producers. A growing number of families with modest herds benefited considerably. Assessing the territory's agricultural resources, Governor Otero's report of 1905 asserted in the ebullient language of the day, "Free lands, the finest climate in the world, irrigation, churches, schools, railroad facilities, home markets, good prices, extensive range, are all factors which help to make the life of the farmer and stock grower in New Mexico pleasant and prosperous." Politician, promoter, and sheepman, Otero was a notable Hispanic connected to the sheep industry through the last years of the territorial period when Anglos had taken on leadership of the industry to a considerable extent. During his years as governor, he ran a large ranch in Guadalupe County in partnership with territorial secretary J. W. Reynolds. There was more than a grain of truth in his assessment of the sheep industry, although the governor failed to note the deteriorating range conditions in some areas, still regarded as a secondary issue. The sheep population had tripled, and wool production had increased by a factor of thirty since 1860 while the human population had doubled.[86]

The two-component structure, however, did not eliminate all the risk in an inherently risky industry. It shielded sheep ranchers only somewhat from the moderately unstable markets that were the norm. Hard times for the sheep growers still came and went with regularity.

The Panic of 1893 devastated the western sheep industry for several years. The well-capitalized operations survived and eventually recovered. But many smaller operations did not.

The Wool Tariff

The US wool tariff was a matter of central importance for the western wool industry. Many growers believed they could not operate without a protective tariff. The American tariff has a long history. From the time of the Republic's inception, laws had been enacted by Congress imposing tariffs upon various imported goods. The laws, revised periodically, were intended primarily to provide the revenue needed to fund the federal government and did so until the passage of the federal income tax law in the early twentieth century. They also operated, at least in principle, to protect embryonic American industries, yet unable to compete successfully with cheaper foreign imports, by raising the price of the imported commodities in American markets to or beyond a competitive level. Wool and woolen goods were important commodities covered by the tariff, and the US tariff on wool was an important consideration, and at times a source of considerable anxiety, for American wool growers throughout the post–Civil War period.

Curiously, the wool tariff and the woolen tariff operated at cross purposes. The wool tariff was intended to benefit American producers by raising the price of wool on the US market, but it could be detrimental to woolen manufacturers, who then had to purchase their raw material at artificially elevated prices. In the absence of a wool tariff, the woolen manufacturers would be able to purchase inexpensively produced, imported wool at less than the cost of domestic wool to the detriment of American wool growers. America's wool growers always favored a high wool tariff. The woolen tariff, on the other hand, was intended to benefit the manufacturers, and the innumerable mill workers in their employ, by increasing the price of woolens on the American market. But of course, it would be detrimental to American consumers at large, who were thus required to purchase their woolen goods at a

66 SHEEP AND THE MARKET ECONOMY

higher price. America's woolen manufacturers always favored a higher woolen tariff and opposed a high wool tariff.

The tariff was a major, and sometimes bitterly debated, political issue almost from its inception through the early years of the twentieth century. The threat of tariff reduction was ever present. Wool growers grew nervous whenever Congress started considering the tariff. In early 1908 Solomon Luna, now president of the newly formed New Mexico Wool Growers Association, led a small delegation to Washington and appeared before the House Ways and Means Committee to lobby, successfully as it turned out, for retention of the wool tariff. Four years later he met with the president and a group of senators concerning the same issue.[87]

Before the Civil War, the tariffs averaged around 20 percent of the value of the subject imported goods. With the coming of the war, Congress increased the tariff substantially to help the finance the Union war effort. After the war Congress maintained the tariff at the high wartime level and held it more or less steady at around eleven cents per pound throughout the remainder of the territorial period, roughly half the cost of the wool abroad. This had the intended effect of raising US wool prices, although by a lesser amount than the tariff. The high wool tariff was supported in Washington by an influential midwestern farm bloc, but it benefited most the producers in the Far West with their large herds and low production costs. Congress removed the tariff briefly during the period 1893–1897, a time of heightened controversy over the tariff. Ordinarily this would have been a significant blow to New Mexico wool growers. But, in fact, the free period coincided with the Panic of 1893, which devastated the sheep industry. It is possible the free importation of wool during this short time had, under the circumstances, little effect on western producers. The restoration of the wool tariff in 1897 was unquestionably a relief to all American growers.[88]

The wool tariff was a continuing benefit through the territorial period to New Mexico sheep growers, both the landed, large-scale producers and a growing number of families of modest means with their

Sheep and the Market Economy 67

comparatively small herds. And it remained beneficial, even essential, to wool growers in the late twentieth century. It was part of an increasingly strong connection between the federal government and the sheep industry.[89]

Wool Production at the End of the Territorial Period

At the turn of the twentieth century the United States was the world's third largest wool producer, accounting for about 10 percent of the total production. Nine western states and territories were producing nearly 60 percent of the nation's wool. And New Mexico, facing stiff competition from other western states and territories, accounted for about 10 percent of the western production. American wool production, now an important component of the nation's economy, was absorbed in its entirety by the domestic mills. The roughly 30 percent of the wool that was imported was primarily carpet wool, like that produced by *churros*, but no longer profitable for American growers. Overall, American mills were utilizing about 15 percent of the world's production. By 1890 America's consumption of wool, estimated at 8.75 pounds per capita, was the largest of any nation in the world. New Mexico wool helped make this possible.[90]

STOCKING THE WESTERN RANGES

In the years following the Civil War, the Great Plains–Rocky Mountain region, not just New Mexico, was becoming recognized for its fine grazing land. Alexander Majors, principal in the storied western freighting firm of Russell, Majors, and Waddell, asserted in 1870: "The country west of the Missouri River is one vast pasture, affording unequalled summer and winter grazing, where sheep, horses, and cattle can be raised with only the cost of herding." Another typically optimistic government report of 1870 described the entire Rocky Mountain region from New Mexico to Montana as a land of "perennial pastures, 'boundless, endless, gateless,' where cheap beef and mutton

68 SHEEP AND THE MARKET ECONOMY

may be raised to feed the millions of laborers who are to develop the wealth of this continent." The optimism was not unjustified. Opportunity abounded. Large tracts of fine, cheaply attainable grazing land were opening up in the West and soon beckoning immigrant stock growers as never before. The government report, quoting Majors, went on to assert that the nation's wool production needed to spread west if it was to flourish: "We must of necessity . . . if we grow wool at all, develop the resources of the great interior pasture land [the Great Plains and Rocky Mountains]." In contrast, conditions in the East and Midwest, where land prices were increasing rapidly, were turning less attractive, even inhospitable, for sheep growers. Rising land prices were, however, only one of a confluence of economic and technological developments that began to unfold immediately before the Civil War and would have a profound effect on the sheep industry, giving rise, as they did, to a vast increase in American sheep and wool production together with a geographical shift of the industry into the trans-Mississippi West. And New Mexico's *churros* would play an important and unique role.[91]

Agricultural Developments in the Midwest

The expansion of America's rail network into the Midwest in the 1850s set off the chain of developments. Up to this time, midwestern farms were congregated in the river valleys so as to be near the water highways over which they transported their crops to market, an expensive, time-consuming practice. The railroads penetrating the Midwest rendered such inefficient transport practices obsolete. They could transport midwestern agricultural produce for the first time to urban eastern markets relatively quickly, safely, and inexpensively. As farms now needed only to be reasonably near a rail line, farmers started taking up lands much farther from the rivers. Large areas of the Midwest opened up for agriculture as a result.

As conditions in the Midwest were becoming more favorable for farming, America was undergoing rapid industrialization, which

Sheep and the Market Economy 69

created a growing army of urban factory workers needing to be fed. Even as their numbers grew, the midwestern farms did not sufficiently meet an expanding urban market for their crops. The prices for farm produce rose, and a wave of farmers pursuing new opportunities took up homesteads in the Midwest, diminishing the availability of good farmland while driving up land prices. However, a relatively large amount of pastureland was required for commercial livestock production, utilizing the grassy meadows of midwestern farms. Particularly critical, the winter feeding of farm-raised livestock, a necessity in the eastern winters—long and often brutally cold—became more expensive, considering the increasing value of the land that had to be dedicated to growing feed. A further development that finally rendered eastern sheep growing unattractive to many farmers was the precipitous post–Civil War drop in the price of domestic wool.[92]

The rapidity and extent of these inauspicious changes caught sheep farmers by surprise. According to one government report, "thousands of flock masters have quit the business in disgust." Many, faced with ruin, sold off their stock in panic. Others continued production, but the eastern sheep industry as a whole underwent a steady decline that continued through the 1890s and into the early twentieth century. Sheep growing made less and less economic sense in the Midwest and the East. Breeding sizable herds on the farms simply became too expensive.[93]

If sheep production became less profitable, agriculture became more so. In response to the opposing price trends of agricultural produce and wool and the increasing land costs, wool growers in the East and Midwest redirected their efforts away from sheep to more profitable crops, grains in particular. Others moved their sheep operations west. This is not to say that sheep growing ceased altogether in the East. Until the early1880s the small farms east of the Mississippi River dominated commercial mutton and lamb production. Shipments were small, buyers were numerous and small scale, and the produce entered the meat market through local butchers.[94]

70 SHEEP AND THE MARKET ECONOMY

The Far West Beckons

In New Mexico land prices were held down by "a deep and acknowledged distrust of land titles" under the recently adopted American legal system. A substantial portion of the privately claimed land, some 35 million acres as it turned out, had unsettled titles. A legacy of the Spanish-Mexican land-grant system, this retarded homesteader immigration, giving ranchers a few more years to dominate the range that they otherwise would not have had. In the 1860s and into the early 1870s an undivided interest in a Spanish-Mexican grant land could be acquired for as little as thirty cents per acre. Well situated land with clear title could be had for $3 per acre. But much of the territory's land was freely open for occupancy. Before 1880 many ranchers simply used unclaimed portions of the public domain without establishing legal ownership in any way. Rights of occupancy were recognized on a first-come-first-served basis. As described by West Texas sheep rancher Winifred Kupper, your range was yours "though you hadn't paid a cent for it. It was yours by unwritten law because you'd got there first." Ranchers were expected, however, to keep their sheep on their own range and not let them stray onto a neighbor's. Conversely, it was sometimes necessary to defend one's own range from intrusion by other stockmen with the help of a gun. In a similar fashion, many Hispanic families owned their lands by Spanish occupancy custom. Following the annexation, Hispanic herders in many areas of New Mexico retained control of the traditional grazing areas they had long been using. Such lands would have included the common lands on community grants and unclaimed lands that had become US public domain. The US Census of 1880 noted that New Mexico had a substantial contingent of widely ranging, largely Hispanic, nomadic herders who owned no home range.[95]

The lure of cheap land drew Anglo sheepmen, refugees from the eroding opportunities in the East, to the West, including New Mexico. Even when grazing tracts were purchased, the entry costs were altogether manageable for many sheepmen. Writing in 1881, promotional writer General James S. Brisbin made the observation that the young farmer of the East could no longer afford the farm his father had acquired a generation earlier. The opportunities of the past were gone, it seemed. He continued, "What has been occurring in the East during the last two hundred years is now occurring in the West, only with ten fold more rapidity." He further asserted, "No industrious man can make a mistake in moving west."[96]

By the mid-1870s, with the considerable suppression of Indian hostilities and an increased realization of the value of New Mexico land, prices did begin to climb.[97] Land values continued increasing in the 1880s with the arrival of the railroads and the economic boom they engendered. Hispanic grantees who had sold out at rock-bottom prices would later believe that they had been cheated. Despite the price rise, Anglo stockmen continued to find ways to acquire large tracts of New Mexico land cheaply.

Western lands would not even be fully useful for grazing until their nomadic Indian occupants were pacified. Large continuing losses of livestock and significant, if less frequent, losses of human life were endemic. When forced to it, Hispanic sheepmen had expanded out from their river kingdom with considerable trepidation, despite the immense tracts of unused rangeland beckoning them. When the Civil War started, Indian raiding increased throughout the West. Wagon trains no longer attempted to cross the plains without military escort.[98]

By 1870, the US Army had suppressed the hostilities of the nomadic tribes throughout much of the trans-Mississippi West, in the process removing those Indians from their ancestral hunting grounds and placing them on reservations. The campaign would continue into the 1880s. In the same general period, American hunters removed vast populations of buffalo from the western plains, slaughtering them primarily for their hides and tongues, but also to feed railroad laborers and to weaken Indian resistance by depriving the nomadic tribes of their most important resource.[99] For their part, the ranchers taking up the lands could now concentrate their resources on raising livestock rather than defense against Indian raids. And their livestock did not have to compete with wild buffalo for the available forage. The combined Indian and buffalo removal, aside from moral and ecological

72 SHEEP AND THE MARKET ECONOMY

considerations, which were expressed only weakly at the time, opened vast tracts of inexpensive western rangeland for domestic livestock. And those lands came to be more heavily stressed by the domestic herds than they ever had been by the buffalo, substantially altering the vegetation in many areas. In this sense the western ranching industry was built, to a significant degree, upon land stolen from the nomadic tribes and then modified uncontrollably.

The western rangeland possessed specific attributes that made it the prime grazing land that it was. As Santa Fe trader Josiah Gregg's reported in 1844: "by far the most important indigenous product of the soil of New Mexico is its pasturage. Most of the high-table plains afford the finest grazing in the world being mostly clothed with different species of nutritious grass called *grama*." The western environment was overall better adapted to sheep growing, and stock growing in general, than the East.[100]

Under the prevailing climatic conditions, the western grasses, in particular, were indeed superior. Where there is sufficient rainfall, east of the 100th meridian, natural grasses remain green and full of sap throughout the summer until the coming of frost. When the frost strikes in the fall, these grasses lose their nutritional qualities and can no longer sustain livestock. As a result, eastern farmers had to provide winter feed for their livestock for as much as six months of the year, a considerable expense, as previously noted. In the West the feed promised to be free year around and seemingly inexhaustible. Abundant grama grass (genus Bouteloua) ranged from Texas through Arizona and north to Colorado. It was said to withstand dry weather better than any other grass. Also valuable for grazing, buffalo grass (genus Buchloe) ranged north and south from Canada to Mexico and east and west from the Rocky Mountains into Kansas. Use of the western grasses required no human intervention. In the words of Brisbin, "it is unnecessary to cut hay, for the grass cured on the ground and always at hand is better than any hay in stacks." Indeed, during the summer and fall, the grasses in the West cure—that is, dry out—before the coming of the first frost. The nutritional value of the grasses is then locked in. In a good

Sheep and the Market Economy   73

year the dried, uncut grass of the western range would sustain a herd adequately during the winter months, despite the cold temperatures.[101]

Shelter facilities, needed in the East to protect livestock from the harsh eastern winters, were unnecessary in the West. The midwestern stockyards installed sheds to protect the sheep from the elements. Farther west, where shelters were not essential, the expense was avoided. Livestock could be run freely on the open range or in feed lots, exposed to the elements year around, at least in most years. Winter losses from inadequate forage or freezing storms were usually sustainable. Western ranchers only started building shelters in the late nineteenth century when increased competition demanded that winter losses be cut to a minimum.[102]

A further benefit for sheep growing in the West was that the large expanses of available land allowed for substantially larger herds than the farm environments of the East, introducing money-saving economies of scale. And if good land was cheap, so was labor. The availability of cheap, skilled labor had been an important factor in New Mexico sheep growing since its inception and remained important in the post–Civil War era. As in the past, a skilled herder in the West could manage 1,000 head or more on the open range. A government report of 1869 described the situation rather bluntly: "Ample labor to meet the demands of the rude pastoral industry of the Territory [New Mexico] is supplied by the emancipated peons at low rates. Owing to the small outlay required, sheep husbandry continues profitable under the primitive conditions still existing, not withstanding the distance of the markets." Sheep owners could, at the time, secure skilled Hispanic herders for $10 per month and board (less than $250 in 2020 dollars). Keeping labor costs low was important, even essential, for sheep growers through the remainder of the nineteenth century.[103]

Churro Seed Stock

Cheap land, cheap labor, good grass, a comparatively moderate climate, and developing transport capabilities helped make the West attractive

74 SHEEP AND THE MARKET ECONOMY

for growing sheep. The cheap, acclimated sheep abundantly available was another major, even essential, factor. In this regard New Mexico played a decisive role in western sheep production beyond the territory. The prolific New Mexico *churros* could be used to assemble a commercially viable flock quickly. Before 1869 the ewes could be purchased for $1.25–$1.75 per head, an attractive price despite the animals' small wool output. The low cost made it possible for men of modest means, who might otherwise have been unable to do so, to take up western sheep ranching.[104]

As it turned out, New Mexico *churros* constituted seed stock for building herds throughout much of the West. Before the Civil War, growers drove New Mexico sheep in small numbers for this purpose to Mormon farms in Utah, to the Nevada silver mines, and, after 1858, to the Colorado mining districts. They also drove flocks to Kansas, Nebraska, Missouri, and Fort Laramie, Wyoming, on a very small scale for both meat production and breeding. During this period New Mexico sheep came to be recognized as a desirable commodity.[105] Some western sheepmen built their flocks exclusively from *churros*.

Eastern sheep also contributed to western herds. Like the *churros*, the eastern sheep were also cheap following the post–Civil War collapse of the wool market. In their worst years, 1867–1869, midwestern and eastern flock owners sold off their herds en masse at $1–$2 per head for animals that had been selling for as much as $20–$40 per head only a short time earlier—during the war. These sheep, generally bred up wool producers, were then either slaughtered or driven west to help stock the open ranges. Eastern farms also provided wool-producing rams used to upgrade western flocks for increased wool production. Thus, graded stock from the eastern and midwestern farms, as well as *churros*, contributed to the western gene pool.[106]

The initial capital investment for a commercially viable western sheep ranch, including land and livestock, was relatively modest through the 1880s. Annual operating expenses for open-range grazing were likewise low, labor costs being a major component.[107]

The Sheep Industry Moves West

The confluence of economic developments in both the East and the West opened the way to an expanded, capital-intensive, and altogether more efficient national sheep industry. The push created by low wool prices and high land and feed prices in the East combined with the pull of low-cost western land, labor, and stock were the factors that shifted America's livestock industry to the West, the shift playing out over a comparatively compressed time frame. The center of commercial sheep and wool production shifted from the eastern farm belts to the Rocky Mountain–Great Plains region and the Pacific Coast, expanding outward from the two pre–Civil War centers of sheep breeding, New Mexico–southern Colorado and the more recently developed California-Oregon area. In the 1870s a contingent of midwestern sheepmen, from the Ohio Valley in particular, emigrated to California, Colorado, and New Mexico. Large herds of wool producers owned by an increasing number of growers stocked government lands. New Mexico's wool production doubled in the 1880s (figure 2.1). The new generation of growers was part of a larger postwar wave of western migration.[108]

While the easterners concluded that commercial sheep production no longer made economic sense and sold off their herds, western growers, sometimes acquiring those same herds, believed that, to be profitable, they simply had to maintain larger herds, production costs being low. Low production costs combined with increasingly efficient shipping facilities and the economies of scale possible for large open-range operations gave rise to a profitable post–Civil War western wool industry. Wyoming stockman J. A. Moore reported in 1870 after eleven seasons that he could produce wool for less than half what it had once cost him in Ohio and elsewhere in the East. According to other contemporary sources, the annual cost of keeping sheep in the West was in the range of twenty-five to seventy-five cents per head, while the cost in the East and Midwest was about $2 per head. In the early 1890s, production costs in New Mexico were reported to be cheaper on a per-head basis than in any other area west of the Mississippi River with

76 SHEEP AND THE MARKET ECONOMY

the exception of Texas, even though the annual lamb production per breeding ewe might have been somewhat lower than elsewhere. Western growers prospered in the 1870s, even though sheep prices were low. Southern Colorado grower Don Felipe Baca, who began raising sheep in 1864, reported that his wool clip covered all his annual running expenses. The sale of his wethers on top of that resulted in pure profit. New Mexico sheepmen were now profiting substantially from both wool and live sheep.[109]

Although profits were still possible with low-cost mutton production, many western sheepmen in the post–Civil War period concentrated on wool, at least until the late 1880s. According to the Las Vegas *Stock Grower*, the older sheep-producing states, with their higher production costs, Missouri, Illinois, Wisconsin, and Indiana in particular, could not compete in either wool or mutton production with "the range states," including New Mexico, and the feeder states Kansas and Nebraska. By the 1890s the wool and sheep production east of the Mississippi River had declined substantially, despite growing national markets.[110]

As was the case with the other western states and territories, New Mexico's sheep industry grew under the impetus of expanding national markets for meat and wool. The New Mexico sheep population more than tripled between 1867 and 1883 because wool had become truly profitable (figure 1.2).[111] Ever more rangeland was brought into production. The newcomers to New Mexico employed the traditional Spanish, open-range grazing practices best suited to the territory at the time. Land remained cheap or free even as ranching took hold on a much larger scale than in the past.

The territory's role was, however, unique. It supplied breeding stock for flocks throughout the West, starting in the late 1860s and continuing into the 1880s. *Churros*, particularly ewes, were employed to establish flocks in Colorado, Utah, Wyoming, Kansas, and Nebraska.[112] Until about 1880 sheep growing in New Mexico and southern Colorado was still largely controlled by Hispanics—wealthy, large-scale producers but also a growing population of small-scale owner-herders. Elsewhere sheep growing was an Anglo endeavor.

Sheep and the Market Economy 77

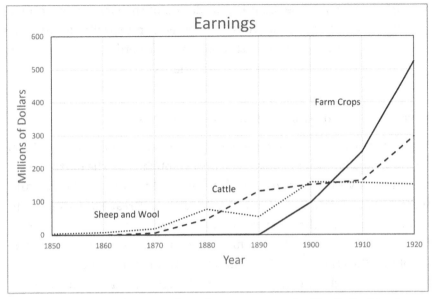

FIGURE 2.3. New Mexico annual earnings versus year by decade for live sheep and wool, cattle, and farm crops, 1850–1920. Annual earnings from live sheep and cattle are estimated to be produced by the sale of 30 percent of the total inventories. Earnings from cattle were negligible before about 1870 and did not surpass sheep earnings until after 1880. From 1890 on, cattle earnings surpassed or were at least comparable to sheep and wool earnings. After about 1900, the earnings from agricultural crops increased rapidly and surpassed both sheep and cattle earnings around 1905. Data are from US census reports, 1850–1920, and New Mexico Department of Agriculture, *New Mexico Agricultural Statistics*, 44, 56; Rocky Mountain wool prices for 1860–1900 are from Sypolt, "Keepers of the Rocky Mountain Flocks," appendix 3, 326. Dollar amounts have been converted to 2020 dollars using the annual Consumer Price Index for the United States.

Anglo flock owners were, during these times, possessed of an unshakable optimism about the future, and that optimism was an important key to their success. It fostered aggressive expansion and capitalization at a time when the industry would benefit most from it. The sheep industry spread throughout the Rocky Mountain–Great Plains region with extraordinary speed. Despite the popular imagery favoring the cowboy and cattle, the sheep industry was, at the very least, an equally

78   SHEEP AND THE MARKET ECONOMY

important part of the economic foundation of the West between 1870 and 1900 (see figure 2.3). It brought a degree of prosperity to innumerable New Mexico families, with their modest herds, and continuing wealth to the landed families with large herds.

Churros and the Expansion of the Western Sheep Industry

In the post–Civil War years there was a tremendous demand for sheep in the West wherever flocks were being established for the first time. As a result, New Mexico *churros*, well positioned to address the demand, were driven throughout the Rocky Mountain–Great Plains region to establish ranches. The sheep drives out of New Mexico, curtailed during the Civil War, resumed on a much larger scale than before.[113] They involved altogether more sheep than the California drives of the 1850s.

Stocking of the western ranges had begun gradually during the 1850s when New Mexico speculators and sheepmen exported some 700,000 sheep to California and another 100,000 to Colorado, Kansas, Nebraska, and Wyoming combined, while boosting the territory sheep population by about 500,000. After the war, peaking during the 1870s, innumerable western sheepmen purchased herds of breeding livestock in New Mexico and trailed them to their ranches.[114]

These post–Civil War sheep drives have been chronicled in detail elsewhere and will only be summarized here. By 1876 New Mexico was exporting 350,000 "Mexican" sheep annually by trail to Wyoming, Kansas, and Nebraska. The numbers increased steadily thereafter until 1885, when sheep exports, shipped increasingly by rail, reached a maximum of approximately 1 million head annually, "principally to Texas" at this point. In the 1870s the aggregate sheep population of Idaho, Montana, Utah, Wyoming, Nevada, and Colorado increased from 190,857 to 1,407,916, a sevenfold increase due significantly to *churro* imports, according to US census data.[115]

Colorado was the first area to be extensively stocked using New Mexico sheep. By the time of the Civil War, Hispanic New Mexicans had expanded their homeland into southern Colorado, and the southern third of the territory had already been stocked with *churro* herds. A handful of Anglo sheepmen began to arrive during and immediately after the war. Some of them established large flocks using *churros*. By 1871 there were several large Anglo outfits in Colorado and Wyoming. Some but not all of the early Anglo ranchers employed rams imported from the East to build their herds. In 1880 Colorado sheepmen imported 61,420 sheep, 50,000 of which were trailed in from New Mexico. The New Mexico ewes, readily bred up for increased wool production, were highly regarded as seed stock. The Bennett Brothers of Livermore, Colorado, got an average fleece of about 10 pounds from their 1,000 head in 1877.[116]

The sheep industry swept north, penetrating Wyoming upon the completion of the transcontinental railroad. Here sheep growing was an Anglo operation from the beginning, but New Mexico *churros* again played an important role. According to one government report, Wyoming growers imported 22,000 stock New Mexico sheep in 1880. Wyoming territory was well suited for sheep, with good grazing on over half its land area. And although it got off to a comparatively late start around 1870, it had the second-largest sheep population of any state or territory by 1900. One Wyoming sheep outfit grew into the huge Warren Livestock Company. Wyoming and also Montana had a significant effect on the New Mexico industry when they provided serious competition.[117]

The "Big Freeze" of 1886–1887, which devastated the cattle industry over large areas of the North, had remarkably little impact on Wyoming sheep ranchers, sheep being better able than cattle to withstand drought and freezing conditions. Prior to that time, cattle had been the favored livestock in the territory. Afterward many cattlemen, wiped out and lacking the financial resources for a fresh start, entered the sheep business, which required substantially less capital. The notable Swan Land and Cattle Company, originally of Cheyenne, survived when many other outfits collapsed. But after years of failure to realize its pre-1886 profitability, the company began in the early twentieth century to make substantial investments in sheep.[118]

80   SHEEP AND THE MARKET ECONOMY

Wyoming proved superior to the older areas, including New Mexico, for growing, if not breeding, sheep. By 1903 Wyoming and Montana sheep were valued at $2.58 and $2.31, respectively, while New Mexico sheep were valued at $1.98 on the average.[119] Clearly, New Mexico had not kept up with developments elsewhere in the West, due in part to environmental considerations. While it benefited considerably from the growth, the territory's monopoly on Rocky Mountain sheep slipped away. Even as their industry expanded, within a decade New Mexico ranchers became an integral part of, and were even enveloped by, a large Rocky Mountain–Great Plains industry of national importance that was dominated by Anglos.

The sheep industry next swept eastward across the Great Plains. The first permanent herds in western Dakota Territory were started in the early 1880s with flocks from New Mexico and Colorado. Thousands more head were driven from New Mexico to Texas in the early 1880s and sometimes traded for cattle. Over a twelve-year period, Kansas sheepmen imported about 1.5 million head from New Mexico and the Texas Panhandle, then occupied by Hispanic sheepmen. During 1880 alone, some 228,900 sheep were trail driven from New Mexico to Colorado, Kansas, and Nebraska, significantly surpassing in size the annual drives to California during the 1850s. And an additional 30,000 head were driven that year to Arizona Territory and 15,000 head to Texas. Between 1870 and 1900 3 million to 4 million head in all were exported from New Mexico to serve as seed stock elsewhere.[120]

Although some Anglo sheepmen built their first herds entirely from *churros*, it became a widespread practice to build flocks by breeding churro ewes with graded rams imported from the East and California, just as in New Mexico and for the same reason—that is, to develop a robust, open-range flock that produced an optimum combination of wool and mutton, an optimum that varied from year to year with changing market conditions.[121] In either case, New Mexico sheep constituted an important component of the initial breeding stock. By the early 1880s, with sheep herds throughout the Rocky Mountains and Great Plains well established, the demand for *churros* died down, and

Sheep and the Market Economy   81

New Mexico sheep exports for stocking purposes dropped off substantially. The West dominated sheep and wool production in America from this point on.

In the post–Civil War period, the sheep industry matured on several fronts. Sheep and wool merchants became increasingly important, and capitalization became a central feature in both the mercantile and the ranch operations. This is the subject of the following chapter.

3

THE INDUSTRY MATURES

New Mexico's sheep industry underwent major changes during the latter decades of the territorial period. Mercantile capitalism, the arrival of the railroads, commercial banking, the adoption of winter feeding, and the establishment of sheep growers organizations all had important consequences. The business side of sheep raising—shipping, marketing, and financing—took on the features that would be recognizable today. And ranching operations were capitalized. Important social changes accompanied these developments. At the same time, detrimental environmental changes on the rangelands, brought on by heavy grazing, were appearing through much of the territory. However, an early business arrangement that predated the territorial period was influential and helped make sheep growing a successful commercial endeavor.

https://doi.org/10.5876/9781646425471.c003

THE PARTIDO SYSTEM

As New Mexico's flocks proliferated in the eighteenth century, labor shortages developed. Sheep-owning families with their poorly compensated peon and *genizaro* herders were sometimes hard pressed to manage their growing stock holdings. Necessity drove them to adopt an ancient system of livestock management, called the *partido* system in Spanish. The earliest written record of a *partido* contract in New Mexico dates from 1766 and refers to an agreement made six years earlier. The practice grew steadily. In 1819 Bartolome Baca had 8,000 sheep under contract.[1]

The partido system was a livestock leasing arrangement that was well adapted to a cash-scarce economy with plenty of open rangeland; it was basically a sharecropping system. Under the *partido* system in its most basic form, an ambitious but poor man, the *partidario*, would essentially rent a flock of sheep from his patron for a fixed period, typically three to five years. The *partidario* was required to care for the sheep, often about 1,000 head, and to return to his patron as rent a fixed number of lambs and wethers each year, typically 20 percent of the number of ewes in the flock. And in later years the rent might include some fraction of the annual wool output. The *partidario* was entitled to retain the remaining offspring and wool as compensation for his labor. At the end of the contract the *partidario* was required to return to the patron a replacement herd equivalent to the original rented herd—that is, the same numbers of ewes and wethers, each of the same age and condition as the original flock. If all went well, and this was a big "if" in New Mexico, a *partidario* would, over a period of years, build up a significant herd of his own. Don Jose de Escudero described such a situation as he saw it in 1849. The *partidario* "could construct a house, and take in other persons to help him care for and shear the sheep. . . . The milk and sometimes the meat, from said sheep provide him sustenance; the wool was spun by his own family into blankets, stockings etc., which could also be marketed, providing an income. Thus the wealth of the shepherd would increase until the day he became like his overseer, the owner of a herd. He, in turn, would let

84 THE INDUSTRY MATURES

out his herds to others after the manner in which he obtained his first sheep and made his fortune."[2]

The system, however, favored the patron. The *partidario* assumed most or all of the risk in raising the sheep. In a surviving 1882 written contract from Bernalillo County between patron Cristobal Armijo and *partidario* Jesus Armijo y Jaramillo and his wife Altagracia Lucero de Armijo, the *partidario* received "two thousand new white sheep without defect" for which he was to pay an annual rent to the owner of two pounds of wool per head, "clean and in honest conformity to the accepted customs." He was also to guarantee the 2,000 ewes against all losses except the "invasion from Indians that are at war against the United States." As collateral for the loan of the ewes, Armijo y Jaramillo was required to mortgage his "property, houses, lands, goods and furniture both present and future, until the end of the last payment and to its fulfillment." One harsh winter storm or one devastating Indian raid might severely diminish or destroy totally a leased flock, wiping out an entire year's increase or worse. If the *partidario* was unable to meet his obligations to his patron, he was liable to fall into debt peonage. It was the opinion of Charles Lummis, on the basis of information he gathered in the late nineteenth century, that this was the norm rather than the exception, that *partidarios* were almost always reduced to peones. In his pessimistic view this was the mechanism by which New Mexico society "gradually fell apart into two classes—sheep owners and sheep-tenders." Whatever the case truly was, becoming a *partidario* was a calculated risk at best. The widespread use of *partido* contracts over a 150-year period suggests that many of those contracts were successfully fulfilled.[3]

Through the post–Civil War years, when the sheep industry was expanding rapidly, the *partido* system flourished and was adopted in modified form by Anglo sheep growers and merchants. Acting, in part, as patrones for the territory's growing number of independent, small-scale sheep growers, Anglo mercantile capitalists employed the system, much like their Hispanic forebears, to secure skilled herders cheaply, while shifting the risk of actually raising sheep from their own shoulders and onto their *partidarios*. Under these *partido* contracts, some but not all of the negotiations were conducted in cash.

MERCANTILE CAPITALISM

Mercantile establishments, dealing in general merchandise imported from the East, had come to New Mexico with the opening of the Santa Fe Trail. Many more opened after the annexation. Sheep and wool were not commodities of overriding importance for these operations in their early years. But the merchants soon found themselves dealing in sheep because they were an important medium of exchange in the cash-scarce economy. Some accumulated large herds as an adjunct to their mercantile activities. After the Civil War wool became, for many merchants, the single most important component of their business. The mercantile community grew for the remainder of the nineteenth century.[4]

The merchants addressed a growing need within the industry. As the territory's sheep population increased, ever more people were raising sheep, and the handful of large-scale Hispanic growers that had dominated the industry in the past was joined by a much larger contingent of small- and intermediate-scale, independent Hispanic growers together with an influx of immigrant Anglo sheepmen. It is believed that the smaller Hispanic operators, owner-herders, were the successful *partidarios* who had achieved independence from their patrons.

The number of stock growers was in any case amplified by freed herders when captive servitude and peonism had essentially disappeared by the end of the 1870s. Several antislavery political forces seem to have coalesced to contribute to this development before, during, and after the Civil War. Political sentiment in the territory in favor of slavery had largely dissipated during the Civil War as Union victories mounted. Antislavery forces in the East had redoubled their campaigns when they came to fully understand southwestern slavery. Congress expanded abolitionist legal doctrine beyond the Thirteenth Amendedment. The territory's political leaders, long having considered

86 THE INDUSTRY MATURES

the benefits of statehood, had seen continuing slavery as detrimental to that movement. They opposed it more strongly than ever in the post–Civil War years. From this point on, slavery, without political or even general public support, ceased to be an important part of territorial life, although isolated cases persisted for decades thereafter.[5]

Only the large-scale growers had the wherewithal to transport and sell their own produce in the distant markets, as they and their forebears had done during the days of the Camino Real and the California drives. The growing contingent of smaller-scale sheepmen, largely uneducated, Spanish-speaking, unconnected with the outside world, and having negligible financial resources in what was becoming a capital-intensive industry, became dependent on New Mexico's growing community of mercantile capitalists to market their produce.[6]

Dealing in wool and live sheep became an important, distinct component of the sheep industry. Well-connected and well-informed merchants, largely but not exclusively Anglo, assumed leadership roles in the sheep industry. They eventually were marketing the bulk of New Mexico's wool, linking growers to eastern commission houses and woolen mills.[7]

The Hispanic monopoly in sheep production, characterized by immense ranches linked to land grants, slipped away. Many of the landed *rico* families carried on as in the past; a few patrones became successful sheep and wool merchants, particularly those who had been active in the Santa Fe trade. But the number of *rico* growers was, if anything, diminishing, some of the old family fortunes being diluted by inheritance customs.[8] Many leading families, with their fortunes tied up in land and livestock, lacked the capital resources needed to engage in the lucrative mercantile activities.

The mercantile operations had become well established by the time of the Civil War and the expansion of the wool industry that followed. Their basic modus operandi was straightforward. They bought general merchandise wholesale in the East, transported it west, and sold it in New Mexico at higher western retail prices. They established relationships with suppliers in New York City, Philadelphia, Baltimore, and

St. Louis and with wool brokers in Boston and Philadelphia. Typical of such arrangements, New Mexico merchant John Dold transacted a considerable amount of business with New York City merchant-wholesaler Leon Arnold & Co. while Las Vegas–based Charles Ilfeld sold his wool to Gregg Bros. of Philadelphia and purchased merchandise from several eastern companies. The merchants usually traded the merchandise they brought back from the East for the agricultural produce and livestock of the numerous small ranchers and farmers in their respective areas, hard currency remaining scarce in New Mexico until the railroads arrived.[9]

The merchants opened operations in all the larger towns. Eventually mercantile outlets were scattered throughout the territory. Their customer base was mostly Hispanic. These establishments became part of a growing national commercial network, emanating from the industrial cities of the Midwest and the East and extending into the West and ultimately into isolated, rural, Hispanic New Mexico.[10]

Many of the mercantile capitalists were recently arrived in the territory, well educated and well connected. Notable among these businessmen was a small but influential community of German-Jewish immigrants with long family traditions in merchandising extending back to Europe. As a mark of their success, Jacob Amberg's store on the northwest corner of the Santa Fe Plaza was said, by 1864, to be the "most commodious and elegant building in New Mexico." The Charles Ilfeld Company, headquartered on the Las Vegas Old Town Plaza, was for many years New Mexico's largest mercantile operation. A key to his success, and that of many of his cohorts, was the large amount of capital, extraterritorial in origin, that he had at his disposal.[11]

A few Hispanic merchants were extraordinarily successful. New business opportunities opened by the Santa Fe Trail enabled some of the old mercantile families to expand their operations and further increase their wealth. Active after the annexation, one of the most successful Hispanic merchants was Belin-based Felipe Chaves, a well-connected, well-educated cousin of J. Francisco Chaves, who built his fortune upon a foundation of preexisting family wealth. He was, for a

88 THE INDUSTRY MATURES

time, one of the richest men in the territory. Like other elite Hispanic merchants, his operations were essentially indistinguishable from those of his Anglo cohorts. He likely entered the wool business before or during the Civil War. Chaves's operation, whenever it was launched, expanded rapidly during the postwar period when he made large sales in Kansas and Missouri. He shipped 7,642 pounds of wool to Philadelphia in 1869, his first documented wool transaction. Nine years later he shipped 192,668 pounds out of New Mexico, a twenty-fivefold increase. He is known to have driven herds of sheep east also. And like many of his Hispanic cohorts, he remained active in sheep ranching.[12]

Business practices in territorial New Mexico were always somewhat schizophrenic. While the merchants employed up-to-date methods in their business negotiations with the outside world, their dealings with local sheep growers, involving considerable barter, diverged slowly from tradition. Often finding themselves in possession of considerable numbers of sheep that they needed to hold for a time prior to shipment to market, the merchants became sheep owners out of necessity, not choice. Their inclinations to the contrary, and somewhat unique to the western sheep industry, they became involved in every aspect of sheep production.

Prior to about 1875, Charles Ilfeld typically had a relatively modest herd of 3,000–5,000 sheep. But by 1890 his holdings had increased to 17,000 head that he let out under *partido* contracts. He reached a maximum in 1905 of 86,000 head, which he rented out to forty-four *partidarios*. Ilfeld held most of his *partido* sheep in San Miguel County. He hired his herders in Las Vegas and received more requests for *partido* contracts than he could fill. He generally turned down Anglo applicants, preferring to deal with local Hispanics who were his customers. Similarly, the Bond brothers held over 18,000 head under *partido* contracts in 1900 and had $36,000 (over $1 million in 2020 dollars) invested in sheep. The *partidarios* were now often required to secure the necessary grazing lands themselves, although some merchants, including the Bond brothers, leased private or government lands for their *partidarios'* use.[13]

FIGURE 3.1. Lieutenant Colonel Jose Francisco Chaves, New Mexico, 1903? Photograph by J. M. Crausbay Studio, courtesy of the Palace of the Governors Photo Archives (NMHM/DCA), 027132

90   THE INDUSTRY MATURES

Not all *partido* contracts were successfully concluded. An assessment of just how many went unfulfilled is difficult to make. Records of the Ilfeld Company provide some hint, however. By the late nineteenth century some 35 percent of Ilfeld's herders had fallen progressively deeper in debt to the company, which carried over their accounts from year to year.[14]

Theft by *partidarios* was an occasional problem. Sometime around 1898 Charles Ilfeld became aware that some brothers under a *partido* contract had been selling off small quantities of his sheep from time to time. The company decided, after unsuccessful efforts to stop this practice, to take back the sheep. A letter written by Max Nordhaus, Ilfeld's brother-in-law and right-hand man, describes the situation: "We have previously been informed that they [some *partidarios*] have sold small numbers ranging from 10 to 25 and although we have raked them about this—time and again—we did not care to take the sheep from them, since we know [now] that they are trying to dispose of them in such a wholesale way we surely have to take decided steps against them. We have today written Wm. Hunter to *at once* take possession of our sheep." On another occasion, a *partidario* sold 900 Ilfeld sheep, a substantial loss for the merchant.[15]

Sometimes merchant-*partidario* relations took on a "wild West" character. In 1892 Wagon Mound merchant John Justus Schmidt got wind that one of his *partidarios*, J. D. Gallegos, was planning to quietly relocate to Raton, taking the rented sheep with him. To prevent the theft of his sheep, Schmidt obtained a restraining order from the court in Las Vegas, apparently frustrating Gallegos. Sometime later when Schmidt and his family left town by buggy to attend to some business, Gallegos followed them, and an altercation ensued. The herdsman caught up with the buggy, threatened Schmidt with a rifle, and then shot him after he jumped clear of the buggy. Mortally wounded, Schmidt was able to shoot Gallegos with a derringer before he died.[16]

As the markets continued to grow, meat packers and wool commission houses became more aggressive and sent buyers, specialists, out to western sheep-growing regions including New Mexico. Buying wool was challenging. The buyers had to inspect and judge each individual lot on the hoof and offer a purchase price based on its estimated sale price in the East, usually months in the future. They needed a thorough, up-to-date knowledge of international crop data. The well-known lack of uniformity of American wool created added difficulty. Wool and sheep buying was characterized by uncertainty, instability, and risk.[17] The independents imposed a degree of competition upon established general merchants, who were nevertheless able to continue operating successfully by expanding to the more remote areas of the territory.

COMMERCIAL FINANCING

The sedentary general merchants were the first bankers in New Mexico. Before the railroads, the sales of general merchandise and food supplies to army personnel had been quite profitable for the territory's merchants. The fact that the sales were paid for in cash or its equivalent, still a scarce commodity, amplified the importance of that market. A commerce in bank drafts ensued since sales to the US government were often paid for with such drafts—that is, checks drawn on eastern banks and backed by the US government. The expansion of the sheep industry in the post–Civil War period could not have occurred without the introduction of secure bank drafts and the monetary exchange they engendered. And since monetary exchange was the purview of the merchant, its introduction was instrumental in shifting leadership of the sheep industry from the large-scale ranchers to the merchants. It was, in the view of Parish, the most important factor in shifting sheep industry dominance from the producer to the merchant.[18]

As the sheep industry expanded and capital requirements grew, the merchants began providing rudimentary banking services for their sheep-growing suppliers, advancing them money for supplies, payrolls, or the purchase of livestock at the beginning of the growing season and settling accounts at the end of the season when their produce was sold. Frank Bond entered into such arrangements on a fairly large scale. For many years the merchants remained the sole source of credit

92 THE INDUSTRY MATURES

for the territory's sheep growers, even for some of the larger operations. Venceslao Jaramillo, a politically prominent member of a leading sheep-ranching family, is known to have had a business relationship with Frank Bond.[19]

The mercantile firms sometimes became full-service financial agents for their growers. Besides advancing needed operating funds, they honored bank drafts used by their clients to pay herders and buy equipment, and they negotiated leases for grazing lands. They were sometimes purchasing agent, sales agent, real estate broker, and banker all rolled into one and all expedited by their control of the flow of money and credit between East and West.[20]

Banking was a risky business in these early years. If a borrower failed to pay off his loan when due, the bank might confiscate his livestock or wool. This was the fate of wool grower Eusebio Garcia y Ortiz, who ran up a debt of $1,716 to Otero, Sellar & Co. of Las Vegas, substantially larger than the annual expenses of $1,000 he incurred running his band of 3,500 head. The company then took an advance assignment of his 7,000-pound wool clip to be delivered after shearing. This they were authorized to sell and to apply the proceeds to Garcia's indebtedness.[21]

With the rapid growth of the western sheep industry and the concomitant demand for financing, New Mexico's merchants eventually found themselves unable to provide the loans needed by their many farming and ranching client-suppliers. Requiring ever larger amounts of capital, they began borrowing from a variety of sources, including eastern wool commission houses, western feeder farmers, midwestern slaughterhouses, and occasionally private investors. The Bonds are known to have obtained a substantial loan, about $22,000 ($680,000 in 2020 dollars), from private Santa Fe investor Abraham Staab in 1902.[22]

Commercial banking began in New Mexico in 1870 when a group of partners, including Lucian Maxwell, founded the First National Bank of Santa Fe (FNBSF) with the proceeds from the sale of the Maxwell Land Grant. Loans to sheepmen were an important component of the business. On another front, Don Miguel A. Otero, politically prominent partner of Otero, Sellar & Co., sold out his interest in the company and, together with several other local businessmen, established the San Miguel National Bank of Las Vegas in 1881. A major part of this bank's business also involved loans to sheepmen. The western banks were usually small, and their high interest rates discouraged livestock financing, although that became a considerable part of their business. New Mexico's sheep industry thus played a role in the development of banking.[23]

A word about the marketing and financing of cattle—territorial New Mexico's other important livestock export in the post–Civil War years—is in order here. New Mexico merchants rarely dealt in cattle on a large scale, although they had sold cattle at Indian reservations and various US Army forts starting on the eve of the Civil War. By the 1870s cattlemen were employing a network of trails for the romanticized cattle drives to the Great Plains rail junctions, where they sold their herds directly to dealers. After adequate rail service was in place, New Mexico cattlemen shipped their livestock out of the territory by rail to Chicago slaughterhouses and other markets. Ilfeld chose not to deal extensively in cattle because of the long delay in completing sales during which cattle prices could fluctuate even more wildly than sheep prices. The business was too risky for his tastes. Many other New Mexico merchants likewise chose to limit their cattle dealings.[24]

Unlike the case for sheep, absentee investors were an important factor in the Rocky Mountain cattle industry. They visualized the growing cattle business as new, exciting, and promising and expressed little interest in sheep, as the cattle bubble raged.[25] Sophisticated investors on the East Coast and in Europe, men who had never been west of the Mississippi River, poured their resources into large cattle ranches, and the early returns did seem promising.[26] These investors, like cattlemen on the range, considered the sheep industry shabby, disreputable, and altogether unworthy of their attention. The sheep industry was, of course, old, and the fortunes it had produced, although real, were modest by gilded-age standards. Western sheepmen, to their benefit, could often get started and operate without wealthy absentee investors since the sheep business was less expensive to enter than cattle ranching.

94   THE INDUSTRY MATURES

THE RAILROADS

The extension of the nation's railroads into the West after the Civil War had an immense, transformative impact on the region's economy. They were a critical factor in the expansion of the western sheep industry. They made possible the utilization of the West's fine grazing lands as never before. Snaking their way west across the Great Plains, they soon provided fast, safe, and relatively cheap transport for western livestock to the eastern and midwestern slaughterhouses in Chicago, Omaha, Kansas City, and elsewhere. They also efficiently transported western wool to the East Coast textile mills (figure 2.1).[27]

The US Army forts with their cash payrolls and monetary exchange services had been the first steady source of capital in the territory. Three decades later the railroads brought the first infusion of corporate capital. Their cash payrolls provided a second source of hard currency, giving merchants, sheepmen, and society in general increased liquidity, which they badly needed. Describing his first Sunday on the job at a Chamita store in 1883, Frank Bond recalled years later, "Sunday was the big trading day in the week when the people came to church, and I recall on the first Sunday we took in so much silver the till had to be emptied. There was not much other money in circulation that day apparently. It was more money than I had ever seen before."[28]

The fact that a railroad traversed New Mexico at all was a fortuitous accident. The territory's modest commerce over the Santa Fe Trail, which their line would supplant, was of little interest to AT&SF officials building west from Kansas. However, the territory lay along the path to southern California and its much larger, rapidly expanding economy. California business would justify the line; New Mexico was a passive beneficiary. When the AT&SF linked up with the Southern Pacific Railroad in Deming in 1881, the nation had a second transcontinental line. And New Mexico's sheep industry, now connected to national markets by rail, was once again well situated by chance to take advantage of serendipitous extraterritorial developments.

The benefits provided by the railroads came to the territory gradually. The sedentary merchants, along with independent Santa Fe Trail traders, had been shipping wool east over the Santa Fe Trail in small quantities since the late 1850s. As the AT&SF extended across the plains of Kansas and into Colorado, the Santa Fe Trail, along which the rails were being laid, became, in effect, ever shorter. The trail's eastern terminus shifted continually westward over a fifteen-year period with the advancing tracks. Sheep and cattle drives from New Mexico to the railheads became practical.

The territory's sheep were, in small numbers, initially driven to recently established railheads in Missouri for shipment to markets farther east. By 1877 the AT&SF had reached Animas, Colorado, providing service to the East via Kansas City. In the same general period, the Denver and Rio Grande Western Railroad (D&RGW) established a competing terminal at El Moro, Colorado, providing connections to markets in St. Louis and Chicago. The travel time from El Moro to Kansas City via Denver was about fifty hours for a heretofore unimaginable savings in the time and labor. Charles Ilfeld, one of the first to do so, began shipping wool in quantity east out of the Great Plains railheads around 1874.[29] Around the same period, before the arrival of the railroads in New Mexico, many sheepmen drove herds to railheads in Kansas and Colorado to be shipped on to meat packers in Chicago, Philadelphia, and other large cities.

After the AT&SF reached Animas, only a comparatively short wagon haul from New Mexico was required to get wool to a rail terminus and thence to Boston and Philadelphia brokers. When the line reached Las Vegas, it rendered the Santa Fe Trail commercially obsolete. Las Vegas and later Albuquerque, with their rail access, became major shipping centers.

The railroad was a critical factor in the expansion of the territory's mercantile operations, and by extension its sheep industry.

The roads slashed transport costs. They enabled merchants to ship live sheep to the midwestern slaughterhouses and wool to northeastern dealers safely, quickly, and, most important, profitably in much larger quantities than in the past. They provided access to far more outlets than the sheep trails ever had and opened up important new

96 THE INDUSTRY MATURES

markets for the territory's produce, although freight rates became a continuing source of complaints from stockmen in the following years.

The introduction of double-decked stock cars made rail shipping of live sheep even more efficient. The railroads were employed to transport New Mexico sheep not only directly to the markets but also north to Wyoming and Montana for fattening in the rich summer pastures and east to feeder farms in Kansas and Nebraska.

The increased security the railroads provided for an inherently high-risk business was significant. The trail drives of the past had been quite hazardous. Losses on the great drives down the Camino Real were always considerable, and sheepmen simply had to sustain those losses. Weather, predators, and trail conditions, once important sources of danger on the drives, became largely irrelevant with the arrival of the railroads.

After the railroads arrived, New Mexico's wool and sheep exports exploded. Annual wool exports expanded from 4 million pounds in 1880 to 15 million pounds 1910, a factor of nearly four (figure 2.1). Not surprisingly, the Charles Ilfeld Company moved toward a specialization in sheep and wool and, to a much lesser extent, cattle and other livestock starting in the late 1880s. After shearing time during Las Vegas's halcyon years, the main trail into town from the eastern plains would be backed up for four or five miles with wool-laden wagons. Charles Ilfeld and Gross, Blackwell & Co. were, in 1900, each weighing in 100 wagons per day with wool to be shipped east by rail.[30] To the west, Frank Bond was shipping large quantities of wool out of Espanola over the D&RGW.

FEEDING

A new practice that would have major repercussions within the New Mexico sheep industry began in the mid-1860s, a practice made possible by the development of mercantile capitalism and the railroads and which made the industry more productive and more efficient. A few ranchers began growing crops to feed their livestock. Later New

Mexico ranchers discovered it to their advantage to ship their sheep out of the territory to be fattened on feeder farms prior to sale. The recovery of the mutton market in the late 1880s, which had been in decline since the Civil War, accelerated the development. Seeking a supply of winter mutton to feed America's growing urban populations, Chicago and Kansas City meat-packing families initiated farm feeding of western sheep as a commercial enterprise, but it was soon taken over by private feeder-farmers specializing in the activity.[31] Winter feeding provided, for the first time, western mutton for consumption during the first three months of the year, since range sheep always lost weight during the winter and were not profitably marketed at that time.

An early Colorado feeding operation was reported by Civil War general William T. Sherman. On an inspection trip through Huerfano County in 1866, he visited a feeder farm with thousands of acres under cultivation, which served to feed 3,000 head of cattle, 5,000–6,000 sheep, and numerous horses. An industry of commercial proportions that specialized in feeding lambs and young sheep until they were ready for market spread through the Rocky Mountains and Great Plains over the following decades and flourished after about 1890.[32]

Before the advent of feeding, western sheep were generally grazed throughout their production cycle on the open range but still in a relatively circumscribed area. The land and the fodder it provided were free, or nearly so, and in a good year supplied the livestock all their required sustenance. Grass was still abundant in many parts of the West; the sheep were dispersed, adequately fed and healthy, and losses were usually light. Such operations were, however, not very efficient. Competition grew with the expanding markets. Traditional grazing practices became less profitable as market requirements became more exacting. More proactive attention to growing conditions was needed, even demanded. When summer droughts and overly harsh winters arrived, as they did with some regularity, sheep became thin and weak, not suitable for market even when they survived the winter, an increasingly unsustainable situation for growers. Under these circumstances, assisted feeding was beneficial, particularly during the first three months of the year. Feeding was found to produce heavier animals, which were better able to withstand the winters and brought higher market prices. Furthermore, fed sheep matured faster and could be sent to market sooner, reducing production costs.[33]

Western growers, including those of New Mexico, started in the mid-1880s driving sheep in large numbers to feeder farms to be fattened at locations better suited for this activity. Shipping lambs, not just mature sheep, to feeder farms became practical with the advent of rail transport, giving western growers a new outlet for their produce, since lambs in the care of their mothers had always proven difficult to trail drive and were thus not readily marketable prior to this.

Breeders found the new practice more profitable than raising livestock to full maturity on the open range, even after their profits were shared with the feeder farmers, while feedlots proved to be quite profitable for the farmers involved. Just prior to the Panic of 1893, the New Mexico sheep industry was flourishing, in part due to the extraterritorial demand for its feeder stock.[34]

Alfalfa and grains were the most common forage crops grown for sheep. The emergence of the Colorado sugar beet industry in the late 1890s—on irrigated lands—also had an important effect on the feeding industry in that area when it was discovered that beet tops and the residue beet pulp, a by-product of the sugar-refining process, made good feed for both cattle and lambs.[35]

Farm feeding, as it was practiced in the West, owed its success to the fact that the southern ranges were best utilized for breeding livestock, while the northern plains and valleys were best for fattening. The grasses in the southern regions, which included New Mexico, had sufficient nutritive value for building bone and muscle but lacked the sugar and starch needed to build up the level of fat then desired. The fields farther north produced better grass for fattening. But the northern areas have colder winters that can extend well into spring and are subject to sudden, extreme climate changes, rendering them unsuitable for breeding livestock. Cold, windy spring weather, during the first month after birth, could cause significant losses of the newborn.[36]

New Mexico had always been a good breeding area with its comparatively stable weather patterns, mild springs, and ample green grass needed by the ewes. Late in the year, when the weather on the ranges became colder, was the best time to ship sheep to the feed-growing areas to be fattened. New Mexico ranchers thus came to specialize increasingly in breeding. The Santa Fe *New Mexican*, ever optimistic, predicted that New Mexico would become "the great breeding ground of the Southwest."[37]

New Mexico sheepmen sent their flocks to several different feeding areas—Colorado, Nebraska, and Kansas, where the needed forage crops were readily grown, being popular destinations. By the early 1890s typically about 25 percent of the New Mexico sheep inventory was sold every year and shipped by rail or trail driven to feeder farms or ranches. The practice of sheep feeding beyond New Mexico's borders grew steadily through the 1920s.[38]

A thriving feeding industry developed in Colorado at a relatively early date following the introduction of alfalfa into the territory from New Mexico in 1863. Commercial-scale operations were in place by the mid-1880s, when crop surpluses along the Platt and Arkansas Rivers proved useful for feeding livestock. Western-bred sheep, many from New Mexico, but also from Wyoming, Idaho, California, and Colorado itself, and smaller numbers of cattle were brought into the irrigated areas to feed on the alfalfa and corn.[39] Lambs purchased in New Mexico and shipped by rail to Colorado were fattened in feeding pens for four to six months prior to being forwarded for sale in the Kansas City and St. Louis markets.

Colorado sheep feeding received a boost in 1889 when a rail shipment of 2,400 "Mexican" lambs belonging to New Mexico growers E. J. and I. W. Bennett became stalled in Walsenburg, Colorado, by a blizzard. When the weather finally cleared, the lambs were in such poor condition that the brothers decided to ship them to Fort Collins where they could recoup on cheaply available alfalfa. Finally shipped to market in Chicago, they brought an excellent profit. The brothers must have been delighted, as they then expanded this modus operandi, feeding

100 THE INDUSTRY MATURES

3,500 "Mexican" sheep the following season. Word of their success got around, and Fort Collins developed into another important feeding center. Lamb feeding in the Fort Collins area was described in the late 1880s as "the most profitable industry the farmers of this county ever engaged in." Lambs surpassed wool as the Colorado sheepman's main source of income.[40]

Following the Panic of 1893, which devastated the Colorado feeding industry, H. C. Abbott trailed 10,000 sheep partly from Folsom, New Mexico, into Las Animas, giving rise to a spring lamb industry in that area. The first lambs for rebuilding the Fort Collins feeding industry after the panic came from New Mexico in 1896. The Sargent family of Grant County, Wisconsin, was quite active in the San Luis Valley, where the Colorado sheep industry had started. One of the sons, Ed Sargent, entered a business arrangement with Frank Bond and eventually had sheep on feed all over Colorado and northern New Mexico. Besides individual sheepmen, New Mexico mercantile companies became involved in Colorado feeding. Both Gross, Kelly (previously Gross, Blackwell) and the Moulton-Ilfeld Company of Albuquerque were active in the Arkansas Valley. The Colorado feeding industry grew steadily for the remainder of the nineteenth century.[41]

Feeding started in the Platt River Valley of central Nebraska in the late 1870s with a New Mexico flock and spread to the North Platte area of western Nebraska in the late 1880s when irrigation ditches were built. By this time Nebraska, where fertile, unused farmland in several areas was taken up to grow feed crops, led the nation in the number of range-bred sheep on feed. Most of the state's farmers replaced their range stock with pen-fed farm flocks. The *Stock Grower and Farmer* of Las Vegas reported that over 12,000 head of New Mexico sheep had been shipped to a single Nebraska feeding outfit in the first seven months of 1897. More than one million sheep were being readied for market by Nebraska feeders in the same period. The larger Nebraska feeders typically held 10,000–25,000 head. The feeding industry spread to other parts of the region, notably Kansas, where flocks were first developed in the late 1870s.[42]

The feeder industry was driven by the feeder farmers themselves. By the late 1880s farmers in all the feeder states, even Iowa and Minnesota, were sending buyers to New Mexico, seeking not just feeder stock but also breeding ewes. Fort Collins feeder and US senator William A. Drake began his highly successful operation in 1892 with 15,000 sheep purchased in Albuquerque, illustrative of the large capital requirements required in this new endeavor. By the early 1900s Fort Collins feeders were traveling to Espanola in August to purchase lambs from the Bond brothers and continuing on to Wagon Mound and Las Vegas to further fill out their needs. Interestingly, the "Mexican" lambs, preferably six to eight months old, still widely grown in New Mexico, were described as the most sought after by Colorado feeders, *churros* having been found to respond well to feeding. And their superior meat was desired by a broadening base of consumers. As mutton once again became a more important market commodity than wool, their light fleeces were not an important issue.[43]

Land issues also contributed to the rise of the feeding industry. Land had always been critically important for sheep raising. The growing scarcity of rangeland, and the grass it supported as more and more stockmen placed more and more sheep and cattle on the ranges, was detrimental for all ranchers and an important factor in the adoption of feeding. Furthermore, widespread deterioration from overstocking was generally reducing the stock-carrying capacity of considerable existing rangeland. In New Mexico land scarcity became even more critical starting around 1880 as homesteaders immigrating to the territory in substantial numbers started taking up the best unclaimed tracts. According to Carlson, the growing land scarcity forced *ricos* who had expanded their sheep operations onto the public domain to move their livestock back onto their grants, thus limiting their herd sizes. As discussed below, the federal government exacerbated the situation with a misguided land policy that channeled good western rangeland into what proved to be marginal dryland farms, resulting in further overstocking of sheep and cattle onto the remaining, mostly inferior rangelands. Naturally growing forage became altogether too

102 THE INDUSTRY MATURES

scarce, and sheep growers had little choice but to become more proactive in feeding their flocks. Shipping their stock out to feeders before they were fully grown helped New Mexico ranchers contend with diminishing availability of good rangeland.[44]

On another front, the construction of large-scale irrigation projects in the late-nineteenth- and early-twentieth-century West opened up new agricultural areas, notably along the Platte and Arkansas Rivers, and was important in the development of feeding in these areas. Irrigation projects came late to New Mexico, but when they did, feeding took hold. By the late 1880s alfalfa crops were being grown for feeding purposes in the Las Cruces area. And by 1910 about 300,000 sheep were on feed in New Mexico. But the initiative did not develop to a great extent in this period.[45]

The adoption of sheep feeding in the West was part of a larger overall process occurring in America at the time. The nation's agriculture was becoming more sophisticated and more efficient. Each section of the country was beginning to recognize what it could do best and to specialize accordingly, making optimum use of its available resources. By 1900 specialized farming particularly suited to the soil, climate, and geographical location was taking hold nationwide. The emergence of a Rocky Mountain–Great Plains feeding industry was an early manifestation of that process.[46]

Feeding enterprises employed a variety of financial arrangements. For the numerous small-scale growers in New Mexico, feeding transactions were often carried out through a local merchant. Charles Ilfeld began contracting sheep he amassed from small-scale growers with feeders starting around 1890. A few New Mexican merchants like Frank Bond owned and operated feeder farms elsewhere. Feeder farms were capital intensive and required substantial financial resources, which often took the form of loans from commercial lending institutions. The feeding business did not lend itself to small-scale family operations.[47]

The western feeder industry was well established by 1900. It linked the territory more strongly to the regional and, ultimately, national economy, just as the banking industry had done earlier. With the advent of feeding, within an industry of growing complexity, New Mexico sheepmen lost control of one phase of mutton and lamb production to capital-intensive, Anglo-owned feeder farms outside the territory. New Mexico Hispanics became an ethnic minority within the western sheep industry they founded and once monopolized.

ENVIRONMENTAL CHANGES

As the sheep industry expanded, a new level of environmental changes manifested itself, although few seem to have been seriously concerned or even aware of the importance of the developments, at least until the final years of the territorial period. Considerable changes in vegetation throughout the territory with long-term consequences, brought about in large part by heavy grazing, were appearing. The productivity of many tracts of rangeland would be diminished. Many blamed the changes on the weather. This was only part of the explanation.[48]

The vegetation of New Mexico seems to have been comparatively stable for centuries until the arrival of the first Europeans in the sixteenth century. Thereafter grazing began to take its toll in the immediate vicinity of some settlements, gradually at first. Then, following the annexation and the vast increase in the sheep population, the rate of change of the vegetation increased considerably. These more recent changes were due to a range of human activity: logging, farming, fire suppression in the twentieth century, and grazing. Farming in eastern New Mexico was a major factor in reducing the grassland in that area.

The poor grazing in the vicinity of some villages reported by members of Kearny's army may have been a localized condition resulting from exceptionally heavy use. Typically the changes in vegetation that New Mexico underwent can be characterized by changes in pattern rather than additions or losses of major types of flora. Some types of vegetation moved onto ground previously covered by another type. Forest and grassland, particularly, diminished considerably, to be replaced by other types of vegetation. Most relevant to the sheep industry, the

104   THE INDUSTRY MATURES

extensive Plains-Mesa grasslands, productive lands dominantly covered in blue grama grass (*Bouteloua gracilis*), the territory's best grazing grass, gave way under heavy grazing to less productive classes of forage for livestock.[49]

In the most widespread transition grasslands gave way to what natural vegetation biologist William Dick-Peddie has designated desert scrubland. Of the two important classes of desert scrubland, Great Basin desert scrub is found largely in the northwestern part of the state and consists predominantly of various types of sagebrush and saltbush—shadscale, greasewood, fourwing saltbush, and notably big sagebrush, palatable for livestock but not as nutritious as grass—on sparsely covered ground with little grass. The other important class, Chihuahuan desert scrub, predominantly creosotebush, is spread across the southern part of the state and extends south into Mexico. Desert grassland, a transition vegetation between Plains-Mesa grassland and desert scrubland, which is widely scattered across western and southern parts of the state, took over other large areas of New Mexico. Considerable areas of desert grassland persist today, not having transitioned further into desert scrubland. It consists commonly of a sparse layer of black grama grass with scattered desert forbs and shrubs of wide variety. The forbs and shrubs replaced the more palatable grasses for a significant reduction in the productivity of the land.[50]

Elsewhere, juniper savanna, characterized by widely scattered low trees in a sparse grass groundcover, is the most common replacement vegetation for grassland, sometimes advancing both upslope and downslope. In some areas of northern New Mexico, sagebrush advanced upslope, from the lower, dry side of the grassland, while juniper advanced downslope, giving rise to open juniper-sagebrush woodland where grass had once grown. In the north-central part of New Mexico, near the Rio Grande at Taos, the *bajadas* (erosion slopes) are commonly covered by savannas of juniper and big sagebrush. In a few parts of New Mexico various other desert shrubs are mixed with juniper. Also, alien species have been inadvertently introduced into former grasslands, replacing native species less able to withstand heavy grazing. Much of today's juniper savanna may have been grassland up to about 1880.[51]

The disappearance of grasslands in New Mexico has occurred over a period of decades and has been very uneven. Writing about the southern Sangre de Cristo Range, DeBuys has asserted that there is "not a single meadow, cirque, or bald divide" where the original, native flora "remains intact." Farming in this area has been seriously degraded by the dryer, eroded lands. In contrast, "extensive" and "good quality" grasslands were still to be found in the southern portion of the territory into the twentieth century. In fact, much of the loss of foliage has occurred in the early years of the twentieth century, although conditions leading to the changes were created decades earlier. Change continues. Much of the forest, woodland, and grassland of New Mexico is today in some stage of succession.[52]

Juniper Savanna Creation

Considerable progress has been made in understanding the vegetation transitions. Generally, range conditions depend on rainfall, history of previous use, the kind of management of stock, and the type of animals involved. The primary factor in the vegetation changes is moisture availability—precipitation, the ability of the land to hold it, protection from drying winds and the sun. Overgrazing destroys the capacity of the land to absorb and store water. The transformation of grasslands into savannas of trees and desert shrubs is understood to progress following a "water catchment" phenomenon, as described by Dick-Peddie, a process very common on the grasslands and scrublands in New Mexico. In the first phase of the process grass cover is reduced when the lands are overgrazed and cannot recover sufficiently between usages. When the animals consume the grass down to the ground, including the seeds, the grass is rendered unable to reproduce and thins out. Bare spots open up. The exposed bare ground allows rainwater to flow rather than infiltrate the ground where it falls. The compaction of the ground by the sheep's small hooves further reduces water absorption. The flowing

106 THE INDUSTRY MATURES

water accumulates in small depressions in the land, causing more water than normal providing more-than-normal water in these areas, favorable to the establishment of junipers. The raised land areas receive less water less-than-normal water than they normally would under grass cover. Only "desert shrubs" are supported in these areas, predominantly big sagebrush in the north and snakeweed and rabbit brush in the south. Erosion increases, accelerating the process. And juniper savanna takes over the grasslands, a common, widespread phenomenon throughout the West. Juniper savanna is less productive for livestock than the grassland it took over. It persists to this day in many areas.[53]

Arroyo Cutting

Before the annexation, the rangelands of the territory showed little evidence of the intense accelerated erosion and the creation of gullies or arroyos that occurred later in the century. The large sheep herds of the Mexican period seem to have caused little erosion. This has been attributed to the above-normal precipitation during the 1820s and 1830s, which provided the rangelands with higher carrying capacity generally and thus less stress on the lands from the herds. It should be noted, however, that the conditions in any specific area might diverge widely from this general assessment. This is not to say that there were no arroyos before this time. They were simply not nearly as widespread as they later became. Some arroyos are understood to be prehistoric. Some are known to have developed before 1870 and the rapid sheep buildup that followed.[54]

Before 1850 climatic factors may have started a tendency toward decreased vegetation. In any case, a long period of below-average rainfall in the 1870s and 1880s was followed or else overlaid toward the end of the period by particularly heavy summer rains with flash floods. At the same time, sheepmen were stocking the rangelands with unprecedentedly large numbers of sheep. The abundance of arroyos seen today throughout the Southwest is believed to have been caused by this rather unique chain of events.[55]

The dynamics of arroyo cutting are similar to the dynamics of juniper savanna creation. First, the abnormally dry conditions during the 1870s and 1880s combined with heavy grazing to weaken the vegetation groundcover. This, together with livestock, caused soil compaction, produced runoff, and decreased the infiltration of rainwater into the soil. With runoff instead of infiltration and abnormally heavy rains, miniature drainways of rainwater and dirt were created, leaving much of the soil surface dry after the sun came back out. Under these circumstances, the root systems of the existing foliage were starved, exacerbating the degraded groundcover. Plants died and bare spots opened up. The newly developed catchments of the miniature drainways held sufficient water for junipers to become established. The increased runoff over the hard, sparsely covered land caused erosion and led ultimately to the creation of arroyos. As the erosion continued, more and more gullies across the grasslands developed, and the juniper density increased. Juniper savanna, which has a higher moisture requirement than grassland, advanced comparatively quickly into the grassland via the erosion gullies. A hotter, dryer microclimate resulted.[56]

Arguably the most infamous case of channel cutting occurred on the Rio Puerco, which has one of the most eroded river channels in the West. The Puerco Valley had been known for its fine grazing, with large sheep and cattle herds, as early as the 1760s. But it was abandoned in 1823 due to Navajo raids. Subsequently, the Navajos may have grazed their sheep in the area. Hispanic herders began using the area again sometime after 1860 when the Navajo as well as the Apache threat had subsided. Farmers from the Rio Grande Valley quickly populated the irrigable land. By 1880 some 10,000 acres of the upper Puerco Valley, in the general vicinity of the village of Cuba, were under irrigation, supporting several smaller subsistence farming communities.[57]

The Puerco Valley was ecologically fragile and could not withstand the levels of human activity imposed without considerable change. The soil composition was particularly susceptible to erosion. Deep channel trenching along some stretches of the Puerco began long before 1850

108 THE INDUSTRY MATURES

and may have been climate related. Kearny's men observed river channels ranging from ten feet to as deep as twenty-five feet along some portions of the river. Heavy grazing and flash floods in the following years led to "more extensive erosion." Grazing well beyond the carrying capacity of the Puerco basin, which had given rise to numerous trails channeling stormwater to the river, is widely believed to have been the main cause of the accelerated incision in later years. Above Cuba, near the Puerco headwaters, a chain of arroyos developed having the appearance of corduroy. They extended from the valley, across uncultivated rangeland, and up to the top of the surrounding mountains. The main deepening and widening of the Rio Puerco started in 1885–1890, eventually extending along the entire length of the river to a depth of twenty-five to thirty feet.[58]

Disaster ensued. By 1925 fewer than 3,000 acres of the valley were still in agricultural production, the Puerco running wilder than in the past and having washed out dams, rendered head gates to irrigation ditches inoperable, and cut into the canyon so deeply that gravity-dependent irrigation was becoming difficult. Erosion eventually swept away much of the valley's floodplain cropland. By the mid-twentieth century irrigation below Cuba was impossible. The village's farmers and stock growers abandoned the area. The Rio Puerco Valley is essentially a desert today.[59]

Navajo Land Degradations

Arguably the most serious degradation of grazing lands occurred on or near the Navajo Reservation. Following the Navajo's return from incarceration at Bosque Redondo, the federal government provided substantial consignments of sheep, as noted previously. The sheep multiplied. The US Census of 1890 estimated the Navajo sheep and goat population at 1.6 million. Under a heavy burden, the grazing lands on what became the Navajo Reservation degraded quickly. Because goats, horses, cattle, and sheep each favor different forage, much of the heavily used land was thoroughly grazed.[60]

A succession of academic and government investigators, passing through parts of the reservation in the early twentieth century, reported widespread range degradation from overgrazing. Tracts throughout western New Mexico, it was reported, had been "eaten pretty clean." One report noted that the blue grama grass had been "killed out by sheep" to a large extent. The frequent back-and-forth drives of family herds from home to pasture had created trampled pathways and largely denuded the ground in the immediate vicinity of the water sources. At the same time, Yale University geologist Herbert Gregory found good, sometimes excellent, grasslands in the unpopulated areas with little water. But the populated, well-watered areas of the reservation were "much overgrazed." Reporting on an extended tour of western New Mexico in 1904, including a sweep through the Navajo Reservation, the territory's leading botanist, Professor E. O. Wooton of the New Mexico College of Agriculture and Mechanical Arts, noted severe overgrazing wherever he went, exacerbated by an extraordinarily long, six-year drought. He found the worst conditions in the area near Gallup outside the reservation and on the eastern margins of the reservation, which he described as "nearly denuded of grass." This land degradation, as it turned out, was a disaster in the making for the Navajo.[61]

SOCIAL CHANGES

Social changes came to New Mexico along with the growing Anglo population and the evolving leadership of the sheep industry. While the merchants assumed in part the role of the sheep-growing patron and employed *partidarios*, they also provided the villagers in their area a link to the outside world. With their specialized knowledge and connections, they sold the local produce in national markets at the best prices possible. And like the landed patrones of the past, they extended credit, or cash advances in later years, to their suppliers on produce for future delivery. They sometimes provided translation and rudimentary legal services. And, of course, they provided the household

THE INDUSTRY MATURES

merchandise and farm supplies needed by their customers, employing their wholesale sources in the East and Midwest. The merchants did not, however, generally assume the political or the social leadership roles of the traditional patron.

The *pastores* and small-scale producers, for their part, exercised an increasing degree of independence from their former patrones. In so doing, they exchanged one master for another, in a sense, one generally more impersonal but also more systematic, efficient, and arguably less exploitative, particularly when an element of competition among merchants was present. It was a relationship with which the herders were familiar and comfortable. While the merchants assumed a greater role in territorial life, the leadership and power of the traditional patrones eroded, as discussed above.

Sheepmen who did not embrace the developments coming to their industry did so to their own detriment. The added effort and initiative required for specialization within an increasingly competitive and exacting market was apparently too great an undertaking for some of the old, landed sheep-growing families as well as smaller-scale marginal operators. Some *ricos*, appearing to have simply run out of steam, sold their grant lands to ambitious speculators and ranchers, both Anglo and Hispanic, and relocated to the towns. Recalling his youth in Albuquerque around 1900, Harvey Fergusson, grandson of merchant Franz Huning, gave a rather harsh assessment of these relocated families: "I lived in Old Town among people who belonged to the past—surviving families of the old Mexican aristocracy who still cherished their pretensions and their hand-hammered silver."[62]

In the twentieth century some of the sons and daughters from the landed families entered the middle class and likewise relocated in the towns. Some assimilated socially and culturally into the Anglo upper and middle classes. Indeed, territorial New Mexico's first Hispanic governor, Miguel A. Otero Jr., the son of businessman, political leader, and sometime rancher Don Miguel A. Otero and his Anglo wife from South Carolina, himself married an Anglo lady woman from Minnesota. And as noted previously, his political associate, J. Francisco Chaves, had married an Anglo lady he met in California. Because sheep growing was traditionally a family enterprise, such assimilation adversely affected Hispanic representation in the industry.[63]

SHEEPMEN'S ORGANIZATIONS

In the drive for efficiency, growers assumed a new, increased concern for the health of their herds, an issue also for the national reputation of New Mexico's sheep, which had become important. The most common and widespread sheep disease during the territorial years was scab. A contagious, parasitic disease, scab develops over a period of weeks after infection, causing the shedding of wool and finally death of the animal. It can be spread to a healthy animal through contact with an infected one or with an area over which an infected flock has passed. A single diseased sheep can quickly infect an entire herd. Scab had been a concern from the time sheep were first introduced to New Mexico, although the dry southwestern climate tended to suppress the incidence of the disease, which usually struck during the damp winter months.

As long as the range was sparsely stocked, herders had been able sustain their operations without addressing the disease systematically. However, as the range became more densely stocked in the late nineteenth century, ongoing preventative measures became necessary. This took the form of dipping once or twice a year, whereby the sheep of an entire herd were driven in succession through a trough filled with a disinfectant chemical solution. By this time effective dips, commonly containing sulfur and lime, had been developed, and the dipping process eradicated any infestation in a properly dipped herd but did not inoculate the sheep against future infection. To maintain healthy herds, it was thus necessary that all the herds in any given area be dipped periodically. Dipping was a significant expense. The necessary dip ingredients, facilities, and labor added to the cost of sheep growing. The larger operations had made dipping part of their annual ritual and sometime built their own dipping facilities. Sheepman Montegue Montague Stevens built an elaborate dipping facility at Horse

112 THE INDUSTRY MATURES

Springs that he rented out to neighboring growers. All too many of the marginal, less profitable outfits did not dip their herds. Their owners earned the enmity of those who did. Responding to the changing conditions, the New Mexico Territorial Legislature established the New Mexico Sheep Sanitary Board in 1897. The board actually had a twofold role. It was tasked with enforcing regulations for herd inspections and disease control in general and also with registering the ear markings and brands of the territory's herds. The original three-member board, appointed by the governor, included Solomon Luna as president, W. S. Prager, of the prominent Roswell mercantile family, and J. Manuel Gonzales, soon to be replaced by Las Vegas merchant Harry W. Kelly, while Harry F. Lee of Albuquerque was employed as secretary.[64]

The board undertook a territory-wide campaign to combat scab. To that end, it appointed range inspectors, experienced sheepmen all, to oversee the dipping of every herd in the territory and to file with the board a written report for each dipping they witnessed. By 1900 about forty-five inspectors, a mix of Hispanics and Anglos spread throughout the sheep-growing parts of the territory, had been appointed. The legislative act established stringent regulations for dipping the territory's herds. The inspectors, compensated with territorial funds, were given the authority of deputy sheriffs regarding sheep matters and could order a diseased herd to be dipped at the owner's expense or quarantined until the disease was eradicated. If the owner of a diseased herd was not forthcoming with the dipping costs, the inspector could take possession of the herd until the payments were made.[65]

In this period, the US Department of Agriculture took on an active role in regulating the nation's sheep industry, enforcing federal laws more stringent and comprehensive than the territorial laws to fight the spread of scab and other diseases and, more generally, to establish an increasingly necessary degree of government oversight of the industry. The department introduced federal inspectors, augmenting the network of territorial inspectors. In 1904 Luna, who was working closely with the Bureau of Animal Industry of the Department of Agriculture, issued an order—"To the Sheep Growers of New

Mexico"—informing them of the federal regulations. The growers were advised that all "flocks in the territory" were to be dipped within the following two months using government-approved dip solutions. Diseased flocks were to be dipped immediately and then a second time ten days later. All dipping was to be overseen by a federal inspector, if available, and a territorial inspector otherwise. The owners of all "public dipping places" were required to have a permit from the Sanitary Board. If "immediate and vigorous action" was not taken, all sheep in New Mexico would be quarantined and none permitted to enter or leave the territory, a measure that would have devastated an industry so heavily dependent on exports. Any owner who did not comply would be subject to "a heavy fine." The campaign was popular with sheepmen and continued for the remainder of the territorial period. Dipping was another expense to be borne by growers as the sheep industry capitalized, and it gave rise to another connection between governments and the industry. In its other capacity the board operated as a registry for the markings and brands of the territory's sheep owners.[66]

Closely following the establishment of the Sheep Sanitary Board was the New Mexico Wool Growers Association, launched in1906. The association was not entirely new in that it was a spin-off from the New Mexico Stock Growers Association, founded in 1884. The Stock Growers Association was dedicated to protecting and advancing the interests of the territory's stock growers and dealers. This included enforcement of the stock laws, many already on the books in New Mexico at the time. These laws covered such matters as theft, trespass, branding, and disease control, issues that were later taken up by the sheepmen. By the early twentieth century the stock growers' organization was proving to be too general to meet the needs of sheep growers, and some of the same men who had led the establishment of the Sheep Sanitary Board founded the New Mexico Wool Growers Association. Solomon Luna was elected first president of the new organization. Along with Luna, A. D. Garrett was chosen vice president, and Harry F. Lee became secretary and treasurer, a paid position like the one he held with the Sheep Sanitary Board. By late 1907 the association, based in Albuquerque, had nearly 300 members, a

114 THE INDUSTRY MATURES

mix of Hispanic and Anglo sheepmen spread throughout New Mexico, paying annual dues of $10, a rather stiff fee at the time.[67]

The association, as it evolved, was, to a large extent, a lobbying organization with, at times, a significant presence in Washington, DC. Western sheepmen were coming to the realization that government, territorial and national, was beginning to exert considerable influence on their industry, and they came to understand that the larger their organizations and the more growers involved working together, the more clout they would have with lawmakers. The association increased its strength by joining the National Wool Growers Association, and it established lines of communication with other western wool growers' organizations. It held annual conventions in Albuquerque. And it communicated resolutions voted on at the annual conferences to influential politicians and government officials in Santa Fe and Washington, often to good effect.

The association addressed the wool tariff, a continuing issue with wool growers everywhere; regulations and grazing fees on the National Forest Reserves, discussed below; the freight car shortage that occurred annually during the brief sixty-day period of outgoing wool shipments; and freight rates, always too high. Working closely with the New Mexico Sheep Sanitary Board and the Bureau of Animal Industry of the Department of Agriculture in Washington, it also addressed sheep diseases. It did not, however, take a position on the environmental degradation caused by overgrazing, which was now becoming serious in many areas. Success came indirectly when, in late 1908, the National Wool Growers Association successfully obtained a reduction in grazing fees on the Forest Reserves. Later the national organization successfully secured lower railroad freight rates for western wool growers.[68]

Not surprisingly, one of the first, and continuing, issues the association dealt with was land. A bill had been introduced in the US Congress to extend the leasing arrangements then in effect on the National Forest Reserves to all the public rangeland. Sheepmen throughout the West had found the rules governing use of the reserves overly constraining and were strongly opposed to the "lease law." Many feared that it would have a devastating effect on their industry, rendering sheep growing completely unprofitable. Taking up the cause, in early 1907 Luna, together with a delegation from the association, joined forces with sheepmen's delegations from other states and spent over a month in Washington lobbying against passage of the law.[69] The effort was successful, the bill died, but the threat still hung over the territory's sheepmen.

In early 1908 the National Wool Growers Association held a large meeting in Helena, Montana, to which New Mexico again sent a sizable contingent and where the land issue was again a major topic of consideration. As it turned out, western sheep growers successfully delayed the land legislation through the end of New Mexico's territorial period. The association was still fighting when another "lease law" was introduced in Congress in 1912, just as New Mexico was entering statehood. The New Mexico sheep industry had entered a new era in which livestock legislation and government policy would be increasingly influential in how business was conducted.[70]

RANCH CAPITALIZATION

In a 1902 report government livestock expert E. V. Wilcox reviewed the various safeguards sheep ranchers would have to put into place if they were to see attractive profits in the future. He then asserted that individuals with "sufficient capital and industry" to implement those safeguards would be the ones to realize the profits.[71] By the late nineteenth century western sheep ranching was indeed becoming increasingly capital intensive. A new range of capital investments and more highly specialized skills and knowledge were required to meet increased competition and more demanding market requirements. Sheepmen could no longer depend entirely on New Mexico's natural resources, nature's bounty, for raising their herds. The remaining open range, beginning to show considerable degradation and growing ever more crowded, first with livestock and later with homesteaders' farms, could no

116 THE INDUSTRY MATURES

longer serve as a year-around home and feed trough for the herds. The expansion of the sheep industry in other western states and territories introduced a degree of competition heretofore absent so that successful ranching required greater efficiency. Profit margins became thinner.

Under increasingly demanding conditions, only the financially strong prospered. The capital requirements worked to the detriment of those sheep growers, both large- and small-scale, including landed Hispanic families, whose wealth remained tied up in their lands and unimproved herds. Raton sheepman Daniel Troy observed that the number of sheep growers in his area decreased during the fifteen years prior to 1892, the small owners being forced out. He also asserted that the "improved" flocks, then called for, required improved care, employing expensive investments and fairly paid, clothed, and fed "American" (i.e., strictly Anglo) labor. As discussed previously, some *rico* families sold their private grants to Anglo speculators, others simply walked away, although they must have done so with considerable bitterness. Those leading Hispanic families with capital continued to operate, but their numbers, never great, did not grow.[72]

Entering the territory in increasing numbers, Anglo stockmen with access to some capital, and a little good fortune, prospered to varying degrees, following the advice of government reports to keep smaller flocks of higher-quality stock, which meshed with the new economic realities. New Mexico sheep ranching thus underwent a major transition, both economic and social, starting in the late nineteenth century, a transition that depended on unprecedented levels of capital investment.[73]

Land

Starting in the 1880s or perhaps even earlier, the most basic capital investment for sheepmen, beyond actual livestock purchases, was the acquisition of land. Forced upon ranchers by a growing scarcity of good grazing land, ownership enabled sheepmen to better control their grazing areas, construct permanent facilities, and thus work toward stabilizing production, combating the large, unpredictable year-to-year profit fluctuations characteristic of the range industry. Although New Mexico production costs, as estimated in 1890, for farm-raised, selectively breed sheep (sixty cents per year) were twice those for the open-range *churros* still being produced by Hispanic sheepmen (thirty cents per year), with land a major part of the added expense, ownership led to greater profits.[74] Land acquisition could be a challenge. It could be acquired in several different ways, ethical and unethical, legal and illegal. Two different classes of land figured importantly: Spanish-Mexican land grants and US public domain.

The land grant system of the colonial and republican periods was a frontier exigency that populated the lands and brought them into production without many legal niceties; Spanish Civil Law, Roman based, provided the general framework of land tenure. The sheep industry of New Mexico, which collapsed following the Pueblo Revolt, was reborn on grant lands after the Reconquest. The grant system also supported and propagated the *rico* class and, by extension, the commercial sheep industry those families created. After the annexation, the incompatibility of the Spanish-Mexican system and the American legal system, English based and now the law of the land, left the grant lands vulnerable to acquisition by Anglo-American newcomers. In a highly controversial development Anglo lawyers, speculators, and stockmen acquired Spanish-Mexican land grants at an astounding rate to the detriment of the Hispanic grantees.[75]

Frequently, Anglo ownership initially fell to the land speculators and lawyers, many with influential political connections. The speculators employed a combination of more or less subtle legal procedures and aggressive lobbying in Santa Fe and Washington to get title to the grant lands they sought, with little concern for the Hispanic occupants. A great deal of chicanery was involved. Conversely, Hispanic grantees sometimes lost their lands because they lacked political clout and the financial resources to engage skilled, aggressive Anglo lawyers to defend their interests in the American courts. Sometimes they were

118   THE INDUSTRY MATURES

able to secure viable legal representation, but having insufficient cash resources, they paid dearly for those services with land, a substantial fraction of their tracts being taken up as attorneys' fees. The ownership determinations by the courts were, in the end, largely arbitrary and unfair.[76]

A few of the best-positioned *rico* families held onto their land, as was the case of the Chaves family. With their claims in San Mateo unconfirmed, Manuel Antonio Chaves and his half-brother Roman A. Baca sent Manuel's son, Amado Chaves, back to Washington in 1882 to defend their acquisitions. A well-educated attorney, he worked long and hard to obtain a patent for the grant, which covered over 200,000 acres, and ultimately prevailed.[77]

Most Hispanic families could not muster such legal talent, and many lost courtroom battles for their property. Others sold out cheaply when they were unable to pay newly imposed property taxes. Private grants fell to Anglos through other paths. When a patriarch died, ownership was distributed among the children and surviving spouse. Some or all the heirs often chose to sell their inheritance, as was the case with the Maxwell Grant. A similar situation transpired in the case of the Pablo Montoya Grant. Speculators and lawyers, in a complex series of transactions, acquired the grant, 530,000 acres previously confirmed by Congress and later to be patented, by purchase or as legal fees from six of the seven grant heirs in 1868. Their total financial outlay was no more than a few thousand dollars. They in turn sold this and other grant lands to flamboyant entrepreneur and land promoter Wilson Waddingham in 1870 for tens of thousands of dollars. He used the lands to form part of the massive Bell Ranch, southeast of Las Vegas. Eventually, many of the grants, both community and private, ended up in the hands of Anglo stockmen. Not surprisingly, sheep-growing resources that had once been Hispanic controlled came under Anglo control. Hispanic sheep interests diminished; Anglo interests grew.[78]

The changes in landownership were frequently conflict ridden. For the new Anglo owners, the presence of Hispanic settlers, squatters, and trespassers on the grant was often a source of continuing conflict.

When Harvard-educated John Greenough and James Brown Potter, New Haven investors, assumed control of the failing Bell Ranch in 1893, they discovered that about seventy long-term resident Hispanic families were living in villages on the grant and using some twenty miles of river frontage to raise their sheep, thus depriving Bell livestock of grass. The situation was unacceptable for the new owners, as good grazing land and water frontage were growing scarce. The resources had become too valuable for the new owners to share. The Bell management determined therefore to use the grant in its entirety. The land's Hispanic occupants, who had once lived under their patron's protection, were left in an ambiguous, insecure, and altogether difficult situation. In the end the Bell organization simply bought out the families with ten or more years of tenure, encouraging those families to file homestead claims on nearby public domain. Apparently, the program proceeded peaceably, although it is hard to imagine that these families were not distressed over the development. Documentation available for one family, the Munizes, indicates they received $200 cash plus ten foals worth $50 in exchange for their holding. By 1898 most of the settlers were gone from the grant. The new owners brought the huge ranch up to high standards of efficiency, enabling it to operate successfully for the next half century.[79] Ultimately, the bulk of the Spanish-Mexican land grant acreage fell into Anglo hands. The spirit of Manifest Destiny provided all the moral justification the land-seeking Anglos needed for this questionable and controversial shift in landownership.

Considering the other major source of land in New Mexico, much of the land taken up by the expanding sheep industry had, from the time of the annexation, been US public domain, the suppression of Indian raiding by the US Army having opened immense grazing tracts on these lands beyond the extent of the Spanish-Mexican land grants. Just as the Anglo acquisition of land grants has been highly controversial, so has the acquisition of public lands since much of the land in question was claimed illegally. The public lands that were eventually devoted to sheep included extensive tracts east and west of

120 THE INDUSTRY MATURES

Albuquerque, lying somewhat south of the bulk of the grants. Farther west Solomon Luna employed large tracts of public land for his herds.[80]

The critical factor in the acquisition of public lands from the federal government, even when illegal means were resorted to, as they often were, was some capital outlay, if not mainly for the land itself, then for livestock and other necessary expenditures, a situation that favored stockmen with ready cash. And once land was legally owned, it was subject to taxation, while a period of years might be required to develop a profitable ranch on the land. To be successful, ranchers might have to be able to pay taxes for a time before profits were realized.

Several paths, both direct and indirect, to public land acquisition existed. The railroads sold off their grant lands along their rights-of-way. The federal government, at times, made available for sale to the public both military and Indian lands. Cash was not always necessary. Land might be purchased with scrip, which had been issued to veterans by the federal government in compensation for military service. Land could also be purchased at public auction, possibly because of a previous claimant's tax arrears. And it could be bought from a private owner, possibly a failed homesteader who had managed to prove up his entry or a claimant under the Desert Land Act who could sell his claim at any time. Reminiscing in the early twenty-first century about her family history, sheep grower Roe Lovelace asserted that her family built their ranch in the Corona area of Lincoln County in part from the acquisition of homesteads, sometimes trading a wagon and a mule for the land of a failed homesteader. Anglo stockmen who began immigrating to New Mexico after the Civil War sometimes chose this path because it provided clear title outright, unlike the government land offerings with strings attached. This often enabled them to acquire the better available grazing tracts. These more affluent individuals, men like Luna's neighbor, Montague Stevens, brought the necessary funding into New Mexico from elsewhere, England in Stevens's case. At the other extreme, many cash-poor grant heirs, caught in a rapidly evolving financial environment, with their assets in the form of overgrazed land and marginally improved livestock, lacked the capital resources to purchase

The Industry Matures   121

additional, newly available land. The end result, again, was that Anglo sheep interests expanded more rapidly than Hispanic interests.[81]

Much of the public land claimed through the various federal programs was dedicated to grazing. Some, perhaps most, of these acquisitions were illegal. Ranchers often exploited the Homestead Act of 1862 and the Preemption Act of 1841. They proved to be valuable tools for New Mexico stockmen, although that was never intended by the lawmakers.[82] Congress passed the homestead laws as a path to populating the western regions of the country with productive, small-scale farmers and their families. The laws did not apply to nonagricultural lands, which constituted much of New Mexico. However, before the advent of mechanized irrigation, the 160-acre tracts available under the Homestead Act were completely inadequate for farming in the Southwest. Unsurprisingly, the federal government disposed of little public land in New Mexico before 1880.

Starting in the 1880s the situation changed. Ranchers with the necessary financial resources circumvented the homesteading restrictions by purchasing scrip, directly or indirectly from the veterans to whom it had been issued, and used it to purchase waterfront land at $3.50–$6.00 per acre. Others followed a different path. Much of the watered land that cattlemen acquired in New Mexico was obtained illegally, exploiting the homestead and preemption laws. The widespread practice has been described in detail by Westphall. Anglo sheepmen followed similar practices. By law, the 160-acre homesteads were to be continuously occupied and devoted to farming by the claimants for five years before they could file for a patent (deed of ownership). The laws were, however, easily exploited by western stockmen, who never occupied or farmed the tracts they claimed. While illegal, the process was easy and basically risk free. A rancher might first file a claim for land entry under the Homestead Act. He was not required to prove that he had satisfied the conditions for claiming title until the end of the five-year residency period. Thus, even if he never acquired title through a patent, he still could claim sole usage of the land for at least five years, provided the fraud was undiscovered, invariably the case. This

122 THE INDUSTRY MATURES

practice had the effect of tying up the land for years, devoting it strictly to grazing, and preventing anyone else from filing a claim or using it until the tract was again opened for entry. Ranchers often found this procedure for reserving land satisfactory for their purposes.[83]

With little competition from farmers whose numbers were still small, stockmen, aided by the collusion of public officials, sought particularly the quarter sections along streams or with springs needed to water their stock. Then, having secured the essential water rights, they gained control of large, unclaimed expanses of surrounding dry grazing land needed for their herds. The dry tracts alone, without water rights, were of no value to an encroaching rival, be he rancher or farmer, without mechanized irrigation, an expensive development of a later era. The dry tracts would remain unclaimed and open for grazing for many years. Montague Stevens described the situation succinctly: "As regards the amount of land a rancher owned compared with the acreage of his free range, it was very small and consisted mainly of the actual land on which was living [running] water such as creeks or springs." This land, the "home range," would often be the site of the ranch headquarters. Cattle rancher woman, Agnes Morley Cleaveland describes her family's "ranch," much of it actually public domain, as adjoining that of Stevens, although their dwellings were located seventy miles apart! Miguel A. Otero Jr. and J. W. Raynolds acquired a thirty-mile strip along the Salado River in Socorro County, which in turn give them control over a thirty-square-mile square area.[84]

Claimed stretches of waterfront could be readily expanded by exploiting the Preemption Law, which required only a six-month period of occupancy. An applicant could easily engage a bogus entry-man for that period so as to appear to be satisfying the letter of the law. Describing the situation in the Datil area, west of Magdalena, in the mid-1880s, Cleaveland noted that every site of "living water" in the area had been promptly homesteaded after the area was surveyed, only a few years earlier, and many families had supplemented their homestead with an additional 160-acre claim under the Preemption Act of 1841. She noted further that although it was not permitted under the law to sell or transfer these claims until final title was secured, this ruling was easily evaded. Most of the original homesteaders in her area, in short order after the receipt of land, sold their [would-be] patents to one of the large, open-range ranching outfits. This seems to have been common practice throughout the territory. Among westerners, there was a widespread disrespect for the federal land legislation. Seemingly few had serious compunctions about breaking federal statutes to acquire public lands, which must have appeared inexhaustible into the 1880s.[85]

Westphall has shown that by the 1890s a substantial fraction of the New Mexico public domain had been acquired fraudulently by ranchers since there were too few farmer-settlers in the territory to account for the number of homesteads that had been allotted. Cattlemen sometimes acquired title to public domain land that had been used by Hispanic herders for generations but never filed on. Some stockmen created ranches by first engaging a number of men, possibly employees, or possibly just fictitious names, to file contiguous homestead, preemption, or desert land claims. The false claimants would, if necessary, testify in court on each other's behalf that they were residing on or using the lands for agricultural purposes, as required by law. As soon as possible, the rancher behind this charade would buy out all the fictitious claimants, which had been the intent all along, thus carving out a large tract of rangeland for minimal financial outlay. The questionable practices did, for better or worse, enable many stockmen to go into business in New Mexico without a large financial outlay for land, while putting the land to a use for which it was better suited at the time.[86]

Westphall makes a good argument that the poorly conceived, unworkable, unpopular, inconsistently enforced land laws opened the way for widespread corruption.[87] Only in the late 1880s and early 1890s did public land transactions become normalized, as genuine homesteaders started arriving in New Mexico in substantial numbers and taking advantage of the homestead laws as they were intended. With the laws on their side, they were able to claim and take up some of the best lands

124   THE INDUSTRY MATURES

then available, an important factor in ending open-range ranching. Stockmen were then forced to approach landownership legally.

Reflecting the various difficulties, less than 60 percent of the New Mexico homestead entries were ever finalized.[88] This exacerbated the uncertainty in landownership first introduced by the grants and helped to keep New Mexico land prices low. Congress failed to provide adequate legislation to accommodate the western ranching industry as it assumed national importance, and perhaps even more seriously, Congress was little concerned about it. With a proper legal title under American law, land took on increased value because it could then be readily bought and sold on the open market, without any preexisting obligations. The federal government gave away 623,000 acres of US public domain in New Mexico, once the hunting grounds of nomadic tribes, and sold another 648,000 acres. The railroads eventually sold 356,000 acres of their deeded grant lands. Suffice it to say that the post–Civil War expansion of New Mexico's important sheep industry rested on a foundation of at best questionable, and often clearly fraudulent, land transactions.

Facilities and Operations

With the growth of markets and competition, costly new field facilities were required to counter inefficiencies that could no longer be dismissed. Labor costs increased as labor requirements became more exacting and competing employment options appeared. And while financial leadership in the industry shifted to the well-capitalized merchants, sheep ranches could still be quite profitable. Under evolving conditions, sheepmen needed to invest in fencing, wells, windmills, shearing pens, and a myriad of other items. Some undertook the growing of winter feed, alfalfa in particular, which necessitated farming equipment, seed purchases, and irrigation systems. Outdoor sheep camps had to be updated with the construction of permanent buildings.[89] Selective breeding using expensive, graded rams became necessary, not simply desirable, to meet the changing demands of the national wool and lamb markets. Sheep diseases were no longer sustainable and had to be combated aggressively, necessitating costly dipping facilities.

By the late nineteenth century, fencing became an important requirement, and a major expense, for an efficient sheep ranch. The introduction of barbed wire, invented in DeKalb, Illinois, and patented in 1874, made range fencing possible for the first time in New Mexico, where materials for any other type of fence were scarce and would have been prohibitively expensive. The railroads made it possible to economically ship the heavy rolls of barbed wire into the territory, which were too heavy for ox-drawn wagons, and both ranchers and farmers adopted fencing remarkably quickly. Fences altered the character of the rangeland irreversibly and revolutionized the western livestock industry. The introduction of fences on the western range was, however, a conflict-ridden process. Strongly, even violently, opposed by stockmen in the beginning; fences disrupted their traditional grazing practices. Ranchers eventually embraced the new technology when they came to appreciate its uses. The advent of fencing ultimately led to more orderly operations and generally greater, more stable profits. Fences were a critical factor in bringing open-range grazing in New Mexico, and throughout the West, to a close.

Barbed wire fences began to appear in New Mexico around 1880. Ranchers initially used fences to keep intruding livestock and stockmen off their range or cropland and preserve it for their own stock. Sheepmen[90] soon discovered, however, that a more important function of fences was to contain their own livestock rather than to exclude intruders.

Fences provided an array of advantages for sheep growers. They reduced labor and equipment expenses significantly. By containing flocks, fences reduced the need for herders. Two range and fence riders could do the work of ten herders. And the need for camp tenders, camp equipment, pack burros, and the like was eliminated along with the long-distance annual treks on the open range. Fenced livestock could be better protected and fed in winter. Fencing could be

126 THE INDUSTRY MATURES

employed to restrain and isolate breeding stock. All other factors being equal, fenced grazing land could carry 25 percent more sheep per acre since the land was utilized more uniformly. Fences made possible pasture rotation, reducing the damage from overstocking. Fenced watering places remained in better condition generally. Sheep and cattle could be raised together more readily in carefully managed enclosed pastures. On the negative side, fences could also lead to more heavily degraded land when too many animals were concentrated in a confined area.[91]

An important advantage of fencing for wool growers was the cleanliness of the wool produced, because fenced flocks did not crowd together in their own dust as much as range herds. Moreover, without the bunching typical of range herds, it was found that fenced-in lambs got more food and gained more weight. The practice of holding an entire herd of sheep in a small, compact, and thus food-scarce pen during lambing and shearing was eliminated, solving the longstanding problem of weight losses during these periods. If the fenced pastures were irrigated and seeded with grass, they could hold considerably more sheep per acre than open rangeland. The sheep ranches with fences would see increased profits over the long term. The value of barbed wire for westerners cannot be overestimated.

Many of the first fences were illegal. Ranchers did not restrict themselves to installing barbed wire on their patented home-range tracts. It was a widely accepted practice for New Mexico stockmen to fence tracts of public range that they had become accustomed to using, land they considered part of their "ranch." In an attempt to eliminate the practice, the fencing of public lands was declared illegal by territorial law in 1882. But the law was ineffective in many areas. Perpetrators could get around it easily because the fences were generally in remote areas where few people, and only rarely law officers, ventured. The practice was, besides, essentially a continuation of the custom of first-come-first-served usage rights. The big cattle growers with rosters of intimidating cowboys on their payrolls could readily suppress any local protests against their fences.[92]

By 1883 large stock companies in the territory were putting up fences on the public domain. The Bell Ranch together with several thousand acres of surrounding public domain, de facto part of the ranch, was completely fenced by 1889. Cleaveland noted that ranchers in her area around Datil enclosed their lands with as much barbed wire as they could afford. Her family fenced in their water hole and large tracts of adjoining rangeland, which in her words they used "by custom" but did not actually own. Some 3.5 million acres of public domain in New Mexico were being acted upon or under investigation for illegal fencing from 1885 through 1888. By 1900 the western range was crisscrossed everywhere by barbed wire.[93]

The initial cost of constructing sheep-proof fences was high, a significant deterrent for small-scale ranchers. Cleaveland noted that fences cost more than the land itself in her area. In 1880 Cimarron's *News and Press* reported that New Mexico attorney Frank Springer installed eighteen miles of fencing on his Colfax County ranch. Likewise, H. M. Porter installed thirty-two miles, and Chase and Dawson thirty miles on their ranches in the area. The average cost of the cattle fencing, the case here, was $130–$140 per mile. Expenditures of this magnitude were out of the question for growers having only a few hundred head. The news story went on to predict, a little too soon as it turned out, that within five years it would become the "almost universal custom to fence all ranches."[94]

If fences made ranches more profitable, they made life more difficult for those ranchers without them. Once they had become relatively common, fences broke up the range and often restricted the route from one open section to another, making it more difficult for any herder to utilize the remaining public rangeland. Open-range herding then required more time and labor than in the past. Starting around 1890, the proliferation of fencing had the effect of leaving many New Mexico *partidarios* and small-scale sheepmen "fenced out" of rangeland they had long been using. In frustration, they sometimes resorted to violence.

A wave of fence cutting swept through New Mexico and elsewhere in the Southwest. This was mainly an activity directed against large-scale

128   THE INDUSTRY MATURES

stock growers who had erected fences, both Anglo and Hispanic, by small-scale herders, whose marginal operations were most adversely affected by the fences. Fencing was one of the issues that gave rise to the *Gorras Blancas* and rampant fence cutting in San Miguel and Guadalupe Counties starting in the late 1880s. When Fabiola Cabeza de Baca reported that the *Gorras Blancas* had cut miles of fencing on her family's ranch, she was probably not exaggerating. The "fencing out" of smaller operators accelerated during 1900–1910.[95]

The social consequences of fencing the range should not be overlooked. Fencing ultimately helped bring about a more cooperative and stable farming and ranching society. The fences designated land claims unambiguously and thus suppressed range wars as well as less dramatic land conflicts.[96]

Watering crops and livestock had been a major challenge in semi-arid New Mexico since Spanish colonial times. The colonists learned to harness the forces of nature to provide their villages with water. They built *acequias* to channel river flow to their nearby fields and dug wells for domestic use, but beyond that made no technological progress in water procurement. The industrial revolution, which swept through the United States beginning in the late eighteenth century, produced a wave of technological innovation, including mechanized irrigation, which had an immense effect on both farming and ranching in New Mexico and throughout the West. During the late nineteenth century advancing irrigation technology rendered reservoirs, commercially useful wells, and windmills, at long last, practical and affordable in the West. As in the case of barbed wire, the railroads transported windmills to New Mexico for the first time.

The reservoirs utilized the occasional flood waters in the streams, heretofore untapped. Wells and windmills to pump underground water to the surface and also artesian flow were used to fill livestock watering tanks and to irrigate fields.[97] Until this time, possession of water frontage had given ranchers control of the surrounding dry rangeland. However, those lands farthest from water were often lightly used. This was an inherent inefficiency in the open-range system. Large tracts of otherwise good grazing land were simply too far away from water for either stock growing or farming. The advent of wells and windmills greatly ameliorated this situation.

By 1900 many New Mexico sheep ranchers had drilled wells and installed windmills, an expensive proposition. Others would continue to do so well into the twentieth century. James Hagerman and Charles Eddy irrigated John Chisum's old ranch area in southeastern New Mexico in 1889. Mechanized irrigation opened great expanses of heretofore unused rangeland. Livestock could now congregate around a water tank on a segment of otherwise dry land and utilize the surrounding dry range more fully. Sheep could be more evenly distributed over the land, and herd sizes could be increased. Sheep growers could concentrate more on the demands of increasingly competitive markets and less on basic range conditions. In any case, more efficient use of the land became increasingly necessary after homesteaders began to take up rangeland and natural water frontage on the public domain.[98]

With increased demands for efficiency and a resulting professionalization, the labor requirements on sheep ranches became more exacting. Government livestock experts discussing the direction in which the industry was headed in 1892 encouraged owners to personally supervise the care of their flocks in the interest of maximizing profits. When Waddingham's Bell Ranch went into bankruptcy and was taken over by East Coast investors, they hired as on-site general manager Irish-born Arthur J. Tisdall, a knowledgeable, experienced sheep and cattle grower and, apparently, also a first-rate businessman. Tisdall, in turn, hired as "range manager" Englishman Jack Culley, a graduate of Oxford University. During the dry winter of 1894–1895, a critical time for the operation, they successfully introduced large flocks of sheep onto the ranch, which they considered the optimum livestock under the prevailing conditions. Eventually, they turned around the failing operation and put it on the road to success. Combining East Coast money with European managerial know-how on a New Mexico ranch proved to be a formula for success in this case. Such managerial talent was not cheap; sufficient funds were needed to pay competent

130 THE INDUSTRY MATURES

managers. In a more down-to-earth approach, many of the successful operations were, as in the past, family enterprises in which a few individual family members shared managerial responsibilities.[99]

More demanding labor requirements were not restricted to the managerial levels. The labor situation in New Mexico had changed significantly since the Civil War. Cheap, skilled herders were no longer so readily available, particularly with the disappearance of captive Indian slavery and peonism. Knowledgeable, responsible herders became harder for sheepmen to find, particularly for seasonal employment, while labor expenses increased. And now ranchers needed cash on hand to pay the temporary work forces fairly and attract competent workers.

Lambing, which lasted about a month to six weeks in the early spring was a critical operation for sheep growers that strongly affected their success in the coming year. Peggy Sultemeier, who grew up on a combined sheep and cattle ranch near Santa Rosa in the early twentieth century, remembered lambing as a "delight." In the increasingly competitive economy, a high survival rate for newborns was essential. Typically, however, no more than about 85 percent of ewes, and frequently many fewer, produced viable offspring each year. Greater losses might be hard to sustain. For a successful season, sheepmen needed to hire temporary lambing crews on a cash basis, a practice that became increasingly difficult as Hispanic villagers, who had once eagerly sought seasonal work in the sheep camps, chose other employment options in the expanding Southwest economy. If a birthing crew was inept or unmotivated, lamb survival could drop precipitously, resulting in deep cuts in the sheepman's profits.[100]

Shearing costs were another expense incurred about the same time of year—sometimes before, sometimes after lambing. Skilled shearers were, like skilled birthing crews, essential for successful wool production. Poorly skilled or unmotivated shearers would not obtain the full fleece weight from an animal, and their clumsy work would lead to additional mortality of the mature sheep.

The industrialization and capitalization of New Mexico sheep production in the latter decades of the territorial period are illustrated at both the mercantile level and on the ranches by the well-documented experiences of three prominent Anglo sheepmen, Frank Bond, Montague Stevens, and Thomas Catron. The following three chapters, each drawing on extensive personal correspondence, focus on these three men and their experiences with sheep. The well-documented activities of Frank Bond and his brother, G. (George) W., exemplify the role of mercantile capitalism and the maturation of New Mexico's sheep industry. The establishment, growth, and success of the Bond enterprises are the subject of the following chapter.

4

FRANK BOND'S SHEEP EMPIRE

"I am a stock-man. I gamble in wool, also speculate in land, lend a little money, make some money, and lose some."[1] So wrote Frank Bond. The well-documented activities of Frank Bond and his brother G. (George) W. exemplify the role of mercantile capitalism and the maturation of New Mexico's sheep industry. By the last decades of the nineteenth century, mercantile companies had spread widely throughout the territory and had, in large part, taken on leadership of the sheep industry. Frank Bond's organization became the largest, most successful, and most influential of the territory's sheep and wool enterprises. Operating from his Espanola headquarters for over forty years and from Albuquerque thereafter, he built a mercantile empire extending from the San Luis Valley of Colorado east into Nebraska and south through much of New Mexico.

First established as a general mercantile concern, the Bond company was soon deeply involved in live sheep and wool. The operation was

https://doi.org/10.5876/9781646425471.c004

innovative, complex by contemporary standards, capital intensive, and extraordinarily profitable. Frank Grubbs, in his corporate history, succinctly and accurately described the Bond enterprises as "not only intricately interlocked corporate organizations but also numerous joint venture arrangements for buying and selling wool and sheep." The Bond organization, a step considerably beyond the comparatively simple, independent mercantile operations of the Santa Fe Trail era, was well adapted to the New Mexico economy of the late nineteenth and early twentieth centuries. Its operations mirrored the nation's sheep business, which was becoming increasingly complex and capital intensive during this period, developments ultimately driven by the demands of expanding national and international markets into which New Mexico was drawn. The story of Frank Bond and the Bond empire provides a quick look at a slice of life in territorial New Mexico in its final decades and illuminates what the sheep business was like for the insiders at this time.[2]

Frank Bond was born in 1863 and grew up on a farm in Argenteuil County, Quebec Province, Canada. His correspondence from his long business career indicates a stern but fair, highly disciplined workaholic of a somewhat secretive bent. At age nineteen or twenty he joined his older brother, George, who was working at a general store in Chamita (San Juan Pueblo). Entering into partnership, the brothers soon bought out a small mercantile firm located in the recently established town of Espanola, population 150. The business, renamed G. W. Bond & Bro., was well situated, as the town was becoming a rail terminal of importance since the arrival of the Denver & Rio Grande Western Railroad. It is believed that the brothers were initially financed by a loan from their father in Quebec, possibly of about $25,000, a considerable sum at the time (about $700,000 in 2020 dollars).[3]

The brothers were typical of many Anglo businessmen who came to New Mexico after the Civil War in that they had no long-standing antecedents, family or friends, in New Mexico but through some unclear channels had learned about the economic opportunities in the territory. Smart, ambitious, and hardworking, they also possessed the

FIGURE 4.1. Sheepman Frank Bond and his son, who much later took over the family business. Courtesy of the Center for Southwest Research, Pictorial Archives, UNM

sense of adventure, and the stomach for risk, to pursue the opportunities offered. The brothers are not known to have had any prior involvement in merchandising or, for that matter, the sheep business. Like many of their Anglo cohorts, the Bond brothers seem to have been well educated and possessed of a family background of affluence. They were fluent in French and Spanish as well as English. Frank was less than delighted by what he saw upon his arrival in New Mexico. Reminiscing years later about the stagecoach ride from Santa Fe to Espanola in 1883, he noted, "The country seemed to me a perfect desert, and the people we met, with their few burro loads of wood and sacks of grain in tanned buffalo sacks, seemed so poor that I was by no means very favorably impressed with my new home."[4]

If the Bond brothers were not atypical of a new class of New Mexico immigrants, their father also bore much in common with many absentee investors in the West. Western business organizations during this period, even those running large cattle ranches, were often basically closed circles of family and friends. The younger men served as on-site managers while the older men, more often than not, remained in the East, providing financing and attending to other necessary business matters.[5]

The brothers' mercantile operation seems to have been successful from the start, growing quietly for its first decade. And like other New Mexico mercantile capitalists, the brothers found themselves, in time, dealing in wool and live sheep and in possession of herds of significant proportions. The earliest clear indication of wool dealings in the company records is dated 1897, but Frank Bond recalled years later that the brothers were buying up, and marketing at a small profit, most of the wool grown in their part of the country during the Panic of 1893.[6] They purchased what they called "outside" wool from local growers. And they acquired wool as rent due from their *partidarios*, to whom they had contracted out their own flocks. The Bond sheep generally produced to the partners' credit two pounds of wool per head, indicating a degree of breeding for increased wool production. The brothers gained leverage in the trade by controlling access to the

136 FRANK BOND'S SHEEP EMPIRE

D&RGW rail service, over which they shipped both wool and sheep to eastern markets.

The Bonds' first entry into the live sheep business also occurred no later than 1893. Like other New Mexico merchants, the Bonds accepted sheep from their customers in exchange for merchandise or to satisfy standing debts. And to care for that livestock, they employed a modified *partido* system, eventually enlisting Hispanic herders throughout New Mexico and the San Luis Valley. The earliest existing Bond *partido* contracts date from 1895. The brothers rented sheep out in the fall for periods ranging from one to five years, but most commonly for three years. The *partidario* assumed the entire risk in caring for his rented flock, including losses from bad weather, poor range conditions, and disease. Like Charles Ilfeld, Frank Bond assumed the role of patron, while his *partidarios*, accustomed to the situation, operated much as they had in the past. And like the traditional Hispanic patrones of the past, the Bonds maintained control over their flocks through *partidarios* who were indebted to them financially. The Bond contracts were not uniform but, being granted on an individual basis, were adapted to local conditions. The brothers required the wives of their *partidarios* to also sign the contracts. Should the herder be unable to fulfill the terms of his contract, he would be left in debt to the Bonds at the end of the contract period.[7]

THE MONEY FLOW

When the Bond brothers commenced operations in Espanola, they found it absolutely necessary to extend credit to their customers; the bulk of their sales, in Espanola as well as at other branches they established later, were in fact made on credit. The Bonds also found it necessary to extend advances to their wool suppliers, usually in the late spring or early summer, against deliveries in the fall. Likewise, their *partidarios* needed credit, in addition to sheep, to get started. The brothers' financial commitments became considerable as they entered into a growing number of *partido* contracts. By the end of 1890 the partnership had extended $10,266 in credit. This practice grew rapidly. By 1898 they had extended $55,000 or more in credit out to their customers. In 1911, at the time of the partnership dissolution, Frank Bond was carrying $420,000 ($11 million in 2020 dollars) in the form of notes and bills receivable. This amount was far beyond the lending ability of most western enterprises but ultimately enabled the Bonds to take on more business and continue to grow. The Bonds, like other New Mexico merchants, provided an interface between the traditional, smaller-scale Hispanic sheep growers and the often volatile sheep and wool markets of the East.[8]

For many years the Bonds sold or consigned their wool to the Boston commission house of Brown & Adams. Much like their mercantile cohorts, they employed a few different financial arrangements. Sometimes they purchased wool outright with their own funds or in partnership with another investor and sold it outright to their Boston dealer. At other times they would not sell but instead consign a particular lot of wool to the dealer, who then sold it on commission to the New England textile mills, the dealer reducing his risk but often also his profits by operating solely as a commission merchant. Most commonly, the Bonds would purchase wool in the West with partial or full financing from their Boston wool house. The advantage of this was that the eastern dealer was often able to borrow money in the East at a relatively modest rate and then turn around and loan it to Frank Bond at the higher rate of 6 percent interest. Bond would then turn the money around again, loaning it to his suppliers against future deliveries. If he borrowed from a western bank, which he often had to do, he would have to pay the higher prevailing interest rate, 8 percent or more.[9] When the Bonds put up some of the money and the commission merchant put up the rest, the risk in this inherently risky business was shared.

Pursuing this sort of arrangement, the Bonds took out the advances from their eastern wool dealers in the late spring or early summer on fall deliveries, the loan collateral being the unshorn New Mexico wool. They employed a similar procedure to finance their feeding operations. At the beginning of the winter feeding season, they borrowed funds, typically from John Clay's livestock commission firm, Clay, Robinson

138 FRANK BOND'S SHEEP EMPIRE

& Co. of Denver, which they used to provide lambs and cash for feed to their feeder ranchers in Colorado and Nebraska. They compensated the feeder $50 per month plus 15 percent of the profits when the sheep were sold. And they paid off the loan in the form of fattened sheep delivered to the dealer at the end of the season. Capital had become not just convenient but essential for the functioning of the New Mexico sheep industry.[10]

During times of particularly uncertain markets, western buyers like the Bonds would be reluctant to sink their own funds into advance wool purchases, not knowing whether they would experience a profit or loss on the sale at the end of the growing season. Under such trying circumstances, the eastern dealers might, out of necessity, simply provide all of the necessary funds and engage their western suppliers, like the Bonds, simply as on-site wool buyers. Another practice, undertaken in uncertain times, was for the eastern wool dealer to guarantee a minimum price to the western merchant, shielding him against loss. In both these scenarios the eastern dealer assumed a higher degree of risk than normal practice against the possibility of realizing higher profits at the westerners' expense. In February 1915, Frank Bond made such an agreement of guaranteed price with Brown & Adams, something he rarely did. They guaranteed him his costs plus the first cent per pound of any profit on the wool while reserving for themselves the next half cent of profit. Additional profits, if any, would go to Bond, although the tone of the letter suggests this was unlikely.[11] Thus, in this instance, Bond relinquished potential profits in return for a guaranteed price support, which would protect him from losses. It was a crude form of insurance policy. The New Mexico merchants thus had procedures for hedging their investments in uncertain times, rendering a risky business a bit less risky. Sheep growers had few such options to protect themselves in a bad year. Needless to say, these arrangements involved close relationships between the New Mexico merchants and the commission houses 2,000 miles and several days' travel away. Good communications and financial know-how were essential. These new complications are one of the reasons why marketing sheep and wool became the purview of a specialist, the merchant. The grower, unless he operated on a fairly large scale, could not continue to be his own dealer. By the late nineteenth century the New Mexico wool grower was absorbed into a nationwide financial network.

During the Panic of 1893, the Bonds were forced to accept ewes as payment on debts, for which they gave a credit of $1 per head, despite the depressed going price of only fifty cents per head. During another run of tough times in 1901, the brothers experienced a loss of $1,868 in a wool transaction with Brown & Adams, having paid by preagreement with their New Mexico growers more than the wool was actually selling for on the eastern market by the time it was shipped. In 1903 the situation was even worse. Brown & Adams sold 557,646 pounds of wool for the Bonds and their partner in the deal, Fred Warshauer, for a loss of nearly $10,000 ($300,000 in 2020 dollars). The Bonds, being well capitalized, were able to sustain an occasional annual loss such as this in one component of their business. Their wool profits in 1904 and 1905 more than offset the losses of 1901 and 1903, as discussed below. At the opposite extreme, their suppliers—small, independent, undercapitalized, mostly Hispanic—might be thrown out of business by one particularly bad year. Like Charles Ilfeld, the Bond brothers chose, when necessary, to forgo immediate profits and take losses in the interest of keeping their suppliers solvent, loyal, and a source of future profits both as wool and livestock producers and as customers at their general stores. This was an act of survival more than altruism. Despite the occasional losses, the Bonds' overall business, including general merchandise, live sheep sales, and *partido* contracts, was always profitable, although the profits varied widely from year to year.[12]

EXPANSIONS

The Bonds expanded steadily over the years, establishing several branch operations. In 1892, after eight years in business, they bought out an existing mercantile establishment in Wagon Mound when the owner, John Justus Schmidt, was killed, as noted above. George then relocated

140 FRANK BOND'S SHEEP EMPIRE

to Wagon Mound and managed this operation for over a decade until 1904 while Frank remained in charge at Espanola. The brothers capitalized the Wagon Mound branch at just under $40,000, drawing largely upon accumulated profits from the Espanola store but with an additional $8,000 loan from their father at the modest annual interest of 4 percent. Like the Espanola headquarters, the new Wagon Mound branch at first dealt principally in general merchandise; but within about two years it was holding $3,300 worth of sheep in Fort Collins, Colorado, feed lots. Its sheep holdings increased more than tenfold in value over the next few years to $46,000 in 1898. By 1900 Wagon Mound had 30,000 sheep out on *partido* contracts. In its first year of operation the branch realized a 20 percent return on the Bonds' initial capital investment. And during its first decade of operations, 1893–1903, the branch usually produced an annual return in the range of 18–40 percent. This is a huge sustained return by twenty-first-century business standards and indicates what was possible for a conservatively run, well-capitalized operation in New Mexico at the time.[13]

After 1914 the bulk of the profits were coming from sheep and wool, as was also the case for the other Bond branches. The territory truly could be a land of opportunity. In later years the brothers transferred additional capital infusions from Espanola to Wagon Mound to further expand that operation. The free flow of capital between their branches, these two and others that they established later, greatly facilitated the company's operations and expansions. During their partnership the brothers occasionally took out short-term bank loans when an immediate need for cash arose. They borrowed from private investor Abraham Staab and the First National Bank of Santa Fe, with which they had a close, long-term relationship. This was a practice they tried to minimize because of the high interest rates for such loans. However, their expansions were, like the Wagon Mound acquisition, always financed with accumulated past profits, never by bank loans or through public offerings of stock or bonds like a modern corporation.[14]

Up until this point, G. W. Bond & Bro. had remained a simple partnership between the two brothers. The expansion demanded that an additional manager be hired. To help run the Wagon Mound branch, the Bonds brought in an old family friend from Quebec, Archibald (Archie) MacArthur, employing a strategy then typical of western businesses. In a similar scenario Charles Ilfeld had brought several of his brothers to New Mexico, who later established an independent mercantile operation in Albuquerque. The Spiegelbergs did likewise. And Ilfeld also brought his brother-in-law, Max Nordhaus, over from Germany, eventually placing him in charge of his Las Vegas headquarters. In a more atypical move, the Bonds also employed in a managerial capacity a family outsider, former Schmidt employee and Wagon Mound native Manuel Paltenghe.[15]

Upon the arrival of railroads on the eastern plains of New Mexico, the Bonds established a branch operation in Cuervo, fifteen miles east of Santa Rosa, on the newly built Rock Island rail line—the Chicago, Rock Island, and Pacific Railroad. They employed another outsider, Andy Wiest, to manage that operation. They had serious competition here. The Charles Ilfeld Company established a similar branch in 1904 in Santa Rosa. The Bonds financed the Cuervo start-up with $10,000 of accumulated profits from the Wagon Mound store.[16]

In Taos the same year, the Bonds acquired the long-established mercantile establishment of Alexander Gusdorf in partnership with Gusdorf's younger brother Gerson and Justin H. McCarthy, the latter two men providing the on-site management and investing some of their own funds. Thus was born the Bond, Gusdorf, and McCarthy Company, initially capitalized at $30,000, predominantly with Bond funds. The partners made an agreement never to sell their interest to an outsider without first offering it to the other associates on the same terms.[17] And in fact Gerson Gusdorf sold out his share to the other stockholders in 1907. This acquisition was notable for the mixed ethnicity of the owners, Canadian, Jewish, and Anglo-American, which was not atypical of New Mexico mercantile enterprises of this era. The extraordinary challenges and rewards of frontier enterprises often drew together talented men of diverse backgrounds in pursuit of common opportunities. The Bonds' Antonito partner, Fred Warshauer, was also Jewish.

142 FRANK BOND'S SHEEP EMPIRE

Not all the expansion was in the form of branch stores. In 1907 Frank Bond built, at a cost of about $1,000, a sheep-loading complex with pens, scales, and a camp house in Servilleta, thirty-eight miles north of Espanola on the D&RGW line. Sheep were thereafter driven from the various grazing locations in the region to this loading site for rail shipment out of New Mexico. The scales, a new expense, became necessary when sheep began to be sold by weight rather than by the head around the turn of the twentieth century, so the animals had to be weighed prior to loading. In another significant capital outlay, Bond built a sheep-dipping facility in Espanola for about $3,500 in 1911.[18]

The Bonds had cautiously departed from the family business modus operandi when they hired able outsiders for important positions. In 1904 the Bonds took another major step and incorporated the Wagon Mound operation with themselves, MacArthur, and Paltenghe as shareholders, establishing a procedure that they would employ repeatedly in the future as they opened new branches. The new corporation was called the A. MacArthur Company, as MacArthur now became the on-site general manager while George Bond departed for Trinidad, Colorado. MacArthur and Paltenghe were actually the largest shareholders, at least on paper.[19] The Bonds incorporated the Cuervo branch the same year as Bond & Wiest with Andy Wiest as stockholder–general manager.

The specific procedure employed by the Bonds to bring in their key managers as stockholders was innovative. They would first issue the man a block of stock. Since these employees generally had no funds of their own to pay for the stock, they were allowed to give the Bonds a note, or an I.O.U., for the amount needed.[20] Then, instead of turning over the stock certificates to the employee, the Bonds retained the certificates as collateral for that note. In this way an employee with no funds of his own became a part owner of the store he managed and would share in future profits. Over a period of years he would be able to pay off his note to the Bonds using the profits resulting from his own managerial efforts. The arrangement provided a powerful motivation for the employee to perform his duties well. In the meantime he was paid a salary, typically $75–$100 per month (about $2,800 in 2020 dollars) for a general manager, which was quite substantial for the times. Thus, no cash or even stock certificates initially changed hands. The Bond brothers, holding all the certificates, thus maintained ultimate control over the new corporation and their managers.

Frank Bond strengthened his leadership position further by making personal loans to his various store managers, who would then be doubly indebted to him. He directed branch operations from his Espanola office while his employee-stockholders oversaw the day-to-day operations. As the Bonds employed this procedure to finance and consolidate control over a succession of branches, each new enterprise constituted an individual corporation, with the stock owned by the brothers, their key managers, and a mix of preexisting Bond corporations. The actual cash used to capitalize each new initiative came from the accumulated profits of previously established branch corporations. Just as the Wagon Mound branch was initially financed by the Espanola operation, it in turn financed other Bond start-ups in later years.[21] This arrangement made possible considerable operating flexibility since the Bonds were not beholden to any outside investors and could effortlessly transfer cash as needed from one of their corporations to another. Wagon Mound was only one of a series of successful partnerships Frank Bond formed with talented, proven family outsiders.

In 1906, two years after the Wagon Mound reorganization, the Bonds incorporated their Espanola store as the Bond & Nohl Company, with the Bond brothers and Louis F. Nohl as principal shareholders. Nohl, another outsider, had joined G. W. Bond & Bro. in 1900 under some sort of profit-sharing arrangement, and over time he had assumed much of the day-to-day management of the store. Frank Bond retained a separate business, still part of the G. W. Bond & Bro. partnership, on the same site, buying and selling wool, overseeing his numerous *partido* contracts, negotiating lamb feeding agreements, and looking after the overall financial and organizational matters for his growing empire. Bond & Nohl handled all the merchandising, the sheep trading, and the financial aspects of the feeding operations, a developing activity for the company.[22]

144 FRANK BOND'S SHEEP EMPIRE

While George was establishing what was to be a very profitable sheep and wool operation in Trinidad, the Bonds undertook another new initiative in Colorado. A few years earlier, around 1903, they had entered a partnership agreement with Fred Warshauer of Antonito, Colorado, sharing profits fifty-fifty in wool deals in New Mexico and southern Colorado. Even earlier, during the winter of 1894–1895, they had begun placing lambs with feeders in Colorado through their Wagon Mound branch, and they negotiated feeding contracts in Nebraska as early as 1902. After about 1908, they became actively involved in the winter feeding of lambs, forming a three-way partnership with Warshauer and E. S. Leavenworth of Wood River, Nebraska, who owned a feeding ranch. That year they had over $100,000 ($2.8 million in 2020 dollars) worth of sheep on feed with Leavenworth and more with another feeder. Several other New Mexico growers had arrangements with Wood River feeders. The Bonds maintained a decade-long, and quite profitable, partnership with Warshauer, with whom Frank became particularly close. In 1909 Frank acquired a 270-acre feeder ranch in Wood River, where he fed 20,000–25,000 head. He expanded his operations a few years later, leasing additional land in Lexington, Nebraska, for feeding purposes. The considerable capital outlay required for these feeding operations, which included not only the cost of the lambs but also the cost of feed (corn, hay, alfalfa), was quite substantial as was the cost of cash advances provided to the ranchers in the fall. To finance his operations in the winter of 1914 Frank Bond took out a loan of $65,000 at 9 percent ($1.8 million in 2020 dollars) from Clay, Robinson in Denver, a measure of the financial commitment needed. Earlier, during 1911, his most active year up to that time, Bond and his feeding associates had a total investment of $283,000 ($7.9 million in 2020 dollars). Frank continued doing business with Warshauer's company, the Warshauer-McClure Sheep Company, after his friend's death—by suicide—in 1913.[23]

In 1911, after twenty-eight years in business together, the Bond brothers ended their partnership; thereafter Frank became the sole senior managing proprietor of the business, although he continued to take on new partners from time to time. George retained his financial interest as a stockholder but relocated to Idaho and California to pursue other business opportunities. Frank's personal net worth at this time was in excess of $500,000 ($13 million in 2020 dollars), a considerable fortune at the time. During the best year of their partnership, 1905, the brothers had cleared nearly $100,000 in profits. At the time of the partnership dissolution, Frank had in his own account 37,296 head of sheep valued at $112,000 out on *partido* contracts. Considering his various partnerships, he held an interest in a total of 52,244 sheep, rented out under ninety separate contracts to individuals in and around Espanola and Taos, where most of the Bond sheep were grazed, and Antonito, Colorado. To manage his large holdings, he went into partnership with various individuals and other mercantile companies who oversaw the various *partido* operations in their localities. The sheep were generally run in small flocks, either on public lands, with Bond paying grazing fees, or on land grants. With grazing rights on the public land becoming permanent after three years, Bond took particular care to count and report to the forest authorities all his sheep and *partido* contracts and thus protect his grazing resources from being taken over by another stockman.[24]

The Bonds made their first move to the south in 1905 with the establishment of a mercantile branch in Encino, Torrance County, south of Albuquerque. The branch was dealing in sheep and wool within a few years and remained profitable through the remainder of the territorial period. Frank Bond continued expanding during the early years of statehood. In mid-1914 he opened a branch in Albuquerque that dealt strictly in sheep, wool, hides, and pelts, but no general merchandise. Following his usual policy, Bond incorporated the business, taking on three of his managers as shareholders. This start-up is notable for its new general manager and shareholder, Walter Connell. Connell was a Fordham University graduate with years of experience merchandising and wool buying in New Mexico and banking in New York. In its first full year of operation, 1915, the Bond-Connell Sheep & Wool Co., as it was called, sold 151,000 head of sheep, 455,000 pounds of wool, and 305,000 pounds of hides and pelts for a net profit of over $20,000, a staggering return on the initial capitalization, thought to be $25,000. Additionally, the company was still holding a considerable inventory of sheep, wool, hides, and pelts at year's end. Following this success, Bond established the Bond-Sargent Company in Grants, New Mexico, a site chosen because of its proximity to the Navajo Reservation with its large sheep population. This branch developed into one of the most successful of the Bond enterprises. Its successor, the Bond-Gunderson Company, was still in operation in the early 1960s.[25]

LAND

During the early years of the twentieth century, the brothers, under George's initiative, invested or speculated in land, mostly in southern Colorado. A few years earlier, however, they had started to acquire land in New Mexico. With growing sheep populations in San Miguel and Leonard Wood (later Guadalupe) Counties and the pending arrival of railroads, the Bonds acquired at least six ranches in the area around 1900. In 1900 they also purchased a 63,000-acre segment of the Preston Beck Grant, only one of their grant-land acquisitions in New Mexico, for $43,000. At one point they were holding as many as 30,000 head of sheep on the Beck land, but they sold the tract in 1907 for a profit of over $20,000. A few years later, in 1909, they acquired a 270-acre feeder ranch in Wood River, Nebraska, for $65,000. Despite all their land acquisitions, their business was never dependent on huge tracts of grazing land, as was also the case with Charles Ilfeld. They held some of their tracts for a comparatively short time. In some cases they seemed more intent on land speculation than the acquisition of good grazing land for their flocks. Landownership on a large scale was no longer a prerequisite to wealth and influence in New Mexico.[26]

BUSINESS POLICY

By the early twentieth century, G. W. Bond & Bro. had moved beyond its initial two-man management structure and had a substantial number of salaried employees, including several of managerial status, with no

Frank Bond's Sheep Empire 147

Bond family connections. It has been estimated that Bond & Nohl had about ten or twelve salaried employees at Espanola, presumably a typical number for an active branch operation. Among the Bond employees were store managers, bookkeepers, and, on account of Frank's voluminous correspondence, stenographers as well as store clerks, general handymen, warehouse clerks, and general laborers. Bond & Nohl always employed one or two "native clerks." Frank Bond paid his stenographers as much as $75 per month, fluency in both Spanish and English being desired, and his bookkeepers as much as $100 per month ($2,800 in 2020 dollars), generally recruiting bookkeepers and stenographers from out of town. An important position in his organization was that of "outside man," a sort of assistant manager tasked with buying sheep from the growers, contracting for wool, making collections, and acting as general foreman in the field. For many years this position at Bond & Nohl was held by Leandro Martinez, who also was a small shareholder in the company. Frank Bond always paid his store managers $75–$100 per month, a good salary at the time, and for key men he augmented this with a profit-sharing arrangement, including stock in the branch corporation, as described above. Business hours were long. The Bond & Nohl store was open six days a week, usually closing at 10:00 p.m. The sheep and wool business could be quite profitable—it certainly was for the Bond brothers—but the efforts required to fully realize the potential gains were considerable.[27]

Frank Bond was a hands-on manager; he kept close watch on every detail of his empire and, not averse to physical labor, supplied his own labor when it was called for. He often personally supervised the loading of sheep onto railroad cars, rising at 3:00 a.m. to serve as his own foreman, working at what has been described as a "fast dogtrot" all day long. For a single shipment in October 1913, Bond loaded an estimated 27,000 head of sheep at his Servilleta facility into thirty railroad cars per day for a period of three successive days. Frank Bond was totally dedicated to business and would do whatever was necessary for success. He asserted in a letter to his brother George, "in fact, I wouldn't trade my job with anybody." When he was not working, he was bored and unsettled.[28]

CHALLENGES

The Bond enterprises faced several challenges that were characteristic of sheep- and wool-dealing mercantile operations. Consideration of these various challenges, which are well documented for the Bond enterprises, provides some insight into what working in the New Mexico sheep industry may have been like.

All the Bond companies, as with all weather-dependent businesses then and now, experienced widely fluctuating profits from year to year, despite being quite conservatively managed. At Bond & Nohl annual net profits between 1906 and 1915 ranged from $3,400 to $29,400. The Bonds' wool partnership with Warshauer lost $10,000 in 1903, as previously noted, and then yielded $25,000 profits in 1906, $46,000 in 1908, but only about $12,000 in 1911. Such fluctuations were a fact of life that never abated and derived in part from the inherent instability of the national sheep and wool markets. And that brought the matter of capital reserves to the forefront of financial considerations. Capital was, of course, needed just to keep the company operating smoothly. The brothers routinely moved funds back and forth between their various enterprises as needed. But during extraordinarily tough times when expenses exceeded income, capital reserves were totally essential for survival.[29]

Volatility imparted considerable risk for investors in the widely touted, and occasionally realized, business opportunities found in New Mexico and the West in general. When Fred Warshauer died, Frank Bond advised the man's widow not to invest any more of her money in sheep or wool, noting that he would not want his own wife to do so if he died. Expressing a similar sentiment in his will, Solomon Luna advised his wife to liquidate the family business and invest the proceeds in conservative securities. In any case, soon after his death in 1912, she relocated to California. When Frank Bond's own wife expressed an interest in investing her personal funds in sheep, he instead purchased for her secure bonds paying 5 percent.[30]

Frank Bond believed that the high risk could only be counteracted by close attention to the business. In answer to an inquiry from a

Kansas City businessman who was considering investing in sheep, Bond replied, "I consider this line of business very dangerous, and [it] requires very careful watching. Three of our renters have lost this winter over half of their flocks on account of heavy snows. . . . I would advise you very strongly to have nothing to do with sheep, unless you can give the matter your personal attention. . . . We make money out of sheep, but we make it because we give them close attention, otherwise it could not possibly be done."[31]

Up-to-date market information was critical for success in sheep and wool negotiations, particularly as the markets could be quite volatile. Information retrieval was thus an important, continuing activity for western merchants. Valuable industry news and advice was provided to them by their East Coast commission houses. Specifically, the eastern establishments provided up-to-date news on domestic market trends and the effects of foreign wool production on markets in Britain (London and Liverpool), Australia, and other parts of the world. They discussed such matters as the wool tariff, wool manufacturers' current problems, and the condition of wool clips in various parts of the United States at the time.

The Bonds, like other western wool merchants, were dependent on the eastern wool houses for such trade information. Bond's informants transmitted information west in the form of long, coded Western Union telegrams or detailed letters. Max Nordhaus received intelligence from an eastern wool house by telegraph but also directly from his boss, Charles Ilfeld, who by the 1890s was spending his winters in New York City. Adolph Letcher, Ilfeld's onetime partner now living in Baltimore, also sent his wool and sheep market forecasts to Nordhaus, who in turn forwarded them to his New Mexico suppliers. The westerners would generally seek out and attach themselves to an eastern dealer in whom they had confidence, giving him the bulk of their business year after year and thus securing for themselves a reliable information source.[32]

Although the Bonds dealt almost exclusively with the Boston wool house of Brown & Adams for many years, they later shifted their

150   FRANK BOND'S SHEEP EMPIRE

business to the Boston firm of Hallowell, Jones & Donald. Early in that shift, Frank Bond advised his branch manager, Andy Wiest, to shift some of his wool sales over to H, J & D primarily to diffuse competition that company was creating but also so that the Bond & Wiest branch would "get the posting from H, J & D as well as that of B & A," thus securing two important streams of information.[33] While the Bonds benefited from the information they received, they took pains not to pass it on to their competitors. In numerous letters to his partners and various other business associates containing important information, Frank Bond admonished the recipients to keep the information to themselves.

New Mexico's sheep and wool merchants seem to have gotten along well generally, although competition was endemic. The harsh conditions of the frontier gave rise to a considerable degree of cooperation among businessmen. Each major wool buyer seems to have had an agreed-upon geographical area in which to operate exclusively. Frank Bond believed that invading another merchant's territory would hurt his business as much as the other merchant's when that man reciprocated. He asserted decisively, "We leave the other fellow's territory absolutely alone knowing that if he so desired he would probably do us just as much damage as we could him." Nevertheless, conflicts sometimes arose. Around 1903 Harry W. Kelly of Gross, Kelly & Co. encroached on Bond's turf, offering higher wool prices than Bond. Kelly, whose operation was smaller than Bond's, was able to offer higher prices to New Mexico growers at the time because he was selling directly to East Coast woolen manufacturers and receiving higher prices than Bond did from Brown & Adams. The matter had apparently blown over by 1907 when Kelly was once again selling his wool through a Boston broker. Competition had many manifestations. When Charles Ilfeld inquired about renting Bond's unused Cabra store building around 1904, Bond refused, believing that Ilfeld was intent on developing a branch to compete with his Cuervo store.[34]

Debt collections were a continuing headache. Since most of the general merchandise sales at the Bond branches were made on credit, the company usually valued accounts receivable on the company books at less than 100 percent. In the late 1890s, the Bond brothers valued the loans they extended and the accounts receivable on their books at seventy-five cents on the dollar, thus assuming that 25 percent of the debt owed them would never be repaid. However, by 1912 they raised the figure to ninety cents on the dollar. These discounts, which were determined by a careful annual analysis of the company books, appear to have been overly conservative, if consistent with the Bonds' business practices. In fact, Bond & Wiest had to write off only 4 percent of its loans in 1912. Nevertheless, at various times, Frank Bond engaged attorneys, collection agencies, and investigators to collect debts. On one particularly dramatic occasion, a Bond employee seized an entire herd of cattle for the purpose of settling a long-standing debt just as the animals were being driven through Espanola. The herd belonged to a particularly recalcitrant pair of debtors described as two "irascible spinsters."[35]

When loans were not promptly repaid, it was usually because the borrower was going through hard times, not because he was attempting to avoid his financial responsibility. The harsh realities of territorial life forced, to an extent, a generally cooperative social and business environment. Frank Bond described his experiences with his Hispanic suppliers and customers after many years in business: "They [the Spanish-American people] were extremely honest about paying their bills, and to this day in case of a death in the family, a son will pay his father's debt, or a father the son's. They look on this as a personal obligation." He added a note of caution, however, with his assertion that very little money was lost dealing with his customers "if you do not give them too much credit."[36]

The economic history of the West is a history of panics and bank failures. The inherent volatility of the western sheep business was exacerbated by bank failures when they occurred. Frank Bond recounted his experiences during the Panic of 1907—the so-called Roosevelt Panic—when numerous banks were failing and several checks he had received from feeders, advances on sheep deliveries, were refused by his Santa

152   FRANK BOND'S SHEEP EMPIRE

Fe bank. Unbeknownst to the feeders, their banks had failed and their checks were worthless. Bond, in turn, was unable to pay for the lambs scheduled for delivery at Servilleta, which were to be shipped out to the feeders. He described the situation that ensued: "I recall going up to Servilleta to receive lambs from a bunch of our old customers. I told them about the panic and the position we were in, that we could borrow the money to pay for the lambs, but if they did not need all the money we would appreciate it if they would wait until the lambs were marketed next spring. One of the biggest men spoke up at once and said he did not need a cent, and I could keep all his money, and there was not one but what left part of his money with us. . . . I never forgot how those Spanish-Americans stood by me in our time of need. . . . I will say for our old time Spanish-American people that they are the most loyal people I have ever met, and if you get their confidence, they are your friends always."[37]

The Bond enterprises had an important influence on the economies of large parts, if not the entirety, of New Mexico as well as parts of southern Colorado and Nebraska. They dominated the wool business wherever they set down. In later years the Bond branches in Roswell and Albuquerque would handle the bulk of the wool produced in New Mexico.[38] The Bond businesses flourished well into the twentieth century, but the surviving family liquidated their holdings around 1954, nine years after Frank Bond's death.[39]

The Bond empire exemplifies the capitalization, and subsequent control, of the sheep industry at the mercantile level. The capitalization of New Mexico's sheep ranches brought about major changes in how they would operate and what would be required to establish and maintain a successful ranch. It was another process that acted to shift industry dominance from Hispanics to Anglos. The life of Montegue Montague Stevens illustrates the growing role of capitalization for the sheep ranches by the late nineteenth century.

5

MONTAGUE STEVENS, GREAT PROMISE AND HARSH REALITY

Western Socorro County stockman Montague Stevens left a collection of letters, spanning over three decades, to his friend and business partner, army officer Leonard Wood, in which he discussed in extraordinary detail New Mexico sheep ranching—its promise and the risks, hardships, and challenges—at the turn of the twentieth century. Stevens employed his own and his wife's considerable inherited wealth together with Wood's investment to build a large and notably innovative ranching operation.[1]

STEVENS'S BACKGROUND

Montague Stevens was born in London in 1859 to an extraordinarily wealthy family. His father, a general in the British army, had spent many years stationed in India, where he amassed his wealth. Stevens's mother had inherited a fortune of her own. He attended Cambridge

https://doi.org/10.5876/9781646425471.c005

University, where he received two degrees, one in mining engineering and one in law. General Stevens had intended for his son to join his brother's law practice in London. However, during college Montague went on a hunting trip to Wyoming and fell in love with the American West. Upon his twenty-first birthday, he inherited about $100,000 ($2.4 million in 2020 dollars) from his mother's dowry and immigrated to America, leaving behind forever the predictable, comfortable, circumscribed existence of a London barrister. He also left behind an even larger fortune, as his father, angered by Montague's decision to forsake a law career, disinherited him.[2]

By 1882, with the cattle boom in full swing, Stevens was raising cattle in the high valleys of the Mogollon Mountains and purchasing ranches from earlier settlers in the general area of today's town of Reserve, New Mexico. Stevens was one of a cohort of cattlemen who came to the area over a very short period and transformed it into cattle country. Up until this time, the area had been sheep country, the growers Hispanics who had never purchased or homesteaded the lands they were using. Within a few years Stevens was running some 8,000 head of cattle. His situation was not altogether unique. He was one of a number of English cattlemen who came to New Mexico in this period. He learned the cattle business from the ground up, riding with his cowboys, and became best friends with his foreman and hunting buddy, Texan Dan Gatlin, with whom he shared many adventures that he later wrote about. Stevens met General Nelson Miles and his junior officer, Leonard Wood, in 1885 during the Apache wars, when several detachments of soldiers under Miles's command were stationed on his range. Wood was a trained physician, a graduate of Harvard Medical School, and later attended graduate school at Georgia Tech. He played a prominent role in the Spanish-American War and rose to the rank of general in the US Army.[3]

Stevens was well on his way to becoming a western cattle baron when double disaster struck. First, he shot off his left arm in a hunting accident and almost died. Then the horrendous winter of 1888–1889 killed 90 percent of his cattle. This disaster nearly ruined Stevens financially and probably would have been the end of his ranching career if Gatlin, who had saved up some money, had not rescued him by buying up his remaining cattle and otherwise helping him rebuild his operation.[4]

Broke and despondent, Stevens ended his engagement with his beloved English-Irish fiancé, thinking she would not want him under the circumstances, and spent the next several years working to recover his losses. Due to a confluence of low cattle prices, overstocked ranges, and large mortgages in addition to the killer winter, many of the other cattlemen in the area simply went bust during this period. For her part, Stevens's former fiancé married a wealthy, abusive Englishman who conveniently soon died, but not before giving her tuberculosis. Helen Gordon Dill, left in poor health, and Stevens eventually reunited and were married in Leonard Wood's New York City home in 1896. She gave up a considerable inheritance from her first husband's estate when she remarried but still had about $120,000 of her own ($3 million in 2020 dollars).[5]

Shortly after his marriage, Stevens switched from cattle to sheep and entered a financial partnership with Wood, assuming the on-site, managerial responsibilities himself. He succinctly summed up his reasons a few years later: "experience has proved that cattle raising in these parts is a failure at the best." As for sheep, he continued, "they have always paid to run, no matter how low wool or mutton might have been." In this time period, Englishmen are known to have raised sheep on a large scale in other parts of New Mexico also.[6]

LAND ACQUISITION

Stevens undertook sheep ranching in a very systematic manner. His first order of business was to acquire grazing land. Land was readily available in western Socorro County at this time because so many cattle ranches had recently failed and their extensive tracts were being foreclosed by mortgage companies or being sold off cheaply by the defunct outfits. The mortgagees were mostly nonresidents who knew nothing about the country and were anxious to divest themselves of their ranches, now unproductive but still liable for taxes.[7]

Stevens identified a property he wanted, the S.U. Ranch, and got himself appointed co-receiver for the bankrupt operation. Two London-based companies held mortgages on the ranch that had gone into default. They added up to about $80,000, largely tied up in livestock. In his new capacity Stevens worked closely with the mortgage companies and their high-powered attorneys in Denver. He hoped to purchase the property, including the livestock, from the mortgage companies.[8]

Stevens's most immediate problem, however, was in dealing with a Judge Hamilton, a corrupt federal judge presiding over the bankruptcy. The judge had a scheme for milking money out of the property and, to that end, had appointed a co-receiver he could control, a man named Smith, who, according to Stevens, could barely read. Smith was later murdered, and Hamilton then appointed a Mr. Balmey as his replacement.[9] The judge attempted to bypass Stevens by means of a fraudulent sale—on paper only—of the cattle below market price to a friend, a Mr. Bruton. To gain possession of the cattle, the judge and his friends did not plan to actually put up any money, which they apparently did not have. The plan was for Bruton to immediately turn around and sell the cattle at the market price to a legitimate buyer for cash at about $1–$2 per head above the fraudulent purchase price. Judge Hamilton and his circle of friends stood to clear in the range of $8,000–$16,000, the difference in price between the fake sale and the legitimate sale of the 8,000 head. The mortgage companies would be paid the smaller amount, the fraudulent sale price, for their cattle and thus be swindled out of the money the judge and his friends got. This was not in the best interest of Stevens and Wood because a smaller amount of the mortgages would be paid off by the sale, which they would have to make up if they were to purchase the property at a later date.

To counter this possibility, Stevens requested that Wood put up $10,000 and, at the same time, wrote his sister in England to send him money. Wood immediately sent Stevens a check. This would enable him and Wood to put up real money and outbid Bruton in the upcoming court-ordered sale of the cattle at public auction. When the court proceeding actually occurred, Stevens simply presented Wood's check for $10,000 as a down payment for the cattle. This apparently bluffed out the Hamilton-Bruton ring, which had no cash to put up. No cattle were actually sold at that time though.[10] Instead, the attorneys for the mortgage companies pressured Judge Hamilton to empower Stevens to sell the cattle privately on behalf of their clients. Stevens believed he could sell off the dry cattle immediately for about $30,000–$40,000.

It might seem that this would be the end of the affair, but it was not. Hamilton attempted then to somehow resuscitate his scheme and remove Stevens as co-receiver on the basis of some sort of trumped-up charges, leaving his man Balmey as sole receiver. The situation was even more unsettled than this would indicate. Balmey was also postmaster of Socorro, a political appointment, and had apparently intercepted some important letters from the Denver attorneys addressed to Stevens, which concerned filing charges against Hamilton with federal authorities and initiating a federal investigation of the judge. In a later letter Stevens asked Wood to report Hamilton privately to US Attorney General McKenna, hoping for a federal investigation. No action was taken, as it was later determined that sufficient evidence to remove Hamilton from the bench was lacking. Apparently, several New Mexicans who had had unpleasant dealings with him did not want to openly oppose the judge and testify against him since he wielded considerable local influence. This was particularly true of lawyers with cases slated to come up before him. The proceedings dragged on for well over a year. But Stevens eventually gained control of the property, stocked it, and later purchased it. Having large amounts of ready cash and influential friends in Washington helped.[11]

STOCKING THE RANGE

Stevens's next step was to stock his range with sheep. He anticipated correctly that McKinley would be elected president in 1896, the wool tariff would be reinstated, and wool and sheep prices, depressed at the time, would go "up at a bound." He was understandably anxious to buy quickly while prices were still comparatively low. He considered buying a flock of heavy-fleeced California ewes but was uncertain whether they could tolerate the harsh New Mexico range conditions. So instead he shifted his attention to a flock of Arizona Merinos, which sheared a heavy seven- to eight-pound fleece. The Arizona sheep dealers were anxious to sell at a relatively low price.[12]

In the meantime, Stevens's sister sent him $3,100 ($98,000 in 2020 dollars).[13] But his hands were temporarily tied, as the English mortgage companies, concerned that the cattle sales might not cover their initial investments, would have to approve Stevens's proposed sheep purchases. At this point, one of the Denver attorneys traveled to London to negotiate with his clients and to clarify their conditions for the sale of the cattle and Stevens's purchase of sheep to be grazed on the property. As it turned out, Stevens sold half the cattle to a Kansas bank president and purchased the other half himself, deferring his sheep purchase until the fall. The cattle he sold were to be delivered in several shipments over a period of a year and a half, and the mortgage companies were determined to put off the sale of the land until the cattle were completely gone.

As the S.U. Ranch was not to be sold for some time, Stevens managed to lease the property from the mortgage companies and stock it with his own sheep. As rent, he agreed to pay the annual property taxes, about $250 per year. With Stevens's funds now tied up in cattle, it was agreed that Wood would put up $5,000 ($150,000 in 2020 dollars) toward the purchase of 5,000 head of sheep, the minimum number for a profitable operation in Stevens's assessment. To manage the sheep, he estimated further that it would be necessary to hire "one good white man" at $30 per month. In the meantime he delivered the first S.U. cattle shipment of 2,000 head to the Magdalena rail terminal in late July or early August. He then bought the Arizona herd, 3,750 ewes at $1.60 per head, and 100 graded rams at $5.00 per head. Wood put up $5,000, Stevens $1,500, for the purchase.[14]

Stevens then hired a Mr. Hayes at $30 per month as majordomo and two "Mexican" herders for the two herds he thus constituted. On the

150-mile drive from Arizona to the ranch, Hayes died, and Stevens had to hire another majordomo quickly. In this period Helen's father visited the ranch and gave her $5,000, apparently to invest in sheep. Later, in November of 1896, Stevens bought another flock of 1,080 sheep in Albuquerque, apparently upgraded *churros*—improved Mexican sheep—that produced five-pound fleeces.[15]

By the late summer, sheep and wool prices had started their climb in anticipation of McKinley's election. The following spring Wood sent out another check to Stevens, this time for $3,000. In late March Stevens made another large purchase of 3,300 mature ewes, 400 yearling ewes, and 1,200 wethers, for which he made a down payment of $4,500, the balance to be paid in July when the wethers and wool were sold. He described these as seven-pound sheep, apparently also upgraded *churros*. This third sheep purchase turned out to be a major headache. The dealer attempted to substitute inferior ewes for the ones he had agreed to sell, and Stevens had to go to a great deal of trouble to get the man to live up to the original agreement. Then the delivery of the stock was late. When the matter was finally settled, the partners were holding about 8,000 ewes.[16]

LAMBING, SHEARING, AND SALES

In anticipation of the 1897 spring lambing, his first, Stevens read everything on the subject he could get his hands on and started building a dipping facility. About 5,000 lambs were born during the lambing. The survival rate after two months was an above-average 85 percent, losses having been sustained due to dipping, blowflies after ear-marking, coyotes, and the like. With lambing completed, shearing yielded 42,000 pounds of wool. After investigating the possibility of selling the wool through a Boston dealer, the partners marketed it in New York City through Wood's brother, Jacob H. Wood. Like other large-scale New Mexico growers, Stevens dealt directly with East Coast wool brokers, bypassing local merchants like Charles Ilfeld and Frank Bond.[17]

By this time operating expenses were beginning to add up. The cost of the lambing had been $500; the cost of the shearing had been over $200; and the cost of shipping the wool to the rail junction in Magdalena was $250. Stevens hoped to realize $4,000 from the sale of the wool, of which $2,000 was needed for the final payment on his last sheep purchase.[18] Presumably he got this money. Jacob Wood sold the partners' wool shipment in late 1897 or early 1898. It was a successful first year.

EXPENSES GROW

A new opportunity for land acquisition arose in the spring of 1897. Apparently, prior to declaring bankruptcy, the S.U. Cattle Company had made an $800 down payment on two other ranches on the Rio Tularosa below the S.U. range. An amount of $1,200 was coming due to finalize the purchase, but the mortgage companies were balking at this further expenditure. Stevens suggested to Wood that they buy these two ranches. By owning the ranches, Stevens believed that the partners would "virtually own the heart of the S.U. range and practically prohibit anybody else from bidding on the S.U. ranches when they went up for sale, and I think it will therefore enable us to make our own terms with the mortgagees for the purchase of them." The bulk of all these "ranches" was, in fact, dry rangeland in the public domain, which would be controlled by the tracts owned and patented along the Tulerosa, the essential water source for the livestock. By late spring Stevens had indeed negotiated the purchase of the two ranches, one for $450 and the other for $650, freeing the mortgage companies from sinking additional funds into the properties.[19]

In the fall of 1897 before the first year's wool was sold, Stevens had additional, apparently unforeseen expenses that were adding up. And the monthly operating expenses for his four flocks were now running $300. He asked Jacob Wood to advance him $3,000 on the upcoming sale of the wool. And he asked Leonard Wood to invest another $1,000 in the ranch, which Wood did. The good news was that sheep prices were rising rapidly, essentially doubling since the first purchases. Also, Stevens made $1,200 on the sale of his calves from the S.U. cattle he owned, which he invested immediately in sheep. In December, after dipping, Stevens moved his sheep to a leased winter range at a 5,000-foot elevation, about seventy miles northeast of his headquarters ranch.[20]

At this point, Stevens encountered another challenge, the acquisition of heavy-fleece rams. He had already acquired about ninety Merino rams, which he had used the previous season and planned to use again on the "common ewes." Now, to boost his wool production further, Stevens sought Shropshire rams, copious wool producers. He needed forty or fifty, but to get the best price, $15 per head delivered in Magdalena, it was necessary to buy an entire railroad car of one hundred and fifty. Such rams purchased individually or in small lots were considerably more expensive. To this end, Stevens made an agreement with his neighbor, Solomon Luna, to share a full carload; Stevens ended up with forty-seven, and Luna took the rest, about one hundred.[21]

Stevens then turned his attention back to land. In particular, he was in the market for a winter range of lower elevation than the 6,000- to 8,000-foot elevation of the S.U. range, which had good grass but underwent a killer winter about every ten years. During the horrible 1888–1889 winter, Luna lost 19,000 out of his 40,000 sheep, and this loss occurred on his range of 8,000-foot elevation. The snow had gotten so deep that he was unable to drive his flocks to lower elevations where the weather was milder; they died in place. Hoping to avoid such a disaster, Stevens searched extensively and found two ranches for sale, "the Blain ranches on the Baca places," that satisfied his requirements. He used Wood's most recent $1,000 investment to make the down payments, $400 and $450, on the $2,500 properties.[22]

EARLY SUCCESS

By the fall of 1897, Stevens had 10,923 sheep, divided into four flocks. He also had eighty "fine Merino bucks," the rams constituting a fifth flock. A large herd such as this was desirable, as Stevens reported: "Of course the more sheep we have the cheaper and better we can run them." This

162 MONTAGUE STEVENS, GREAT PROMISE AND HARSH REALITY

herd was, nevertheless, much smaller than the massive *churro* herds held by some Hispanic sheepmen in years past. Anglo sheepmen tended generally to have smaller herds of more highly graded sheep. Montague Stevens was no exception. His was, in fact, a fairly typical holding for New Mexico's Anglo sheep ranchers, whose herds numbered from 5,000 to 30,000 head.[23]

Stevens's sheep had done well over the winter of 1897–1898 on the leased lower-elevation land. By the early spring he was still in the market for winter pastureland. He found some properties in foreclosure on or near Alamosa Creek near the town of Luna. The Spur Ranch, as they were called, was available at a cost of $4,500, payable in three installments. Stevens believed the tracts could hold 50,000–100,000 head. Cattle investors had paid $60,000 for them a few years earlier. One tract consisted of about thirty patented claims of 160 acres, which controlled the grazing over a twenty-square-mile area, with houses on site that would be useful for "our Mexican herders' families." The property also included 200 acres of "fine farming land" with water for irrigation. Stevens then requested a loan of $1,000 from Wood for the purchase at 6 percent interest, to be paid off when his brother, Jacob, sold their wool in July (1898). Sometime later, after he acquired the property, Stevens made the Spur Ranch his headquarters. It was 125 miles from Magdalena, four days' travel in winter; mail delivery took from four to seven days. In the meantime he had sold the partners' remaining interest in the yet unsold S.U. cattle to Dan Gatlin.[24]

In the spring of 1898 Stevens achieved a lamb crop of nearly 100 percent, his second lambing season, for a projected income of $4,000–$5,000 in future sales. He proudly boasted that his lamb crop was the highest percentage that the area had ever seen, a typical lamb crop in the area being 70 percent. And he had been able to do this with only one third of the usual labor costs by employing an innovative system of movable wire fences, which he had developed himself. To his satisfaction, Stevens discovered that his graded sheep were easier to herd and the lambs sold for 15–25 percent more than the common lambs. He proudly reported to Wood that their sheep were so large that only 155 could be loaded onto a stock car whereas 175 was the usual load. They were, he claimed, "the finest that ever left Magdalena."[25] As for wool, the Arizona Merinos, which the locals had predicted would do poorly on the open range, had in fact each produced $1 worth of wool, on average, while the common "Mexican" sheep were producing about forty cents' worth. He did concede that the common sheep would do better on the open range under "unfavorable conditions," which, of course, had been an important factor in the adoption of the *churro* three centuries earlier.

The partners now had about $40,000 ($1.1 million in 2020 dollars) invested in the business, which Stevens believed was worth $50,000–$60,000 at the time. Wood, having served as a brigade commander during the recently concluded Spanish American War—his command included Theodore Roosevelt's Rough Riders—was now a brigadier general and military governor of Cuba. His mind was on matters other than sheep.[26]

After two years in the business, a rather overconfident Stevens concluded that "the sheep men out in this section know very little really about sheep." The men he was referring to were mostly Hispanic "small holders" following traditional practices that had never been challenged. He further wrote that the "old sheep men out here" hold "many misconceptions." They ran their sheep near their ranches at the same elevation year around, while he was finding that the key to success with graded sheep was to run them at low elevations in winter, where there was little snow, and at high elevations in the summer, where it was cool and shady. Unquestionably, up-to-date sheep-growing methods were slow to penetrate rural New Mexico. However, Stevens may have been overly critical of his neighbors.

DISASTER STRIKES

If Stevens's reports to Wood sounded too optimistic, too self-assured, they were. With the flocks in good order and his wife experiencing health problems, he accompanied her back to England in December of

1898 so she could see her family's eminent doctor. While they were away, the worst winter in years swept through the West, causing large sheep losses from Wyoming south into Texas, New Mexico, and Arizona. In January 1899 Stevens's weather-weakened sheep contracted scab from some diseased traveling herds. His foreman quickly exhausted the inadequate supply of sheep-dip chemicals that was stored at the ranch for combating the affliction, and the supplier in Magdalena ran out. It was a month before a new shipment arrived. At that point the foreman dipped the flocks during very cold winter weather, causing substantial losses. Upon his return in April 1899, Stevens, frustrated and angered by the losses and the man's poor judgment, fired his foreman.

But Stevens's problems had just begun. Matters worsened when winter was followed by "the driest spring on record." Stevens reported that there was no rain or snow between February and July. There were forest fires, but no new grass came up. And with green grass lacking, the spring lamb losses were devastating, the weakened ewes producing only 2,500 lambs. Many of the ewes, having no milk, abandoned their lambs. Out of 16,000 head at the start of winter, 6,000 had perished by mid-summer. Next, with his herds severely depleted, his fall wool clip was only 40,000 pounds whereas he had anticipated 120,000 pounds. Overall, the ranches suffered a $30,000 loss in sheep and wool. In his own words, Stevens, contrite and stressed, described himself as having worried until he didn't have "the power to worry any more." Resuming personal oversight, he stayed out at his sheep camps almost every night following his return from England. In a separate short letter to Wood in the summer of 1899, he wrote, "I have been nearly worked to death." Despite the disaster, one of his sheep sheared sixteen and a half pounds of wool, as noted above. He proudly sent a wool sample to Wood.[27]

LESSONS LEARNED

In the aftermath of the disaster Stevens admitted to himself and to Wood that they had not been adequately prepared for the inordinately harsh conditions they had just experienced. He had seen the considerable potential for profits in sheep but now recognized, for the first time, the barriers. He stated, "I think there is no business [here] or anywhere else for that matter that pays better than the sheep business provided you are fixed to run it right on every point, otherwise you are always liable to serious loss." He admitted further that he had possessed "not the least conception at the time" of the risks in raising sheep when he entered the business. He noted that the profits in sheep were "so great because the risks are so great, unless you are properly fixed." It was the failure to prepare for every contingency that kept "everyone" from entering and prospering in the business. A rancher might not need every one of his safeguards as various contingencies arose, but he would never know which one might be essential. All of them had to be in place if his operation was to be secure. And money was needed for this. "But to be fixed for every contingency that might arise it naturally needs lots of capital which of course we haven't had," Stevens wrote.[28]

In Stevens's assessment one needed about $40,000 to start a secure, stable sheep operation, although others had done it successfully with "much less." In those cases, an element of luck was involved, "sheer good luck" in Stevens's words. He concluded that those who enjoyed "a series of good seasons combined with good prices for wool and mutton" in the first years after they entered the business were most likely to succeed. The "principal cause" of the many failures in sheep growing in the past was "lack of sufficient capital."[29]

REBUILDING

After his losses, Stevens began to address his newly appreciated need for various safeguards. In particular, he considered growing his own winter feed, which would have prevented the worst of the terrible losses he had just undergone. He saw this as possibly the most important of the safeguards he had heretofore lacked. Specifically, he was thinking of employing the agricultural sections of the Spur Ranch to grow alfalfa and other feed grasses. But the start-up cost to plant 300 acres was $1,000–$1,500, money he didn't have. At this point, Stevens found himself in even more serious financial straits than in the past. He and his wife had now invested over $25,000 ($800,000 in 2020 dollars) in their sheep ranches. To rebuild his flocks and, at the same time, create the expensive new safeguards he envisioned, he needed cash but had no immediate personal resources. Forced to take his least favored option, he borrowed money from an Albuquerque bank, some amount over $12,000. A source of continuing anxiety, it would be many years before he was able to pay off this loan. And Wood invested another $1,000 in December 1899, bringing his total investment up to $10,000.[30]

Stevens now also understood that he needed a better dipping facility, one that included a building that could house overnight the 800–1,000 sheep dipped each day, allowing them to dry off safely, since exposure to subfreezing weather and cold winds could kill the wet sheep during the night. With such a facility, sheep could be dipped any time of year, whenever a flock became infected, scab having become a persistent problem due to the increasingly crowded range. The location of the dipping facility was important. It had to be accessible to driven flocks in the harshest winters, never isolated by deep snowdrifts. Stevens built his facility at his recently acquired ranch at Horse Springs, midway between his summer and winter range. It cost $2,500, which he took out of the $8,000 his wife invested in the ranch using funds she had brought back from England in April of 1899—$14,000, apparently from her father. Having built the most advanced dipping facility in the area, Stevens earned about $500 the first year it was in operation, dipping the flocks of other local sheepmen, including 36,000 head for Luna. In later years Catron sheep were also dipped at the facility. This was in stark contrast with the self-destructive practice of some local sheepmen, who refused to dip their flocks, or did so improperly, despite the recent territorial law demanding it on a yearly basis. Stevens expressed considerable frustration over this widespread negligence, as did many other responsible sheepmen whose flocks were subject to infection.[31]

Some of Stevens's other capital expenditures paid off quickly. To reduce the cost of shipping wool the ninety miles from his shearing camp to Magdalena, which had been running about $1,000 per year, he purchased four large freight wagons and ten mules to pull them for $625. Then he was able to hire teamsters to drive his wool to the rail depot for less than $375, so his outfit paid for itself within a year.[32]

Summarizing their highest-priority capital requirements in a seventeen-page letter to Wood, after their first three years in business, Stevens listed good summer range, which included the S.U. Ranch; good winter range, which included the Garland and Spur Ranches; good sheep-dipping facilities, the Horse Springs facility; and hay growing, which required a good irrigation system and had been heretofore neglected.[33] He understood now that sheep needed to be maintained in good condition at all times so they could tolerate any weather that came along, be it a sudden winter cold snap or summer heat and drought. Feeding and dipping were expensive but necessary to this end.

Stevens had been learning fast. He "studied every book, pamphlet, etc. that I could possibly get hold of and besides making a very close study of conditions as they exist here I have tried numberless little experiments in order to get at the right way of doing things and I am pleased to say I have succeeded in many ways in doing things not only infinitely cheaper but infinitely better than they were ever done before, at any rate in this section." Stevens was looking ahead to a prosperous future.

UPS AND DOWNS

By the fall of 1900 things were looking up again. As Stevens described the stock, "Our herd is without exception, the finest herd in these parts both in the quality and size of the sheep." With the ranches apparently flourishing, Stevens hoped to accept an invitation from Wood to visit him in Havana, but that would have to wait until the spring of 1901 after the "backbone of the winter" was broken. He never took the trip. Stevens, perhaps spooked by his previous experience, had not become sufficiently comfortable about taking another extended leave from his ranches. With his growing awareness of the large element of chance in western sheep growing, the gamble inherent in the business, he shifted direction and began devoting ever more of his energy to developing his agricultural resources. During the previous spring he had dammed up a stream running through his land and created a reservoir capable of irrigating 500 acres. He had dug several miles of irrigation ditches and built flumes to carry water across the streambed. He also put up several miles of fence to keep loose range stock off his hayfields. It was slow, expensive work, which he undertook despite now being in debt. In his own words, it was "one constant expense and outlay for several years." The farm implements Stevens needed were expensive, and he had just purchased a sawmill for $300, a move to combat the high price of the lumber for his farm structures. Lacking the resources to seed all his agricultural lands at the time, Stevens rented out sixty acres on shares and planted only eighteen acres of alfalfa on his own. But by the end of 1902, he had planted 250 acres of rye to be used in the following spring and summer.[34]

At the same time, Stevens found himself faced with a new, very different type of complication. The federal government established a national forest reserve that took up about half of his "range and ranches" (i.e., land that he never owned but considered part of his ranches). The end result, after months of uncertainty, was that he now had to obtain a grazing permit to run a restricted number of sheep on the reserve, his former "ranch land," and then only between April 1 and September 1, as described below.[35] The agricultural lands that he did own lay within the boundary of the newly established reserve, making it almost impossible to get his sheep from outside grazing areas to his farms for winter feeding since that would require that the floaks be driven illegally across reserve land.

From this point on, Stevens seemed to come up against an endless sequence of setbacks and few successes. Some of his misfortunes were beyond his control. In 1901 drought in the corn belt decimated the corn crop and, along with it, the market for feeder lambs throughout the midwestern feeding region. In 1902 drought in Colorado drove the price of alfalfa so high that it made no sense to feed it to lambs, eliminating the market for feeder lambs in Colorado. As a result, there was little or no market for New Mexico feeder lambs two years in a row.[36]

In the late spring of 1903 another killer blizzard struck suddenly in Montana. In a period of forty-eight hours, hundreds of thousands of lambs and mature sheep were lost. As Stevens described it, "many sheepmen lost the results of years of toil." In New Mexico it was just another bad winter, fortunately, but the damage, such as it was, left an even deeper and more lasting impression on Stevens than his many past difficulties. After eight years raising sheep, he understood clearly the inherent insecurity of sheep ranching in all its ramifications. More generally, he now possessed a comprehensive understanding of the entire business, the risks and the benefits. Once so optimistic, he became quite pessimistic about the industry. As he wrote to Wood, "You may go rapidly ahead for a time (like we did at the start) and then like a thunderbolt in a clear sky, you may get a back-set from which it takes years of patient toil to recover . . . the constant worry and anxiety for fear of sudden calamity, even when things seem to be running most smoothly, is beyond belief except to those who have tried it."[37]

INVESTMENT SUMMARY

By 1902 Montague Stevens and his wife had invested about $30,000 in their sheep ranches, while Wood had put up $10,000 ($1.1 million total in 2020 dollars). He held a total of 6,000 acres of patented lands, which he estimated were worth anywhere from two to ten times their purchase costs. Stevens believed the total operation—the land, the capital equipment and facilities—was now worth far more than the start-up costs. But he seems never to have had any excess cash on hand to pay the dividends Wood had hoped for. He reinvested all the ranch profits year after year, increasingly redirecting his efforts to developing his agricultural resources. With 500 acres under irrigation, his goal was to develop a feeding operation for raising high-quality lambs. By this time, however, Stevens was plagued by an entirely new matter, a growing labor problem that he had not anticipated.[38]

LABOR PROBLEMS

By the late 1890s Stevens was finding it increasingly difficult to hire good herders. He lamented in his correspondence that the Hispanic sheep herders that he was now able to hire were, with few exceptions, lazy, mean, and irresponsible. Continuing, he noted that in his first years after entering the sheep business, he had been able to readily hire competent, responsible herders; "Now they will only work for a month at a time. When they get a few dollars, they quit and go off to some plaza to drink and gamble," he complained to Wood. This development was indeed real and did not occur without reason. New Mexico sheepmen were facing serious competition for labor for the first time. And that was almost certainly an important factor in how they viewed their employees. The western railroads and mines and the Colorado sugar beet farms had started employing Hispanic labor on a large scale, as discussed below. The effects seemed to have hit western Socorro County rather suddenly. As Stevens described the situation, these options drew the most ambitious, energetic, and responsible men away from New Mexican villages on a seasonal basis, leaving behind the marginal workers. The men who had been the ablest, most reliable herders secured employment wherever railroads were being built or sugar beets grown. The sheepmen simply could not match the wages being offered elsewhere.[39]

Open-range sheep growing had always depended on cheap or even free labor, and the supply was disappearing. Many Hispanic men who stayed behind in the villages owned modestly successful small farms and ranches and were not overly anxious to hire themselves out, although many certainly had the skills to do so. The large-scale sheepmen had to make do, to a considerable extent, with the available unambitious men who stayed behind or drifted back home after they found out how hard the new jobs were. During the first years of the partners' operation, starting in 1895, there had been a ready supply of good Hispanic herders, although otherwise "totally illiterate and ignorant." They were, Stevens observed, happy to be employed once again herding sheep after being economically marginalized for so many years by the cattle takeover in the area. But after the turn of the century, the available labor force had deteriorated.[40]

Not only herders but supervisory employees became hard to find. In years past, Stevens noted, he had employed a few "really good" Hispanic foremen, apparently men who demanded and received what he considered a fair amount of work from the herders under their supervision. But now, he reported to Wood, if he had a good foreman, the workers would gang up and "all work against him" and demand his discharge. Likewise, if there was a particularly responsible, hardworking man on the crew, the others would demand he be discharged. Stevens responded in frustration by firing whole crews at a time and, consequently, found himself in a constant state of hiring. He found it necessary to hire men who lived along the Rio Grande, 150 miles distant, where there was still an adequate labor supply. He would then transport them by wagon to his ranches.[41]

The most difficult time to hire workers was during the April–May lambing period when extra men were needed at all the sheep ranches. And, once hired, laborers could be difficult to retain on the job. Steven asserted, "If the least little thing happens to offend one of them the whole lot may go on strike and leave you in the middle of lambing, and there were no others to be hired." To compound his difficulties, incompetent, careless shearers were killing 200–300 of his sheep each season while presenting similar labor problems. It was becoming necessary to contract and pay laborers in advance, and then they did not always show up as agreed. The courts provided no recourse. By his own account, Stevens, always shorthanded at lambing, at times put in twenty-four-hour days for two or three days running during the month to six-week period.[42]

During dipping one year Stevens precipitated a general strike when he fired a recalcitrant employee. The same scenario repeated itself some weeks later during shearing. Stevens then hired a replacement crew of "good Indian shearers," who competently sheared about half his stock and then abruptly departed. He found out subsequently that the local Hispanic shearers had threatened to kill the Indians if they did not quit. Under the circumstances Stevens had to hire another Hispanic crew, substandard in his assessment, to finish the job. The contrast to the peon-patron relationship, widespread only a half century earlier, where the peon was totally beholden to his master, could not have been more dramatic. Stevens was bitter because he believed the kindness and fair treatment that he felt he had extended to his workers over the years was to no avail. He claimed that "man after man has quit me because he said 'I worked him to death.'" He felt betrayed.[43]

Solomon Luna managed his men more successfully than Stevens. As Stevens reported to Wood, Luna's men were beholden to him because many had worked for his father and their families lived on his land at Los Lunas. And like peones many were also in debt to him for an aggregate of several thousand dollars. Longevity in the business clearly had its advantages. In describing Luna's modus operandi, Stevens noted that although Luna generally "treated his men very well," he controlled them through fear. He occasionally would beat a recalcitrant herder. If a man seriously failed him, Luna would have the man thrown in jail on some pretext and left there for a few months awaiting trial. Then the man would, upon Luna's order, be turned loose with an admonishment to mend his ways and made an example for the other herders. According to Stevens, Luna's unopposed political power and influence in the region was such that he could get things like this done on the quiet.[44]

WITHDRAWAL FROM SHEEP RANCHING

Stevens's problems had become overwhelming by late 1903. His herders were losing 20–25 percent of his lambs before fall, severely cutting into his profits. At some point his Hispanic foreman, a good man whom he had employed for years, quit, fearing for his life, according to Stevens, the herders under him having become so unruly. To make matters worse, another drought had badly hurt all the stock growers in the region. The Rio Grande south of Albuquerque had run dry. The spring lamb crop had been poor. Also, sheep and wool prices had gone into a steady decline. Stevens began pulling out of the sheep business in the summer of 1903. His letters suggest that it was primarily his labor problems that drove him to this action.[45]

Over the next few years, with 400 acres under cultivation and employing "a few pretty good men" to work on his farms, Stevens withdrew entirely from sheep ranching, selling his remaining stock and leasing his ranges, water rights, and dipping facility to Luna for about $2,500 a year, an arrangement that continued for several years. He used the proceeds to pay off the bank loan he had taken out upon his return from England in 1899. He put a handful of his best men to work in his lumber mill, now a commercial operation. His ranches now added up to about 6,300 acres, 600 acres of which was farmland, about forty patented quarter sections in all, scattered over an area seventy miles by twenty-five miles. He estimated the land was now worth at least $30,000, his sawmill and farm machinery $4,000, and his remaining livestock (not sheep) $3,000, while taxes on the land ran about $500 annually. In total he believed the entire operation, after nine years, was worth something over $50,000 ($1.5 million in 2020 dollars), at most only a bit more than the original investment but a considerable amount of money at the time.[46]

Stevens had not made the financial killing he hoped for, despite his innovations and near superhuman efforts. However, in 1909 he sold some of his land, including the two Baca Ranches, at a considerable profit.[47] He claimed in his correspondence that many other large-scale sheepmen in the area were also quitting the business on account of labor problems. In any case, the practice of open-range sheep growing was coming to an end.

The small-scale Hispanic sheep enterprises in the area persisted. Modestly profitable family operations with few if any wage employees, the smaller operations avoided the worst of the growing labor problems. Children were brought up in the business. During lambing, entire extended families, both men and women, would work together and get the job done.

In the years following Stevens concentrated on farming and continued growing alfalfa. He eventually settled primarily into his lumber business but retained some of his ranches. His friends and fellow ranchers in the area, Dan Gatlin and Ray Morley, Agnes Morley Cleaveland's brother, also experienced considerable ups and downs. Stevens's later letters often allude to the many ranchers in the area who had gone bust. For his part, Stevens made a decent living in sheep ranching but worked tremendously hard for it. He remained for decades a prominent figure in western New Mexico until he and Helen relocated to Albuquerque, with the support of their son, to live out their final years in relative comfort.[48]

During this period the western sheep industry began to undergo another sea change, this time in financing. As capital requirements increased, large-scale ranchers could no longer depend on family and friends to finance their operations. Following the lead of cattle ranchers with their greater capital requirements, sheep growers began to seek the services of extraterritorial financial institutions. This development is illustrated dramatically by Thomas Catron's conversion of his defunct American Valley Company from cattle to sheep. This is the subject of the following chapter.

6

THOMAS CATRON AND FINANCING A WESTERN SHEEP RANCH

Thomas B. Catron is one of the most prominent and controversial figures in New Mexico history. Attorney, land speculator, and businessman, he was also a dominant figure in the territorial Republican Party for over four decades.[1] Often drawing on his political connections, he was involved in some way with essentially every major industry in the territory during the late nineteenth and early twentieth centuries. Among his many identities, he was a rancher of sorts.

Unlike Frank Bond and Montague Stevens, Catron relied heavily on commercial lending institutions for his sheep-growing endeavors, although he also drew from his considerable personal financial assets. As such, the large body of correspondence that Catron left sheds light on that new development, which would become an important part of how ranches and farms in New Mexico would operate, right up to the present. The correspondence illustrates, furthermore, the role of its iconic grazing industry in bringing New Mexico into the US financial community.

https://doi.org/10.5876/9781646425471.c006

The letters, like the Stevens correspondence, also present a vivid picture of the considerable risks, barriers, and frustrations in establishing a large western ranching operation, a considerable undertaking by the twentieth century. The territory remained the land of opportunity only for those with the good credit required to borrow the large sums of money needed for such endeavors. At the same time, sheep growing was moving away from traditional, open-range grazing and toward the capital-intensive management of highly controlled, well-cared-for, bred-up stock, as practiced today. Competition from other parts of the West together with growing national markets for mutton, lamb, and wool demanded as much.[2]

CATRON'S BACKGROUND

Thomas Benton Catron was born in Lexington, Missouri, near Kansas City and the head of the Santa Fe Trail in 1840. His was a comparatively well-connected and prosperous frontier farm family. His father had a cousin who was a US Supreme Court justice and a distant relative was the mother of a US president. Catron attended the University of Missouri, graduating in 1860, a time when few Americans went beyond grammar school. With the coming of the Civil War, he joined the Confederate Army as an artillery officer and saw considerable action throughout the war. After the war he returned briefly to Lexington, where he studied law privately. Then, barred from practicing law in Missouri on account of his Confederate service and at the encouragement of college classmate Stephen B. Elkins, he departed for New Mexico and the promising opportunities of the West, arriving in Santa Fe in 1866.[3]

Catron soon established a law practice and became active in territorial politics. He proved himself to be an exceedingly capable attorney and was soon flourishing. His cash-poor clients often paid for his services with their only marketable asset: land. Not surprisingly, he quickly became a major landowner himself and wealthy by territorial standards. He is known to have held an interest in an extraordinary number of Spanish-Mexican land grants.[4]

FIGURE 6.1. United States Senator and Attorney Thomas B. Catron, Santa Fe, New Mexico, 1915? Courtesy of the Palace of the Governors Photo Archives (NMHM/DCA), 050364

178 THOMAS CATRON AND FINANCING A WESTERN SHEEP RANCH

In the ensuing years Catron held many important public offices. Subsequent to his ranching endeavors, following statehood he served as one of New Mexico's first US senators. He was controversial almost from the outset of his career and was involved in several notable scandals, in particular, a double murder near his ranch, discussed below. In his turn-of-the-century correspondence Catron emerges as a tough, fearless, contentious risk-taker of unshakable determination.

INVOLVEMENT IN RANCHING

In parallel with his political activities, Catron engaged in a succession of generally successful business ventures, often in partnership with Elkins. Catron's interests included a few modest cattle operations starting in the late1860s. Then, with the western cattle bubble growing out of control, he entered ranching in a much larger way. The American Valley Company would occupy him for over two decades. In 1885 he bought into the preexisting but troubled operation in western Socorro County, now Catron County, on Largo Creek, south of today's town of Quemado and north of Montague Stevens's and Solomon Luna's ranches. The ranch founder, John P. Casey, had named the area American Valley. He established the American Valley Company ranch, starting in 1881, by employing the common practice of filing fraudulent homestead and preemption claims of water-controlling tracts, expedited in this case by territorial surveyor general and ranch partner Henry M. Atkinson. Catron provided legal services for the outfit almost from the time of its inception. The company connections extended almost immediately to Washington, DC, where Elkins used his influence to help secure patents for the land claims.[5]

The ranch was an open-range operation, employing expanses of dry public lands controlled by water sources on a few patented or claimed tracts. In 1886 Catron and Atkinson, no longer in public office, joined forces with William B. Slaughter, a brutal Texas cattleman who had driven a large herd into the area, to take over the operation from Casey, who had fallen into financial difficulties. Catron, together with Atkinson, Slaughter, and a minor forth partner, Henry L. Warren, incorporated the operation in 1886, issuing 3,978 shares of stock having $100 par value. Slaughter received initially around 75 percent of the stock, recognizing his ownership of the bulk of the livestock and some land. Catron and Atkinson each contributed some land and livestock and split the remaining shares. No cash actually changed hands among the three principals. The stock was heavily "watered" in that the capitalization on paper, $397,800, was about three times the true value of the outfit, which consisted of 9,000–10,000 head of cattle, claimed ownership of about 7,000 acres of land, and other miscellaneous assets. This amounts to about $11 million in 2020 dollars.[6]

The operation was launched under a cloud of scandal. Earlier, in May 1883, when two men with land claims in the area that Slaughter wanted for his ranch refused to sell out to him, they were murdered by Slaughter employees. Two of the alleged perpetrators were apprehended and tried for murder but released after two successive trials ended in hung juries. Local lore had it that a single dissenting juror had been bribed to break a unanimous guilty verdict.[7]

Following the 1886 incorporation, Slaughter assumed on-site management of the operation, which did poorly from the outset. A period of overly harsh weather conditions—summer drought followed by excessively cold winters—took its toll on the herd. At one point Slaughter removed parts of the herd to better rangeland in other territories and states, only to sustain substantial losses elsewhere. In the end only about 4,000 head were ever actually sold. As the cattle were liquidated, the income was issued in the form of stockholder dividends, eventually summing up to $11 per share. Devastating weather had hit early on after the incorporation, so the operation never gained the solid financial footing that might have carried it through hard times. By about 1893 Slaughter had returned to Texas and the ranch had been abandoned, except for "Mexicans and bands of tramp sheep," leaving behind an estimated 200 head of feral cattle to roam the immense range. Significantly, the company did not declare bankruptcy, as many ranches in the area did. The demands upon Catron increased when

Atkinson died within the first year, leaving behind a pregnant wife and his financial affairs "in an almost hopeless condition." Ada Atkinson returned to her family home in Lincoln, Nebraska, and, short of funds, resumed her former profession, school teaching.[8]

ADA ATKINSON AND RANCH REBIRTH

Against all odds Catron resuscitated the ranch starting in 1899, exhibiting an unrelenting determination to make the operation succeed. Now approaching age sixty, old by the standards of the day, he had shown this trait in the realm of politics, where he fought an unending succession of political battles to retain his considerable influence. Catron's return to ranching was an outgrowth of his drawn-out relationship with Ada Atkinson. He had promised to buy out her late husband's interest in the ranch and then, forever short of cash, bickered and stonewalled her and her lawyers for years before the contending parties reached a settlement fifteen years after Henry Atkinson's death.[9]

Catron's dealings with Ada Atkinson provide a glimpse into his business methods. In 1896, while he was serving as New Mexico's delegate to the US House of Representatives, he wrote to Ada's attorney, Neill B. Field, claiming that a block of American Valley Company stock—150 shares, then in the attorney's possession—belonged entirely to him, although it appeared to have been jointly owned by him and Atkinson. "That stock belongs to me," Catron claimed on the basis of verbal agreements with Ada's late husband. He continued his letter with a convoluted explanation of why the stock documentation made no mention of his sole ownership, and he demanded that Field turn the stock certificates over to him immediately along with the dividends that had previously been paid to the Atkinson estate. Field, in response, advised Catron that no payments would be made to him "in advance of a complete adjustment of all your claims." Catron continued to press his claim. There is, of course, no way to determine whether the claim was legitimate; Henry Atkinson had died ten years earlier. Many of the written contracts Catron signed seem to have been overlaid with verbal agreements, a cause of never-ending contention and delays in his wide-ranging business activities. A final settlement of the Atkinson estate with Catron was not reached for another five years![10]

When a settlement finally appeared imminent, Ada sent Charles H. Elmendorf, a Nebraska accountant with some sort of cattle interests, as her representative to close out her affairs in New Mexico with Catron. The estate involved land in both New Mexico and Nebraska. Considerable conflict arose over the amount due from Catron as a result of the curious fact that the lands Catron and Atkinson had contributed to the ranch's operation were never legally conveyed to American Valley Company ownership. The situation was further complicated by the fact that the Atkinson lands were mortgaged. After much legal wrangling, the parties finally agreed that having paid off the mortgage loan, Catron owed the estate $7,426.12 (about $240,000 in 2020 dollars).[11]

It might seem that this should have been the end of the affair, but it was not. With the monitory amount determined, Catron gave the Atkinson estate four notes adding up to $8,000, but no cash, which Ada claimed she needed badly to remove a lien on her recently constructed house. And when the notes came due, Catron failed to make the scheduled payments. After more wrangling and with an overdue payment of $500 in September 1901, Ada's attorney threatened legal recourse. A few months later Elmendorf transferred by check $6,121 in American Valley Company funds to the Atkinson estate, finally satisfying the debt. The Atkinson affair was typical of Catron's often troubling financial transactions. Contentions over verbal agreements, delays, worthless checks, and inadequate documentation would persist throughout the American Valley Company's remaining existence.[12]

CONVERSION TO SHEEP

Catron was apparently impressed by Elmendorf and hired him in May 1899 to take charge of the ranch and bring the American Valley

182   THOMAS CATRON AND FINANCING A WESTERN SHEEP RANCH

Company back to life. What followed was one of the longest, and strangest, relationships of Catron's career. The massive collection of surviving correspondence between the two men, predominantly from Catron's end, reveals a great deal about contemporary business practices associated with New Mexico ranching and the way Catron pursued them.

The men quickly determined to raise sheep rather than cattle. Veteran sheepman John D. Patterson assured Elmendorf that the sheep industry had never been more promising.[13] Many cattle ranchers had been reluctant to make this transition. New Mexico's cattlemen were largely Anglos from Texas who viewed sheep growing as a dishonorable occupation, the purview of "Mexicans," whom they held in low esteem and with whom they did not wish to be associated in any way. Many other cattle ranchers made the switch, swallowing their pride in the aftermath of the devastating winter of 1886–1887, the "Big Freeze" and "The Great Die-Up," that decimated innumerable herds throughout the Rocky Mountain region.

The general strategy for restarting the company was to buy up all the outstanding stock, purchase more land with water access, a continuation of the Atkinson buyout, and, of course, stock the ranch with sheep. This was to be financed through the sale of bonds to eastern and midwestern investors.

Catron had long been involved in land speculation and was intent on securing a water monopoly in the American Valley, which he had up to that time only partially accomplished. He charged Elmendorf with the task of purchasing the remaining tracts of watered land needed to realize that goal. For his part, Catron was largely preoccupied, as he often would be, with political activities and his law practice. Elmendorf, working more or less independently, was generally able to acquire the desired tracts for $1.50–$2.50 per acre. He also obtained a large quantity of scrip for about $4.00 per acre. These land acquisitions were part of a larger shift in the New Mexico grazing industry. With the arrival of ever more legitimate homesteaders in New Mexico during this period, the public range was being taken up on a much larger scale than in the past and would eventually be unavailable for free grazing. To protect themselves, better-positioned ranchers were redoubling their acquisitions of patented land, a considerable expense.[14]

The American Valley land acquisitions seem to have gone smoothly. By October 1899 Elmendorf reported that the company now held a total of 12,000 acres of patented land (nineteen square miles), which would control two or three million acres of dry public rangeland. In a "History of the Company," a document probably prepared by Elmendorf and written a few years after the relaunch, it was claimed that this land could carry 100,000 sheep.[15]

Shortly thereafter, in early 1900, Catron took on Elmendorf as a partner. Catron became president of the reconstituted American Valley Company with 60 percent ownership and liability, while Elmendorf was supposed to take on the remaining 40 percent as secretary and treasurer. In a late-1901 letter Catron claimed he had invested $40,000 of his own funds in the company prior to the relaunch, which the company then owed him with interest.

Although the recapitalization was to be financed by the sale of bonds, substantial start-up funds were needed immediately. With Elmendorf short of cash, Catron assumed full responsibility for the immediate expenses associated with reestablishing the operation, with the understanding that Elmendorf would soon settle up and purchase his 40 percent interest.[16]

Without delay, Catron took out a short-term loan—four months' duration—for $10,000 from First National Bank of Santa Fe to cover the additional land acquisitions, stock buybacks, and other miscellaneous expenses.[17] Once bond sales got underway, the loan would be readily paid off, or so the thinking went. Unfortunately, bond sales faltered. When the FNBSF loan came due, Catron was without funds to pay it off and was required to take out a series of expensive extensions and additional larger loans over the next ten years.

The Washington connection persisted. Although Elkins was not formally an investor in the American Valley Company at this time, Catron kept him apprised of the company's activities while hounding him for

184 THOMAS CATRON AND FINANCING A WESTERN SHEEP RANCH

an appointment to the office of US Attorney. In years past Elkins had used his influence in Washington in securing patents for the claimed land tracts. And within a few years he had a substantial stake in the relaunched company.[18]

With the partnership agreement consummated, the partners continued the whirlwind of activities that had begun with the new land purchases. To clear the way for the bond sales, Catron initiated an aggressive campaign to consolidate ownership of the company. In 1900 he bought out his surviving partner, Slaughter, who was now in financial difficulty, taking over his assets and assuming his debts for only $3,000. At the same time Catron charged Elmendorf with the task of buying back the rest of the outstanding American Valley Company stock. The buy-back was somewhat complicated. As was the case with the Slaughter shares, blocks of stock had been used over the years as collateral for loans and were in the possession of several lenders. Tracking down these shareholders, Elmendorf, like Catron earlier, bought their shares for pennies on the dollar plus any unpaid dividends in recognition of the fact that the American Valley cattle company had essentially failed. The two partners thus became sole owners of the company.[19]

Aside from land acquisitions and stock buybacks, Elmendorf was soon directly involved in bringing the ranch back into operation. He set up a sawmill and made additional improvements, including fencing and irrigation development, employing laborers at $1 per day and two range riders assigned to trespasser removal from the property. He began stocking the range with a few local sheep purchases, and by about June 1900 he was in communication with Clay, Robinson concerning market conditions for lambs and wethers. He was investigating the purchase of bucks in Ohio; he was also involved with sheep purchases and loans in San Angelo, Texas. And he still had matters to attend to in Omaha, where settlement of the Atkinson estate dragged on.[20]

Catron also charged Elmendorf with placing the company bonds, an activity he would pursue for the next several years and a matter of particular concern to Catron. A considerable infusion of money was essential to get the reorganized company up and running on the large scale that the partners envisioned. Elmendorf assured Catron he could sell the bonds readily to this end. The initial plan was to sell 200 bonds, valued at $1,000 each. And Elmendorf claimed, from the outset, that he had buyers in Buffalo, New York, who would buy $175,000 in bonds at 6 percent. This would take some time. Bringing the ranch back into operation was more immediately pressing, and acquiring sheep took on a high priority.

The partners made their first large sheep purchase in San Angelo, Texas, borrowing the $9,000 (about $240,000 in 2020 dollars) needed for the purchase from local lending institutions. By August 1900 the 8,000 head were on the trail to New Mexico under the supervision of a majordomo hired by Elmendorf. A rather large number, 460 head, were lost on the drive, a harbinger of the ranch's future. Over the next few years Elmendorf made additional large purchases in San Angelo and Kansas City. By the spring of 1901 there were apparently about 10,000 head on the range. But there were also large losses in this period. A year later, subsequent to a large purchase in Kansas City, it appears there may have been about the same number of sheep at the ranch.[21]

BOSQUE DEL APACHE

In December 1900, just as the ranch was getting stocked and while the Atkinson settlement was still underway, Catron undertook the largest of the land transactions, purchasing the 60,117-acre (ninety-four square miles) Bosque del Apache Grant from Elkins and London investor John B. Collinson, who had acquired the tract in 1871. Initially Collinson had put up all the money for the purchase in exchange for a two-thirds interest, Elkins to be indebted to Collinson for his one-third interest and to oversee the property. Elkins, in turn, hired Catron as managing agent for the grant in exchange for half of Elkins's share of the profits when the property was sold. The grant turned out to be a money sink; the lease income never covered expenses. As a consequence, Catron paid out of his own pocket the Socorro County property taxes for many years, which had added up to $19,000 by 1900. When

Collinson refused to reimburse him for that expenditure, he responded by suing Collinson in the Socorro County court jurisdiction. In a resolution of the conflict, Catron agreed to purchase the grant from Collinson for $35,000 (about $950,000 in 2020 dollars).[22]

The down payment was to be $5,000, and the balance was to be paid off within three months; Elmendorf was to sell the tract for a profit and so obtain the funds needed for the pledged payments or else to sell company bonds to that end.[23] Collinson drove a hard bargain; the purchase agreement stipulated that if any payment was not made on schedule, all previous payments toward the purchase were forfeited and the agreement nullified. Thus, if Catron failed to fulfill the agreement, his $19,000 in tax payments would be a total loss in addition to any payments he had made toward the purchase. Elmendorf had assured him that sufficient American Valley Company funds would be available to honor the contract.

When Elmendorf failed to sell the property or any American Valley bonds, Catron, lacking sufficient liquid assets, faced a considerable loss. Very unhappy with Elmendorf's inaction, Catron admonishing him severely: "I assure you that I am becoming to be very much disgusted at your delay in getting out the deed of trust and the bonds. There can be no reason for your tardiness except you are preparing to cramp me out of existence." A few days later, continuing with other grievances, he wrote: "You have not taken any steps whatever about those lost sheep. They will certainly have to be accounted for by some one." Several weeks later, no payments having been made and the situation growing desperate, he wrote, "I do not like your way of doing business. It is not such a way as inspires confidence. I cannot see what you have done with the money of the American Valley Company which you have had. Is it your purpose to simply compromise me, embarrass me and tie me up, and have everybody plauge [sic] me for the payment of debts."[24]

Catron, having failed to make the payments, was able to get an extension on the payment schedule—twice—in the following months. In exchange, Collinson imposed upon him a $2,500 penalty to keep the deal alive. In the spring of 1901, well past the contracted payoff date, an increasingly impatient Collinson, with Elkins's intervention, forced upon Catron a revised payment schedule. Now $5,000 was to be paid immediately, and thereafter $2,500 was to be paid on the fifteenth of each month. Catron cabled two payments ($5,000 and $10,000) in quick succession to Collinson but immediately thereafter fell behind in his payments. And Elmendorf was no help. On one occasion Catron transferred $3,000 to Elmendorf, then residing in New York City, apparently for one of the monthly payments to be forwarded to Collinson. But Elmendorf ignored his partner's wishes and allocated the money elsewhere, much to Catron's consternation.[25]

Through the spring of 1901 Catron and Elmendorf continued to harbor high hopes that the needed money would be provided by the sale of American Valley bonds. Elmendorf claimed that he had a major bond deal underway that would provide $60,000 in three months' time and so informed Collinson. In the fall, claiming the deal was about to close, he assured Catron that there would be "smooth sailing" thereafter.[26]

By fall of 1901 no bond sales had been consummated, the company had produced little if any income, and Catron still owed Collinson $20,061.87. He had failed to make the payments due in London as scheduled and was getting quite worried, and a protracted flurry of angry telegrams and letters between Catron, Elmendorf, and Collinson ensued. Fuming over the short payments, Collinson threatened, through his New York agent, to sell the grant to another party. In the genteel language of the English investor, he wrote Elmendorf, "It would be most impolitic for me to delay taking steps to complete other arrangements which have been proposed to me." Catron somehow managed to wire $13,000 to Elmendorf on October 16, but Elmendorf only forwarded $10,000 to Collinson on October 25 instead of the entire amount, as Catron expected. It is unclear what Elmendorf did with the remaining $3,000, a considerable amount of money to be unaccounted for.[27]

Catron was now severely short of funds. A few days earlier, he had mortgaged his large personal library for $5,300 for ten days and used the funds for an overdue payment on a sheep loan from the Waco State Bank, San Angelo, Texas, which was threatening legal action.[28]

To make matters even more uncomfortable for Catron, he had agreed by this time to the settlement of the Atkinson estate but had yet to make any cash payments to Ada Atkinson, which were coming due. In an unrelated business matter, he was late on a loan payment of $5,600 to the Alliance Company of Dundee, Scotland, in early 1901.[29] And he was soon to become enmeshed in the settlement of the estate of his former business associate, Wilson Waddingham, and owed the estate a considerable amount of money.

Catron was not taken completely by surprise by the unfortunate turn of events. Noting that Elmendorf had consummated no bond sales and becoming increasingly desperate, he demanded that Elmendorf get a loan to cover the payments due Collinson. This proved to be difficult for Elmendorf, and he was not immediately successful. In the fall, at what seems to have been the last minute, Catron complaining bitterly that his credit was tapped out, Elmendorf miraculously did get a $20,000 loan from the Continental Trust Company of New York, to which he gave forty American Valley bonds (face value, $1,000 each) as collateral. He used the money to pay off Collinson ($10,253.25) and the obligation to Ada Atkinson in November 1901.[30]

Catron had met his match with Collinson, who held his feet to the fire and forced him to honor the purchase contract in a comparatively timely fashion despite the delays. Including his previous tax payments, Catron now had over $56,000 (about $1.5 million in 2020 dollars) invested in the grant.

The reasoning behind the Bosque del Apache Grant purchase is somewhat unclear. It seems to have been initiated as a strategy for Catron to recover his tax expenditures for the tract. But it quickly evolved into an expansion of the American Valley Company rangeland, a very large expansion. The conclusion of the Bosque del Apache deal gave the company an impressive 72,000 acres (112 square miles) of patented, or claimed, rangeland, but that was a meaningless statistic. The purchase of the grant was a poor allocation of resources on more than one level. The timing was poor. Money that went toward the purchase might well have been used for operating funds that were needed to get the ranch up and running on the scale necessary to justify the already-large start-up costs. The location was wrong. As the tract was situated on the Rio Grande, over 100 miles from the heart of the ranch in American Valley, it never functioned as a productive part of the operation. Catron had acquired more land for the ranch than he would ever bring into production.

RANCH CONDITIONS DETERIORATE

If the finances were precarious, conditions at the ranch went downhill from the outset. In early 1901, as the Bosque del Apache purchase was getting underway, ranch manager John V. Morrison, desperate for operating funds, presented a disturbing picture to Elmendorf, then soliciting bond investments in Buffalo. The herders had not been paid and were threatening to turn the sheep loose if not paid soon. He was understandably finding it hard to hire and retain herders; local people were losing confidence in the company. As early as July 1900 a disgruntled employee walked away from his job, stealing the doors and windows of the house that the company provided for him. Unpaid bills were piling up. The sawmill had not been put into operation. The log wagons Elmendorf bought were worthless beyond repair. Morrison was away from the ranch and wrote that he would not return until he could pay his men. Shortly thereafter, when Elmendorf made a quick visit to Santa Fe to attend to some business matters, he returned to New York without visiting the ranch, despite the growing crisis. Compounding difficulties at the ranch, seed money needed to plant crops was delayed in delivery. And the plow that had been ordered turned out upon delivery to be worthless and had to be returned.[31]

Three months later the men had finally been paid, but conditions had not improved. The ranch account was overdrawn. The sawmill had still not begun to operate. And Morrison needed funds to hire the extra men needed for the spring lambing. Instead, men were quitting.

Supplies were needed, and creditors had received no word from Elmendorf, who was responsible for the mounting bills. One local merchant began taking sheep pelts as security for unpaid bills. Neither cash nor credit was available to make the next payroll.[32]

By the end of May 1901, less than a year after the first large livestock acquisitions, sheep were dying; there were reportedly only 2,362 ewes and 110 bucks on the range, half the herd unaccounted for. And they were being tended by five men whereas one or two would have been sufficient. The mill, recently put into operation, had stopped; with no supplies, the loggers were quitting. Expenses were greatly exceeding the sheep and wool income. Elmendorf had run up $10,000 in expenses, which he failed to account for in his correspondence with Catron.[33]

By November 1901 the men, unpaid and quitting, were becoming unruly. Morrison, pursuing a strategy that Stevens also employed, was finding it necessary to go all the way to the Rio Grande to hire new men. Trespassers were bringing their sheep onto the range, and company checks were being refused. A forlorn Morrison wrote to Elmendorf, "I don't believe you realize just what the situation has been out here."[34] Elmendorf's bland letters to Morrison provided no meaningful guidance. He never showed a great deal of interest or concern for ranch operations.

In late 1901 the company sold 14,118 pounds of wool, not a particularly large quantity, through E. J. McLean & Co., Santa Fe. But the merchant, aware of the company debts, forwarded the proceeds directly to a creditor, bypassing Elmendorf entirely. A few months later McLean was holding another 3,000 pounds of American Valley wool unsold because it had shrunk so extraordinarily much during the scouring process that the sale of the wool in Boston would not even cover the cash advance the broker had paid Elmendorf.[35]

Always sidestepping the very real problems facing the ranch, Elmendorf complained to Catron about the squatters coming onto their range, a matter he knew obsessed the senior partner. He noted that the "Mexican" people on the ranchland had used it for so long that they regarded the American Valley Company as trespassers and had tried to keep the company off the land since 1883. This was probably true. The American Valley Company was underutilizing the range in any case. Grasping for approval, Elmendorf boasted to Catron that he had gotten rid of "a good many undesirable people" over the previous two years, an irrelevancy.[36]

Elmendorf not only neglected to act on the appalling conditions at the ranch but also failed, in large part, to transmit the bad news, or much of any news, to Catron. On several occasions Catron had requested "full details about the business at the ranch" and received little satisfaction. Sensing that all was not well and angry about Elmendorf's lack of communication, Catron fired off a sequence of berating letters to his junior partner: "I cannot understand why you do not write me as per our understanding. I have only received four letters from you in over two months. You agreed to write every two days and tell me everything. The letters you have written have been mere subterfuges they give no information and each of them had to be drawn out by a telegram. This course of procedure must stop. I will not tolerate it longer." Catron nevertheless continued the arrangement for another eight years as their relationship deteriorated.[37]

In early 1902, in one of his rare references to sheep, Elmendorf reported that there were 2,812 head on the American Valley range, confirming earlier reports that the ranch was severely understocked. Some 2,500–3,000 sheep were reported as "lost." By this time, Catron noted, Elmendorf had paid out more money to local merchant Becker, Blackwell & Co. for ranch supplies than the value of all the sheep.[38]

FINANCIAL PROBLEMS

Elmendorf may have had little good news for Catron. Remarkably, the picture he painted for a New York City bond broker during the summer of 1902 was in startling contrast to the reports he had been getting from the ranch. He boasted that the "fine sheep," 2,326 head, had produced 22,130 pounds of wool, an impressive 9.5 pounds per head, and the "other sheep," 3,415 head, had produced 20,635 pounds for over 6 pounds per head, which was still impressive. The wool had been sold at Magdalena for 12.5 cents per pound, as high a price as had been paid anywhere in New Mexico that year. There had been an 80 percent lamb crop the previous spring, and he had just purchased an additional 5,039 sheep in Kansas City.[39] This may well have been a high point in the ranch operations. However, no bond sales resulted from the glowing report.

In early 1903 the company borrowed another $10,000 from FNBSF to buy sheep, 4,372 head as it turned out. The purchase, Elmendorf's responsibility, had left $1,256 unspent that should have been returned to the bank. But instead Elmendorf retained it, much to Catron's dismay. The purchases brought the sheep count up to 14,000. They were valued at $3 per head ($42,000). But during 1902 Elmendorf spent $30,000 that he was again unable to account for. And his range manager still had to take out an $800 advance on the wool that year with Gross, Kelly in order to pay the men for lambing and for other expenses. Solomon Luna, Catron's sometime political ally, with herds in the same general area, got word to Catron that his ranch was being very poorly run, his on-site managers were being grossly overpaid, and no ranch so operated could ever be profitable. Certain that he was getting the runaround from Elmendorf, a frustrated Catron implored him, "Tell the truth at least to me."[40]

In the summer of 1904 the company sold $3,000 worth of wool and some wethers, another paltry sale that would have hardly made a dent in the debts piling up. The head count was down to fewer than 8,000 after four years, insufficient to sustain the operation. And according to Catron's assessment in the following spring, 1905, Elmendorf had lost since the relaunch a staggering 15,000–16,000 head, for which he had no explanation! The herd had not multiplied and was apparently being replenished by continuing costly purchases.[41]

BOND SALES FALTER

The relaunch of the American Valley Company involved taking on a massive amount of new debt. To that end, the company had worked

FIGURE 6.2. Politician and sheep rancher Solomon Luna, New Mexico, 1896? Courtesy of the Palace of the Governors Photo Archives (NMHM/DCA), 050606

through the necessary financial arrangements to sell bonds, giving in 1901 the Continental Trust Company of Denver a trust deed to secure payment on 200 bonds valued at $1,000 each.[42]

Selling the bonds turned out to be more difficult than either partner had imagined. Elmendorf had begun efforts to place the bonds as early as mid-1900. He ran into problems immediately. There is a hint in Catron's correspondence that Elmendorf did not know enough about the ranch to be an effective bond salesman. He had no experience in far western stock growing and, residing in New York and Kansas City, never spent much time at the ranch. The more or less sophisticated eastern and midwestern investors he approached were consistently unmoved. It is clear also that Elmendorf was withholding information. When a potential lender was scheduled to perform an on-site inspection of the ranch, Elmendorf advised his range manager to keep quiet about the business, particularly some recent sheep losses. Elmendorf would be present and do all the talking.[43]

But Elmendorf was up against some truly substantial barriers. In late 1900 a New York City bond broker informed him that the company bonds would be unsalable in New York due to uncertainties in the future of the wool tariff. If Congress were to reduce the tariff, the value of the American Valley Company, with its critically important wool sales, would be depreciated greatly at once. The broker noted also that Elmendorf's estimate of livestock losses seemed too low, which may have been true. He also asked Elmendorf why the company, already so large and successful, as he had been given to understand, wished to incur new debt obligations. Furthermore, upon investigating the company records, the broker identified an "impairment" of $200,000 and wanted an explanation.[44]

A year later, the climate for marketing bonds had not improved. In response to Elmendorf's inquiries, New York City bond broker Edgar Mels wrote, "I have received reports from my Philadelphia and Boston correspondents regarding your bonds and regret to say that they declare it practically impossible to do anything with them. The price asked, the short tenure and low interest are all against the sale." By mid-1902 Elmendorf had attempted to sell bonds in Kansas City, St. Louis, Buffalo, New York City, and Philadelphia, all to no avail.[45]

Catron sent Elmendorf, now residing in Kansas City, a flurry of castigating letters. "I want you to get that sale through," he wrote concerning a deal that had, according to Elmendorf's reports, been in the works for a year and a half. In a typical response to Catron's complaints, Elmendorf replied, "When I write to you that I am doing what I can, and making progress, it is not satisfactory. I know what you want is results, and I am striving each day as earnestly as I can to bring about results to be satisfactory to you."[46]

Later, in 1902 or early 1903, Elmendorf finally managed to sell $25,000–$30,000 worth of bonds, but Catron asserted that he had put up for the company $40,000–$50,000 of his own money in the same time frame. When Elmendorf sold some bonds in New York in 1904, it seems that he did not forward the proceeds to Catron, who was then scrambling to borrow more money and could have used the bond proceeds. Two years later, in early 1906, Elmendorf claimed he had sold $40,000 worth of bonds and had four other investors lined up for similar amounts. Nothing came of this.[47]

Catron continued to be deeply dissatisfied with Elmendorf's infrequent and misleading reports. Venting his frustrations, he wrote, "You have agreed with me that you would write me in detail of everything, yet I get nothing but generalities from you." Catron had concluded by mid-1902 that Elmendorf was unreliable. He had written to his wife, Julia, then living in Malaga, Spain, with two of their sons, "I have about lost confidence in him [Elmendorf]."[48]

BANK LOANS

By late 1903 there had been no improvements in the company's financial health. With bond sales faltering, Catron shifted tactics in favor of bank loans to recapitalize the operation. And he charged Elmendorf with negotiating the new loans, now critical to the company's survival. He had previously taken out a confusing array of loans more or less connected with the ranch. Now, although the company had more recently negotiated loans from FNBSF to restart the operation, this source was exhausted. Catron had tapped out his credit at that institution ($27,000–$30,000), having borrowed over 10 percent of the bank's assets. Now he took on increasingly large loans from several additional sources, scrounging up money wherever it could be found while claiming that the company owned "about one-half million dollars worth of property" in New Mexico. He took out loans from the First National Bank of Albuquerque ($20,000), Bank of Commerce, Albuquerque ($6,000–$8,000), Fidelity Trust Company of Kansas City ($30,000–$35,000), Bank of Commerce, Kansas City ($6,000), New Haven County National Bank ($4,000), with which he was involved in settling the Waddingham estate, Gross, Kelly & Co. ($5,000), Silver City National Bank ($10,000), private investor Gustave Becker ($8,500), and a Mrs. Perea ($4,000), although not all at the same time. By his own assessment, the company's debt mounted to $70,000–$80,000 (about $2.4 million in 2020 dollars) by late 1904 while the ranch was "bringing in thin money." Catron now claimed he had $150,000 of his own money tied up in the company.[49]

Interestingly, several of the bank loans were collateralized using the unsold American Valley bonds—the bonds were thus converted into cash after all, although, typically, at half their face value. The Fidelity Trust loan was secured by a mortgage on the Antonio Ortiz Grant, in which Catron had a large interest. He had also mortgaged his interest in the Mora Grant to that institution, taking out a $20,000 mortgage at 7 percent interest in 1901. Around 1906 he mortgaged a portion of the Anton Chico Grant that he claimed as his own.[50]

This strategy did not go well. With little income, one loan after another went into default. Catron seems to have been skilled at putting off creditors, but he was successful only up to a point. His considerable political clout in New Mexico counted for little in the greater financial world. The correspondence, dreary, repetitious, and angry, reveals a trail of loan defaults, extensions and renegotiations, penalties, legal fees, threats of legal action and actual suits, threats of livestock attachment, and, unsurprisingly, deteriorating relationships with lenders.[51]

By early 1903 two notes to FNBSF were past due. A year later Catron received a summons from Socorro County for unpaid taxes, long a bugaboo for owners of unproductive New Mexico property. This was an unexpected embarrassment. At that time Catron was able to obtain a high-interest $50,000 loan from a Denver source, which he used immediately to pay off a large preexisting debt and unpaid taxes on his land holdings. With no improvement in the American Valley Company's prospects by early 1905 and payments overdue, the Bank of Commerce, Albuquerque, threatened to attach $45,000 in stock Catron held in another entity, the Valles Grandes Company. A lien was placed on all of his property in Socorro County. And at the same time, the Silver City Bank brought suit against him for nonpayment.[52]

He wrote to Elmendorf in anger, "You seem to make no effort whatever to relieve me. I am here standing the brunt of these suits." In this period Becker also threatened suit, and Catron was able to get a delay of execution only at a cost of $2,000–$3,000 in penalties. He claimed that the foreclosures destroyed his credit in New Mexico and cost him over $50,000 in extra expenses. By mid-1906 the FNBSF loans were again in arrears and the bank was threatening suit. Catron implored Elmendorf to get some money to the bank, noting that "Palen [R. J. Palen, bank president] says he cannot believe me and he won't believe you, that we are both a pair of liars." In early 1907, after endless negotiations and nonpayments, Palen sold off some Socorro County bonds that Catron had pledged as collateral for the loans. Catron seems to have pacified the banker because he had still had an active $18,000 loan from FNBSF a year and a half later, although Palen was threatening to call it in.[53]

With funds always running short, Catron asserted to Elmendorf, "I have nothing in the world except my income from my legal services to rely on and that is hardly enough to pay my family and office expenses." This was not true. Catron had, in fact, been feeding personal funds into the company since its relaunch, $87,963.59 ($2.4 million in 2020 dollars) by his own estimate in mid-1906, drawing on income from his successful investments. He periodically sold lumber cut on his Mora Grant property through Gross, Kelly and used the proceeds for

198   THOMAS CATRON AND FINANCING A WESTERN SHEEP RANCH

American Valley loan payments. For his part, Elmendorf was witnessing one bond sale after another fall apart and one bank loan after another go into default. Over the years of the partnership Elmendorf never came up with the funds to pay for his 40 percent share of the ranch while residing in New York and Kansas City hotels on company funds.[54]

DESPERATE MEASURES

Conditions at the ranch were as dismal as the finances. Over a period of seven years, by early 1907 the company had spent a total of about $50,000 purchasing sheep and had little to show for it. The herd still had not multiplied and was down to a pathetic 2,500 head. Ranch profits, essential to address the massive debt piling up, were never realized. The company was in a downward spiral from which there was no escape. In desperation, Catron borrowed $2,500 from his brother, George, in Lexington, Missouri. He requested a $2,000 loan from his brother-in-law, W. G. Walz, in El Paso, Texas. He borrowed $2,000 from Elkins and then, unable to repay it, requested an extension while claiming that Elmendorf was about to get a large loan that would provide payment. In the same period Elmendorf, himself short of funds, borrowed $2,000 for personal expenses from Elkins. Elkins granted the loan, believing Catron would back it up in case Elmendorf failed to pay it off. As it turned out, Elmendorf indeed defaulted, and Catron claimed he lacked the funds to cover the debt, worsening his often-strained relationship with Elkins. As the company's future became increasingly uncertain, Catron involved himself in a sequence of dubious money-raising schemes orchestrated by Elmendorf. Nothing came of any of them, and cost Catron, by his own assessment, several thousand dollars.[55]

LIQUIDATION

Elmendorf's failure to sell enough bonds and profitably manage the New Mexico ranch had placed the company in severe financial straits.

The sheep holdings had never grown to anywhere near the size necessary to sustain the company. For years Catron had mined his personal resources to keep the company going; but that could not continue indefinitely. Furthermore, from early 1909 on, he became increasingly involved in the New Mexico statehood movement, which occupied much of his time and energy. And his wife, in poor health for some time, died late that year. The company was, in the same period, turned over to Judge C. H. Stoll, Lexington, Kentucky, who controlled a modest stock interest. Stoll put the company into receivership. Two years later, the Bosque del Apache Grant, now mortgaged, was threatened with foreclosure. From the two-person stock distribution in 1900 there were by mid-1910 at least six principal stockholders or bondholders, as the securities had been used rather freely to collateralize loans and changed hands in the transactions. Elkins, not an original investor, now held 1,160 shares.[56]

On August 4, 1911, the inevitable happened. The company was sold at auction for $150,000 to a syndicate that included Catron himself. Elmendorf was now completely out of the picture. The "costs, expenses and preferred debt" took up $32,000 of the proceeds. The outside bondholders were projected to receive something less than sixteen cents on the dollar for their bonds. Catron had high hopes of buying back the entire property for $350,000 within the next six months, but this was not to be. He did, however, manage to retain the Bosque del Apache Grant. So ended Catron's foray into sheep ranching. He lost roughly $100,000 (about $3 million in 2020 dollars) on the ranch by his own reckoning.[57]

At the turn of the twentieth-century, New Mexico was undergoing a period of rapid but uneven change. In some respects, the territory was still the Wild West with rampant land fraud, egregious murders, a corrupt court system, and open-range grazing. In contrast, it was simultaneously being absorbed into the generally orderly, well-established American, even international, financial community. This was particularly true for the territory's grazing industry. The American Valley Company had financial connections in New Mexico, Texas, Colorado,

Nebraska, Missouri, Massachusetts, Connecticut, Washington, DC, New York, London, and perhaps elsewhere. Catron's sheep-ranching sojourn, even though the ranch ultimately failed, illustrates the growing need for commercial financing in the sheep industry and the concomitant challenges. The days were long past when a sheepman, to get on the road to success, needed only a large flock of *churros*, cheap, unsupervised *partidario* or peon labor, and access to the seemingly boundless public range. It was no longer always possible for ranchers to rely on their own resources, family, and friends to finance their operations, although it was still done. Maintaining good relations with bankers became part of the sheep business.

The failure of Catron's sheep operation is another matter; it is easy to see Catron's mistakes in hindsight. The relaunch of the American Valley Company would have been an expensive and risky financial proposition under even the wisest management and the most favorable economic conditions. Thomas Catron did not devote sufficient attention to his sheep-growing enterprise. Preoccupied with his law practice and politics, his true passions, he traveled continuously and rarely visited the ranch. He took on an inexperienced, marginally competent partner, assembled an extraordinarily large ranch, and then failed to build up his herd to the level necessary to sustain the operation. All in all, the mistakes were a recipe for the disaster that followed. When Catron's sheep business came to an end, after twelve years, he had other matters on his mind. Within a year's time, when New Mexico was granted statehood, he would be heading to Washington as one of New Mexico's first the US senators.

COMPARISONS

A comparison of the experiences and operations of the entrepreneurs described in these three chapters is instructive. There are points of both similarity and difference. All three men came to New Mexico from elsewhere as young men. They were well-educated, well-connected risk-takers from more or less affluent families. Bond and

Stevens were active, hands-on managers, attentive to every detail of their operations. Catron was not, designating the management of his ranch to others. The three men were all prolific letter writers and left behind a considerable body of business correspondence. Stevens and Catron both started out raising cattle and later switched to sheep as more promising after their cattle ranches faltered. The Bonds never dealt extensively in cattle.

The Bond brothers, acting as middlemen between slaughterhouses and wool dealers and mostly small- and intermediate-scale Hispanic growers, prospered from the start. With conservative, conscientious management, they became exceedingly successful in a fundamentally risky business. And they became quite wealthy. Stevens was a moderately successful rancher and seems to have suffered from a sequence of inordinate setbacks that occurred before his operation was well established. He eventually left the sheep business for other financial pursuits. Catron's ranch was a financial disaster almost from the start and eventually failed. Thereafter, he devoted himself to his political career.

Land was a critical issue for all three men. Stevens and Catron expended considerable effort to secure waterfront tracts that could control large expanses of dry grazing land. Bond was less dependent on large grazing tracts. He secured land for the use of his *partidarios* and for feeding operations as the need arose. The Bond land acquisitions, however, may have been speculation-driven to a considerable extent.

Beyond land acquisitions, stock acquisitions constituted an important part of the operations of both Stevens and Catron. Stevens, particularly, expended considerable time, effort, and expense to obtain desirable stock. The Bonds, of course, acquired livestock as a natural adjunct to their business.

The men differed somewhat in their hiring practices. The Bonds started out as a partnership of the two brothers. Later they brought in a family friend as a branch manager and then, apparently with considerable care, hired men outside their circle of family and friends for important positions. Eventually, after many successful years, Frank took over sole overall management of the business. Stevens worked alone employing a range of unrelated people as needed: range foremen, herders, birthers, shearers, and farmworkers. Catron, much to his detriment, formed a partnership with a man he met through a business transaction and turned over the management of his ranch and most of its business affairs to him. Both Stevens and Catron suffered from labor shortages, often having to settle for marginally skilled, irresponsible, or dishonest workers. Bond controlled his herders through their financial obligations to him but was forced to sustain some losses on his *partido* contracts.

Perhaps the most notable differences between the three men concerned their financing. Like all western producers, they faced the stiff competition stimulated by the growing opportunities in mutton, lamb, and wool production during the last decades of the nineteenth century. And it was important for them to adopt the most efficient and profitable methods of sheep growing. That necessitated considerable capital investment. In fact, all three men required and employed substantial extraterritorial sources of capital to establish and then expand their operations. Their varying approaches exemplify, to an extent, an evolution in financing toward practices that would be familiar to the ranchers and farmers of today.

The Bond brothers launched their mercantile operation in 1883, buying out a preexisting business with funding from their father in Canada. And they received an additional cash infusion from their father some years later. Otherwise, they financed the expansion of their business with retained earnings. They used short-term loans from local banks, Denver livestock dealers, and Boston wool merchants to meet running expenses. *Partido* contracts also constituted an important part of their business. They avoided large loans from commercial financial institutions.

Montague Stevens got into the cattle business about 1882 and converted to sheep in 1896 using inherited wealth brought from England, both his own, his wife's, and possibly that of other family members. He supplemented this with a substantial investment from his wealthy friend and passive business partner Leonard Wood. Stevens was a strong advocate of innovation and technological advances. He reinvested all his ranch income into expansions and capital improvements. His operation was beset almost from the beginning with considerable difficulties. He had to take out a commercial bank loan from a New Mexico institution that he was unable to pay off for several years. The continuing debt made him uncomfortable, and he was greatly relieved when he was finally able to pay it off. Carrying debt, even in a large stock business, was not an acceptable modus operandi to Stevens or to Bond.

Catron's financing was more consistent with today's practices. When he became involved with the American Valley Company in 1885, the ranch, then a cattle operation, was capitalized by issuing stock. Later, after conversion to sheep in 1899, the ranch was recapitalized with large bank loans from commercial institutions, several outside the territory, when an attempt to sell bonds faltered. Catron also provided additional cash infusions to the ranch from his considerable personal wealth. His *modus operandi* was modern in the sense that mortgages on farms and ranches are today a common feature of the business. Large, standing debts were a way of life for Catron in his extensive land dealings. His indebtedness, however, eventually got out of control and led to the loss of his ranch.

The risk factor in the sheep business was always considerable. It was lower for merchants like Bond than for ranchers, however. Bond was able to negotiate the ups and downs of the markets and the weather better than the ranchers. His business was broad enough with merchandising and a wide customer base that he had a cushion for meeting hard times. He was not so strongly linked to the seasonal labor imperatives that tormented Stevens and Catron. In contrast, the ranchers' production of sheep and wool had to be sustained steadily year after year for continued success. A poor year for whatever reason could be devastating.

As it turned out, open-range grazing, as Bond, Stevens, and Catron employed, would soon be a thing of the past. This is the subject of the following chapter.

7

THE END OF THE OPEN RANGE

In the final sentence of his seminal essay, "The Significance of the Frontier in American History," Frederick Jackson Turner states, "And now, four centuries from the discovery of America, at the end of a hundred years of life under the Constitution, the frontier has gone, and with its going has closed the first period of American History." Turner's meaning is clarified by recalling that he launched his essay with a quote from the superintendent of the US census of 1890 to the effect that a "frontier line" no longer existed and all the wide expanses of unsettled lands in America had disappeared.[1]

The disappearance of the frontier as envisaged in the superintendent's comments was an irrefutable fact. A clear and comparatively immediate manifestation of the closing of the western frontier was another important transformation of the New Mexico's livestock industry. Cattle and sheep raising on the open range, the tradition since Spanish colonial times and adopted by Anglo newcomers under

https://doi.org/10.5876/9781646425471.c007

Mexican sovereignty, became a thing of the past within a generation. Henceforth, livestock would be raised in fenced pastures on farms and ranches or on leased federal lands under controlled conditions, a modus operandi that continues down to the present. This transformation was part of a complex of interrelated national developments that gained momentum in the late nineteenth century: industrialization, capitalization, labor reorganization, technological advances, and changing demographics.[2]

LAND USAGE

Land and how it was used were the immediate factors driving the transformation. Open-range herding, depending solely on naturally growing forage and natural water frontage, required very large tracts of land for commercially viable operations. But by the late 1870s, the New Mexico livestock industry had expanded to the extent that land was taking on an element of scarcity. In the same period, largely as a result of technological advances, open-range grazing no longer constituted the most efficient use for much of the territory's land. Writing at the turn of the century, Chester Whitney Wright described the practice as "an unnecessary waste" of land.[3]

At this point, farming was beginning to make more efficient use of the land. Farming would soon surpass the New Mexico grazing industry in commercial importance, farm crops surpassing in value both cattle and sheep production in the first decade of the twentieth century. (See figure 2.3 for a comparison of sheep and wool, cattle, and farm-crop earnings in New Mexico.) The tipping point was reached in the 1890s when an array of land-related developments rendered open-range practices largely unsustainable. Competition for land between ranchers and homesteaders, small-scale nomadic herders, and national forest allocations all played a role. The degradation from overstocking of the diminishing public domain was an additional factor pushing ranchers off unclaimed rangeland. New efficiencies made possible by fencing, wells, windmills, well-equipped dipping facilities, and other technological advances drew stock growers onto privately owned tracts.

During the Spanish colonial period New Mexico's herders had grazed their sheep on the land grants and unclaimed outlying areas. As long as ownership of the grants remained uncontested, the herders' most critical tasks were to defend themselves and their hardy flocks against Indian raiders and the sometimes harsh physical environment, major but ultimately manageable detriments. Under the pressures of a growing population and the concomitant need for more grazing land, first the herders and then entire communities spread out from the Rio Grande Valley, as described above. Any claims to the lands by Indian tribes were disregarded by the Hispanic settlers and later negated by the Americans. By the time of the annexation, Hispanic sheepmen held usage claims to large grazing tracts both within and outside the established grants. The lands legally unclaimed under Mexican sovereignty became public domain under the US government.

The first large wave of Anglo stock growers, largely Texas cattlemen who came to the southeastern portion of the territory after the Civil War, usually found ample open rangeland for their herds on the public lands. Thereafter access to public lands generally followed the western custom of first-come-first-served, which, among its other shortcomings, led to overstocking and subsequent range deterioration.[4]

For a time, sheepherders, mostly Hispanic, and cowboys were usually able to keep out of each other's way. But as more Anglo stockmen arrived in the territory, the range became heavily stocked and access to grazing areas became contested. Cattlemen were pitted against sheepmen, and large-scale growers of both cattle and sheep were pitted against small-scale growers.[5] In the most extreme cases, brutal land skirmishes occurred. Although an uneasy peace usually prevailed, as evidenced by the post–Civil War growth of both cattle and sheep interests in New Mexico and throughout the Rocky Mountain–Great Plains region, this simmering, conflict would not persist indefinitely. A new factor totally upset the situation.

HOMESTEADERS AND AGRICULTURE

The arrival of homesteaders threatened both sheepmen and cattlemen and added a new dimension to the land conflict when the homesteaders started taking up expanses of land that had once been the sole domain of the stockmen, lands that the stockmen never actually owned. In New Mexico homesteading brought about a significant decrease in the aggregate acreage available for grazing. With the land laws on their side, homesteaders were a far greater threat to New Mexico cattle and sheep interests than those two factions ever were to each other.[6]

Homesteading got off to a late start in New Mexico, beginning significantly around 1880. This was due in part to the fact that the Spanish-Mexican land grants had long since taken up much of the best arable land. With a conservatism forged by over two centuries of survival under very harsh conditions, fearful and resentful of Anglo incursions, the *pobladores* maintained a precarious hold over their lands for a considerable time after the annexation.[7]

If many Anglos considered landownership in New Mexico undesirable because of title uncertainties, the grant system had worked adequately in the preannexation subsistence economy.[8] Nevertheless, apart from the legal considerations, it could not have persisted for long in the cash and credit economic order that came with the annexation. Title uncertainty was a deterrent to forward-looking Anglo settlers, who wished to establish farms and homes and raise families on the land. Lands without clear title might be confiscated by a rival claimant through legal maneuvering with the help of a skillful, well-paid lawyer. The inability or unwillingness of the US courts and Congress to address them promptly or fairly exacerbated the title difficulties.

While the mass of unsettled titles held land prices low to the advantage of stockmen and their land-intensive industry, by about 1884 nearly every tract of good grazing land in the territory had been claimed, legally or by custom, for sheep, cattle, or horses. Government investigators concluded that the amount of rangeland in use peaked about this time. Government livestock expert E. V. Wilcox later

208 THE END OF THE OPEN RANGE

concluded that *all* public lands suitable for grazing were occupied by 1900 and that traditional open-range grazing had reached a limit.[9]

Important developments in the late nineteenth century rendered farming more attractive than in the past and served to diminish remaining concerns over land titles. The homestead laws together with the placement of large tracts of grant lands into the public domain by the Court of Private Land Claims, active during the period 1891–1904, provided additional farmland with clear title. Aside from title considerations, mechanized irrigation opened large areas of New Mexico for farming. Commercial agriculture then began to take hold. During the first decade of the twentieth century, the territory experienced a large expansion in its farming population. Mechanized irrigation converted large expanses of dry rangeland into viable farmland so that farming penetrated areas that had once been devoted solely to grazing. The aggregate acreage available for grazing was thus reduced.[10]

Just as it had made possible an expanded sheep and wool industry, the nation's growing rail network expedited farming by providing ever more efficient transport of farm produce to the important markets in the Midwest and the East, removing a barrier that had stood since Spanish colonial times. Besides shipping farm produce, the railroads provided fast, comparatively convenient transportation to New Mexico for immigrating homesteaders, their livestock, and their farm equipment. The railroads also sometimes transported winter feed from the farms where it was grown to ranch country where it was needed.[11]

Homesteaders, responding to a combination of advancing technology, favorable land laws, and the declaration of nearly 33 million acres to be public domain, claimed some of the best public grazing tracts and water resources in New Mexico, public policy having, in effect, given them priority over ranchers. In 1890–1900 the population of the territory grew by about 22 percent. In the following decade, 1900–1910, the population grew explosively from 195,000 to 327,000, a 68 percent increase, due largely to an influx of Anglo farmers (see figure 1.1). The number of farms in New Mexico increased by 176 percent in the 1890s and by 189 percent in the 1900s, an eightfold increase over the two-decade period.[12]

Agricultural production exploded (figure 2.3), while the sheep population held roughly at around 3 million from the 1890s until World War I (figure 1.2). Stockmen, already squeezed, came under steadily increasing pressure from the homesteaders. In the words of John Clay, "Its [the open range's] death rattle was echoed over its broad acres in three words, 'the dry farmer.' You can fight armies or disease or trespass, but the settler never. He advances slowly, surely, silently, like a great motor truck, pushing everything before him."[13]

RANGE DEGRADATION

As homesteaders claimed the most desirable lands, landless stockmen crowded their herds of sheep and cattle onto the ever smaller tracts of the inferior land that remained in the public domain. Overgrazing, if it had not already taken its toll, followed, and the resulting degradation of the public lands became more acute. Farmers grazing their small livestock holdings on the public lands near their homesteads exacerbated the degradation. From the early 1880s many Rocky Mountain ranchers had disregarded the dangers of overgrazing and placed too many animals on the rangeland they controlled, sacrificing long-term sustainability of the land for short-term profits. Wiser growers looked on in alarm and frustration as they witnessed the steady range deterioration. In the words of twentieth-century sheepwoman Roe Lovelace, "If you overgraze you're in trouble. You don't have a ranch." At a time when public domain was becoming scarce, its stock holding capacity in terms of the heads per acre that it could support was diminishing. Few if any ranchers possessed the resources to prevent their irresponsible neighbors from degrading the land in their area.[14]

The crowding of livestock onto the remaining public lands was largely the work of smaller, less affluent, even impoverished growers without the resources to purchase their own land. These herders—"drifters," as landowners called them with their "tramp" or "arab" flocks—utilized

210 THE END OF THE OPEN RANGE

the range heavily, often trailing their small herds far to the north in the summer and far to the south in the winter in an increasingly desperate search for free fodder. Their flocks denuded unclaimed lands during the summer, rendering them useless for landowning stockmen who still continued to employ some public tracts for winter grazing.[15]

These marginal herders introduced a new level of conflict over land. Many of them, with no permanent base of operations and no home range, paid no county taxes and purchased no supplies from local merchants, rendering them despicable to established ranchers, farmers, and merchants alike. A government publication characterized them as a "public nuisance." According to the Troy Brothers of Raton, their "arab" flocks were diseased and spread scab. Living day to day, they exploited whatever land they could find and demonstrated little concern for conserving the range resource over the long term. By the early 1880s the drifters had become a serious problem for all well-established open-range stockmen. Although conscientious sheep growers could do little about these invaders, cowmen sometimes ran them off at gunpoint. The nomadic herders eventually disappeared when their marginal operations became completely unsustainable.[16]

Homesteading in New Mexico did not have the effect anticipated by the land laws. In many cases the early homesteaders, like the sheep-growing drifters, damaged the lands they used. Homesteaders were not always able to obtain irrigated land. Dryland farming, which many early homesteaders took up, was a disaster. The first wave of immigrant farmers that found their way to the territory crested during the wet years immediately following 1900, when prospects appeared bright. A double tragedy resulted when the homesteaders, in New Mexico and elsewhere, discovered for themselves that they could not build a successful dry farm on a quarter section in the semiarid West. Many gave up and abandoned their homesteads after a few heartbreaking years, but often not before their plows had destroyed the underlying deep root system of the native grasses, which efficiently utilized the limited natural water supply.[17] These were the very grasses that had long sustained the range livestock. The plowing furthermore opened up the soil and released its natural moisture into the dry western air, and the winds subsequently eroded away the loosened, dried-out topsoil.

When the dryland farmers departed, as most of the first wave did, they often left behind horribly damaged land that, like the overgrazed rangeland, would not recover and be productive again for decades. Of no use for agriculture as it was then practiced, these lands were likewise of no use for livestock, making for a further reduction in available grazing land. One unsympathetic government report characterized the first homesteaders in the semiarid regions as "poor men who have no cattle." A well-intentioned government program went awry. Some of the unsuccessful farmers took up livestock growing and survived. Others with sufficient resources built their own irrigation systems and survived as farmers.[18]

CONFLICT

The arrival of homesteaders in grazing country produced considerable conflict, as might have been expected. Established stockmen and merchants sometimes welcomed the homesteaders, provided them with water rights, and otherwise helped them get started, confident that they would probably soon fail and sell their land cheaply, providing an inexpensive addition to the stockman's holdings.[19] Contentious interactions were more common. The conflicts caused by fencing, the breakup of grazing tracts, and the blockage of long-established trails became more acute with the influx of farmers. Moreover, when a farmer acquired public water frontage, it became unavailable to stockmen. In time it became impossible to drive a herd from New Mexico to the grazing tracts of Colorado or farther north, as had once been common practice. Ultimately, rail shipment became the sheepman's only remaining option.

STOCKMEN ON THE DEFENSIVE

When homesteading did finally become well established in New Mexico, it had a dramatic impact on ranching. Within a comparatively

212 THE END OF THE OPEN RANGE

short time farmers literally crowded out the open-range stockmen. With their grazing lands disappearing, stockmen found themselves on the defensive for the first time. Fabiola Cabeza de Baca described the situation at the high point of farmer immigration to the Ceja-Llano region in eastern New Mexico: "Hardly a day went by but some new family arrived, until nearly every inch of ground was taken." The homesteaders were taking up land that her family had long used for growing sheep and cattle. Sheepmen found it increasingly difficult to find any land open for grazing or even for temporary sheep holding. Writing in 1909, Bond partner Andy Wiest wrote, "We know of no other land this side [east] of the Pecos where 5,000 head of sheep could be grazed, all available land is being taken up rapidly by the homesteaders, this means that the sheep business in this section [the area north of Cuervo] will soon be a thing of the past." At a more official level, and somewhat belatedly, the 1917 New Mexico Blue Book asserted, "Important changes affecting the livestock industry of New Mexico are now in progress, the result of homestead entries and agricultural expansion. The open range is being steadily reduced, and in time will become a thing of the past."[20]

By 1900 much of the better grazing land and natural water sources had indeed been claimed under one of the federal programs. Both Anglos and Hispanics participated in the homesteading process. The remaining public rangeland, degraded and subject to increased competition, became ever harder for any individual stockman to occupy and control. Ownership proved to be the long-term solution to the diminishing land availability. As early as 1880 Gordon reported that Anglo sheepmen in Colfax, Mora, and San Miguel Counties were filing homestead and preemption claims to establish their home ranges. The process accelerated in the following years. In the late 1880s and continuing through the early 1890s, stock growers throughout the West, those with the most foresight and some available capital, began to extend their legal holdings beyond the 160-acre tracts of water frontage that they had once found adequate. At the same time, land prices were increasing.[21]

As sheepmen moved their operations onto patented tracts, their growing practices changed. H. M. Taylor's 1889 government report, first noted that western sheepmen were settling on titled lands to a much greater extent than ever before while farmers and cattlemen were likewise acquiring titled land at a great rate, then discussed how sheepmen could prosper under the new conditions. The report asserted, "The tendency of the times is for the sheep raiser of the West to acquire range by purchase, then to gradually work towards a proper system of stock farming, changing his methods as means and intelligence dictate. Sometimes this causes a decrease in the flock, but it generally leads toward safety for the investment, and more uniformity in the amount annually derived as income." The report further noted that raising sheep on fenced pastureland could reduce the risks and uncertainties. Additional considerations included combating scab, predators, and poisonous plants, all of which could be addressed more expeditiously by restricting flocks to privately owned fields.[22]

Sheepmen, pushed off the shrinking open range and required to adapt to sheep growing on smaller tracts of land, were also ultimately forced to adopt the recent advances in range management, no longer just an option. The more conscientious and more financially sound sheepmen accepted the range-management goal of maximizing livestock production "consistent with conservation of the range resource." This was a major undertaking of a technical character. It involved mapping range resources, estimating grazing capacities and forage production, prescribing types and numbers of livestock best suited to each land parcel, and developing systems of grazing usage, fencing, and irrigation. Stockmen began, moreover, to systematically address range restoration through artificial reseeding, burning, weed control, and soil and water conservation. Such sophisticated range management became imperative on account of the wide-ranging distressed land conditions of the late 1890s. Stockmen called on the federal government for assistance, and the US Department of Agriculture began to undertake scientific studies of grass and forage.[23] For their part, the farmers who crowded out the sheepmen would eventually bring about

214 THE END OF THE OPEN RANGE

more efficient food production from the land. They also quickly outnumbered the ranchers.

For the next several years most New Mexico sheepmen, including the *ricos*, still held title to only small tracts and grazed their livestock on nearby public lands. Those stockmen who would not or could not purchase land and address the new array of requirements, which were expensive, would be left behind. In the words of Cabeza de Baca describing the situation she had witnessed in the Ceja-Llano region, "The few cattle and sheepmen who were left [after the arrival of the homesteaders] and had not been foresighted [and bought land], had to diminish their herds and they also had to live on credit from the country store. One by one, they also disappeared." She described the herders still running sheep on the Llano as late as 1915 as "sad people, these men, for their days on the Llano were numbered." Her father had actively purchased land to preserve the family's ranching operation.[24]

NATIONAL FOREST RESERVES

A second federal policy caused further reductions of grazing lands. By the late nineteenth century many Americans, including influential politicians, were becoming alarmed by the rampant exploitation, even theft, of the nation's natural resources by private interests, particularly the timber industry. It was felt that these resources needed to be protected for future generations. In response, Congress, taking an increased interest in conservation and "reclamation," passed the Forest Reserve Act of 1891. This act allowed the president to set aside, and close off from public use, lands in the public domain as reservations or National Forest Reserves, as they were designated. The administration of the reserves fell initially to the Department of the Interior. The immediate intent of the reserves was to protect the designated tracts from flooding and erosion as well as overexploitation of the timber resources. Over the following decade many substantial tracts of the public domain were declared National Forest Reserves. Later, as president during the years 1901–1909, Theodore Roosevelt spearheaded this growing conservation movement, asserting, "The conservation of natural resources is the key to the future. It is the key to the safety and prosperity of the American people." Roosevelt's beliefs were fortified by his observation of range degradation during his years raising cattle in North Dakota. The reserves were renamed National Forests in 1907, and on a single day in that year Roosevelt established twenty-one new national forests, 40 million acres in the West, laying the foundations for the nation's national park system.[25]

Grazing on public lands had been banned in 1894, but the law was unenforceable and ignored. These lands included much of the traditional western summer range, where sheep were fattened for market or for the coming winter. Then in 1897 cattle but not sheep were officially allowed back on the range, an apparently meaningless development. The situation for sheep ranchers improved somewhat in 1905 when the forest reserves were transferred to the Department of Agriculture, and the federal government began, in 1906, issuing annual grazing permits through the recently established US Forest Service. The seasonal grazing fees imposed were modest (twenty to thirty-five cents per head for cattle and five to eight cents per head for sheep), but with specified cattle and sheep allotments, the number of animals and the months of the year for which grazing was permitted on each leased tract were restricted, reducing its usage from the past. Stockmen—their grazing lands, lands they had in some cases been using for decades, effectively diminished and now more expensive to utilize—were outraged. They mounted legal challenges in California and Colorado opposing the federal program that went all the way to the Supreme Court, but the government prevailed. Roosevelt defended the program, which he believed would benefit small-scale ranchers and homesteaders fighting both large cattle operations and landless, itinerant sheepmen. Public lands available for homesteading also diminished.[26]

When a forest reserve, later to be incorporated in the Cebola National Forest, was established in western Socorro County, Ray Morley, Montague Stevens, and many other ranchers obtained grazing permits. They were ordered to remove the fences they had put up on the public

216 THE END OF THE OPEN RANGE

lands. According to Cleaveland, the ranchers in the area were shocked and incensed by the order. They felt the directive was a violation of their "natural rights," but they complied. Her brother took down miles of fencing. In addition to fences, some ranchers had constructed various structures on the public land that they were ordered to remove. They considered these structures legitimate capital investments. Having to remove their fences and buildings constituted an additional, apparently unforeseen expense. An Arizona sheepman, commenting on the establishment of the National Forest Reserves around 1903, asserted, "From a wool grower's and a mutton raiser's point of view it is a decidedly wrong and dangerous condition of affairs."[27]

The program was ultimately successful on several levels. The policy did benefit the flora and fauna on the reserves, as intended. By 1914 the national forest land was supporting 50 percent more livestock per acre than ten years earlier, and 29,000 stock growers had grazing permits for 1.6 million cattle and horses and 7.6 million sheep and goats. Under systematic federal range management, the range in some badly overgrazed areas was, over a period of years, restored. The national forests became self-supporting; grazing becoming a secondary resource for the federal government, as the Forest Service had hoped. Also, by this time, the range wars between cattle and sheep interests had ended, ranchland had increased in value, forage production had increased, the grazing industry had been stabilized, and the quality of stock produced had generally improved.[28]

The National Forest Reserves and the associated grazing fees constituted one component of the steadily growing network of connections between the federal government and the sheep industry.

SMALL-SCALE GROWERS

No component of the sheep industry was as strongly affected by the diminishing grazing resources as the small-scale, commercial Hispanic growers from the villages of New Mexico and southern Colorado. They had profited from the post–Civil War export economy in sheep and wool. But their best years had passed. By the turn of the twentieth century the loss of rangeland had for them become acute. The modest grazing fees for use of the National Forest Reserves were beyond the means of many small-scale growers.

As early as the 1880s Hispanic herders were being excluded from lands they had used for decades, even centuries. Continuation of the traditional grazing practices, on the long-established scale, was not an option. Raising modest herds on the shrinking open range ceased to provide the profits and the sustenance necessary for village life. In the future cash would be needed to purchase or lease adequate grazing land, acquire graded-up stock, and otherwise capitalize an up-to-date ranch or farm. And many small-scale sheepmen had never been able to amass any cash reserves, closing off that option. The more prosperous Hispanic farmers and stockmen would expend time and money to take up homesteads if they were so inclined.[29]

Many found homesteading unattractive and, following a new course of action, took up seasonal wage employment, often far from their villages. Starting in the late 1870s some men hired out as herders for large-scale Anglo outfits in New Mexico and elsewhere. John and Thomas Cosgriff, who, starting in 1882, built the largest sheep operation in Wyoming, eventually 165,000 head, employed Adriano Apadaca as their foreman. He was one of a cohort of Hispanic herders that spread throughout the West. After 1876, with the arrival of the AT&SF in Las Animas, Colorado, employment on track crews, constructing and maintaining rail lines, became available for village men. Some villagers went to work in the mines and, much later, in the Colorado sugar beet fields. Soon many were departing seasonally, during the warmer months, to take up these new jobs, which paid more than herding but were more physically demanding. By the late nineteenth century reliable Hispanic labor in New Mexico, once abundant, became difficult for sheepmen to secure, largely a consequence of these new employment opportunities.[30]

In this period, the barter economy, once the norm in the villages, was giving way to a cash and credit economy, an added incentive for the men to take up wage employment. Villagers now needed cash to pay taxes on their land and livestock and to purchase iron cookstoves, bedsteads, farming equipment, and myriad other merchandise now more readily available with the arrival of the railroads.[31]

By the early twentieth century coal mines had opened at several sites in southern Colorado, and seasonal mining jobs in the coal fields became available. Mining paid even more than track work on the railroads. By the turn of the twentieth century there were over 10,000 New Mexico–born residents in Colorado, largely congregated around the mines of Las Animas County. Work in the sawmills of the expanding lumber industry provided another outlet for village men. Some village women relocated to active job sites to work as seamstresses, laundresses, and in a variety of other occupations.[32]

Starting in the 1890s sugar beet companies set up operations throughout much of Colorado, notably in the South Platte and Arkansas River areas. This opened up another new opportunity for wage employment, cropping, thinning, and harvesting sugar beets. By 1909 one quarter of Colorado beet workers were Hispanic. Initially seasonal, beet work soon became effectively permanent. From this time on, entire families began leaving their villages to relocate near the job sites. In later years they formed new communities in the sugar beet districts or nearby towns, entire families sometimes working together in the beet fields. Some, perhaps most, of the younger men from the northern villages who took up wage work at this time would leave commercial sheep growing and the open range behind forever.[33]

NAVAJO STOCK REDUCTION

This section is intended only to provide a brief introduction to an important chain of events that played out in the early twentieth century. The factual material, unless otherwise noted, is drawn from Weisiger.[34]

While the great majority of New Mexico sheep growers, Anglo and Hispanic, revised their methods of production, giving up the open range in favor of controlled conditions, the Navajo followed—or, more accurately, were compelled to follow—a unique trajectory embodied in the federal stock reduction program of the 1930s. The program was part of a complex political process encompassing the development of water resources, the clarification of the boundaries of the reservation, scientifically based rehabilitation of degraded lands, and the interests of Anglo commercial sheepmen operating at the boundaries of the reservation.

When the Navajo were allowed to return home from Bosque Redondo, the reservation then established encompassed an area considerably smaller than their traditional homeland, decreasing the available grazing land. At the same time, the Navajo population began to expand explosively, the number of families eventually increasing fivefold from an estimated 2,000 to 10,000 in the years 1870 to 1930. With the establishment of the reservation, the Navajo became excessively, in retrospect alarmingly, reliant for their subsistence on the single, comparatively dependable resource of sheep and goats, a repetition in some ways of the colonial village economy in the early years of Spanish sovereignty. Family subsistence holdings generally consisted of a few hundred goats and sheep at most, together with a few cows and horses. The reservation land area and water resources were insufficient to support the growing population in this fashion. By the early twentieth century the reservation had been severely overgrazed, and much of the land closest to water sources was denuded of nutritious forage. The practice of grazing near dwellings, traversing a path from home to pasture twice a day, was particularly detrimental to the lands so employed. Erosion, accelerated by cycles of drought followed by excessively heavy rains, contributed significantly to the degradation. The overall productivity of the lands was threatened.[35]

The situation would, if it continued, devastate the innumerable families who depended on their modest herds and, by extension, the tribal grazing lands for their subsistence. The tribe would be left essentially landless, a possibility recognized by government officials. The impending disaster, of course, had roots extending well back into the

220 THE END OF THE OPEN RANGE

territorial period. By the early twentieth century Navajo families were competing intensely for good grazing land.

Federal officials monitoring the developments concluded that stock reduction on a large scale throughout the reservation was the only way to avert disaster. Beginning in the early 1930s, the officials overseeing the reservation subsequently initiated what turned into a multiyear stock-reduction program. They had the force of federal law behind them since the reservation land was the property of the US government under the purview of the secretary of the interior. The Indians possessed only the right to occupy the land. Sadly, the stock reduction was carried out in a clumsy, high-handed fashion with little input from the Navajo and little understanding of the importance of sheep, both economic and cultural, in Navajo society.

In 1933, under considerable government pressure, the Navajo gave up, voluntarily, over 86,000 sheep, which were purchased by the government. But this was a minor sacrifice. As of 1935 it was estimated by government experts that the Navajo lands could carry 560,000 sheep and goats or their equivalent in horses and cattle.[36] However, the equivalent of 918,000 sheep were grazing on reservation land at the time, a number not excessive given the number of mouths to be fed. The Navajo resisted the stock reductions, the losses from economic considerations alone being exacerbated by the cultural significance of the flocks. Voluntary reduction proved inadequate, and the government authorities instigated forced reductions. In 1934 the federal government asked the Navajo to give up half their goats, over 100,000 head, which had no market value but were an important food source. When complications for their disposal arose, thousands of goats and sheep were shot by federal agents and left on the ground to rot. Otherwise, between one third and two thirds of the stock slated for removal were consumed.

Later, in 1937, the federal government divided up the reservation into eighteen grazing districts to better oversee and control livestock numbers. Each family was assigned to a grazing district and was required, without written permission, to keep its flocks within the boundaries of its district. This was intended to limit the maximum

The End of the Open Range 221

number of livestock within each district to the area's carrying capacity. A maximum limit on the number of livestock each family could own was imposed, depending on their grazing district and family size. The Navajo herders were shocked by the low permissible stock numbers when they were finally announced in 1938. The numbers would have the effect of reducing all stock herds to bare subsistence levels while freezing the size of smaller herds until the goals had been met. When the districts were fenced, traditional grazing circuits were curtailed and herders' options diminished, just as had transpired with the advent of fencing elsewhere in New Mexico.

Over the next several years as the reductions were mandated, considerable protest and resistance, accompanied by a degree of violence, followed. A few stock owners who flouted the regulations were arrested and jailed for short terms. More commonly, the Navajo only presented angry petitions to the authorities.[37]

Few Navajo, it seems, understood the horrible bind they were in. It was a complicated and ultimately sad situation, undertaken, as was perceived at the time, as a necessity on the part of the federal government. In time, the reduction allocations were relaxed somewhat, although protests, sometime violent, persisted. In 1943 a reassessment of the legalities of the stock reduction program concluded that the government had overstepped its authority, and the program was terminated. The management of grazing on the reservation was, in large part, turned over to the tribal council, which subsequently suspended the grazing limits. Stock numbers were allowed to increase slowly, but not to the levels of the early 1930s. Remarkably perhaps, by the mid-1940s stock numbers were reduced below the officially designated carrying capacity of the reservation, 450,000 head. This was accomplished by a combination of consumption, the leasing of off-reservation grazing lands, and voluntary sales. By this time the Navajo had become less dependent on goats and sheep for their sustenance.

In the aftermath of the stock reduction program, substantial tracts of Navajo land remained severely degraded. Less nutritious grasses and other vegetation of little value had displaced the grama grass on once

222 THE END OF THE OPEN RANGE

productive land, just as had transpired through much of the West. The lands would not soon recover, even with the herd reductions. Beyond this, the stock reduction program was a devastating experience for the Navajo, particularly the women who owned and cared for a large fraction of the sheep, performed the shearing, and carried out the spinning and weaving of the wool. It left many Navajo angry and fearful. It was an assault on their ability to feed themselves and their identity as pastoralists. Some questioned the desirability of reestablishing, or continuing to raise, their herds. The Navajo stock reduction program would be long remembered as a dark chapter in the tribe's history.[38]

NAVAJO WEAVING

The Navajo had another important resource besides their subsistence herds. A considerable legacy of the introduction of sheep to New Mexico has been the extraordinary weaving of Navajo women. Their wool rugs and blankets, textile artistry of a high order, have garnered international renown. Some of their creations are quite valuable and sought after by serious collectors. Others have been acquired by innumerable tourists to decorate their homes throughout the country. The Navajo weavings of *churro* wool were first marketed to external buyers by Anglo traders during the 1870s. The market expanded in time, particularly with the twentieth-century growth of the southwestern tourist trade, and became critically important for the Navajo economy. At the end of the territorial period it was reported that wool-blanket production, then engaged in by thousands of women, was the most important and remunerative Navajo industry. By 1930 the external market for Navajo weaving had reached $1 million.[39]

Weaving in the Navajo world has a significance beyond its monetary importance, however. An aspect of Navajo culture and spirituality, sheep and weaving have been absorbed into the Navajo creation story, which includes a mythological account of the origins of the loom and weaving tools and plays an important role in the lives and values of the people. The act of weaving wool has deep cultural significance and was, and is today, undertaken with reverence. This connection has been perhaps as important for the weavers as any other aspect of their work.[40]

Sadly, an inordinate amount of the profits, the monetary gain from Navajo weaving, has gone to the Anglo merchants and reservation traders dealing in the wool products rather than the weavers themselves, who have been meagerly compensated for their labor.

SUMMARY

By the end of the New Mexico territorial period, open-range sheep growing had, in large part, come to an end, although it would persist well into the twentieth century in some areas.[41] In the future, sheep would be raised on privately owned farms or on leased government land under controlled conditions, becoming essentially another farm crop.

EPILOGUE

The preceding chapters chronicle the development of New Mexico's all-important sheep industry during the territorial years when it occupied a central place in so many lives. With the US annexation and the opportunities that followed, men like Charles Ilfeld, Frank Bond, Montague Stevens, and Thomas Catron brought about changes on the ground, following the lead of Solomon Luna and Filipe Chaves and many other native New Mexicans who pointed the way to what was possible in semiarid New Mexico. The West's oldest sheep growing region, so isolated and controlled, as it was, by a small cohort of landed families, became integrated into the mainstream US economy with, among its many connections, links to woolen mills in Massachusetts and Pennsylvania, feeder farms in Colorado and Nebraska, meat packers in Chicago, and financial institutions in New York, all under the impetus of the sheep industry. The connections extended into the most remote villages when the sheep and wool merchants made available cash and

https://doi.org/10.5876/9781646425471.c008

Epilogue 225

credit to their suppliers in these areas against future deliveries. This national economic web, together with the advent of commercial banking, which had been boosted significantly by the sheep industry, would help pave the way for later industrial developments in agriculture, mining, and lumbering as statehood was finally achieved.

The economic integration was accompanied by a steadily growing network of relationships between the territorial and federal governments and the territory's sheep economy. These relationships concerned legislation that first regulated and then banned captive Indian slavery and peonism, the US Army presence that rendered the land safe for grazing, the wool tariff that increased prices wool producers would get, homestead legislation, the court system whereby landownership was adjudicated, sheepmen's organizations and dipping requirements, and the establishment of national forest reserves and grazing allotments.

New Mexico held its own against other developing stock-growing regions in the West, contributing significantly to US livestock production, all in response to, and indeed part of, the country's industrialization and the growing army of urban laborers in the East and Midwest needing to be fed and clothed.[1] By the end of the territorial period New Mexico sheepmen and merchants were part of a national industrial complex. At the same time, the benefits at home were widespread and considerable, as they always had been in a way when innumerable New Mexico families were running modest, and in some cases considerable, sheep operations for both profit and sustenance.

The advance of the western sheep industry during the territorial period was astounding, considering particularly that Americans had only become aware of sheep in New Mexico a few decades earlier with the reports of the Pike Expedition. Between 1878 and 1888 the total number of sheep delivered annually to the Chicago stockyards increased fivefold, the increase coming entirely from stock produced beyond the Missouri River. At the time of the annexation, 1846, there were an estimated 377,000 head of sheep in New Mexico and a human population of about 50,000. By 1882 there were about 5.2 million sheep, a fourteenfold increase, while the human population increased to about 120,000, having little more than doubled. Of the states and territories, only Montana and Wyoming had larger sheep populations at the end of the century. At this time, about 8 percent of America's sheep were being raised in New Mexico.[2]

In the same period, at the beginning of the twentieth century, the United States, with less than 5 percent of the world's population, was producing about 10 percent of the world's wool. And some 60 percent of America's wool was being produced in nine states and territories west of the Mississippi, New Mexico contributing about 10 percent of the West's production. Among industrialized countries the United States was the world's largest wool producer by more than a factor of two. America's woolen mills were utilizing essentially all of the domestic production and importing an additional 30 percent of their wool. Overall, they were consuming about 15 percent of the world's production, a measure of the nation's extraordinary prosperity. By 1890 America's annual wool consumption, estimated at 8.75 pounds per capita, was the largest of any nation in the world. The volume of wool consumed in the United States was at this time five times what it had been in 1860.[3]

Wool production in New Mexico had risen from about 33,000 pounds in 1850 to an estimated 17 million pounds in 1909, a 500-fold increase! The average fleece weight had grown from 1 pound or less to 5.5 pounds as a result of selective breeding. During this same period New Mexico's human population increased by a factor of about five, due in substantial part to Anglo immigration. Of the states and territories, Montana and Wyoming were by 1900, just as in the case of live sheep, the two largest wool producers, New Mexico was tied with Idaho for fifth place, trailing only slightly Utah and Oregon (table 2.2).[4]

The prosperity that sheep had brought to New Mexico was not achieved without cost. Overgrazing brought about widespread changes in the vegetation. Replacement vegetation more resistant to heavy grazing penetrated productive grasslands throughout New Mexico and the Rocky Mountain West. Sparse, less nutritious grass cover, juniper savanna, and other types of replacement vegetation of little or no

Epilogue 227

use for livestock have become dominant in many areas. The lands have been crisscrossed by arroyos created by heavy grazing in combination with extreme weather conditions. With diminished ground cover, the lands are today dryer than they once were. A Department of Agriculture report dating from the 1930s noted that after some fifty years of overgrazing, the western range was less than half as productive as it had once been.[5] Only toward the end of the territorial period did these losses begin to be understood and appreciated. Vegetation patterns are still evolving. Further long-term consequences of New Mexico's period of heavy, open-range grazing remain unclear.

Until the last years of the territorial period, New Mexico's lack of surface water continued to favor sheep growing over farming with its much greater water needs. And sheep remained central to the territory's economy and society, even as ownership patterns shifted. As late as 1913, *The New Mexico Blue Book* asserted with only a little exaggeration that "the breeding and raising of sheep [is] the largest industry in our state."[6] Although other states and territories had surpassed New Mexico in sheep and wool production, the territory continued to be an important sheep-growing region, even as open-range grazing was disappearing. As the twentieth century progressed, mining and particularly agriculture expanded significantly, national wool and lamb markets weakened, and sheep ceased to occupy the central place in New Mexican lives that they once had. An ever smaller cohort of dedicated stock growers continued to produce sheep commercially. Within only three decades after the close of the territorial period, New Mexico was launched into a new role, and a new identity, as a center for scientific research and development in support of national defense. An era extending back to the Spanish colonial period had passed.

NOTES

PREFACE

1. Baxter, *Las Carneradas*, 90; "The backbone of industrial husbandry" is understood to mean that sheep husbandry had provided, and continued to provide, a more widespread economic benefit to the people of New Mexico than any other single industry. By this time, mining, if not it's individual mineral subdivisions, and agriculture, if not it's individual crops, had surpassed the state's sheep industry in annual revenues, while cattle were comparable to sheep in revenues. However, cattle and mining were largely controlled by outside investors and a few local entrepreneurs who reaped the bulk of the profits. *The New Mexico Blue Book, 1913,* 24–26, 42.

2. Thos. N. Wilkerson, "Address of Welcome," Second Annual Convention of the New Mexico Wool Growers Association, October 7, 1907, New Mexico Wool Growers Association Records, Archives and Special Collections Department, New Mexico State University Library, New Mexico State University, Las Cruces (henceforth NMWGA); Abelicio M. Pena, Oral History, conducted and recorded April 17, 1996, by Jane O'Cane and Robert Hart, Oral History Program of the New Mexico Farm & Ranch Heritage Museum, Las Cruces, New Mexico (transcript, p. 58), Archives and Special Collections, New Mexico State University, Las Cruces, New Mexico (henceforth FR). A confluence of developments (low market prices and changes in

230 NOTES

predator-control regulations) had forced the stockmen in the area to convert from sheep to cattle, an activity for which they felt no affinity; Weisiger, *Dreaming of Sheep*, 18.

3. According to the most reliable data now available, New Mexico's sheep population grew from a roughly estimated 377,000 in 1850 to 3,535,000 in 1900, a factor of about nine. See *Seventh Census, 1850*, 170; New Mexico Department of Agriculture, *New Mexico Agricultural Statistics*, 44; *Twelfth Census, 1900*, 5:ccxiv. The annual revenues (sheep and wool) grew from very roughly $100,000 ($3.6 million in 2020 dollars) during the best years under Mexican sovereignty to about $5 million in 1900 ($160 million in 2020 dollars), a factor of 40, while the human population of the territory grew from 61,547, including Arizona, to 195,310, a factor of 3.2 between 1850 and 1900. See *Seventh Census, 1850*, 993; *Twelfth Census, 1900*, 1:xlix.

4. Gressley, *Bankers and Cattlemen*; Clay, *My Life on the Range*; Baxter, *Las Carneradas*.

CHAPTER 1: SHEEP COME TO NEW MEXICO

1. Lummis, *Land of Poco Tiempo*, 15; Weber, *Mexican Frontier*, 139n61.

2. Carman et al., *Special Report*, 21, 919; Baxter, *Las Carneradas*, 20.

3. Prior to 1800, wool production was important at the missions, because the padres sought to cloth the Pueblo Indians.

4. Pattie, *Personal Narrative*, 71, 87; Carman et al., *Special Report*, 929–930.

5. Sypolt, "Keepers," 276; Abelicio M. Pena, Oral History, conducted and recorded April 17, 1996, by Jane O'Cane and Robert Hart, FR; Earnesto Carrejo, Oral History, conducted and recorded by Carol Pittman, September 18, 2001, FR.

6. M'Closkey, *Swept under the Rug*, 28; Pittman, "Solomon Luna," 11–12. In another case in 1868, the Denver press reported on a sheep thief who had allegedly slit the throats of two Hispanic herders and hid their bodies. The stolen sheep were identified and in his possession when he was captured by a US Army detachment near Trinidad, Colorado. *Rocky Mountain News*, April 7, 1868.

7. Pittman, "Solomon Luna," 11.

8. Gilfillan, *Sheep*, 37–38.

9. Abelicio M. Pena, Oral History, conducted and recorded April 17, 1996, by Jane O'Cane and Robert Hart, FR; Thomas Cabeza DeBaca, Oral History, conducted and recorded by Ramona Caplan, September 10, 2010, FR; Weisiger, *Dreaming of Sheep*, 79.

10. The *partido* system is described in chapter 3.

11. Sypolt, "Keepers," 269; Gutierrez, *When Jesus Came*, 215.

12. Towne and Wentworth, *Shepherd's Empire*, 269; Edgar B. Kincaid, quoted in Towne and Wentworth, *Shepherd's Empire*, 257.

13. Cleaveland, *No Life for a Lady*, 255.

14. Navajo women had been raising sheep since the early eighteenth century for food and wool, but little is known about the extent of their ownership or their herding

Notes 231

practices at this time. See Weisiger, *Dreaming of Sheep*, 113, 115, 125; M'Closkey, *Swept under the Rug*, 26.

15. Abelicio M. Pena, Oral History, conducted and recorded April 17, 1996, by Jane O'Cane and Robert Hart, FR.

16. Baxter, *Las Carneradas*, 2–3. According to a contemporary account, there were 500 head of cattle and 5,000 sheep, which were consumed during the Coronado Expedition. For more detail, see Horgan, *Great River*, 127–128. Some sheep were left in New Mexico with a few friars who stayed behind and were later killed by the Pueblo Indians. Those sheep disappeared entirely. Hernán Gallegos, quoted in Hammond and Rey, *Rediscovery of New Mexico*, 89.

17. Baxter, *Las Carneradas*, 4. The initial Oñate party consisted of about 600 or 700 individuals: soldier-settlers, their families, servants, and slaves, and Franciscan friars, a heterogeneous population of Spaniards, creoles, *castas* (of mixed blood), and Mexican Indians. They brought along 1,000 head of cattle, 1,000 goats, and about 3,000 sheep provided by the governor, which were probably augmented with some privately owned stock. Interestingly, the original settlement was near the present-day town of Espanola, New Mexico, later headquarters of notable sheepman Frank Bond. Gutierrez, *When Jesus Came*, 57; Fergusson, *New Mexico*, 166; Wentworth, *America's Sheep Trails*, 113.

18. Butzer, "Cattle and Sheep," 45–51.

19. Pedro Bautista Pino, quoted in Carroll and Haggard, *Three New Mexico Chronicles*, 99n.

20. Scholes, "Civil Government and Society," 108. The encomienda was a system of grants of Pueblo tribute, often in the form of labor, to the soldier-citizens. See Gutierrez, *When Jesus Came*, 102–105; Ebright, *Land Grants and Law Suits*, 14–15, 21–22; Dunmire, *New Mexico's Spanish Livestock Heritage*, 40–41.

21. Referring to the Rio Grande in New Mexico, the Rio Abajo is the downriver country and Rio Arriba the upriver country. They are separated by La Bajada Barranca, southwest of Santa Fe. See Nostrand, *Hispano Homeland*, 37. The imports included tools, builder's supplies, various foodstuffs, clothing, and religious articles. Sometimes these caravans brought along additional infusions of livestock. See Scholes, "Civil Government and Society," 110; Horgan, *Great River*, 225–226; Baxter, *Las Carneradas*, 8–9.

22. Woolen stockings and textiles (fabricated by Pueblo coerced labor), salt, livestock, hides, and pinon nuts were shipped south and exchanged in Mexico for dry goods, hardware, tools, and weapons, all essential for survival in the remote northern settlements and all on a rather small scale. Baxter, *Las Carneradas*, 11.

23. Nostrand, *Hispano Homeland*, 38–48; Westphall, *Mercedes Reales*, 19–23; Gutierrez, *When Jesus Came*, 155–160, 166–172, 304. The encomienda system was gradually abolished throughout New Spain in the early eighteenth century because of the depletion of Indigenous populations. See Kessell, *Pueblos*, 174. The repartimiento, a rotational labor draft, was abolished in 1786.

232 NOTES

24. M'Closkey, *Swept under the Rug*, 26; Weisiger, *Dreaming of Sheep*, 106–107, 111, 115–116.

25. Kiser, *Borderlands*, 1–12, 16–17, 32, 66, 92, 99, 167, 172.

26. Over 4,000 ewes, 170 goats, 500 cows, and 150 bulls were distributed. See Baxter, *Las Carneradas*, 13–17, 27.

27. Baxter, *Las Carneradas*, 15–17; Twitchell, *Old Santa Fe*, 151–152; Gonzales, *Politica*, 49–50. The grant system adopted after the Reconquest may have been a continuation of the previous land distribution practice to some extent. The policy promoted settlement and general economic development while providing rudimentary administrative oversight for the colony.

28. Baxter, *Las Carneradas*, 42–49. *Genizaros* often served as domestics as well as farm laborers, soldiers, and artisans, augmenting the labor of the *mestizos*. The *genizaros'* term of service in a Hispanic family was typically limited to ten years, after which they would be freed and could, if they hadn't already done so, intermarry into the lower rungs of colonial society. See Gutierrez, *When Jesus Came*, 148, 151,.171–175, 295; Brooks, *Captives and Cousins*, 123–126; Gonzales, *Politica*, 49–50.

29. Don Jose Agustin de Escudiero, in Carroll and Haggard, *Three New Mexico Chronicles*, 89. The flocks were also sometimes herded, or at least overseen, by the young men of the patron's family, who were required to learn the livestock business from the ground up. These young *ricos* sometimes supervised the sheep drives into Mexico while their elders remained at home.

30. According to the census of 1757, the "Spanish" population of the colony stood at 5,170 individuals. They possessed 2,543 horses, 7,832 cattle, and 47,621 *ganado menor* (sheep and goats). Additionally, there were almost 9,000 Pueblo and Hopi Indians, who owned 4,813 horses, 8,325 cattle, and 64,561 *ganado menor*. See Baxter, *Las Carneradas*, 42; see also Kessell, *Pueblos*, 175.

31. Baxter, *Las Carneradas*, 26, 42, 47–48; Gutierrez, *When Jesus Came*, 300; Meinig, *Southwest*, 14.

32. Baxter, *Las Carneradas*, 52, 59, 68, 72; Simmons, "Chacon," 84. By this time, however, the Pueblo population had been reduced by multiple causes, including European diseases, to about 9,500, a quarter of its pre-Conquest level, so the Hispanics now greatly outnumbered the Pueblos. See Nostrand, *Hispano Homeland*, 54–55.

33. Gutierrez, *When Jesus Came*, 301, 319–320. This export level is corroborated by 1794 church documents indicating that 15,000–20,000 sheep were being trailed south annually, with the numbers ranging up to 25,000 some years. Baxter, *Las Carneradas*, 58–60; Simmons, "Chacon," 85.

34. Simmons, "Chacon," 86–87. In addition to sheep, the trade goods included deer hides, buffalo robes, furs, tobacco, salt, and copper work as reported by Lieutenant Zebulon Pike, the first American observer to report on a New Mexican trade caravan and the important role of sheep in the trade with Mexico. See Pike, *Expeditions*, 631–632, 739. Horgan (*Great River*, 367) lists additional exports, including woolen blankets, dried meat, and strings of red and green chili. See also Pino, in Carroll and Haggard, *Three New Mexico Chronicles*, 106–109. The New Mexicans attended

Notes 233

the January Chihuahua trade fair and returned home in April with horses and mules, fancy textiles, hats, ironwork, hardware, drugs, paper, dyes, and specialty foods, an ever-widening variety of goods. They also brought home imported goods from the Philippines, China, South America, and Europe, as well as some gold and silver. An additional drive departing in August was added later. See Baxter, *Las Carneradas*, 63, 69. The internal trade of New Mexico, which included sale of the imports, was controlled by the rather small base of only 12–14 *comerciantes*, or merchants. Denevan, "Livestock Numbers," 697–699.

35. Baxter, *Las Carneradas*, 44, 72–75.
36. Pino reported in 1812 that 15,000 sheep were being exported every year to Durango with a valuation of around 17,000 pesos, while total exports to Mexico were estimated to be valued at 60,000 pesos. Pino, in Carroll and Haggard, *Three New Mexico Chronicles*, 36. Pino's figures are only to be considered rough estimates but indicate general relationships. See also Simmons, "Chacon," 85–86. Pino's data indicate that the wealthy trading families controlled over 25 percent of the export trade of sheep alone and perhaps much more considering all other commodities. Besides owning most of the colony's sheep, the *ricos* filled most if not all positions of influence and honor and were, as a result, deeply involved in New Mexico's political and religious affairs. See also Gutierrez, *When Jesus Came*, 149, 231, 262, 301; Boyle, *Los Capitalistas*, 7–13; Baxter, *Las Carneradas*, 43–47, 59; Barreiro, in Carroll and Haggard, *Three New Mexico Chronicles*, 109–110; Payne, "Lessons," 402–404, 411.
37. Baxter, *Las Carneradas*, 75–76, 79, 90; Denevan, "Livestock Numbers," 691. The livestock census included 155,000 in the Albuquerque area, 62,000 in the Santa Fe area, and 23,000 in the Santa Cruz area. In addition to the sheep, the colony was reported to have 5,000 cattle, 2,150 mules, and 850 horses. The sheep were valued in New Mexico at 4 reales/head (about fifty cents/head), about half the value in Mexico during good times, and accordingly constituted 54 percent of the total livestock valuation. See Escudero, in Carroll and Haggard, *Three New Mexico Chronicles*, 43.
38. Weber, *Mexican Frontier*, 11; Twitchell, *Old Santa Fe*, 198n; Boyle, *Los Capitalistas*, 23–24.
39. Baxter, *Las Carneradas*, 97, 100–101; Twitchell, *Old Santa Fe*, 217–218; Gregg, *Commerce of the Prairies*, 203–204, 207–209.
40. Baxter, *Las Carneradas*, 95–96, 104, 107–109; see also Weber, *Mexican Frontier*, 140n62.
41. Of these families, the Chaves brothers owned 52,500 head; Antonio Sandoval, 38,500; and the Otero family, 44,500. See Baxter, *Las Carneradas*, 103–104, 107. Records indicate that Manuel Armijo drove 34,916 sheep south over the decade 1835–1845. Boyle, *Los Capitalistas*, 35–44. Between 1826 and 1846, a total of some 400,000 head valued at about 200,000 pesos were driven to Mexico. This constituted 47 percent of the measurable export value for the period, enumerated by Boyle to be 422,907.71 pesos. The bulk of the merchants after 1832 were, however,

234 NOTES

small-scale businessmen trading in a wide variety of New Mexican and Indian products. They controlled only 10 percent of the total trade, which, spread out broadly and thinly as it was, benefited many New Mexican families more than the sheep trade. See Barriero in Carroll and Haggard, *Three New Mexico Chronicles*, 109; Gregg, *Commerce of the Prairies*, 99; Gonzales, *Politica*, 49–50.

42. Gutierrez, *When Jesus Came*, 167; see figure 1.1. Nostrand has concluded that the 1850 census gives an undercount of the New Mexico population and that it was more likely more than 100,000. In contrast, he has described the 1900 census as "extremely accurate." See Nostrand, *Hispano Homeland*, 19–20.

43. Altogether the Spanish and Mexican governments awarded some 22 million acres of grant lands in New Mexico and southern Colorado. It has been estimated that about two-thirds of the colony's population lived on large grants, somewhat more on community grants than private grants. Outside the grants, some 20 percent of the rural population is believed to have lived on small single-family holding claims perhaps of about 10 acres. See Westphall, *Mercedes Reales*, 11–12, 143–144.

44. Denevan, "Livestock Numbers," 698.

45. Montoya discusses this point in the context of the Maxwell Land Grant. See Montoya, *Translating Property*, 35, 142.

46. Barriero, in Carroll and Haggard, *Three New Mexico Chronicles*, 79, 103. Gutierrez attributes the high incidence of Indian raids to retaliation for Hispanic slave raids on the nomadic tribes. See Gutierrez, *When Jesus Came*, 153. If this is true, the policy of bolstering the colonial economy with Indian slave labor had the countereffect of suppressing the important sheep-growing component of the economy.

47. Dick-Peddie, *New Mexico Vegetation*, 18–19; Denevan, "Livestock Numbers," 691–694; Leopold, "Vegetation," 298–308.

48. Brooks, *Captives and Cousins*, 89–90.

49. Brooks, *Captives and Cousins*, 80.

50. Nostrand, *Hispano Homeland*, 70–97, 214–217.

51. Dunmire, *New Mexico's Spanish Livestock Heritage*, 34, 37, 41.

52. Dunmire, *New Mexico's Spanish Livestock Heritage*, 34, 37, 40–41.

53. Dunmire, *New Mexico's Spanish Livestock Heritage*, 34, 41.

54. Brooks, *Captives and Cousins*, 80, 91, 254.

CHAPTER 2: SHEEP AND THE MARKET ECONOMY

1. Prior to Mexican independence in 1821, foreigners apprehended in the then Spanish colony of New Mexico were subject to arrest, imprisonment, and confiscation of their property.

2. At least two earlier visitors from the United States had previously entered New Mexico but attracted little attention. See Fergusson, *New Mexico*, 236; Horgan, *Great River*, 401–407; Pike, *Expeditions*, 631–632, 739–740; Baxter, *Las Carneradas*, 62–63.

Notes 235

3. Weber, *Mexican Frontier*, 130; Nostrand, *Hispano Homeland*, 101; Kiser, *Borderlands*, 8–9.
4. Armijo's motivation for awarding these overly large land grants is a matter of debate among historians. Armijo apparently received a kickback in the form of partial ownership upon awarding the Beaubien-Miranda Grant. See Westphall, *Mercedes Reales*, 45–46. And that may have also been the case with other grants. It is a matter of speculation that he may also have had the legitimate goal of bolstering the defenses of New Mexico from encroaching Americans by creating large buffer areas in the north. See Westphall, *Mercedes Reales*, 56–57.
5. Charles Beaubien was one of the most notable new arrivals in New Mexico prior to the annexation. He had been quite successful in the fur trade, branched out into more general mercantile activities, and then married into Taos high society, securing for himself a position of status, wealth, and influence. Montoya, *Translating Property*, 31, 38, 49–51, 62, 71, 142; Westphall, *Mercedes Reales*, 44–52; Kiser, *Borderlands*, 89, 168. Maxwell was born in Illinois into an influential fur-trading family and later served, along with Kit Carson, as a scout under General John C. Fremont during his western explorations. He settled in Taos in 1844. A man of considerable energy and industry, he became an astute and highly successful businessman, operating largely within Hispanic customs. Wentworth, *America's Sheep Trails*, 237; Haines, *History*, 244.
6. Montoya, *Translating Property*, 50, 75. A detailed investigation of the dynamics of Anglo-Hispanic intermarriage in Mexican California is presented in Pubols, *Father of All*.
7. Westphall, *Mercedes Reales*, 53–56. Other notable Anglo stockmen in this period were Connecticut-born brothers J. L. "Santiago" Hubbell, married into the distinguished Gutierrez family and believed to have owned 103,000 sheep in 1858, and Sydney A. Hubbell married into the Perea family and believed to have participated in the large 1857 California sheep drive and later became a mine owner and prominent jurist. See Baxter, *Las Carneradas*, 143.
8. There was an overlap between the fur trappers and Santa Fe Trail traders during the early years of the trade.
9. Boyle, *Los Capitalistas*, 17; Meinig, *Southwest*, 17–18; Twitchell, *Old Santa Fe*, 215.
10. Boyle, *Los Capitalistas*, 64, 97; Escudero, in Carroll and Haggard, *Three New Mexico Chronicles*, 66; Nostrand, *Hispano Homeland*, 101. Westbound manufactured goods from the eastern United States were shipped by steamboat to trailheads on the Missouri River, where they were transferred to wagons bound for New Mexico and beyond.
11. Boyle, *Los Capitalistas*, 42, 43, 57–61, 96. See also Fergusson, *New Mexico*, 240; Simmons, *Little Lyon*, 64.
12. There were several reasons for the American's commercial success. See Parish, "German Jew," 2, 9–10; Weber, *Mexican Frontier*, 122; Boyle, *Los Capitalistas*, 60–64; Meinig, *Southwest*, 19.

236 NOTES

13. Prior to the annexation, future New Mexican political leaders and sheepmen attending American schools included J. Francisco Chaves, Francisco Perea, Miguel A. Otero Jr., and Solomon Luna.

14. Gonzales, *Politica*, 164–171; Escudero, in Carroll and Haggard, *Three New Mexico Chronicles*, 61–62. Prior to the annexation, the law of the land in New Mexico had been Spanish civil law, which treated land ownership quite differently than Anglo-American common law. This legal disparity and the accompanying divergent social values have given rise to long and bitter land disputes, some of which persist to the present day. See Ebright, *Land Grants and Law Suits*, 69–70.

15. Kiser, *Borderlands*, 62.

16. Emory, *Lieutenant Emory Reports*, 96; Calvin Ross, "Introduction," in Emory, *Lieutenant Emory Reports*, 16.

17. Gregg, *Commerce of the Prairies*, 135; Pattie, *Personal Narrative*, 77–78; Emory, *Lieutenant Emory Reports*, 48–49, 80, 84.

18. Emory, *Lieutenant Emory Reports*, 47, 60; Abert, *Report*, 456–460; Hughs, *Doniphan's Expedition*, 46; Johnston, *Journal*, 565–614; Ruxton, *Adventures*, 188.

19. Hughs, *Doniphan's Expedition*, 46; Leopold, "Vegetation," 300. Sacaton is a xeric southwestern native grass; DeBuys, *Enchantment*, 188–189.

20. Cooke, *Conquest*, 59; Abert, *Report*, 463; Leopold, "Vegetation," 300.

21. Emory, *Lieutenant Emory Reports*, 54; Johnston, *Journal*, 565–614.

22. In the early nineteenth century, the Spanish government maintained a force of 121 paid soldiers at an annual cost of 240 pesos per man, one seventh the US military's cost per man. This small professional force was augmented by a 1,500-man self-equipped militia in which the men typically served forty-five-day terms of service without compensation. See Pino, in Carroll and Haggard, *Three New Mexico Chronicles*, 68–69; Coan, *History*, 360, 399. During the Civil War, General Carleton's force stationed in New Mexico rose to 3,089 men, although it was reduced after the war. Twitchell, *Old Santa Fe*, 324–325; Kiser, *Turmoil*, 126.

23. Bartlett, *Personal Narratives*, 385–386; Gregg, *Commerce of the Prairies*, 99–100; Emory, *Lieutenant Emory Reports*, 80. The penetration of the railroads west of the Mississippi provided critical support for the army's pacification campaign. Parish, *Charles Ilfeld Company*, 37; *Rocky Mountain News*, April 8, 1868.

24. Nostrand, *Hispano Homeland*, 105–108. The army officers were largely American born, although two-thirds of the enlisted men were born in Europe, largely in Ireland and Germany. When the army established a post at Rayado, the principal settlement on his grant, Maxwell rented out quartering for the soldiers and stables for their horses. He also sold food for the troops and feed for their horses and mules, produce of the grant, charging the high prices that this market would bear. In later years, Maxwell supplied the Jicarilla Indian Reservation with livestock and agricultural produce. See Montoya, *Translating Property*, 51, 70.

25. Boyle, *Los Capitalistas*, 113. Glaab, "Business Patterns," 161.

Notes   237

26. In 1859, 63 of the 112 shipments departing Council Grove, Kansas, the Santa Fe trailhead by then, were Hispanic owned. This amounted to 556 wagons carrying over 1,400 tons and accompanied by 779 men. Boyle, *Los Capitalistas*, 96; Glaab, "Business Patterns," 161–162.

27. Allison, "Santa Fe," 181. Pino is remembered for having written a comprehensive report on conditions in the New Mexico colony during the late Spanish period.

28. Simmons, *Little Lyon*, 50–51, 109–114, 147, 200, 205, 211; Lee, *Bartolome Fernandez*, 32.

29. Simmons, *Little Lyon*, 205.

30. Pittman, "Solomon Luna," 41–42; Larson, *New Mexico's Quest*, 245–247, 275, 277.

31. *Rocky Mountain News*, May 17, 1874; Carman et al., *Special Report*, 922; Fergusson, *New Mexico*, 316–317, 343. Other important Hispanic sheep-growing families were Gutierrez, Lucero, Mirabel, Romero, and Yrisarris, while Captain John G. Clancy and Santiago Hubble were prominent Anglo growers. See Sypolt, "Keepers," 43; Wentworth, *America's Sheep Trails*, 114.

32. Jaramillo, *Romance*, 125; Leonard, *Role of the Land Grant*, 60–61.

33. After the war, the trade in merchandise with Mexico recovered. New Mexico merchant-stockman and later political and military leader Francisco Perea was quite active in that endeavor. Starting in 1849 he made several trading expeditions into Mexico, carrying American manufactured goods, some of which he purchased in New York City. At the same time, he was participating in large sheep drives not to Mexico but to California. See Allison, "Colonel Francisco Perea," 215–216; Boyle, *Los Capitalistas*, 65.

34. Sypolt, "Keepers," 26–27. The herds had been illegally sold off by their politically connected overseers. See Weber, *Mexican Frontier*, 66–67.

35. The Old Spanish Trail went from Abiquiu, New Mexico, to Los Angeles through southwestern Colorado, central Utah, and southern Nevada. Some American traders from New Mexico drove the California horses and mules all the way east to Missouri. Hafen and Hafen, *Old Spanish Trail*, 155, 165–169, 185–188, 206, 211. See also Weber, *Mexican Frontier*, 126–127, 134–135; Boyle, *Los Capitalistas*, 41–42; Hafen, "Old Spanish Trail," 149–160.

36. Sheepherders enjoyed an advantage over those transporting inanimate merchandise in that the sheep provided sustenance on the trail for the herders. See Pittman, "Solomon Luna," 13.

37. Baxter, *Las Carneradas*, 112–114.

38. Angney had arrived in New Mexico with Kearney's army and quickly established himself as a political leader, while Alvarez was a successful Santa Fe–based merchant who had been active for many years and, prior to the annexation, had served as US consul in New Mexico. The two men had served together in the territorial legislature. Baxter, *Las Carneradas*, 114–118.

39. Baxter, *Las Carneradas*, 116–119, 122–124. Sheep had several advantages over cattle on the trails to California. They grazed on any available grass as they were driven

238   NOTES

and after watering bedded down for the night, while cattle would spend the night on their feet grazing and rarely got enough to eat. The flocking instinct of sheep made them easier to drive, whereas cattle were subject to stampede due to thunder and lightning storms, Indian raids, predatory animals, and the smell of water if they were very thirsty. Survival on the trail, therefore, was greater for sheep than cattle. New Mexico was the closest important source of meat to California, and that meat was mutton, because the territory had not yet developed a cattle industry of commercial proportions. See Towne and Wentworth, *Shepherd's Empire*, 101; Chaput, *Francois X. Aubry*, 119.

40. Simmons, *Little Lyon*, 114; Pittman, "Solomon Luna," 14; Baxter, *Las Carneradas*, 119–121; Bartlett, *Personal Narratives*, 293.

41. Antonio Jose Luna's wife was the mother of Solomon Luna, later reputed to be the largest sheep grower in New Mexico. Antonio Jose's paternity is in question, although he seems to have always treated Solomon, who eventually took over the family business, as his own. See Pittman, "Solomon Luna," 59. Baxter, *Las Carneradas*, 121–122.

42. Aubry's biographer believes he probably knew nothing about sheep. Bergan, *The Pathfinder*, 34, 152; Chaput, *Francois X. Aubry*, 120. Francis Aubry was a remarkable man in many ways. He acquired legendary status and the title "Skimmer of the Plains" in 1848 when he rode from Santa Fe to Independence, Missouri, a distance of 780 miles, in five days, sixteen hours, allegedly to win a bet. Hardly stopping to sleep, he tied himself in the saddle to keep from falling when he dozed off. He set a distance-speed record that has never been broken. Aubry got his start as a trader in the spring of 1846 with a $600 loan from his employer, a St. Louis merchant. He proved to be an astute businessman and by the time he entered the sheep trade had amassed a personal fortune estimated at $75,000 ($2.4 million in 2020 dollars). See Bergan, *The Pathfinder*, 1, 54, 63; Chaput, *Francois X. Aubry*, 61–69.

43. Christopher Carson, "The Kit Carson Memoirs, 1809–1856," in Carter, *"Dear Old Kit,"* 132–135nn283–285.

44. Bergan, *The Pathfinder*, 131–132, 142, 146, 152, 156, 166; Baxter, *Las Carneradas*, 126–127. Antonio Jose Otero had been appointed New Mexico Supreme Court judge by Kearny. His nephew, Miguel A. Otero Jr., was later appointed governor of New Mexico by President McKinley. Francisco Perea also became prominent in politics, served as New Mexico's delegate to Congress, became friends with President Lincoln, and was present at Ford's Theater the night Lincoln was assassinated. See Vigil, *Los Patrones*, 53–54.

45. Lee, *Bartolome Fernandez*, 35; Bergan, *The Pathfinder*, 156–157, 165, 197–198; Allison, "Colonel Francisco Perea," 216; Twitchell, *Old Santa Fe*, 346–348.

46. Bergan, *The Pathfinder*, 156.

47. Pittman, "Solomon Luna," 13; Baxter, *Las Carneradas*, 139–144.

48. Pittman, "Solomon Luna," 13; *Santa Fe Weekly Gazette*, October 9, 1858, quoted in Lee, *Bartolome Fernandez*, 35. See also Baxter, *Las Carneradas*, 142–145.

Notes   239

49. By 1870 the California sheep population was 2,768,187; Gordon, "Report," 1000, 1005; Bergan, *The Pathfinder*, 156; Baxter, *Las Carneradas*, 147–148; Allison, "Colonel Francisco Perea," 217.

50. Gordon, "Report," 992. The data given are 1852: 40,000, $12–$15 per head; 1853: 135,000, $9–$12 per head; 1854: 27,000, $3–$4 per head; 1855: 19,000, $3–$4 per head; 1856: 200,000, $3–$4 per head; 1857: 130,000, $3–$4 per head; 1858: "small number"; 1859: 0. The last two entries are clearly erroneous. *Seventh Census, 1850*, 170; Baxter, *Las Carneradas*, 143–150; Sypolt, "Keepers," 30.

51. Baxter, *Las Carneradas*, 128. The Perea, Otero, Armijo, Baca, Jaramillo, Luna, Ortiz, and Pino families dominated the California trade, as they had the Mexican trade. For a more extreme assessment of the *rico-pobre* divide, see Kupper, *Golden Hoof*, 24–25.

52. Sypolt, "Keepers," 30; Carlson, "New Mexico's Sheep Industry," 28–29.

53. Davis, *El Gringo*, 205. W. W. H. Davis became United States attorney for New Mexico in 1853. He later served as secretary of New Mexico and for a time as acting governor.

54. The predominant breed of sheep on these small farms was the Spanish Merino. *Report on Manufacturing Industries, Eleventh Census, 1890*, 15.

55. Gregg, *Commerce of the Prairies*, 99. A few Hispanic sheepmen apparently undertook selective breeding on a small scale, but the practice had not become widespread. Gregg, *Commerce of the Prairies*, 99, 165; Webb, *Adventures*, 101. Other Anglos were also critical of the New Mexicans' wool production. See Pattie, *Personal Narrative*, 71–72, 75; Davis, *El Gringo*, 203–205.

56. Simmons, "Chacon," 87; MacCameron, "Environmental Change," 28.

57. Carlson, *Spanish-American Homeland*, 79; "New Mexico's Sheep Industry," 27; Meinig, *Southwest*, 19; *Seventh Census, 1850*, 1008; *Agriculture of the United States in 1860*, 185; US Department of Agriculture, *Report, 1869*, 621.

58. Surdam, "King Cotton," 122, 125, 128. In 1850 the annual valuation of US cotton product manufacture was $65 million, while the corresponding valuation of woolen manufacture was $43 million with an additional $5 million from carpet manufacture, half this production utilizing imported wool. See *Manufactures of the United States in 1860*, xxi, xxii, xxxv, xxvii. The war not only severed the North-South trade in cotton but devastated the South's cotton industry. Military wool consumption alone in 1862 has been estimated at 50 million pounds, well over half the prewar annual production. See *Manufactures of the United States in 1860*, xxxiv.

59. Sypolt, "Keepers," 139, 326. The prices given here are for Ordinary-Medium wool. To help meet the Civil War demand for wool, Iowa, in particular, was populated with sheep shipped west by rail, an initiative that collapsed after the war. See Wentworth, *America's Sheep Trails*, 138–139, 141–142. The increase in the American West's production was mirrored by international production increases, particularly in Australia, South America, and South Africa, as well as the American Midwest. The 1880 Census reports only 619,000 head of sheep in New Mexico, although

240 NOTES

Gordon ("Report," 992) admitted that this figure was inaccurate. F. A. Manzanares, sheep owner and president of the New Mexico Bureau of Immigration, put the number closer to 3 million. See Manzanares, quoted in Carman et al., *Special Report*, 918–919. A 1962 Department of Agriculture report puts the 1870 sheep population at 1,667,000 and the 1880 count at 4,547,000. New Mexico Department of Agriculture, *New Mexico Agricultural Statistics*, 44. See also figure 1.2.

60. *Report on Manufacturing Industries, Census 1890*, 3–4; *Twelfth Census, 1900*, 9:75; Manzanares, quoted in Carman et al., *Special Report*, 918–919; *Agriculture of the United States in 1860*, 185; *Ninth Census*, 74; *Report on the Productions of Agriculture as Returned at the Tenth Census*, 141. The Census reports from this period can be expected to provide general trends but not accurate absolute values; Grubbs, "Frank Bond," 35:172; Coan, *History*, 390; Carlson, "New Mexico's Sheep Industry," 34.

61. Brooks, *Captives and Cousins*, 254–255, 292–293.

62. Manzanares, quoted in Carman et al., *Special Report*, 918–919; the *Santa Fe New Mexican*, September 1, 1862; US Department of Agriculture, *Report of the Commissioner of Agriculture, 1869*, 623.

63. Brooks, *Captives and Cousins*, 331–332, 334; Weisiger, *Dreaming of Sheep*, 22.

64. Brooks, *Captives and Cousins*, 335–336.

65. Brooks, *Captives and Cousins*, 349–354; Weisiger, *Dreaming of Sheep*, 135.

66. *Rocky Mountain News*, April 8, 1868.

67. Kiser, *Borderlands*, 16, 20–21, 57, 62, 80, 82, 100, 142, 145, 151, 164. A detailed treatment of an 1850 US Senate initiative to ban captive Indian slavery, which did not pass, is given in Magliari, "A Species of Slavery."

68. Robert B. Mitchell, quoted in Lee, *Bartolome Fernandez*, 36. The fact that there was any mention of wool in this report is notable. Jones, "Spiegelbergs and Early Trade," 84.

69. Surdam, "King Cotton," 125; Lehmann, *Forgotten Legions*, 40; Sypolt, "Keepers," 139–140, 326. The price drop has also been attributed in part to a decrease in the national wool tariff. During the brief Franco-Prussian War, international wool prices spiked upward but then quickly settled back down afterward.

70. Wentworth, *America's Sheep Trails*, 285.

71. Boyle, *Los Capitalistas*, 92–93.

72. *Manufactures of the United States, 1860*, xxvii; *Twelfth Census, 1900 Census*, vol. 5, *Agriculture*, ccii.

73. Carman et al., *Special Report*, 919. See also Grubbs, "Frank Bond," 35: 171; Coan, *History*, 389–390.

74. Carman et al., *Special Report*, 919; Wentworth, *America's Sheep Trails*, 237; Gordon, "Report," 989; Haines, *History*, 480; *Rocky Mountain News*, August 22, 1878; Carman et al., *Special Report*, 919. See also Grubbs, "Frank Bond," 35: 171; Coan, *History*, 389–390; Carlson, "New Mexico's Sheep Industry," 32.

75. The common Anglo sentiment at the time was that Hispanic sheepmen were not "lazy or indifferent" but were generally about ten years behind the times in adopting modern growing practices. See Carman et al., *Special Report*, 920.

Notes   241

76. Carman et al., *Special Report*, 922, 926.
77. Wilcox, "Sheep Ranching," 98; Carlson, *Spanish-American Homeland*, 81.
78. Carman et al., *Special Report*, 915, 923.
79. Carman et al., *Special Report*, 926; Wentworth, *America's Sheep Trails*, 565–566.
80. Daniel Troy, quoted in Carman et al., *Special Report*, 931–932.
81. Carlson, "New Mexico's Sheep Industry," 33. At this time the estimated sheep population was 4.5 million so that somewhat less than 2 million were likely to be of improved breeds. See New Mexico Department of Agriculture, *New Mexico Agricultural Statistics*, 44. Gordon's 1880 report estimated that 72 percent of the New Mexico flock were "Mexican sheep," the remainder being various grades of Merino. See Gordon, "Report," 991; Carman et al., *Special Report*, 923; *Report of the Governor of New Mexico, 1905*, 8. TA, roll 149; *Seventeenth Annual Report of the Bureau of Animal Industry for the Year 1900*, 589–590; See also Wentworth, *America's Sheep Trails*, 568; Curtiss and Wilson, "Feeding Range Lambs," 466; Stevens to Wood, August 19, 1899, MSC, Folder 2.
82. Carman et al., *Special Report*, 923–924.
83. As reported by Gov. Prince, two bad winters in a row were in part the cause of a reduction in the New Mexico flock from 1.749 million head in 1887 to 1.340 million in 1888, while wool prices rose from 12–14 cents/lb. in 1888 to 18–20 cents/lb. in 1889. Prince's sheep population numbers are erroneous, but his point is valid. *Report of the Governor of New Mexico, 1889*, 14–15; *Report of the Governor of New Mexico, 1890*, 28. TA, roll 121.
84. Wentworth, *America's Sheep Trails*, 445; Sypolt, "Keepers," 150–152; Carman et al., *Special Report*, 923–924. Throughout the 1880s, wool prices were lower than in the previous decade but still adequate for profits. Sheep prices began increasing after 1886 until the Panic of 1893, when they fell and remained low through 1896. Similarly, wool prices fell and remained quite low between 1893 and 1897.
85. American wool was never exported in quantity, but American wool growers were drawn into a market of international extent, foreign imports being a significant factor.
86. *Report of the Governor, 1905*, 9; Otero, *My Nine Years*, 276, 334.
87. Some investigators questioned the efficacy of the wool and woolen tariffs by the late nineteenth century. See Wright, "Wool Growing," 643–647; Harry F. Lee to A. D. Garrett, January 7, 1908, NMWGA; Harry F. Lee to S. W. McClure, January 2, 1912, NMWGA.
88. Taussig, *Tariff History*, 220, 281, 333. The tariff figure applies to Class I unwashed wool, relevant to American producers, and also Class II wool. At this time, wool was assigned one of three classifications: Class I clothing wool, Class II combing wool, and Class III carpet wool. Almost all carpet wool, the coarsest variety, was imported by about 1890. Western wool was largely coarse clothing wool. See F. W. Taussig, *Some Aspects*, IV.XIX.2–11.

242 NOTES

89. N.a., "New Mexican Sheep Ranchers Face Dwindling flocks," *Santa Fe New Mexican*, October 11, 1987, 87.

90. *Thirteenth Census, 1910*, vol. 10: *Manufacturers, 1909*, 33, 107; See also Cherington, "Some Aspects," 341. The remaining 40 percent of the nation's wool was produced by small flocks of less than a thousand head, incidental to general farming east of the Mississippi River. *Twelfth Census, 1900*, vol. 5: *Agriculture*, 673. See also *Twenty-First Annual Report of the Bureau of Animal Industry for the Year 1904* (Washington: Government Printing Office, 1905), 511–512; *Report on Manufacturing Industries, Eleventh Census, 1890*, 31, 34, 69; *US Census, 1910*, vol. 10: *Manufacturers*, 107.

91. Alexander Majors, quoted in US Department of Agriculture, *Report of the Commissioner of Agriculture, 1870*, 303. See also Latham, *Trans-Missouri*, 6.

92. Latham, *Trans-Missouri*, 3–6. The comments here apply to livestock rather than grain production, however. US Department of Agriculture, *Report of the Commissioner of Agriculture, 1870*, 307; *The Las Vegas Stock Grower*, January 1, 1887.

93. US Department of Agriculture, *Report, 1869*, 378; Wright, "Wool Growing," 629.; Latham, *Trans-Missouri*, 6, 70. Feeding sheep on farm-produced grains was later found to be quite profitable in Kansas, Nebraska, and other Midwestern states, as well as the Far West.

94. Wright, "Wool Growing," 631–635; Latham, *Trans-Missouri*, 46–49; Wentworth, *America's Sheep Trails*, 581. See also US Department of Agriculture, *Report of the Commissioner of Agriculture, 1869*, 378–381.

95. Westphall, *Mercedes Reales*, 145, 193–194, 235–236; Kupper, *Golden Hoof*, 81–82. The first-come-first-served custom worked adequately as long as the ranching and livestock populations remained relatively sparse. In later years, it was the root cause of innumerable range conflicts, which occasionally escalated into out-and-out war, where neither of the opposing parties possessed legal ownership of the lands in contention. These land wars could be particularly vicious when sheepmen were pitted against cattlemen. See Steinel, *History of Agriculture*, 147–148. Under Spanish custom and effectively continuing under American rule, continuous occupancy of a tract of public domain for an extended period conveyed ownership. This would, however, have involved comparatively small tracts of land insufficient for raising large herds of any sort. Westphall, *Public Domain*, 18–19, 50–52; Gordon, "Report," 992. The report identifies these nomadic herders as "Mexican."

96. Brisbin, *Beef Bonanza*, 8–10. It must be noted that Brisbin excluded New Mexico and Texas from his discussion. He was apparently unfamiliar with these areas, but his comments apply equally well to them.

97. Westphall, *Mercedes Reales*, 228–229.

98. Russell, *Land of Enchantment*, 101–102.

99. Brisbin, *Beef Bonanza*, 99; Clay, *My Life on the Range*, 43.

100. Gregg, *Commerce of the Prairies*, 82; Latham, *Trans-Missouri*, 8–22.

101. US Department of Agriculture, *Report of the Commissioner of Agriculture, 1870*, 307; US Department of Agriculture, *Report of the Commissioner of Agriculture, 1869*,

Notes 243

619–623; Carman et al., *Special Report*, 925; Gordon, "Report," 960; Brisbin, *Beef Bonanza*, 92–93; US Department of Agriculture, *Report of the Commissioner of Agriculture, 1868*, 460. See also Wilcox, "Sheep Ranching," 90; Gilfillan, *Sheep*, 16.

102. Wentworth, *America's Sheep Trails*, 346–347, 580; Brisbin, *Beef Bonanza*, 92–93.

103. US Department of Agriculture, *Report, 1869*, 620. By 1892, herders were being paid $15–25/month ($480–$740 in 2020 dollars). See Carman et al., *Special Report*, 924. For comparison, in the western highlands and islands of Scotland in the early twentieth century, an immensely different environment, a single shepherd might manage a flock of five hundred to seven hundred head. See Perry, *I Went a' Shepherding*, 16–17.

104. Brisbin, *Beef Bonanza*, 105–106; Gordon, "Report," 1006; *Rocky Mountain News*, June 4, 1869; Carman et al., *Special Report*, 915.

105. Carlson, "New Mexico's Sheep Industry," 28–29.

106. Sypolt, "Keepers," 83, 141.

107. Steinel, *History of Agriculture*, 147.

108. Carlson, "New Mexico's Sheep Industry," 34; Billington, *Westward Expansion*, 597–598.

109. *Rocky Mountain News*, June 4, 1869; September 25, 1869; April 16, 1873. Latham, *Trans-Missouri*, 16, 86; Carman et al., *Special Report*, 921, 924; Randall, *Practical Shepherd*, 97–99; Sypolt, "Keepers," 142. A particularly large East-West discrepancy was reported in 1862 in which the cost of keeping a flock of 3,000 sheep in the East was $7,950, while the corresponding cost "on the plains" was only $1,200. Carlson, "New Mexico's Sheep Industry," 34–35.

110. This was particularly true in Colorado, where from 1865 through 1888, most growers focused on wool and treated mutton only as a by-product. See Sypolt, "Keepers," 94; *Stock Grower*, February 2, 1889; Parish, *Charles Ilfeld Company*, 144.

111. *New Mexico Agricultural Statistics*, 46.

112. Carman et al., *Special Report*, 914.

113. Towne and Wentworth, *Shepherd's Empire*, 168, 181; Wentworth, *America's Sheep Trails*, 258. Sheep were also driven north from Mexico to New Mexico and Texas as part of the expansion. See Lehmann, *Forgotten Legions*, 70–71.

114. Wentworth, *America's Sheep Trails*, 165. For the statistical sources, see *US Census, 1900*, vol. 5: *Agriculture*, ccxiv. Presented here are revised New Mexico sheep populations for 1860, 1880, and 1890. The 1860 New Mexico sheep population was estimated at 972,000, a 500,000 increase over the reported 1850 population of 377,261, which unfortunately was not regarded as terribly accurate. See *Seventh Census, 1850*, 170; Carman et al., *Special Report*, 920.

115. Towne and Wentworth, *Shepherd's Empire*, 165–181; Wentworth, *America's Sheep Trails*, 258–285. Carman et al., *Special Report*, 920. The primary sources of the Montana, Idaho, and western Wyoming sheep were California and Oregon.

116. Anglos settled early in Huerfano County and the South Park–Colorado Springs area. See Steinel, *History of Agriculture*, 146; Gordon, "Report," 1006. See Latham, *Trans-Missouri*, 73, for a list of the prominent sheepmen. Gordon, "Report," 1006,

244 NOTES

1008; Steinel, *History of Agriculture*, 146; *Rocky Mountain News*, April 18, 1866; July 13, 1877.

117. Sypolt, "Keepers," 105, 111. Wyoming sheep growers also imported sheep possessing various desirable qualities from Canada, Ohio, and Vermont, as well as other Midwestern and eastern states. *US Census, 1900*, Vol. 5: *Agriculture*, ccvi. Sypolt, "Keepers," 107.

118. Sypolt, "Keepers," 126, 324 (appendix I); Clay, *My Life on the Range*, 228.

119. *Twentieth Annual Report of the Bureau of Animal Industry, 1903*, 521.

120. Towne and Wentworth, *Shepherd's Empire*, 170–172, 181; Gordon, "Report," 993, 999, 1001, 1008; Wentworth, *America's Sheep Trails*, 273, 286.

121. Carman et al., *Special Report*, 788–789.

CHAPTER 3: THE INDUSTRY MATURES

1. Gregg, *Commerce of the Prairies*, 99; Baxter, *Las Carneradas*, 28–31; Charles, "Development," 79–82. Baca's flocks provided him a yearly income of 1,500 pesos ($32,000 in 2020 dollars). See Gutierrez, *When Jesus Came*, 326. When the British monetary system was abandoned in America, the dollar was based on the Spanish peso (8 reales). The expression "two bits" comes from the value of two reales, or two pieces of eight, about 25 cents. For much of the nineteenth century, the peso and the US dollar remained about equal in value. See Worster, "Significance of the Spanish Borderlands," 4; McCusker, *How Much Is That?*, 43, 61–62, 84–87.

2. Escudero, in Carroll and Haggard, *Three New Mexico Chronicles*, 40–42. One hundred years later, Fabiola Cabeza de Baca, whose wealthy stock-growing family engaged in numerous *partido* contracts, presented a similarly serendipitous view of the system. See Cabeza de Baca, *We Fed Them Cactus*, 57–58.

3. *Partido* contract, Jesus Armijo y Jaramillo to Cristobal Armijo, 1882, Bernalillo County Records, Albuquerque, NM, trans.; Charles, "Development," 85–86; Gutierrez, *When Jesus Came*, 326–327; Lummis, *Land of Poco Tiempo*, 15–16.

4. Parish, *Charles Ilfeld Company*, 42, 112–134 (chapter 9); Carlson, "New Mexico's Sheep Industry," 35–36; Grubbs, "Frank Bond," 35: 194–195.

5. Kiser, *Borderlands*, 15–16, 20–21, 168–170.

6. This development seems to have occurred around the 1880s. The evidence for it is indirect. As noted in chapter 2, government livestock expert Clarence W. Gordon reported in 1880 that three quarters of New Mexico's sheep were being raised by some twenty-one families, about 80 percent of which were Hispanic. By the 1890s, a large fraction of the sheep that Las Vegas merchant Charles Ilfeld dealt in came from small- and intermediate-scale growers. See Parish, *Charles Ilfeld Company*, 120, 124. And the Bond brothers, heavily involved with wool by the late 1890s, had a similar clientele. See Grubbs, "Frank Bond," 35: 176. Montague Stevens reported in 1898 that the sheep growers in his area, western Socorro County, were almost all

Notes   245

"small holders." See Stevens to Wood, August 26, 1898, MSC, Folder 2. Trade journal reports describing the New Mexico sheep industry, edited by William J. Parish, suggest that by the early twentieth century, most of the large sheep outfits were Anglo owned. Parish, "Sheep Husbandry," 37: 201–213, 260–309; 38: 56–77. When the New Mexico Wool Growers Association was founded in 1906, the membership rose quickly to nearly three-hundred sheepmen. See NMWGA, General Comments; Wentworth, *America's Sheep Trails*, 429; Twitchell, *Old Santa Fe*, 322–323. The total estimated sheep population of New Mexico in 1900 was about 3.5 million. See New Mexico Department of Agriculture, *New Mexico Agricultural Statistics*, 44.

7. Carman et al., *Special Report*, 924.
8. Upon the death of a family patriarch, his property was, by custom, left in part to his wife and in part divided equally among his children, male and female.
9. Parish, *Charles Ilfeld Company*, 42–43, 135–136. The merchants became the sole purveyors of imported eastern merchandise, while providing their customers with the only readily accessible markets for their produce. They provided more limited services to the large-scale, sheep-growing *ricos*.
10. Mercantile establishments were opened early on in Taos, Albuquerque, Socorro, and Trinidad, Colorado. Besides sheep and wool, the new establishments, dealt in a variety of other local produce including lumber, hides, and furs. They remained the most prominent type of merchandising outlets for as long as transport to the eastern markets, was comparatively inefficient and New Mexico's population was sparsely distributed. Only in the twentieth century did industrial capitalism, with its great thrust toward specialization, replace the mercantile mode of commerce in the territory. See Parish, *Charles Ilfeld Company*, 35–36, 60–61, 66.
11. Tobias, *History of the Jews*, 51–102; Parish, "German Jew," 1–29, 129–150; Meinig, *Southwest*, 57; Parish, *Charles Ilfeld Company*, 9. By the late 1860s, merchants Elsburg and Amberg were holding $100,000 worth of stock in Santa Fe and Chihuahua, their initial financial resources having come from outside the territory. And they were carrying a debt obligation of $210,000 to New York creditors ($4.3 million in 2020 dollars). See Parish, *Charles Ilfeld Company*, 10.
12. Boyle, *Los Capitalistas*, 73–88.
13. Parish, *Charles Ilfeld Company*, 42, 154, 162, 168. Ilfeld was listed as the owner of 20,000 sheep on the 1900 New Mexico tax role for San Miguel County, NMSRCA; Charles, "Development," 33; Frank Bond to J. Herbert Reeve, April 5, 1915, Frank Bond & Son Records, 1870–1958, Center for Southwest Research, University of New Mexico, Albuquerque, 82:518. Henceforth, the archive is abbreviated as FBC. Grubbs, "Frank Bond," 35: 299–300; Sypolt, "Keepers," 183.
14. Parish, *Charles Ilfeld Company*, 163, 167.
15. Max Nordhaus to A. G. Mills, January 8, 1898, CIC; Parish, *Charles Ilfeld Company*, 166–167.
16. Grubbs, "Frank Bond," 36:138.
17. Cherington, "Some Aspects," 347–348, 351.

246 NOTES

18. The relationship between merchants and the forts is described in Parish, *Charles Ilfeld Company*, 37–38, 45n14.

19. In a typical arrangement, Charles Ilfeld provided funds to Alfred H. Long of Puerto de Luna to purchase sheep in 1898. See Charles Ilfeld Co. to Alfred H. Long, February 17, 1898, Charles Ilfeld Company Records, 1865–1929 (CIC henceforth), Center for Southwest Research, University Libraries, University of New Mexico, Albuquerque, NM, 107:537. The same year, J. G. Clancey requested a loan of $400 from Las Vegas merchant Gross, Blackwell & Co., with whom he had an account, to pay off a note he had given to the San Miguel Bank. See J. G. Clancey to Gross, Blackwell & Co., March 17, 1898, Gross, Kelly & Co. Records (GKC henceforth), Center for Southwest Research, University Libraries, University of New Mexico, Albuquerque, Gross, Kelly & Co. Records (GKC henceforth), Series II; Frank Bond to V. Jaramillo, El Rito, October 8, 1913, FBC, 77:26.

20. Parish, *Charles Ilfeld Company*, 35–36.

21. Eusebio Garcia y Ortiz to Otero, Sellar & Co., November 12, 1880, GKC, Series I; Sypolt, "Keepers," 159.

22. Parish, *Charles Ilfeld Company*, 113, 121; G. W. Bond to Abraham Staab, May 2, 1902; May 31, 1902; February 21, 1903, FBC, 76:5, 8, 22.

23. The original partners were Maxwell, John Watts, Charles Holly, Peter Maxwell, and Henry Hooper. However, they sold control to attorney–land speculator–politicians Steven Elkins and Thomas Catron only months later. See Larry Schweikart, "Early Banking," 3–5; Jones, "Spiegelbergs and Early Trade," 87; Otero, *My Life, 1864–1882*, 151–152, 234. The mercantile enterprise subsequently became Gross, Blackwell & Co. in 1881 and later Gross, Kelley & Co. in 1901. Western banks typically charged a monthly interest rate of 1.5 percent for loans, not only because of the considerable risk of the livestock business but largely because of the shortage of funds available and the resulting competition for loans. Cashier, First National Bank of Santa Fe, quoted in Larry Schweikart, "Early Banking," 13.

24. Cattle markets developed at Ft. Craig and Ft. Fillmore on the Rio Grande, Ft. Union near Las Vegas, Ft. Marcy in Santa Fe, and Ft. Stanton in the Lincoln Mountains. During the war, General Carleton purchased cattle from local ranchers, including Maxwell. See Baydo, "Cattle Ranching," 86; Parish, *Charles Ilfeld Company*, 42.

25. Stevens to Wood, July 5, 1903, MSC, Folder 3, notes the dearth of outside sheep investors; John Clay, who represented English and Scottish investors during the cattle bubble, says almost nothing about sheep in his book *My Life on the Range*, although he is known to have had a business relationship with Frank Bond.

26. Gressley, *Bankers and Cattlemen*, 62–88; Clay, *My Life on the Range*, 22, 77, 80. Many investors lost their entire investment following the horrendous winter of 1886–1887 and the wholesale destruction of cattle herds it brought on. See Clay, *My Life on the Range*, 178–179, 208.

Notes 247

27. Latham, *Trans-Missouri*, 70–71; Brisbin, *Beef Bonanza*, 101. The transcontinental railroad was completed in 1869; the AT&SF Railway reached Las Vegas, New Mexico, in 1879.
28. Bond, "Memoirs," 340. The D&RGW Railroad—the so-called Chili Line from Antonito, Colorado—had reached Espanola, just south of Chamita, in 1880, three years before. See Gjevre, *Chili Line*, 4.
29. Parish, *Charles Ilfeld Company*, 135; Carlson, "New Mexico's Sheep Industry," 36.
30. *Thirteenth Census, 1910*, vol. 7: *Agriculture*, 148, 155; *Report on the Productions of Agriculture as Returned at the Tenth Census*, 141; *Statistics of the Population of the United States at the Tenth Census*, 72; *Report of the Governor, 1905*, 12; Fergusson, *New Mexico*, 321.
31. Wentworth, *America's Sheep Trails*, 158.
32. *Rocky Mountain News*, November 1, 1866; September 10, 1867. The terminology is somewhat confusing in that the term "feeder" was employed to describe both a farmer or rancher specializing in livestock feeding and also a sheep or lamb destined for a feeding facility.
33. Dick-Peddie, *New Mexico Vegetation*, 19. The utility of supplemental feeding was, in fact, recognized in New Mexico as early as 1700, when grasses were grown in the Rio Grande Valley for this purpose. See Wentworth, *America's Sheep Trails*, 496. But the practice did not become widespread at that time. Of course, winter feeding was absolutely required for raising sheep in the East.
34. Clarke, "Lamb Feeding," 277; Carman et al., *Special Report*, 921.
35. Steinel, *History of Agriculture*, 150. Sugar beets were also grown in New Mexico.
36. Taylor, "On Importance," 294–296; Wilcox, "Sheep Ranching," 79–80.
37. Carman et al., *Special Report*, 925; Taylor, "On Condition," 116–117. Interestingly, the south-to-north shipment of livestock mimicked to an extent the natural migration of the once great buffalo herds on the western ranges. The wild beasts ranged north during the summer months for the grass but went south in the winter to breed. Reported in the *Stock Grower*, July 6, 1889.
38. Carman et al., *Special Report*, 924.
39. Steinel, *History of Agriculture*, 150; Wentworth, *America's Sheep Trails*, 265–266, 285. Western sheep-population statistics are given here. A discussion of Colorado cattle feeding is given in Standart, "On Condition," 326–334.
40. Clarke, "Lamb Feeding," 275–277; *The Stock Grower*, February 2, 1889; Steinel, *History of Agriculture*, 150–151.
41. Wentworth, *America's Sheep Trails*, 366–369; Parish, "Sheep Husbandry," 37: 210–213. Florsheim later acquired Steven Dorsey's huge ranch in northeastern New Mexico, when Dorsey went bust, due at least in part to his legal expenses arising from the Star Mail Route trials. See the *Weekly Optic and Stock Grower*, August 5, 1905. Some feeding took place on the Western Slope of the Rockies after the establishment of sugar factories in the region. Clarke, "Lamb Feeding," 275.
42. Taylor, "Conditions," 331. The Nebraska feeding industry served not just New Mexico breeders but also those of Colorado, Wyoming, Idaho, and even Oregon.

248 NOTES

See Wentworth, *America's Sheep Trails*, 158–159, 347–350, 370–371; *Stock Grower and Farmer*, August 7, 1897, 10. Cattle and hog feeding were also important industries in Nebraska. The growth of the Kansas feeding industry is reflected by a sixteen-fold increase of the Kansas alfalfa crop between 1891 and 1904 to meet the needs of the industry, while the alfalfa acreage increased from 34,400 acres to 557,500. See Graham, "Alfalfa," 242.

43. R. F. Hardy, quoted in Heath, "Condition," 318; Wentworth, *America's Sheep Trails*, 362; Clarke, "Lamb Feeding," 276–277.

44. *Report of the Governor of New Mexico, 1910*, 31; (Territorial Archives of New Mexico, Microform Edition (TA henceforth), roll 188; Carlson, "New Mexico's Sheep Industry," 37; Wentworth, *America's Sheep Trails*, 496; Wilcox, "Sheep Ranching," 94–96.

45. *Report of the Governor of New Mexico, 1897*, 371. Described herein are the rapidly developing irrigation projects in New Mexico, which would increase the agricultural capacity of the territory significantly, the raising of alfalfa in particular. *Stock Grower*, January 1, 1887; Parish, *Charles Ilfeld Company*, 177–178.

46. Hicks, "Western Middle West," 66; Wright, "Wool Growing," 641.

47. Parish, *Charles Ilfeld Company*, 118, 127, 132. P. G. Scott, president of the Bent County Bank and a feeder himself, financed feeding operations for a hundred miles in each direction along the Arkansas Valley. See Wentworth, *America's Sheep Trails*, 366–367; Frank Bond to Clay-Robinson & Co., Denver, October 12, 1914, FBC, 80:456; Frank Bond to Clay, Robinson & Co., Denver, CO, February 8, 1915, FBC, 82:13; Frank Bond to E. S. Leavenworth, Wood River, NE, August 23, 1915, FBC, 84:472; Grubbs, "Frank Bond," 36: 291–292.

48. DeBuys, *Enchantment*, 189.

49. The vegetation designations of Dick-Peddie are employed here. Other researchers use somewhat different designations for similar environments. Dick-Peddie, *New Mexico Vegetation*, 18–20, 104–106.

50. Dick-Peddie, *New Mexico Vegetation*, 106–110, 129–132.

51. Dick-Peddie, *New Mexico Vegetation*, 29, 91–93; DeBuys, *Enchantment*, 196.

52. Dick-Peddie, *New Mexico Vegetation*, 18–20, 32, 36; DeBuys, *Enchantment*, 189, 196.

53. Denevan, "Livestock Numbers," 699; Dick-Peddie, *New Mexico Vegetation*, 27–30, 92–93; DeBuys, *Enchantment*, 193–194.

54. An arroyo is a gully that runs intermittently with storm runoff or snowmelt. Arroyos are one of the commonest features of the Southwestern landscape. Denevan, "Livestock Numbers," 702; DeBuys, *Enchantment*, 194.

55. Denevan, "Livestock Numbers," 691–699, 702.

56. Denevan, "Livestock Numbers," 702; Dick-Peddie, *New Mexico Vegetation*, 92–93, 87, 91.

57. Meinig, *Southwest*, 34.

58. DeBuys, *Enchantment*, 189; Nostrand, *Hispano Homeland*, 183; Leopold, "Vegetation," 304.

59. Nostrand, *Hispano Homeland*, 183.

60. Weisiger, *Dreaming of Sheep*, 128–132.

Notes   249

61. Weisiger, *Dreaming of Sheep*.
62. The case of the Pablo Montoya Grant discussed is a good example of this departure scenario. Fergusson, *Home in the West*, 8.
63. New Mexico author Fabiola Cabeza de Baca is a representative of this trajectory. Born into a wealthy cattle and sheep ranching family in the late nineteenth century, she worked as an adult as an agent for the Agricultural Extension Service. See Tey Diana Rebolledo, "Introduction," in Cabeza de Baca, *We Fed Them Cactus*, xv.
64. *1897 Actas de la Asemblea del Territorio de Nuevo Mexico*, 105–110; *1903 Acts of the Legislative Assembly of the Territory of New Mexico*, 108–113. The measure passed with remarkably little fanfare. It is never mentioned in the detailed running account of the legislative activities published in the *Daily New Mexican* during the 1897 session.
65. Solomon Luna, in *Report of the Governor, 1910*, 330; Grubbs, "Frank Bond," 36:287; H. H. Lee to All Inspectors, July 20, 1901, "Records of the Territorial Boards and Commissions," microfilm edition of the Territorial Archives of New Mexico, New Mexico State Records Center and Archives, Santa Fe NM, Roll 95 (TA).
66. Luna, in *Report of the Governor, 1910*, 330; FBC, 76:82 (loose page). The territory imposed a fine of a cent/head. NMWGA Records, 1912.
67. Luna, "The Annual Address of Hon. Solomon Luna," *Addresses at Second Annual Convention of the New Mexico Wool Growers Association*, ***October 7 – October 8, 1907, NMWGA.
68. The association was in communication with Gifford Pinchot, President Theodore Roosevelt's prominent head of the National Forest Service, concerning the National Forest Reserves. See Harry F. Lee to George M. Black, November 7, 1907, NMWGA; Harry F. Lee to George S. Wolker, October 22, 1908, NMWGA; "Resolutions of the 1912 Convention," NMWGA.
69. Harry F. Lee to J. H. Bearrup, June 14, 1907; Harry F. Lee to Eulogio Pacheco, February 16, 1907. NMWGA.
70. Harry F. Lee to A. D. Garrett, January 7, 1908. NMWGA; Harry F. Lee to S. W. McClure, January 2, 1912, NMWGA.
71. Wilcox, "Sheep Ranching," 98.
72. Daniel Troy, quoted in Carman et al., *Special Report*, 931–932. See also Remley, *Bell Ranch*, 99, for a discussion of the economies of scale realized at the Bell Ranch, although this discussion applies most directly to cattle. In their efforts to acquire the Antonio Ortiz Grant, Thomas Catron and Steven Elkins tracked down some of the heirs, a surviving son and several grandchildren relocated in Juarez, Mexico, for the purpose of buying up their shares. TBC, Series 305, Microfilm Reel 5. In situations like these, the obligations to the settlers that went with the private grants were sometimes ignored by the new owners, giving rise to considerable conflict.
73. Olen E. Leonard's 1940 study of the village of El Cerrito and the surrounding area, within the San Miguel del Bado Grant, noted a large decrease in the number of major Hispanic sheep owners after the end of the nineteenth century, a result of

250 NOTES

the loss of the common grant lands to public domain. In the same period, Anglo cattle and sheepmen purchased land and established large ranches on the grant. Leonard, *Role of the Land Grant*, 14, 17–18; Carman et al., *Special Report*, 927.

74. Heath, "Condition," 312.

75. Westphall, *Public Domain*, 49–50. According to Brayer, over 80 percent of the Spanish-Mexican grants were eventually taken over by Americans. See Brayer, *William Blackmore*, 17–19.

76. Remley, *Bell Ranch*, 67–68, 95–97; Ebright, *Land Grants and Law Suits*, 42–43. Attorney John S. Watts received half the massive Pablo Montoya Grant from the heirs in payment for his legal services around 1867. A considerable body of work, including case studies of specific grants, has been devoted to this land-transfer from Hispanic to Anglo ownership. The lands included both the immense common-land tracts of community grants and the private grants that had been traditionally dedicated to livestock grazing, mostly sheep. Fine works on the subject include previously cited works by Ebright (*Land Grants and Law*) and Westphall (*Mercedes Reales*) and by Van Ness and Van Ness, eds., *Spanish and Mexican Land Grants in New Mexico and Colorado*.

77. Bloom, "Necrology."

78. Westphall, *Public Domain*, 49–50, 68; Montoya, *Translating Property*, 52–54; Remley, *Bell Ranch*, 67–68, 97; Westphall, *Mercedes Reales*, 154–156. As was largely the case for the Montoya Grant, much of the grant land initially passed into the hands of Anglo cattlemen but was employed for sheep growing in later years.

79. Remley, *Bell Ranch*, 154, 302–303. Greenough was a cousin of historian Francis Parkman.

80. Julian, "Land Stealing." By the late nineteenth century, substantial sheep-ranching operations had spread to areas outside the periphery of the Spanish-Mexican land grants in today's Union, Guadalupe, Quay, Catron, and Valencia Counties. See *US Census, 1900*, vol. 5: *Agriculture*, 463, 679; Pittman, "Solomon Luna," 41–42.

81. Roe Lovelace, Oral History, conducted October 29, 2007, by Donna M. Wojcik, FR. Remley has noted that many grant heirs, like those of the Pablo Montoya Grant who sold out to Anglo speculators, were cash poor. See Remley, *Bell Ranch*, 39.

82. The Timber Culture Law, in effect from 1873 through 1891, was another vehicle for obtaining western land, but it was never employed extensively in New Mexico. See Westphall, *Public Domain*, 72–76.

83. Parish, *Charles Ilfeld Company*, 175. Scrip was a veterans' benefit. It had been issued to veterans of the Civil War and other wars and could be exchanged for public land without meeting the residence or improvement requirements of the Homestead Act. It was transferable and could thus be purchased by anyone and used to acquire public land. Westphall, *Public Domain*, 42–65, 81.

84. Montague Stevens, quoted by Roy Willoughby, 16, from personal correspondence with Montague Stevens; Cleaveland, *No Life for a Lady*, 226–227; Westphall,

Notes 251

Mercedes Reales, 185–187; Westphall, *Public Domain*, 55–56; Parish, *Charles Ilfeld Company*, 176.

85. Cleaveland, *No Life for a Lady*, 33; Westphall, *Public Domain*, 43–46, 66.

86. Westphall, *Public Domain*, 48–49, 56–60, 62–65.

87. Westphall, *Public Domain*, 53–54.

88. Westphall, *Public Domain*, 65, 79–80, 136–145.

89. Kupper, *Golden Hoof*, 89. In 1902, Thomas Catron, like many other sheepmen, invested in irrigation, a saw mill, a dipping facility, and fencing at his American Valley Company ranch. Thomas B. Catron Papers, Center for Southwest Research, University Libraries, University of New Mexico, Albuquerque, NM (TBC henceforth), Series 601, Vol. 2.

90. This practice followed the custom in rural America, which, unlike that of England, was to fence out livestock and fence in crops to protect them from wandering livestock. See Hayter, "Livestock-Fencing," 12.

91. *Report of the Governor of New Mexico, 1897*, 367–368; Wentworth, *America's Sheep Trails*, 408–409; Towne and Wentworth, *Shepherd's Empire*, 202; Erna Fergusson, 328. Roe Lovelace's family raised sheep and cattle in the same pastures on their ranch in Corona. See Lovelace, ibid.

92. US Department of Agriculture, *Annual Report of the Secretary of the Interior, 1885*, I:471–472.

93. Westphall, *Public Domain*, 111–113, 153; Remley, *Bell Ranch*, 98–99. The Cimarron and Renello Cattle Company fenced 276,000 acres of public domain in San Miguel County. Farther south, Greyson and Borland fenced in 100,000 acres in Socorro County. See also Hayter, "Barbed Wire Fencing," 196; Cleaveland, *No Life for a Lady*, 140, 320.

94. Cleaveland, *No Life for a Lady*, 140, 320. *News and Press* (Cimarron, NM), June 24, 1880. The cost breakdown on a per mile basis reported in the article was about $100 for wire, $16 for posts, $18 for setting the posts, and $8 for stretching the wire and incidentals.

95. Rosenbaum, *Mexicano Resistance*, 99–110, 122; Cabeza de Baca, *We Fed Them Cactus*, 89–90.

96. Hayter, "Livestock-Fencing," 18–20.

97. *New Mexico Blue Book, 1913*, 25–26.

98. Wells in New Mexico generally ranged from 125 to 400 feet in depth. John Cauhape, Oral History, conducted and recorded by Marcie Palmer, April 13, 2001, FR; Fergusson, *New Mexico*, 352; Remley, *Bell Ranch*, 186.

99. Carman et al., *Special Report*, 926. Kupper presents accounts of sheepmen who had achieved extraordinary success but only through hard work and conscientious, hands-on management. See Kupper, *Golden Hoof*, 62–70. Frank Bond expressed similar sentiments, cf. chapter 4. Las Vegas political leader and sheepman Secundino Romero was sent a letter every few weeks by his majordomo, Ricardo Gauna, keeping him apprised of the condition and location of his herds. See Secundino

252 NOTES

Romero Papers, Center for Southwest Research, University Libraries, University of New Mexico, Albuquerque, NM; Remley, *Bell Ranch*, 125–164.

100. Peggy Sultemeier, Oral History, conducted and recorded by Ramona Caplan, July 31, 2004, FR. Typically, about 4 percent of the mature ewes were barren, while about 4 percent–5 percent of them aborted each year. And about 5 percent–10 percent of the lambs born each spring died within the first three weeks. See Gordon, "Report," 990–991; Carman et al., *Special Report*, 923.

CHAPTER 4: FRANK BOND'S SHEEP EMPIRE

1. Frank Bond to M. B. Otero, January 19, 1914, FBC, 77:669–670.
2. Frank Bond's activities additionally encompassed hides, pelts, lumber, feeder ranches, land speculation, and community service. Grubbs, "Frank Bond," 35:173, 36:303.
3. Grubbs, "Frank Bond," 35:174, 177. For his 1958 University of New Mexico master's thesis and the series of *New Mexico Historical Review* articles drawn from it, Frank H. Grubbs painstakingly extracted basic financial data pertaining to the various Bond enterprises by drawing together fragmentary information from a variety of sources, many poorly documented, in the voluminous Frank Bond & Son Records, 1870–1958, at the Center for Southwest Research, University of New Mexico, Albuquerque. Grubbs's work will be cited extensively in this chapter. Documentation of the Bond brothers' first decade in business contained in the collection is rather sparse, however.
4. Bond, "Memoirs," 340.
5. *Las Vegas Stock Grower*, November 20, 1886, 7.
6. Bond, "Memoirs," 347–348.
7. Frank Bond to G. W. Bond, September 19, 1910, FBC, 76:133–136; Frank Bond to J. H. Sargent, October 29, 1913, FBC, 77:155; Frank Bond to J. H. McCarthy, July 2, 1915, FBC, 84:3; Frank Bond to Sostenes Lucero, January 28, 1915, FBC, 81:625.
8. Grubbs, "Frank Bond," 35:179–180, 35:296.
9. Frank Bond to Clay, Robinson & Co., February 8, 1915, FBC, 82:13; Wentworth, *America's Sheep Trails*, 434.
10. Grubbs, "Frank Bond," 35:181; Frank Bond to C. J. Stauder, October 16, 1914, FBC, 80:509.
11. Frank Bond to J. H. McCarthy, February 8, 1915, FBC, 82:12–13.
12. Bond, "Memoirs," 347–348; Frank Bond to Brown & Adams, April 23, 1902; April 25, 1902, FBC, 76:3, 4; G. W. Bond to Brown & Adams, June 27, 1903, August 1, 1903, FBC, 76:40, 48–49; Grubbs, "Frank Bond," 35:182–183, 35:195–196.
13. Grubbs, "Frank Bond," 36:139–143; These figures come from a rather simplistic bookkeeping system that may overstate the returns. Nevertheless, the returns were quite large. See Grubbs, "Frank Bond," 36:141, table 19; 156, table 27; 154–155.

Notes   253

14. Grubbs, "Frank Bond," 36:158, table 29; G. W. Bond & Bro. to A. Staab, February 21, 1903, FBC, 76:22; G. W. Bond to R. J. Palen, June 8, 1903, FBC, 76:38.
15. Parish, *Charles Ilfeld Company*, 101–103; Grubbs, "Frank Bond," 36:140.
16. The branch was first opened in Cabra, twenty-two miles north of Santa Rosa, in 1899 but later relocated to Cuervo (probably in 1902) when the railroad bypassed Cabra; Grubbs, "Frank Bond," 36:231–233.
17. Grubbs, "Frank Bond," 36:325–328.
18. Frank Bond to Fairbanks, Morse & Co., December 3, 1914, FBC, 81:203. Grubbs, "Frank Bond," 36:288, 299. Western New Mexico sheep grower Montague Stevens had invested $2,500 in an extraordinarily well-equipped dipping facility at his Horse Springs Ranch in 1899. See Montague Stevens to Leonard Wood, August 1, 1899, MSC, Folder 2. See also Montague Stevens to Leonard Wood, April 4, 1897, MSC, Folder 2.
19. Grubbs, "Frank Bond," 36:150–151.
20. Frank Bond to Walter M. Connell, July 17, 1914, FBC, 79:374.
21. Grubbs, "Frank Bond," 36:158.
22. Grubbs, "Frank Bond," 35:298–299; 36:274–275, 284, 303.
23. Frank Bond marketed his Nebraska-fed sheep in Omaha. See Frank Bond to Clay, Robinson & Co., October 12, 1914, FBC, 80:457; Frank Bond to H. A. Wiest, June 25, 1913, FBC, 76:169–170; Frank Bond to G. W. Bond, September 19, 1910, FBC, 76:133–136; Frank Bond to H. S. Eaton, March 11, 1914, FBC, 78:423; Frank Bond to J. E. D. Graham, December 31, 1914, FBC, Vol. 81:406; Frank Bond to Clay, Robinson & Co., Denver, Colo., February 8, 1915, FBC, 82:13; G. W. Bond & Bro. to Fred Warshauer, March 6, 1903, FBC, 76:33; Frank Bond to G. W. Bond, February 21, 1908, FBC, 76:93–94; Frank Bond to G. W. Bond, February 21, 1908; September 19, 1910, FBC, 76:93–94, 133–136; Frank Bond to C. J. Stauder, October 16, 1914, FBC, 80:509. Bond borrowed $65,000 at 9 percent from Clay, Robinson for the winter of 1914 and shipped his lambs to the company in the spring. See Frank Bond to Clay, Robinson & Co., February 8, 1915, FBC, 82:13; Frank Bond to E. S. Leavenworth, August 23, 1915, FBC, 84:472; Frank Bond to Walter M. Connell, July 23, 1914, FBC, 79:439–440; Grubbs, "Frank Bond," 35:185, 35:301, 36:284, 36:285, 36:290; 36:291.
24. Grubbs, "Frank Bond," 35:196, table 10, 35:199, 35:299–301.
25. Frank Bond to Walter M. Connell, July 17, 1914, FBC, 79:374; Frank Bond to J. H. McCarthy, July 17, 1914, FBC, 79:371. Grubbs, "Frank Bond," 36:336–345, 37:51, 56, table 55, 37:61.
26. The Preston Beck Grant was part of the Hacienda de San Juan Bautista del Ojito del Rio de las Gallinas awarded to Juan Esteven Pino, son of Pedro Pino, in 1825. He was said to have run as many as 900 cows and 30,000 sheep and goats on the grant. Pino's heirs, plagued by Indian raids, sold the grant to Beck in 1853–1854. The Bonds purchased a relatively small tract within the grant in 1900 from a later owner and ran sheep on that land. Frank Bond to G. W. Bond, March 16, 1910, FBC, 76:123–127; Grubbs, "Frank Bond," 35:199, 36:146–147, 36:289, 36:305–306.

254 NOTES

27. Frank Bond to G. W. Bond, July 17, 1914, FBC, 79:382; Bond & Nohl to K. O. Windsor, March 10, 1915, FBC, 82:318; Bond & Nohl to Geo. J. Constantine, August 31, 1909, FBC, 76:122. This citation is a letter for a job offer for a stenographer at $75/month, with an advance in salary if the employee learned Spanish and learned the business. Frank Bond to J. N. N. Quintana, January 1, 1914, FBC, 77:599; Grubbs, "Frank Bond," 36:292–293.

28. Frank Bond to G. W. Bond, September 23, 1910, FBC, 76:137–139; Grubbs, "Frank Bond," 36:286.

29. Grubbs, "Frank Bond," 36:331, table 50.

30. Frank Bond to Mrs. Fred Warshauer, June 5, 1913; July 2, 1913, FBC, 76:168, 171–174; Grubbs, "Frank Bond," 35:301–302; Pittman, "Solomon Luna," 97–98.

31. Frank Bond to S. H. Wilts, April 5, 1915, FBC, 82:534–535. Wilts was president of the John Page Plow Company.

32. Brown & Adams to Frank Bond, October 16, 1914, FBC, 80:582–584; Brown & Adams to Bond-Connell Sheep & Wool Co., October 13, 1914, FBC, 80:585. A typical letter of this sort in the company records from wool brokers Salter Bros. & Co., Boston, to Frank Bond discusses London wool auctions, US purchases, current domestic needs, Australian shipments to the United States, and Arizona wool prices and supply. Salter Bros. & Co. to Frank Bond, March 19, 1915, FBC, 82:445–447; Parish, *Charles Ilfeld Company*, 138; Frank Bond to Earnest A. Johnston, January 2, 1915, FBC, 81:419.

33. Frank Bond to A. W. Wiest, June 11, 1915, FBC, 83:459.

34. Frank Bond to Warshauer-McClure Sheep & Wool Co., July 28, 1915, 84:238; Frank Bond to Fred Warshauer, February 25, 1903; February 28, 1903, FBC, 76:27–30; G. W. Bond & Bro. to Brown & Adams, June 25, 1904, FBC, 76:67–68; Grubbs, "Frank Bond," 36:242, 36:320–322.

35. Grubbs, "Frank Bond," 36:143, 36:236, 36:280–281, 36:283, 328–329; table 49 gives the actual receivables, charged-off amounts, and subsequently collected amounts from 1905 through 1915 for the Bond, McCarthy Company, the Taos branch. The losses only exceeded 10 percent in one year and were usually far less. Bond & Nohl Co. to K. G. Dunn & Co., February 27, 1915, 82:234; Bond & Nohl Co. to the American Adjusting Company, April 17, 1915, FBC, 82:600; April 29, 1915, FBC, 82:701; Benj[amin] M. Read to Bond & Nohl Co., June 14, 1915, FBC, 83:510; L. F. Nohl to Miss May T. Bryan, March 9, 1914, FBC, 78:404; L. F. Nohl to Miss Clara D. True, March 22, 1915, FBC, 82:418.

36. Bond, "Memoirs," 343.

37. Bond, "Memoirs," 349. See also Grubbs, "Frank Bond," 35:194n.

38. Walter, "Necrology," 273. Frank Bond died in Los Angeles in 1945 at age 82 or 83.

39. The twentieth-century activities of the Bond family in the Valle Grande are described in Martin, *Valle Grande*, 55–72.

Notes 255

CHAPTER 5: MONTAGUE STEVENS, GREAT PROMISE AND HARSH REALITY

1. Western Socorro County became today's Catron County. The Stevens Collection, housed at the Center for Southwest Research, University of New Mexico, Albuquerque, covers a range of matters pertaining to the sheep business, particularly the capital requirements, but also the risks and labor issues in the late nineteenth- to early twentieth century. The letters provide, furthermore, significant insights into a notable rancher's life during this period. They also express his sometimes-harsh assessments of the Hispanic herders and sheepmen he encountered, assessments with which many western Anglos would agree. Stevens wrote *Meet Mr. Grizzley: A Saga on the Passing of the Grizzley*, an authoritative work on hunting dogs and bear hunting in New Mexico.
2. Stevens was born three years before Frank Bond. Stevens, *Rambling through the 1880s*, 15, 82.
3. Otero, *My Life, 1864–1882*, 265; Otero, *My Life, 1882–1897*, 35–40, 52–53. Apparently, a number of wealthy Englishmen settled in Western Socorro County and took up ranching. See Stevens, *Rambling through the 1880s*, 15–17, 49. Similarly, a considerable number of Englishmen settled in West Texas and took up sheep ranching. See Kupper, *Golden Hoof*, 65–70. The Morley family, who developed a notable cattle-ranching operation, arrived in the area during this period. Their experiences, and contact with Stevens, are chronicled in Agnes Morley Cleaveland's memoir, *No Life for a Lady*. Stevens was remarkably well connected. He, Miles, Wood, and painter Frederick Remington hunted together. Some years later Stevens planned a western hunting trip with Theodore Roosevelt, which, however, never took place.
4. Stevens, *Rambling through the 1880s*, 42–44, 83. This is not to be confused with the disastrous winter of 1886–1887, which destroyed cattle ranches farther north, from Montana to Texas. Montague Stevens to Leonard Wood, September 7, 1897, MSC, Folder 2; Stevens, *Rambling through the 1880s*, 44.
5. Stevens, *Rambling through the 1880s*, 83–88, 91–93, 100; Stevens to Wood, August 14, 1905, MSC, Folder 3. Helen Stevens received these funds over a period of several years, investing some of the money in sheep. Like her husband, she was bold, resilient, and self-reliant and apparently had few misgivings about exchanging England, and a predictable life of wealth and privilege, for ranch life in rural New Mexico, three days by buggy from the nearest town, Magdalena—four days if the road conditions were poor. Helen recovered her health to a significant extent in the dry southwestern climate and led an active life as a ranch wife. See Stevens to Wood, March 2, 1897, September 20, 1897, MSC, Folder 2. She died in Albuquerque in 1946 at the age of eighty-two.
6. Stevens to Wood, March 21, 1898, MSC, Folder 2; William J. Parish, "Sheep Husbandry," 37: 265, 304.

256 NOTES

7. Stevens to Wood, May 20, 1897, MSC, Folder 2; Stevens to Wood, August 14, 1905, MSC, Folder 2, 36 pages!

8. Stevens had apparently been running cattle on this property previously, as evidenced by a running notice in the Las Vegas *Stock Grower*. See, e.g., the *Stock Grower*, September 25, 1886. See also Stevens, *Rambling through the 1880s*, 41. The terms were fairly typical for large property transfers in New Mexico. Stevens eventually did purchase the S.U. Ranch land on his own account for an unknown amount; he later sold it, probably the land only, for $6,000. See Stevens to Wood, May 26, 1918, MSC, Folder 3.

9. Stevens to Wood, February 27, 1896; March 24, 1896; April 30, 1896; May 20, 1897, MSC, Folder 2.

10. Wood's check was apparently never cashed.

11. "Judge Field" was possibly Judge Stephen Johnson Field, associate justice of the United States Supreme Court, 1863–1897. Stevens to Wood, April 30, 1896; December 10, 1897; March 21, 1898, MSC, Folder 2; Stevens to Wood, November 4, 1897; December 28, 1897, MSC, Folder 2; Stevens to Wood, October 10, 1897; February 16, 1898, MSC, Folder 2; Stevens to Wood, November 8, 1897; December 10, 1897, MSC, Folder 2.

12. Stevens to Wood, April 30, 1896, MSC, Folder 2; Stevens to Wood, May 9, 1896, MSC, Folder 2.

13. Stevens to Wood, May 31, 1896, MSC, Folder 2.

14. Stevens to Wood, May 31, 1896, MSC, Folder 2. Stevens was prepared to pay about twice what Hispanic herders were then being paid. Stevens to Wood, April 4, 1897, MSC, Folder 2; Stevens to Wood, August 14, 1905, MSC, Folder 3.

15. Stevens to Wood, August 2, 1896, MSC, Folder 2; Stevens to Wood, September 17, 1896, MSC, Folder 2; Stevens to Wood, October 21, 1896, MSC, Folder 2; Stevens to Wood, April 4, 1897, MSC, Folder 2. Later in fall 1896, Stevens took time off to take large party including General Miles bear hunting. See Stevens to Wood, October 21, 1896, MSC, Folder 2.

16. Stevens to Wood, August 2, 1896, MSC, Folder 2; Stevens to Wood, March 5, 1897, MSC, Folder 2; Stevens to Wood, April 4, 1897, MSC, Folder 2; Stevens to Wood, May 20, 1897, MSC, Folder 2.

17. Stevens to Wood, March 21, 1897; April 4, 1897, MSC, Folder 2; G. S. Davis, "Report, The Shropshire Sheep Company," October 6–8, 1897, MSC, Folder 2.

18. Stevens to Wood, July 6, 1897, MSC, Folder 2.

19. Stevens to Wood, March 21, 1897, MSC, Folder 2; Stevens to Wood, May 20, 1897; June 26, 1897, MSC, Folder 2.

20. First National Bank of Albuquerque to Wood, September 29, 1897, MSC, Folder 2; Stevens to Wood, August 1, 1897, MSC, Folder 2; Stevens to Wood, October 10, 1897, MSC, Folder 2; Stevens to Wood, December 10, 1897, MSC, Folder 2. This winter range tract was about fifty miles northwest of Magdalena on Alamosa Creek, which empties into the Rio Puerco.

Notes 257

21. Stevens to Wood, October 10, 1897, MSC, Folder 2.

22. Stevens to Wood, October 10, 1897, MSC, Folder 2; Stevens to Wood, September 5, 1909, MSC, Folder 3.

23. Stevens's holdings, in addition to the rams, now consisted of 8,176 bearing ewes, 2,437 lambs, and 310 wethers. Of these 3,308 were graded Arizona ewes and 4,868 "Mexican" ewes. See G. S. Davis, foreman, Report of the Shropshire Sheep Company, October 10, 1897, MSC, Folder 2; Stevens to Wood, December 10, 1897, MSC, Folder 2; Parish, "Sheep Husbandry," 37:201–213, 260–309; 38:56–77.

24. See Stevens to Wood, August 14, 1905, MSC, Folder 3. This depressed price for the Spur Ranch was confirmed in later correspondence. The property has the earmarks of a ranch illegally constituted from a large number of homesteads. Stevens to Wood, February 1, 1903, MSC, Folder 3; Stevens to Wood, April 21, 1898, MSC, Folder 2.

25. Stevens to Wood, August 1, 1899, MSC, Folder 2.

26. Stevens to Wood, August 26, 1898; August 1, 1899, MSC, Folder 2.

27. Stevens to Wood, January 1, 1914, MSC, Folder 3; Stevens, an extraordinarily robust man despite the loss of his arm, died in 1953 at the age of ninety-four. See Stevens, *Rambling through the 1880s*, 44, 134; Stevens to Wood, August 19, 1899, MSC, Folder 2.

28. Sypolt, "Keepers," appendixes 2, 4, 5, and 6; Stevens to Wood, August 1, 1899, MSC, Folder 2; Pittman, "Solomon Luna," 50.

29. Sypolt, ibid.; Stevens to Wood, ibid.; Pittman, ibid.

30. Stevens to Wood, June 25, 1899, MSC, Folder 2; Stevens to Wood, August 1, 1899, MSC, Folder 2; First National Bank of Albuquerque to Wood, December 11, 1899, MSC, Folder 2.

31. In later correspondence, Stevens stated that the Horse Springs Ranch, the land itself, had cost him $3,300 while the former owners, cattle investors, had paid $25,000 for the property before the cattle bubble burst. See Stevens to Wood, August 14, 1905, MSC, Folder 3; Stevens to Wood, August 1, 1899, MSC, Folder 2.

32. Stevens to Wood, ibid.; Stevens to Wood, August 1, 1899, MSC, Folder 2.

33. Stevens to Wood, written from August 1, 1899, through December 23, 1899, MSC, Folder 2. This seventeen-page letter is the source for the next several paragraphs.

34. Stevens to Wood, September 9, 1900, MSC, Folder 2; Stevens to Wood, August 25, 1902, MSC, Folder 3; Stevens to Wood, August 6, 1904, MSC, Folder 3; Stevens to Wood, December 2, 1902, MSC, Folder 3.

35. Stevens to Wood, December 2, 1902, MSC, Folder 3.

36. Stevens to Wood, December 2, 1902, MSC, Folder 3.

37. Stevens to Wood, July 5, 1903, MSC, Folder 3.

38. Stevens to Wood, July 5, 1903, MSC, Folder 3; Stevens to Wood, December 2, 1902, MSC, Folder 3.

39. Stevens was hardly unique in his low opinion of Hispanic labor. His sentiments were widespread among Anglos at this time. Thomas Catron's majordomo of the

258 NOTES

American Valley Company, Charles Elmendorf, made an almost identical assessment. See Elmendorf to John Morrison, January 25, 1901, TBC, Series 602, Box 1. Anglo farmers in Texas on the lower Rio Grande held almost identical opinions of their Hispanic laborers. See Montejano, *Anglos and Mexicans*, 76–79; Stevens to Wood, August 14, 1905, MSC, Folder 3. See also Leonard, *Role of the Land Grant*, 49, 149–150. Sarah Deutsch has described the late nineteenth- through early twentieth-century exodus from New Mexico villages in considerable detail. See, in particular, Deutsch, *No Separate Refuge*, 20–40.

40. Stevens to Wood, August 14, 1905, MSC, Folder 3.

41. Stevens to Wood, August 14, 1905, MSC, Folder 3.

42. Stevens to Wood, August 6, 1904, MSC, Folder 3; Stevens to Wood, August 14, 1905, MSC, Folder 3. Lambing was always an exhausting period of very long workdays for western sheepmen. See Gilfillan, *Sheep*, 102–103, 129.

43. Stevens to Wood, August 2, 1905; August 14, 1905, MSC, Folder 3. It should be noted that many men found Stevens difficult to get along with, which may have exacerbated his labor difficulties. He drove himself relentlessly and expected much from his employees, who had far less to gain from their jobs. He was a humorless, loquacious man, and his personality traits apparently did not sit well with some people who had to deal with him. See Stevens, *Rambling through the 1880s*, 16, 63.

44. Stevens to Wood, August 14, 1905, MSC, Folder 3; Stevens to Wood, July 5, 1903, MSC, Folder 3.

45. Guy Spears, who owned a ranch in the Datil area in the early twentieth century, complained that nobody wanted employment as a herder and the resulting labor shortage eventually devastated the sheep business in the area. See Guy Spears, Oral History, conducted and recorded by Jacky Barrington, 1981–1983, FR.

46. Stevens to Wood, January 28, 1914; May 26, 1918, MSC, Folder 3; Stevens to Wood, September 5, 1909, MSC, Folder 3; Stevens to Wood, August 14, 1905, MSC, Folder 3.

47. Stevens to Wood, September 5, 1909, MSC, Folder 3.

48. Stevens to Wood, August 6, 1904; August 14, 1905, MSC, Folder 3; Stevens, *Rambling through the 1880s*, 44, 134.

CHAPTER 6: THOMAS CATRON AND FINANCING A WESTERN SHEEP RANCH

1. The Republican Party identified strongly with Lincoln and was the dominant political party in New Mexico throughout the post–Civil War territorial period, when Catron was active.

2. Everything Catron did in his long, active life was infused with bluster, contention, and questionable tactics. His ranching experiences present a particularly dramatic picture of the new financial challenges and how they could be approached.

3. Westphall, *Thomas Benton Catron*, 1–21.

Notes 259

4. Westphall, *Thomas Benton Catron*, 33–73. Catron is remembered today largely as a "land grabber," one of a small group of men, mostly lawyers, who flocked to New Mexico after the Civil War and employed what are widely regarded as unethical or legally questionable means to acquire large tracts of grant land, to the detriment of the grantees and their heirs. As such, he has been identified with the infamous "Santa Fe Ring."

5. Westphall, *Mercedes Reales*, 28, 195; *Thomas Benton Catron*, 87–88, 150–152; *Public Domain*, 56–61. This land was United States public domain, having been in the Mexican public domain prior to the United States–Mexico War. Catron to Neill B. Field, September 22, 1892, TBC 105, 5:349; Catron to W. L. Rynerson, September 22, 1892, TBC 105, 5:352. All citations from the Catron Collection, CSWR, will be designated TBC with a series number. Elkins served as New Mexico's delegate to the US House of Representative from 1873 to 1877. Later, he relocated to West Virginia and became a noted industrialist, secretary of war under President Benjamin Harrison, and a US senator from West Virginia.

6. C. H. Elmendorf to William Watson, April 14, 1900, TBC 105, 18:191–193. It is unclear exactly how much Catron paid the Casey family for its interest in the company. The details are confusing, but it was around $9,000. See Catron to Elmendorf, December 20, 1905, TBC 105, 24:432–435. Catron, always short of cash, applied to an Albuquerque investor for a loan of $1,500–$2,000, which he needed to pay off Casey. See Catron to S. M. Folsom, June 29, 1887, TBC 105, 1:214; Catron to John P. Casey, August 23, 1887, TBC 105, 1:278–280. Catron and Atkinson had contributed about 1,400 head of cattle and about 4,000 acres of land; Slaughter, about 9,000 head of cattle and about 4,000 acres of land. See "American Valley Company Incorporation Papers," August 2, 1886; "Articles of Incorporation of the American Valley Company," August 2, 1886; "Tax Receipt, No. 851," February 10, 1888; "Schedule of Real and Personal Property," March 1888, TBC 611, Box 2.

7. Catron to Field, September 22, 1892, TBC 105, 5:349; Catron to Rynerson, September 22, 1892, TBC 105, 5:352; Westphall, *Thomas Benton Catron*, 154–158; Westphall, *Public Domain*, 60; Otero, *My Life, 1882–1897*, 134–135.

8. Elmendorf to William Watson, April 14, 1900, TBC 105, 18:191–193; Field to Ada Atkinson, November 2, 1896; November 17, 1896, TBC 611, Box 2; Elmendorf to William Watson, April 14, 1900, TBC 105, 18:191–193; Field to Ada Atkinson, November 2, 1896; November 17, 1896, TBC 611, Box 2; Elmendorf to Ed Beeler, October 2, 1899, TBC 601, 1:7; Elmendorf to J. F. Lederer, August 14, 1899, TBC 105, 15:986–987. As of January 1896, the company debts had essentially been paid off. See Field to Ada Atkinson, January 8, 1896; August 7, 1898, TBC 611, Box 2; Elmendorf to J. O'C. Roberts, November 15, 1900, TBC 602, Box 3, Folder R-Z.

9. Thomas Creigh to Elmendorf, March 21, 1901; December 6, 1901; February 11, 1902, TBC 602, Box 2, Folder C; Elmendorf to Ada I. Atkinson, June 16, 1899, TBC 105, 16:11–14.

260 NOTES

10. Catron to Field, December 10, 1896; Field to Catron, December 18, 1896, TBC 611, Box 2; Catron to Field, December 23, 1896, Field to Catron, December 28, 1896, TBC 106, Box 1, Folder 6; Field to Catron, February 25, 1897, TBC 106, Box 2, Folder 5.

11. Clancy to Catron, May 19, 1899, TBC 103, Box 7, Folder 1; Catron to Field, November 30, 1896, TBC 611, Box 2; Creigh to J. O'C. Roberts, October 29, 1900, TBC 602, Box 3, Folder A-E; Elmendorf to Alice Atkinson Smith, December 2, 1901, TBC 602, Box 2, Folder M-Z; Elmendorf to E. W. Irwin, August 9, 1901, TBC 601, 2:46.

12. Creigh to Elmendorf, September 27, 1900, TBC 602, Box 3, Folder A-E; Creigh to Elmendorf, October 27, 1900; December 11, 1900; May 8, 1901, TBC 602, Box 1, Folder C; Ada I. Atkinson to Elmendorf, June 8, 1902, TBC 602, Box 2, Folder A-B; Creigh to Elmendorf, September 16, 1901, TBC 602, Box 2, 1st Folder C; R. J. Palen to Elmendorf, November 9, 1900; November 12, 1900, TBC 602, Box 3, Folder F-P. The funds were obtained from a loan of $20,000 from another source, also used to pay off another debt—to John Collinson—as discussed below. See Elmendorf to Creigh, November 1, 1901, TBC 602, Box 2, 1st Folder C; Creigh to Elmendorf, November 4, 1901, TBC 602, Box 2, 2nd Folder C.

13. John D. Patterson to Elmendorf, October 25, 1899, TBC 602, Box 3, Folder F-P.

14. Elmendorf to Patterson, October 20, 1899, TBC 601, 1:55–57. In fall 1899, as the ranch rebirth was getting underway, Catron was preparing briefs for the US Supreme Court. See Elmendorf to B. F. Deatherage, September 30, 1899, TBC 601, 1:1; Elmendorf to A. E. Macomber, September 7, 1899, TBC 601, 1:17; Elmendorf to Richard D. Powell, September 30, 1899, TBC 601, 1:5; Elmendorf and Catron to Palen, February 17, 1900, TBC 601, 1:129–130.

15. Elmendorf to Patterson, October 20, 1899, TBC 602, Box 3, Folder F-P. (The same letter appears in TBC 601, 1:55–57.) "History of the Company," TBC 601, 1:274; Elmendorf to C. R. Hall, June 13, 1901, TBC 602, Box 2, Folder D-M; Catron to Elmendorf, August 25, 1904, TBC 105, 23:339–340; William J. Parish, "Sheep Husbandry," 37: 201–213, 260–309; 38: 56–77.

16. Catron to Elmendorf, December 19, 1906, TBC 105, 25:341–343.

17. Elmendorf and Catron to Palen, February 17, 1900, TBC 105, 18:129–130.

18. Catron to Steven B. Elkins, March 28, 1900, TBC 105, 17:447. In a 1903 statement proposing the sale of the company to Elmendorf, Catron noted that $50,000 of the proceeds should go to Elkins. By 1910, Elkins is known to have owned 1,160 shares, a substantial block of stock. See Catron to Elmendorf, April 22, 1903, TBC 105, 21:289; Catron to S. P. Allen, May 2, 1910, TBC 105, 29:578.

19. The Slaughter buyout involved the transfer of only 200 shares, the balance of Slaughter's shares having ended up in the possession of others. See Elmendorf to W. E. Moses, April 28, 1902, TBC 601, 2:58–59; Elmendorf and Catron to Palen, February 17, 1900, TBC 601, 1:129–130. (This is also contained in TBC 105, 18:129–130.) Several offers by Elmendorf to buy back the stock held by private investors are contained in TBC 601, 1:249–256.

Notes 261

20. Elmendorf to Charles R. Hall, August 4, 1902, TBC 601, 2:87–89; Elmendorf to Andreas A. Romero, September 8, 1900, Romero to Elmendorf, August 31, 1900; September 15, 1900, TBC 602, Box 3, Folder R-Z; Elmendorf to Clay Robinson & Co., September 17, 1900, TBC 601, 1:372–373.

21. Elmendorf to John D. Patterson, May 21, 1900, TBC 601, 1:236–237; Elmendorf to Concho National Bank, June 29, 1900, TBC 601, 1:268; Elmendorf to San Angelo National Bank, June 29, 1900, TBC 601, 1:269. The company had accounts at two banks in San Angelo, Texas. David Walsh to Elmendorf, August 24, 1900, TBC 602, Box 3, Folder R-Z; Elmendorf to J. B. Williams, November 19, 1900, TBC 601, 1:480–481; Elmendorf to E. Taussig, June 1, 1901, TBC 601, 2:34. In this letter Elmendorf was negotiating to purchase sheep dip for 10,000 head. Elmendorf to John V. Morrison, May 16, 1901, TBC 601, 2:8; Elmendorf to Hall, August 4, 1902, TBC 601, 2:87–89.

22. "Memorandum of Agreement," May 31, 1879, TBC 103, Box 7; Catron to Elmendorf, January 30, 1901, TBC 602, Box 1, Folder C; Elkins to Catron, May 15, 1899, TBC 103, Box 7; Catron to Elmendorf, February 1, 1900, TBC 601, 1:91–94; Catron to Elmendorf, March 31, 1901, TBC 602, Box 1, Folder C; Catron to Elmendorf, September 17, 1901, TBC 602, Box 2, 2nd Folder C; Catron to Elmendorf, December 20, 1905, TBC 105, 24:432–435. "Deed," TBC 602, Box 1, Folder C.

23. Elkins to Elmendorf, December 24, 1900, TBC 602, Box 1, Folder D-F.

24. Catron to Elmendorf, January 26, 1901 (letter misprints the date as January 26, 1900), TBC 602, Box 1, Folder C. The "deed of trust" referred to here seems to have involved Elkins fractional ownership of the grant. Catron to Elmendorf, February 4, 1901, TBC 602, Box 1, Folder C; Catron to Elmendorf, March 22, 1901, TBC 602, Box 1, Folder C.

25. Collinson to Elmendorf, April 12, 1901, TBC 602, Box 1, Folder C; Elmendorf to Collinson, May 16, 1901, TBC 601, 2:11; Collinson to Elmendorf, May 16, 1901; May 17, 1901, TBC 602, Box 1, Folder C; Collinson to Elmendorf, July 16, 1901; Catron to Elmendorf, July 7, 1901, TBC 602, Box 2, Folder C (letter misprints date as July 7, 1902).

26. Elmendorf to Collinson, May 16, 1901, TBC 601, 2:11; Elmendorf to Catron, September 7, 1901, TBC 103, Box 13, Folder 4.

27. Collinson to Brown Bros. & Co., September 3, 1901, TBC 602, Box 2, 1st Folder C; Catron to Elmendorf, September 21, 1901, TBC 602, Box 2, 2nd Folder C; Elmendorf to Collinson, May 16, 1901, TBC 602, Box 1, Folder C; Collinson to Brown Bros. & Co., September 3, 1901, TBC 602, Box 2, 1st Folder C; Collinson to Elmendorf, September 3, 1901, TBC 602, Box 2, 1st C Folder; Catron to Elmendorf, October 16, 1901, Elmendorf to Catron, October 25, 1901, TBC 602, Box 2, 1st C Folder; Catron to Elmendorf, October 23, 1901, TBC 105, 19:221–223.

28. Catron to Elmendorf, April 23, 1901, TBC 105, 18:808; Catron to Elmendorf, September 19, 1901, TBC 602, Box 2, 2nd Folder C; Catron to Elmendorf, October 1, 1901, TBC 602, Box 2, 1st Folder C; Elmendorf to Bank of Waco (incorrectly addressed, should have been Waco State Bank), May 18, 1901, TBC 601, 2:29; Waco State Bank to FNBSF, May 24, 1901, TBC 602, Box 1, Folder R-S.

262 NOTES

29. Catron to Elmendorf, January 21, 1901, TBC 602, Box 1, Folder C.

30. Catron to Elmendorf, April 25, 1901, TBC 105, 18:812; Elmendorf to Collinson, November 1, 1901, TBC 602, Box 2, 1st Folder C; Catron to Elmendorf, October 28, 1901; March 21, 1902, TBC 602, Box 2, 2nd Folder C.

31. John E. Ryan to Elmendorf, July 25, 1900, TBC 602, Box 3, Folder R-Z; John V. Morrison to Elmendorf, January 30, 1901, TBC 602, Box 1, Folder M; Elmendorf to James G. Smith, March 12, 1901, TBC 602, Box 1, Folder T-Z; Smith to Elmendorf, February 23, 1901, TBC 602, Box 1, Folder R-S (one of many letters from January through May 1901); Elmendorf to Smith, March 12, 1901, TBC 602, Box 1, Folder T-Z.

32. Morrison to Elmendorf, April 23, 1901, TBC 602, Box 1, Folder M; Morrison to Elmendorf, May 4, 1901, TBC 602, Box 1, Folder M.

33. Morrison to Elmendorf, May 29, 1901, TBC 602, Box 1, Folder M; Catron to Elmendorf, June 17, 1901, TBC 602, Box 2, 2nd Folder C.

34. Morrison to Elmendorf, November 5, 1901, April 16, 1902, TBC 602, Box 2, Folder D-M.

35. Elmendorf to Catron, September 14, 1901, TBC 103, Box 13, Folder 4; Elmendorf to Catron, October 28, 1901, TBC 602, Box 2, 2nd Folder C; E. J. McLean & Co. to Elmendorf, January 18, 1902, TBC 602, Box 2, Folder D-M.

36. Elmendorf to Catron, April 23, 1902, TBC 602, Box 2, Folder A-B. See also Elmendorf to John E. Ryan, May 21, 1900, TBC 601, 1:232–234.

37. Catron to Elmendorf, October 23, 1901, TBC 105, 19:221–223; Catron to Elmendorf, August 16, 1901, TBC 602, Box 2, 1st Folder C.

38. Elmendorf to Catron, February 12, 1902; March 12, 1902; March 24, 1902, TBC 602, Box 2, 2nd Folder C; Catron to Elmendorf, n.d., TBC 602, Box 2, 1st Folder C; Catron to Elmendorf, April 21, 1902, TBC 105, 19:438–441.

39. Elmendorf to Hall, August 4, 1902, TBC 601, 2:87–89.

40. Catron to Elmendorf, January 10, 1903, TBC 105, 21:18–20; Catron to Elmendorf, February 28, 1903, TBC 105, 21:190–191; Catron to Elmendorf, February 3, 1903, TBC 105, 21:98–99. Solomon Luna had been running a herd of 40,000 head in this period. See Stevens to Wood, September 7, 1897, MSC, Folder 2; Catron to Elmendorf, March 30, 1903, TBC 105, 21:232–233.

41. Catron to Elmendorf, August 29, 1904, TBC 105, 23:345–346; Catron to Elmendorf, August 25, 1904, TBC 105, 23:339–340; Catron to Elmendorf, April 19, 1905, TBC 105, 23:838–841.

42. Catron to W. N. Coler, May 15, 1901, TBC 105, 18:878–879.

43. Elmendorf to Morrison, May 16, 1901, TBC 601, 2:8.

44. Geo. Hastings to Elmendorf, August 22, 1900; August 28, 1900, TBC 602, Box 3, Folder F-P.

45. Edgar Mels to Elmendorf, November 8, 1901, TBC 602, Box 2, Folder D-M. Mels thought he might be able to sell a few bonds. James M. Brown & Co. to Elmendorf, October 24, 1901, TBC 602, Box 2, Folder A-B; Catron to Elmendorf, April 2, 1902; Elmendorf to Catron, April 7, 1902, TBC 602, Box 2, 2nd Folder C.

Notes 263

46. Catron to Elmendorf, April 21, 1902; April 25, 1902, TBC 105, 19:438–441, 461–463, respectively. Catron to Elmendorf, May 16, 1902, TBC 105, 20:34–37; Elmendorf to Catron, March 5, 1902, TBC 602, Box 2, 1st Folder C.
47. Catron to Elmendorf, March 19, 1903, TBC 105, 21:190–191; Catron to Elmendorf, June 17, 1904, TBC 105, 23:191–192; Catron to Elmendorf, March 28, 1906, TBC 105, 24:732; Elmendorf to Catron, April 29, 1901, TBC 602, Box 1, Folder C.
48. Catron to Elmendorf, April 19, 1904, TBC 105, 23:11–17; Catron to Julia Catron, May 16, 1902, TBC 105, 20:16–18.
49. Catron to Elmendorf, March 14, 1901, TBC 602, Box 1, Folder C; Catron to L. C. Nelson and J. M. Nelson Jr., May 28, 1904, TBC 105, 23:111–113; various sources, TBC 602, Box 1, Folder G-L; Catron to Elkins, November 19, 1904, TBC 105, 23:481; Catron to Elmendorf, October 27, 1904, TBC 105, 23:382–383; Catron to Elmendorf, March 28, 1906, TBC 105, 24:732; Elmendorf to E. G. Stoddard, June 4, 1902, TBC 601, 2:80–81; Catron to Elmendorf, September 16, 1908, TBC 105, 28:103.
50. Catron to Elmendorf, n.d., TBC 105, 28:275–277. Catron lost his interest in the Mora Grant in 1913 for unpaid taxes, and he no longer had an interest in the Ortiz Grant at the time of his death. TBC 306, Microfilm HD266 N6 T472 1992, Reel 11. In 1915, the courts overturned Catron's claim of ownership of the Anton Chico tract; it would seem the tract had never been his to mortgage. Catron was still fighting in the courts to reclaim the Anton Chico lands at the time of his death.
51. Catron to Elmendorf, October 29, 1903; April 4, 1904; April 8, 1904; April 14, 1904, TBC 105, 22:200–201, 649–650, 654, 685–687, respectively.
52. Catron to Elmendorf, March 30, 1903, TBC 105, 21:232–233; Catron to Elmendorf, April 19, 1904, TBC 105, 23:11–17; Catron to Elmendorf, May 2, 1904, TBC 105, 23:75; Catron to Elmendorf, June 17, 1904, TBC 105, 23:191–192; Catron to Elmendorf, December 19, 1906, TBC 105, 25:341–343; Catron to Elmendorf, January 5, 1905; January 7, 1905, TBC 105, 23:585, 588–592, respectively; Catron to Elmendorf, January 13, 1905; February 6, 1905, TBC 105, 23:610–611, 658–659, respectively.
53. Catron to Elmendorf, April 10, 1905, TBC 105, 23:805; Catron to Elmendorf, December 20, 1905, TBC 105, 24:432–435; Catron to Elmendorf, May 12, 1906, TBC 24:854–855; Catron to Elmendorf, February 14, 1907, TBC 105, 25:437; Catron to Elmendorf, August 14, 1908, TBC 105, 28:17–18.
54. Catron to Elmendorf, January 30, 1905, TBC 105, 23:642–643; Catron to Elmendorf, n.d., probably May 12, 1906, TBC 105, 24:848–851; Catron to Elmendorf, April 16, 1904, TBC 105, 23:3–5; Catron to Elmendorf, October 27, 1904, TBC 105, 23:382–383; Catron to Elmendorf, April 26, 1905, TBC 105, 23:853–854; Catron to Gross, Kelly & Co., February 4, 1909, TBC 105, 28:197; Catron to Elmendorf, December 20, 1905, TBC 105, 24:432–435.
55. Catron to George M. Catron, June 5, 1904; July 15, 1904; August 9, 1904, TBC 105, 23:220, 247, 299, respectively; Catron to W. G. Walz, November 21, 1904, November 25, 1904, TBC 105, 23:487, 496, respectively. Three years earlier, Walz had transferred $3,000 to Catron for a loan of some sort. See Walz to Catron, September 22,

264 NOTES

1901, TBC, 103, Box 13, Folder 4; Catron to Elkins, November 19, 1904; March 30, 1905, TBC 105, 23:481, 777, respectively; Catron to Elmendorf, August 11, 1904, TBC, 105, 23:311–314; Catron to Elkins, November 19, 1904, TBC, 105, 23:481; Catron to Elkins, March 30, 1905, ibid.; Catron to Elmendorf, December 19, 1906, ibid.; Catron to Elkins, February 23, 1907, TBC, 105, 25:454.

56. Catron to Elmendorf, September 16, 1908, TBC 105, 28:99; Catron to C. H. Stoll, January 19, 1909, TBC 105, 28:178–179; Catron to Rule, January 17, 1911, TBC 105, 30:393–394; Catron to Allen, January 3, 1910, TBC 105, 29:236; Catron to Allen, May 3, 1910, TBC 105, 29:581–582; Catron to Allen, April 23, 1910; May 2, 1910, TBC 105, 29:545, 578, respectively.

57. Catron to Allen, August 5, 1911, TBC 105, 31:159–160. The Bosque del Apache Grant, heavily mortgaged, was still in Catron's name at the time of his death in 1921. See Westphall, *Thomas Benton Catron*, 385n. In 1939, it was acquired by the federal government and converted into a national wildlife refuge. Catron to Elmendorf, June 22, 1909, TBC 105, 28:347–348.

CHAPTER 7: THE END OF THE OPEN RANGE

1. Turner, "The Significance of the Frontier in American History," in *Frontier and Section*, 37, 62.
2. Wright, "Wool Growing," 639; Wilcox, "Sheep Ranching," 98.
3. Wright, "Wool Growing," 638.
4. Culbert, "Cattle Industry of New Mexico," 166.
5. Westphall, *Public Domain*, 120.
6. *Report of the Governor, 1897*, 367–368; Taylor, "Conditions," 331–332. See also Clay, *My Life on the Range*, 338.
7. Parish, *Charles Ilfeld Company*, 174. Homesteading apparently started comparatively early in the Roswell area, although on a fairly small scale. See Shinkle, *Fifty Years of Roswell History*, 72–73, 128–129; Meinig, *Southwest*, 43.
8. Westphall, *Public Domain*, 50–52.
9. Westphall, *Public Domain*. The late-nineteenth-century government report of Carman et al. asserted that because of the unfavorable land laws, New Mexico sheep owners were not building reservoirs or drilling wells, which would have brought more land into production. See Carman et al., *Special Report*, 926; Taylor, "Conditions," 331–332; Wilcox, "Sheep Ranching," 98.
10. *New Mexico Blue Book, 1913*, 25. The growth of agriculture in New Mexico was part of a larger process in which homesteaders took up lands in the semi-arid West, the last public lands still available for homesteading by that time. See Hicks, "Western Middle West," 74.
11. Bryant, *History of the Atchison*, 191–196; Remley, *Bell Ranch*, 193.
12. Large tracts of land placed in the public domain by the courts had been the common-land portions of Spanish-Mexican community grants. Converting this

Notes 265

land to public domain was a massive injustice to the grantees on the part of the federal government. Westphall, *Mercedes Reales*, 271–272. These farming data were compiled by Westphall from the census reports of 1890, 1900, and 1910. For a more complete discussion of the growth of farming in New Mexico in this period, see *New Mexico Blue Book, 1913*, 24–26; Prince, *Concise History*, 213.

13. New Mexico Department of Agriculture, *New Mexico Agricultural Statistics*, 44–46; Clay, *My Life on the Range*, 228. World War I brought about a further reduction of grazing areas in New Mexico when it created a soaring demand for agricultural products. Prices increased correspondingly, and New Mexico farmers responded by increasing production dramatically. From 1916 to 1918, the acreage devoted to wheat production nearly doubled, that devoted to beans quadrupled, and that devoted to other crops, particularly corn and potatoes, likewise increased considerably. See *New Mexico Blue Book, 1919*, 94. For a well-grounded fictional depiction of the confrontation of New Mexico ranchers (cattle in this case) with homesteaders, see Richter, *Sea of Grass*.

14. Meinig, *Southwest*, 66–67. According to one report, Wilson Waddingham, founder of the immense Bell Ranch, placed a large number of cattle on his range that was later considered over twice the optimal number for sustained operations. See Remley, *Bell Ranch*, 4–5, 100, 106; Lovelace, ibid.

15. Wilcox, "Sheep Ranching," 86–87. This scenario as it played out in Wyoming some time after 1880 is described briefly in Clay, *My Life on the Range*, 36.

16. Taylor, "Conditions," 350; Troy Brothers, quoted in Heath, "Condition," 317; Taylor, "On Condition," 106–107; Kupper, *Golden Hoof*, 87–88.

17. Meinig, *Southwest*, 67.

18. See Cabeza de Baca, *We Fed Them Cactus*, 152–153, for a personal account of this land degradation scenario in the Ceja-Llano country of eastern New Mexico. Clay, *My Life on the Range*, 23; Taylor, "On Condition," 106; Westphall, *Public Domain*, 46; Meinig, *Southwest*, 67. A second wave of immigrant farmers arrived ten years later as conditions on the Great Plains once again appeared favorable. They were better prepared and more successful than their predecessors.

19. Westphall, *Public Domain*, 45–46. Cabeza de Baca, *We Fed Them Cactus*, 152–153, gives a personal account of this scenario.

20. Cabeza de Baca, *We Fed Them Cactus*, 152; Andy Wiest, quoted in Grubbs, "Frank Bond," 36:239; *The New Mexico Blue Book, 1917*, 41–42.

21. A list of recent New Mexico homestead patents published in the Las Vegas *Stock Grower* in 1889 includes many Spanish names. See *Stock Grower*, April 28, 1889, p. 8. See also Carlson, "Long Lots," 56. Deutsch, *No Separate Refuge*, 31, describes the downside of homesteading from the Hispanic standpoint. Gordon, "Report," 992.

22. Taylor, "Conditions," 330. The government report, furthermore, described the area once available for grazing sheep as "now very much curtailed." *Stock Grower*, June 8, 1889. See also Wilcox, "Sheep Ranching," 98.

23. Wasser, "Early Development," 63–65.

266 NOTES

24. Carman et al., *Special Report*, 923; Cabeza de Baca, *We Fed Them Cactus*, 133, 153.
25. Wright, "Wool Growing," 638; *Annual Reports of the Department of Agriculture, 1915,* 46; Gonzales, *Politica*, 801; see also Sypolt, "Keepers," 156; Gulliford, *Wooly West*, 63, 77–84; Theodore Roosevelt, quoted in Gulliford, *Wooly West*, 84.
26. Gulliford, *Wooly West*, 80–84.
27. Cleaveland, *No Life for a Lady*, 320–321; Wasser, "Early Development," 67. See chapter 4 for an account of Montague Stevens's experience with Cebola National Forest Reserve. Mr. Morgan, quoted in Reeve, "Sheep Industry in Arizona," 246–247.
28. *Annual Reports of the Department of Agriculture, 1914,* 9–10; "The National Forests," in *Annual Reports of the Department of Agriculture, 1915,* 46–47; Gulliford, *Wooly West*, 65.
29. Deutsch, *No Separate Refuge*, 31, 40; Gonzales, *Politica*, 801.
30. There were, in fact, several reasons for this development. Hispanics were pushed off lands they had long occupied by losses of grant lands to Anglo speculators, degradation of long-overstocked lands remaining in their possession, and human population growth, which had diminished the size of the agricultural long lots allocated to each family on community grants, together with the inability of their patrones to provide competitive compensation for their labor. The matter of ever-narrowing long lots is discussed in Carlson, "Long Lots," 55–57; Nostrand, *Hispano Homeland*, 139–143; Deutsch, *No Separate Refuge*, 18, 31–33; Carman et al., *Special Report*, 920–921; Sypolt, "Keepers," 122–123; DeBuys, *Enchantment*, 167, 180; Gonzales, *Politica*, 801; Gulliford, *Wooly West*, 48.
31. DeBuys, *Enchantment*, 167, 180.
32. Deutsch, *No Separate Refuge*, 33, 35.
33. Deutsch, *No Separate Refuge*, 33–34; Nostrand, *Hispano Homeland*, 147–149.
34. The factual material in this section, unless otherwise noted, is drawn from Weisiger, *Dreaming of Sheep*, 125–235.
35. M'Closkey, *Swept under the Rug*, 42; Denevan, "Livestock Numbers," 700.
36. Each horse or cow counted as four or five sheep in forage consumption.
37. Excess horse ownership was a particular sticking point in the stock reduction program, government officials failing to understand the importance of horses for Navajos as basic transportation and beasts of burden. Following a 1939 court judgment, the federal government rounded up thousands of horses, sending them to slaughter, killing them on the spot, or otherwise allowing them to die.
38. M'Closkey, *Swept under the Rug*, 26.
39. M'Closkey, *Swept under the Rug*, ix, 12, 65.
40. M'Closkey, *Swept under the Rug*, 7, 205–233.
41. J. P. Cauhape, an immigrant sheepman from France, installed wolf-proof wire fencing on his family's ranch near Roswell in 1937 at a cost of around $20,000, eliminating the need for herders. See Cauhape, Oral History, conducted and recorded by Marcie Palmer, April 13, 2001, FR.

EPILOGUE

1. Wilson, "Cattle Industry," 268.

2. *Seventh Census, 1850,* 170; *US Census, Population, 1880,* 72; New Mexico Department of Agriculture, *New Mexico Agricultural Statistics,* 44. After 1880, the sheep population fell off to about 3 million through World War I. *US Census, 1900,* vol. 5: *Agriculture,* cciv, ccvi, 326; Towne and Wentworth, *Shepherd's Empire,* 181; *Stock Grower,* February 2, 1889.

3. Wool consumption was 277 million lbs. for the fall 1899 and spring 1900. *Twelfth Census, 1900,* vol. 5: *Agriculture,* 679. Consumption was 330 million lbs. (in the grease) in 1909; Cherington, "Some Aspects," 340; *Stock Grower and Farmer,* August 19, 1893; *US Census, 1900,* vol. 5: *Agriculture,* 326. The US was the world's third-largest wool producer in 1900, trailing only Australia and Argentina. *The Stock Grower,* March 30, 1889, 9; *US Census, 1900,* vol. 9: *Manufacturers,* 88.

4. *Seventh Census, 1850,* 1008; New Mexico Department of Agriculture, *New Mexico Agricultural Statistics,* 56; *US Census, 1900,* vol. 5: *Agriculture,* 326.

5. United States Department of Agriculture, Forest Service, "The Western Range." US Senate Doc. 199, 74th Congress, 2nd Session, 1936; DeBuys, *Enchantment,* 190, 344.

6. *The New Mexico Bluebook, 1913,* 42.

BIBLIOGRAPHY

MANUSCRIPT SOURCES

CIC. Charles Ilfeld Company Records, 1865–1929. Center for Southwest Research, University Libraries, University of New Mexico, Albuquerque, New Mexico.

FBC. Frank Bond & Son Records, 1870–1958. Center for Southwest Research, University Libraries, University of New Mexico, Albuquerque, New Mexico.

FR. Oral History Program, New Mexico Farm and Ranch Heritage Museum, Archives and Special Collections Department, New Mexico State University Library, New Mexico State University, Las Cruces, New Mexico.

GKC. Gross, Kelly & Co. Records. Center for Southwest Research, University Libraries, University of New Mexico, Albuquerque, New Mexico.

MSC. Montague Stevens Papers, 1894–1950. Center for Southwest Research, University Libraries, University of New Mexico, Albuquerque, New Mexico.

NMWGA. New Mexico Wool Growers Association Records. Archives and Special Collections Department, New Mexico State University Library, New Mexico State University, Las Cruces, New Mexico.

SRC. Secundino Romero Papers. Center for Southwest Research, University Libraries, University of New Mexico, Albuquerque, New Mexico.

https://doi.org/10.5876/9781646425471.c009

270 BIBLIOGRAPHY

TA. Territorial Archives of New Mexico. Microform Edition. New Mexico State
Records Center and Archives, Santa Fe, New Mexico.

TBC. Thomas B. Catron Papers. Center for Southwest Research, University
Libraries, University of New Mexico, Albuquerque, New Mexico.

GOVERNMENT PUBLICATIONS

Territory of New Mexico

1897 Actas de la Asemblea del Territorio de Nuevo Mexico. Santa Fe: Compania Im-
presora Del Nuevo Mexicano, 1897.

1903 Acts of the Legislative Assembly of the Territory of New Mexico. Santa Fe: New
Mexican Printing Company, 1903.

The New Mexico Blue Book, 1913. Issued by Antonio Lucero, Secretary of State.
Santa Fe: n.p., n.d.

The New Mexico Blue Book, 1917. Issued by Antonio Lucero, Secretary of State.
Santa Fe: n.p., n.d.

The New Mexico Blue Book, 1919. Issued by Manuel Martinez, Secretary of State.
Santa Fe: n.p., n.d.

*Report of the Governor of New Mexico Made to the Secretary of the Interior for the Year
1879*. Washington, DC: Government Printing Office, 1879. TA, roll 99.

Report of the Governor of New Mexico to the Secretary of the Interior, 1889. Washington, DC: Government Printing Office, 1889. TA, roll 121.

Report of the Governor of New Mexico to the Secretary of the Interior, 1890. Washington, DC: Government Printing Office, 1890. TA, roll 121.

Report of the Governor of New Mexico to the Secretary of the Interior, 1897. Washington, DC: Government Printing Office, 1897. TA, roll 148.

Report of the Governor of New Mexico to the Secretary of the Interior, 1900. Washington, DC: Government Printing Office, Rosenbaum. TA, roll 148.

Report of the Governor of New Mexico to the Secretary of the Interior, 1905. Washington, DC: Government Printing Office, 1905. TA, roll 149.

*Report of the Governor of New Mexico to the Secretary of the Interior for the Fiscal Year
Ended June 30, 1910*. Washington, DC: Government Printing Office, 1910. TA,
roll 188.

*Second Annual Message of Acting Governor Arny to the Legislative Assembly of New
Mexico*. Santa Fe: Manderfield & Tucker, 1866. TA, roll 98.

Bibliography   271

US Census Reports

Agriculture of the United States in 1860: Compiled from the Original Returns of the Eighth Census. Washington, DC: Government Printing Office, 1864.

Report on the Productions of Agriculture as Returned at the Tenth Census (June 1, 1880). Vol. 3. Washington, DC: Government Printing Office, 1883.

The Ninth Census (June 1, 1870). Vol. 3, *The Statistics of the Wealth and Industry of the United States.* Washington, DC: Government Printing Office, 1872.

Report on Manufacturing Industries in the United States at the Eleventh Census, 1890. Vol. 6, pt. 3. Washington, DC: Government Printing Office, 1895.

Report on the Productions of Agriculture as Returned at the Tenth Census (June 1, 1880). Vol. 3. Washington, DC: Government Printing Office, 1883.

The Seventh Census of the United States: 1850. Washington, DC: Robert Armstrong, Public Printer, 1853.

Statistics of the Population of the United States at the Tenth Census (June 1, 1880). Washington, DC: Government Printing Office, 1883.

Twelfth Census of the United States Taken in the Year 1900. Vol. 1, *Population*, pt. 1. Washington, DC: US Census Office, 1901.

Twelfth Census of the United States Taken in the Year 1900. Vol. 5, *Agriculture*, pt. 1, "Farms, Livestock, and Animal Products." Washington, DC: US Census Office, 1902.

Twelfth Census of the United States Taken in the Year 1900, Vol. 9, *Manufacturers*, pt. 3. Washington, DC: US Census Office, 1902.

Thirteenth Census of the United States Taken in the Year 1910, Vol. 7, *Agriculture, 1909.* Washington, DC: US Department of Commerce, Bureau of the Census, 1913.

Thirteenth Census of the United States Taken in the Year 1910. Vol. 10, *Manufacturers, 1909.* Washington, DC: US Department of Commerce, Bureau of the Census, 1913.

Department of Agriculture Reports

Carman, Ezra A., H. A. Heath, and John Minto. *Special Report on the History and Present Condition of the Sheep Industry of the United States.* Washington, DC: US Department of Agriculture, Bureau of Animal Industry, 1892.

Clarke, Lowell. "Lamb Feeding in Colorado." *Eighteenth Annual Report of the Bureau of Animal Industry for the Year 1901*, 275–278. Washington, DC: US Department of Agriculture, Bureau of Animal Industry, 1902.

Curtiss, C. F., and James W. Wilson. "Feeding Range Lambs." *Fifteenth Annual Report of the Bureau of Animal Industry for the Year 1898*, 469–470. Washington, DC: US Department of Agriculture, Bureau of Animal Industry, 1898.

272 BIBLIOGRAPHY

Graham, I. D. "Alfalfa for the Growing and Fattening of Animals in the Great Plains Region." *Twenty-First Annual Report of the Bureau of Animal Industry for the Year 1904*, 242–267. Washington, DC: US Department of Agriculture, Bureau of Animal Industry, 1905.

Heath, H. A. "Condition of the Sheep Industry West of the Mississippi River." *Sixth and Seventh Reports of the Bureau of Animal Industry for the Years 1889 and 1890*, 247–320. Washington, DC: US Department of Agriculture, Bureau of Animal Industry, 1891.

New Mexico Department of Agriculture. *New Mexico Agricultural Statistics*. Vol. 1. Las Cruces: New Mexico Department of Agriculture with the US Department of Agriculture Statistical Reporting Service, 1962.

Standart, S. H. "On Condition of the Livestock Industry of Colorado and the Territories of the Northwest." *Second Annual Report of the Bureau of Animal Industry for the Year 1885*, 326–334. Washington, DC: US Department of Agriculture, Bureau of Animal Industry, 1886.

Taylor, H. M. "Conditions of the Cattle Interests West of the Mississippi River." *Fourth and Fifth Annual Reports of the Bureau of Animal Industry for the Years 1887 and 1888*, 306–338. Washington, DC: US Department of Agriculture, Bureau of Animal Industry, 1889.

Taylor, H. M. "On Condition of the Range Cattle Industry." *Third Annual Report of the Bureau of Animal Industry for the Year 1886*, 105–124. Washington, DC: US Department of Agriculture, Bureau of Animal Industry, 1887.

Taylor, H. M. "On Importance of the Range Industry." *Second Annual Report of the Bureau of Animal Industry for the Year 1885*, 293–325. Washington, DC: US Department of Agriculture, Bureau of Animal Industry, 1886.

US Department of Agriculture, Bureau of Animal Industry. Fifteenth Annual Report of the Bureau of Animal Industry for the Year 1898. *Feeding Range Lambs*, by C. F. Curtiss and James W. Wilson. Washington, DC: Government Printing Office, 1898.

US Department of Agriculture. *Annual Report of the Secretary of the Interior, 1885*. Washington, DC: Government Printing Office, 1886.

US Department of Agriculture. *Annual Reports of the Department of Agriculture for the Year Ended June 30, 1914*. Washington, DC: Government Printing Office, 1914.

US Department of Agriculture. *Annual Reports of the Department of Agriculture for the Year Ended June 30, 1915*. Washington, DC: Government Printing Office, 1916.

US Department of Agriculture. *Report of the Commissioner of the Department of Agriculture for the Year 1868*. Washington, DC: Government Printing Office, 1869.

US Department of Agriculture. *Report of the Commissioner of the Department of Agriculture for the Year 1869.* Washington, DC: Government Printing Office, 1870.

US Department of Agriculture. *Report of the Commissioner of the Department of Agriculture for the Year 1870.* Washington, DC: Government Printing Office, 1871.

US Department of Agriculture. *Yearbook of the Department of Agriculture, 1900.* Washington, DC: Government Printing Office, 1901.

US Department of Agriculture, Bureau of Animal Industry. *Seventeenth Annual Report of the Bureau of Animal Industry for the Year 1900.* Washington, DC: Government Printing Office, 1901.

US Department of Agriculture, Bureau of Animal Industry. *Twentieth Annual Report of the Bureau of Animal Industry for the Year 1903.* Washington, DC: Government Printing Office, 1904.

U.S. Department of Agriculture, Bureau of Animal Industry. *Twenty-First Annual Report of the Bureau of Animal Industry for the Year 1904.* Washington, DC: Government Printing Office, 1905.

US Department of the Interior. *Reports of the Department of the Interior for the Fiscal Year Ended June 30, 1910.* Vol. 1. Washington: Government Printing Office, 1911.

Wilcox, E. V. "Sheep Ranching in the Western States." *Nineteenth Annual Report of the Bureau of Animal Industry for the Year 1902,* 79–98. Washington, DC: US Department of Agriculture, Bureau of Animal Industry, 1903.

Wilson, James. "The Cattle Industry of the United States." *Eighteenth Annual Report of the Bureau of Animal Industry for the Year 1901,* 267–274. Washington, DC: US Department of Agriculture, Bureau of Animal Industry, 1902.

Congressional Reports

Abert, J. W. *Report of Lieut. J. W. Abert of His Examination of New Mexico in the Years 1846–47.* 30th Cong., 1st sess., House Exec. Doc. 41, 1848.

Emory, W. H. *Notes of a Military Reconnaissance, from Fort Leavenworth in Missouri, to San Diego, in California.* 30th Cong., 1st sess., House Exec. Doc. 41, 1848.

Hughs, J. T. *Doniphan's Expedition.* 63rd Cong., 2nd sess., Senate Doc. 608, 1914.

Johnston, A. R. *Journal of Captain A. R. Johnston, First Dragoons.* 30th Cong., 1st sess., House Exec. Doc. 41, 1848.

US Department of Agriculture, Forest Service. *The Western Range: Letter from the Secretary of Agriculture Transmitting in Response to Senate Resolution No. 289.* 74th Cong., 2nd sess., Senate Doc. 199, 1936.

274 BIBLIOGRAPHY

NEWSPAPERS

Albuquerque Journal, Albuquerque, NM.
Albuquerque Tribune, Albuquerque, NM.
Daily New Mexican, Santa Fe, NM.
El Paso Times, El Paso, TX.
The News and Press, Cimarron, NM.
Rocky Mountain News, Denver, CO.
Santa Fe New Mexican, Santa Fe, NM.
Santa Fe Weekly Gazette, Santa Fe, NM.
The Stock Grower, Las Vegas, NM.
The Stock Grower and Farmer, Las Vegas, NM.
The Weekly Optic and Stock Grower, Las Vegas, NM.

OTHER SOURCES

Allison, W. H. H. "Colonel Francisco Perea." *Old Santa Fe* 1 (October 1913): 210–222.
Allison, W. H. H. "Santa Fe as It Appeared during the Winter of the Years 1837 and 1838." *Old Santa Fe* 2 (October 1914): 170–183.
Bartlett, John R. *Personal Narratives of Exploration and Incidents in Texas, New Mexico, California, Sonora, and Chihuahua*. Vol. 2. New York: D. Appleton and Company, 1854. Reprint, Chicago: Rio Grande Press, 1965.
Baxter, John O. *Las Carneradas, Sheep Trade in New Mexico, 1700–1860*. Albuquerque: University of New Mexico Press, 1987.
Baydo, Gerald. "Cattle Ranching in the Pecos Valley of New Mexico." *Rocky Mountain Social Science Journal* 8 (April 1971): 85–96.
Bergan, Dalton C. *The Pathfinder: The Story of Francis X. Aubry on the Santa Fe Trail and the California–Santa Fe Trail, 1846–1854*. Carpinteria, CA: printed by author, ca. 1983.
Billington, Ray Allen. *Westward Expansion: A History of the American Frontier*. 4th ed. New York: Macmillan, 1974.
Bloom, Lansing B. "Necrology, Amado Chaves." *New Mexico Historical Review* 6 (January 1931): 100–104.
Bond, Frank. "Memoirs of Forty Years in New Mexico." *New Mexico Historical Review* 21 (October 1946): 340–349.
Boyle, Susan Calafate. *Los Capitalistas: Hispano Merchants and the Santa Fe Trade*. Albuquerque: University of New Mexico Press, 1997.
Brayer, Herbert O. *William Blackmore: The Spanish-Mexican Land Grants of New Mexico and Colorado, 1863–1878*. Denver: Bradford-Robinson, 1949.

Brisbin, James S. *The Beef Bonanza or, How to Get Rich on the Plains. Being a Description of Cattle-growing, Sheep-farming, Horse-raising, and Dairying in the West.* With a forward by Gilbert C. Fite in a new edition. Philadelphia: J. B. Lippincott, 1881. New edition, Norman: University of Oklahoma Press, 1959; foreword by Gilbert C. Fite.

Brooks, James F. *Captives and Cousins: Slavery, Kinship, and Community in the Southwest Borderlands.* Chapel Hill: University of North Carolina Press, 2002.

Bryant, Keith L., Jr. *History of the Atchison, Topeka, and Santa Fe Railway.* Lincoln: University of Nebraska Press, 1974.

Butzer, Karl W. "Cattle and Sheep from Old to New Spain: Historical Antecedents." *Annals of the Association of American Geographers* 78 (March 1988): 29–56.

Cabeza de Baca, Fabiola. *We Fed Them Cactus.* 2d ed. Albuquerque: University of New Mexico Press, 1994.

Carlson, Alvar Ward. "Long Lots in the Rio Arriba." *Annals of the Association of American Geographers* 65 (March 1975): 48–57.

Carlson, Alvar Ward. "New Mexico's Sheep Industry, 1850–1900: Its Role in the History of the Territory." *New Mexico Historical Review* 44 (January 1969): 25–49.

Carlson, Alvar W. *The Spanish-American Homeland: Four Centuries of New Mexico's Rio Arriba.* Baltimore: Johns Hopkins University Press, 1990.

Carroll, H. Bailey, and J. Villasana Haggard, eds. and trans., *Three New Mexico Chronicles.* Albuquerque: Quivira Society, 1942. Includes Don Pedro Baptiste Pino's *Exposicion sucinta y sentilla de la provincia del Nuevo Mexico* (Cadiz, 1812); Lic. Antonio Barreiro's *Ojeada sobre Nuevo-Mexico* (Puebla, 1832); and Don Jose Agustin de Escudero's *Noticias historicas y estadisticas de la antigua provincia del Nuevo-Mexico* (Mexico City, 1849). Original Spanish and English translations are given.

Carter, Harvey Lewis. *"Dear Old Kit": The Historical Christopher Carson.* Norman: University of Oklahoma Press, 1968.

Chaput, Donald. *Francois X. Aubry: Trader, Trailmaker, and Voyageur in the Southwest.* Glendale, CA: Arthur H. Clark, 1975.

Charles, Ralph. "Development of the Partido System in the New Mexico Sheep Industry." MA thesis, University of New Mexico, 1940.

Cherington, P. T. "Some Aspects of the Wool Trade of the United States." *Quarterly Journal of Economics* 25 (February 1911): 337–356.

Clay, John. *My Life on the Range.* Chicago: printed by author, 1924. Reprint, New York: Antiquarian Press, 1961.

Cleaveland, Agnes Morley. *No Life for a Lady.* Boston: Houghton Mifflin, 1941. Reprint, Lincoln: University of Nebraska Press, 1977.

276 BIBLIOGRAPHY

Coan, Charles F. *A History of New Mexico*. Vol. 1. Chicago and New York: American Historical Society, 1925.

Cooke, Philip St. George. *The Conquest of New Mexico and California*. New York: G. P. Putnam's Sons, 1878.

Culbert, James I. "Cattle Industry of New Mexico." *Economic Geography* 17 (April 1941): 155–168.

Davis, W. W. H. *El Gringo: New Mexico and Her People*. New York: Harper, 1857. Reprint, Lincoln: University of Nebraska Press, 1982.

deBuys, William. *Enchantment and Exploitation: The Life and Hard Times of a New Mexico Mountain Range*. Rev. ed. Albuquerque: University of New Mexico Press, 2015.

Denevan, William M. "Livestock Numbers in Nineteenth-Century New Mexico and the Problem of Gullying in the Southwest." *Annuals of the Association of American Geographers* 57 (December 1967): 691–703.

Deutsch, Sarah. *No Separate Refuge: Culture, Class, and Gender on an Anglo-Hispanic Frontier in the American Southwest, 1880–1940*. New York: Oxford University Press, 1987.

Dick-Peddie, William A. *New Mexico Vegetation, Past, Present, and Future*. Albuquerque: University of New Mexico Press, 1993.

Dunmire, William W. *New Mexico's Spanish Livestock Heritage: Four Centuries of Animals, Land, and People*. Albuquerque: University of New Mexico Press, 2013.

Ebright, Malcolm. *Land Grants and Law Suits in Northern New Mexico*. Albuquerque: University of New Mexico Press, 1994.

Emory, W. H. *Lieutenant Emory Reports: A Reprint of a Military Reconnaissance*. Introduction and notes edited by Calvin Ross. Albuquerque: University of New Mexico Press, 1951.

Fergusson, Erna. *New Mexico: A Pageant of Three Peoples*. Albuquerque: University of New Mexico Press, 1951.

Fergusson, Harvey. *Home in the West*. New York: Duell, Sloan, and Pearce, 1944.

Freiberger, Harriet. *Lucien Maxwell, Villain or Visionary*. Santa Fe: Sunstone Press, 1999.

Gilfillan, Archer B. *Sheep*. Boston: Little, Brown, 1929.

Gjevre, John A. *Chili Line: The Narrow Rail Trail to Santa Fe*. 2nd ed. Espanola, NM: Rio Grande Sun Press, 1971.

Glaab, Charles N. "Business Patterns in the Growth of a Midwestern City: The Kansas City Business Community before the Civil War." *Business History Review* 33 (Summer 1959): 156–174.

Gonzales, Phillip B. *Politica: Nuevomexicanos and American Political Incorporation, 1821–1910*. Lincoln: University of Nebraska Press, 2016.

Bibliography   277

Gordon, Clarence W. "Report on Cattle, Sheep, and Swine." In *Manufactures of the United States in 1860: Compiled from the Original Returns of the Eighth Census.* Washington, DC: Government Printing Office, 1865.

Greever, William S. *Arid Domain: The Santa Fe Railway and Its Western Land Grant.* Stanford, CA: Stanford University Press, 1954.

Gregg, Josiah. *Commerce of the Prairies: Or, The Journal of a Santa Fe Trader, during Eight Expeditions across the Great Western Prairies, and a Residence of Nearly Nine Years in Northern Mexico.* New York: H. G. Langley, 1844. Reprint, *Commerce of the Prairies: The 1844 Edition*, unabridged in 2 vols., introduction by Archibald Hanna. Philadelphia and New York: J. B. Lippincott Company, 1962.

Gressley, Gene M. *Bankers and Cattlemen.* Lincoln: University of Nebraska Press, 1966.

Grubbs, Frank H. "Frank Bond, Gentleman Sheepherder of Northern New Mexico, 1883–1915." *New Mexico Historical Review* 35 (July 1960): 169–199; 35 (October 1960): 293–308; 36 (April 1961): 138–158; 36 (July 1961): 230–243; 36 (October 1961): 274–345; 37 (January 1962): 43–71.

Gulliford, Andrew. *The Wooly West: Colorado's Hidden History of Sheepscapes.* College Station: Texas A&M University Press, 2018.

Gutierrez, Ramon A. *When Jesus Came, the Corn Mothers Went Away: Marriage, Sexuality, and Power in New Mexico, 1500–1846.* Stanford, CA: Stanford University Press, 1991.

Hafen, LeRoy R. "The Old Spanish Trail, Santa Fe to Los Angeles." *Huntington Library Quarterly* 11 (February 1948): 149–160.

Hafen, LeRoy R., and Ann W. Hafen. *Old Spanish Trail, Santa Fe to Los Angeles.* Glendale, CA: Arthur H. Clarke, 1954.

Haines, Helen. *History of New Mexico: From the Spanish Conquest to the Present Time, 1530–1890.* New York: New Mexico Historical Publishing, 1891.

Hammond, George P., and Agapito Rey, eds. *The Rediscovery of New Mexico, 1580–1594.* Albuquerque: University of New Mexico Press, 1966.

Hayter, Earl W. "Barbed Wire Fencing: A Prairie Invention: Its Rise and Influence in the Western States." *Agricultural History* 13 (October 1939): 189–207.

Hayter, Earl W. "Livestock-Fencing Conflicts in Rural America." *Agricultural History* 37 (January 1963): 10–20.

Hicks, John D. "The Western Middle West, 1900–1914." *Agricultural History* 20 (April 1946): 65–77.

Horgan, Paul F. *Great River: The Rio Grande in North American History.* 4th ed. New York: Rinehart, 1954. Reprint, Austin: Texas Monthly Press, 1984.

Jaramillo, Cleofas M. *Romance of a Little Village Girl.* Albuquerque: University of New Mexico Press, 2000. Originally published San Antonio, TX: Naylor, 1955.

BIBLIOGRAPHY

Jones, Hester. "The Spiegelbergs and Early Trade in New Mexico." *El Palacio* 38 (April 1935): 81–89.

Julian, George W. "Land Stealing in New Mexico." *North American Review* 145 (July 1887): 17–31.

Kelly, Daniel T., with Beatrice Chauvenet. *The Buffalo Head: A Century of Mercantile Pioneering in the Southwest*. Santa Fe: Vergara Publishing, 1972.

Kessell, John L. *Pueblos, Spaniards, and the Kingdom of New Mexico*. Norman: University of Oklahoma Press, 2008.

Kiser, William S. *Borderlands of Slavery: The Struggle over Captivity and Peonage in the American Southwest*. Philadelphia: University of Pennsylvania Press, 2017.

Kiser, William S. *Turmoil on the Rio Grande: The Territorial History of the Mesilla Valley, 1846–1865*. College Station: Texas A&M University Press, 2011.

Knowlton, Clark S. "Patron-Peon Pattern among the Spanish Americans of New Mexico." *Social Forces* 41 (1962–1963): 12–17.

Kupper, Winifred. *The Golden Hoof: The Story of the Sheep of the Southwest*. New York: Alfred A. Knopf, 1945.

Lamar, Howard Roberts. *The Far Southwest, 1846–1912: A Territorial History*. Rev. ed. Albuquerque: University of New Mexico Press, 2000.

Larson, Robert W. *New Mexico's Quest for Statehood, 1846–1912*. Albuquerque: University of New Mexico Press, 1968.

Latham, Hiram. *Trans-Missouri Stock Raising: The Pasture Lands of North America: Winter Grazing*. Omaha: Daily Herald Steam Printing House, 1871. Reprint, Denver: Old West Publishing, 1962.

Lee, Floyd W. *Bartolome Fernandez (September 2nd, 1767), Pioneer Shepherd on the Hills in New Mexico*. New York: Newcomen Society of North America, 1954.

Lehmann, V. W. *Forgotten Legions: Sheep in the Rio Grande Plain of Texas*. El Paso: Texas Western Press, 1969.

Leonard, Olen E. *The Role of the Land Grant in the Social Organization and Social Processes of a Spanish-American Village in New Mexico*. Albuquerque: Calvin Horn, 1970.

Leopold, L. B. "Vegetation of the Southwestern Watersheds in the Nineteenth Century." *Geographical Review* 41 (1951): 295–316.

Lummis, Charles F. *The Land of Poco Tiempo*. New York: Charles Scribner's Sons, 1893. Reprint, Albuquerque: University of New Mexico Press, 1952.

MacCameron, Robert. "Environmental Change in Colonial New Mexico." *Environmental History Review* 18 (Summer 1994): 17–39.

Magliari, Michael F. "'A Species of Slavery': The Compromise of 1850, Popular Sovereignty, and the Expansion of Unfree Indian Labor in the American West." *Journal of American History* 109 (December 2022): 521–547.

Bibliography 279

Martin, Craig. *Valle Grande: A History of the Baca Location No. 2*. Los Alamos, NM: All Seasons Publishing, 2003.

McCusker, John J. *How Much Is That in Real Money? A Historical Commodity Price Index for Use as a Deflator of Money Values in the Economy of the United States*. 2nd ed. Worcester, MA: American Antiquarian Society, 2001.

M'Closkey, Kathy. *Swept under the Rug: A Hidden History of Navajo Weaving*. Albuquerque: University of New Mexico Press, 2002.

Meinig, D. W. *Southwest: Three Peoples in Geographical Change, 1600–1970*. New York: Oxford University Press, 1971.

Montejano, David. *Anglos and Mexicans in the Making of Texas, 1836–1986*. Austin: University of Texas Press, 1987.

Montoya, Maria E. *Translating Property: The Maxwell Land Grand and the Conflict over Land in the American West, 1840–1900*. Berkeley: University of California Press, 2002.

Nostrand, Richard L. *The Hispano Homeland*. Norman: University of Oklahoma Press, 1992.

Otero, Miguel Antonio. *My Life on the Frontier, 1864–1882: Incidents and Characters of the Period when Kansas, Colorado, and New Mexico Were Passing through the Last of Their Wild and Romantic Years*. New York: Press of the Pioneers, 1935. Reprint, Albuquerque: University of New Mexico Press, 1987.

Otero, Miguel Antonio. *My Life on the Frontier, 1882–1897*. Santa Fe: Sunstone Press, 2007. Facsimile of original 1939 edition.

Otero, Miguel Antonio. *My Nine Years as Governor of the Territory of New Mexico, 1897–1906*. Santa Fe: Sunstone Press, 2007. Facsimile of original 1940 edition.

Parish, William J. "Sheep Husbandry in New Mexico, 1902–1903." *New Mexico Historical Review* 37 (July 1962): 201–213; 37 (October 1962): 260–309; 38 (January 1963): 56–77.

Parish, William J. "The German Jew and the Commercial Revolution in Territorial New Mexico, 1850–1900." *New Mexico Historical Review* 35 (January 1960): 1–29; 35 (April 1960): 129–150.

Parish, William J. *The Charles Ilfeld Company: A Study of the Rise and Fall of Mercantile Capitalism in New Mexico*. Cambridge, MA: Harvard University Press, 1961.

Pattie, James Ohio. *Personal Narrative of James O. Pattie*. Cincinnati, OH: E. H. Flint, 1833. Reprint, Missoula, MT: Mountain Press, 1988.

Payne, Melissa. "Lessons from the Rio Abajo: A Colonial Patron's Contested Legacy." *New Mexico Historical Review* 80, no. 4 (Fall 2005): 397–416.

Perry, Richard. *I Went a' Shepherding: Chapters in the Life of a Shepherding Naturalist and His Wife in the Western Highlands and Islands*. London: Lindsay Drummond, 1945.

280 BIBLIOGRAPHY

Pike, Zebulon Montgomery. *The Expeditions of Zebulon Montgomery Pike*. Vol. 2. Edited by Elliott Coues. Minneapolis, MN: Ross & Haines, 1965. Originally published in 1810.

Pittman, Lucretia. "Solomon Luna: Sheepmaster and Politician of New Mexico." MA thesis, St. Louis University, 1944.

Prince, L. Bradford. *A Concise History of New Mexico*. 2nd ed. Cedar Rapids, IA: Torch Press, 1914.

Pubols, Louise. *The Father of All: The de la Guerra Family, Power, and Patriarchy in Mexican California*. Berkeley: University of California Press; San Marino: Huntington Library, 2009.

Randall, Henry S. *The Practical Shepherd; A Complete Treatise on the Breeding, Management and Diseases of Sheep*. 7th ed. Rochester, NY: D. D. T. Moore; Philadelphia: J. B. Lippincott, 1863.

Reeve, Frank D., ed. "The Sheep Industry in Arizona, 1905–1906." *New Mexico Historical Review* 38 (July 1963): 323–342.

Remley, David. *Bell Ranch: Cattle Ranching in the Southwest, 1824–1947*. Albuquerque: University of New Mexico Press, 1993.

Richter, Conrad. *The Sea of Grass*. Philadelphia: Curtis Publishing, 1936.

Rosenbaum, Robert J. *Mexicano Resistance in the Southwest: "The Sacred Right of Self-Preservation."* Austin: University of Texas Press, 1981.

Russell, Marian. *Land of Enchantment: Memoirs of Marian Russell along the Santa Fe Trail*. Evanston, IL: Branding Iron Press, 1954. Reprint, Albuquerque: University of New Mexico Press, 1981.

Ruxton, George F. *Adventures in Mexico and the Rocky Mountains*. London: John Murray, 1847.

Scholes, France V. "Civil Government and Society in New Mexico in the Seventeenth Century." *New Mexico Historical Review* 10 (April 1935): 71–111.

Schweikart, Larry. "Early Banking in New Mexico from the Civil War to the Roaring Twenties." *New Mexico Historical Review* 63 (January 1988): 1–24.

Shinkle, James D. *Fifty Years of Roswell History—1867–1917*. Roswell, NM: Hall-Poorbaugh, 1964.

Simmons, Marc. "The Chacon Economic Report of 1803." *New Mexico Historical Review* 60 (January 1985): 81–88.

Simmons, Marc. *The Little Lyon of the Southwest: A Life of Manuel Antonio Chaves*. Chicago: Swallow Press, 1973.

Steinel, Alvin T. *History of Agriculture in Colorado, 1858–1926*. Fort Collins, CO: State Agricultural College, 1926.

Stevens, George Richard Montague. *Rambling through the 1880s—And Beyond*. Santa Fe: printed by author, ca. 1983.

Stevens, Montague. *Meet Mr. Grizzley: A Saga on the Passing of the Grizzley.* Albuquerque: University of New Mexico Press, 1944 (c. 1943).

Sunseri, Alvin R. "Sheep Ricos, Sheep Fortunes in the Aftermath of the American Conquest, 1846–1861," *El Palacio* 83 (Spring, 1977): 3–8.

Surdam, David G. "King Cotton: Monarch or Pretender? The State of the Market for Raw Cotton on the Eve of the American Civil War." *Economic History Review*, n.s., 51 (February 1998): 113–132.

Sypolt, Charles M. "Keepers of the Rocky Mountain Flocks: A History of the Sheep Industry in Colorado, New Mexico, Utah, and Wyoming to 1900," PhD diss., University of Wyoming, 1974.

Taussig, F. W. *Some Aspects of the Tariff Question.* Cambridge, MA: Harvard University Press, 1915. On-Line Resource: econlib.org/library/Taussig. https://www.econlib.org/library/Taussig/tsgSTQ.html.

Taussig, F. W. *The Tariff History of the United States.* 5th ed., rev. New York: G. P. Putnam's Sons, 1910. On-line Resource: Books. Google.com. https://oceanof pdf.com/authors/frank_william_taussig.

Taylor, A. J. "New Mexicoan Pastores and Priests and Priests in the Texas Panhandle, 1876–1915." *Panhandle-Plains Historical Review* 57 (1984): 65–79.

Tobias, Henry J. *A History of the Jews in New Mexico.* Albuquerque: University of New Mexico Press, 1990.

Towne, Charles Wayland, and Edward Norris Wentworth. *Shepherd's Empire.* Norman: University of Oklahoma Press, 1946.

Turner, Frederick Jackson. *Frontier and Section: Selected Essays by Frederick Jackson Turner.* Edited by Ray Allen Billington. Englewood Cliffs, NJ: Prentice-Hall, 1961.

Twitchell, Ralph Emerson. *Old Santa Fe: The Story of New Mexico's Ancient Capital.* Santa Fe: Santa Fe New Mexican Publishing Corporation, 1925. Reprint, Santa Fe: Sunstone Press, 2007.

Van Ness, John R., and Christine M. Van Ness, eds. *Spanish and Mexican Land Grants in New Mexico and Colorado.* Manhattan, KS: Sunflower University Press, 1980.

Vigil, Maurilio E. *Los Patrones: Profiles of Hispanic Political Leaders in New Mexico History.* Washington, DC: University Press of America, 1980.

Walter, Paul A. F. "Necrology, Frank Bond." *New Mexico Historical Review* 20 (July 1945): 271–273.

Wasser, C. H. "Early Development of Technical Range Management, ca. 1895–1945." In "Agriculture of the Great Plains, 1876–1936: A Symposium," edited by Thomas R. Wessel. Special issue, *Agricultural History* 51 (January 1977): 63–77.

282 BIBLIOGRAPHY

Webb, James Josiah. *Adventures in the Santa Fe Trade, 1844–1847.* Glendale, CA: Arthur H. Clark, 1931. Reprint, Lincoln: University of Nebraska Press, 1995.

Weber, David J. *The Mexican Frontier, 1821–1846: The American Southwest under Mexico.* Albuquerque: University of New Mexico Press, 1982.

Weisiger, Marsha. *Dreaming of Sheep in Navajo Country.* Seattle: University of Washington Press, 2009.

Wentworth, Edward Norris. *America's Sheep Trails: History, Personalities.* Ames: Iowa State University Press, 1948.

Westphall, Victor. *Mercedes Reales: Hispanic Land Grants of the Upper Rio Grande Region.* Albuquerque: University of New Mexico Press, 1983.

Westphall, Victor. *The Public Domain in New Mexico, 1854–1891.* Albuquerque: University of New Mexico Press, 1965.

Westphall, Victor. *Thomas Benton Catron and His Era.* Tucson: University of Arizona Press, 1973.

White, Richard. *Railroaded: The Transcontinentals and the Making of Modern America.* New York: W. W. Norton, 2011.

Worster, Donald E. Wright. "The Significance of the Spanish Borderlands to the United States." *Western Historical Quarterly* 17 (January 1976): 5–18.

Wright, Chester Whitney. "Wool Growing and the Tariff since 1890." *Quarterly Journal of Economics* 19 (August 1905): 610–647.

INDEX

Locators with an *f* indicate a figure, locators with a *t* indicate a table, and locators with an *n* indicate a footnote.

agriculture: and alfalfa, 98, 99, 102, 124, 144, 165, 168, 173, 248*n*42; and colonists' economy, 9, 49; and cotton, 24; and farm crops, 77*f*, 99, 100, 102, 108, 144, 165–66, 167, 189, 205, 223, 248*n*42, 265*n*13; and farming, 12, 15, 16, 22, 28, 33, 35, 54, 64, 68, 69, 102, 103, 105, 124, 128, 129, 168, 173, 205, 208–9, 211, 213–14, 227, 265*n*12; and feeder farms, 92, 96–100, 102, 224; and grazing resources, 27, 53; growth of, 227; and homesteaders, 210–12, 264*n*10; and increase of production, 265*n*13; and industrialization, 225; and irrigation, 20, 23, 102, 108, 124, 128, 168, 208, 211; and land, 10, 20, 22, 27, 28, 55, 64, 68, 69, 108, 123; and long lots, 266*n*30; in the Midwest, 68–69; and missions, 10; modernization of, 208; and Native Americans, 13, 23, 55; and Nebraska,

224; and Platte River, 102; and produce, 69, 87; and Pueblos, 23; and Rocky Mountain–Great Plains feeding industry, 102; and the Southwest, 121; and sugar beet farms, 170; and supply networks, 28; and transportation, 50. *See also* Colorado; cotton; United States

Alvarez, Manuel, 40, 43, 237*n*38

A. MacArthur Company, 142

Amberg, Jacob, 87

American Valley Company, 174, 178, 179, 180, 181–84, 188. *See also* Catron, Thomas

Anglo-American common law, 30, 236*n*14

Angney, William Z., 40, 41, 237*n*38

Apadaca, Adriano, 217

Arizona: border of, 37, 54; grass in, 72; and sheep, 158, 163; sheepmen in, 216; and S.U. Ranch, 159; Tucson in, 42; and

284 INDEX

winter of 1899, 164; and wool prices, 254n32; and wool production, 57t, 216

Arkansas River, 26, 99, 102, 218

Armijo, Ambrosio, 41, 42

Armijo, Cristobal, 84

Armijo, Governor Manuel, 20, 27, 233n41, 235n4

Armijo y Jaramillo, Jesus, 84

Atkinson, Ada, 180, 181, 188

Atkinson, Henry M., 178, 179, 179–81

Aubry, Francis X., 42, 43, 46, 238n42

Baca, Bartolome, 83

Baca, Don Felipe, 76

Baca, Roman A., 36, 117

Baca Ranches, 6, 173

banking, commercial, 82, 91–93, 102, 103, 140, 145. *See also* Catron, Thomas; sheep industry

Bank of Commerce, 197

Barriero, Licenciado Don Antonio, 21, 52

Beaubien, Charles (Carlos), 27, 235n5

Beaubien, Luz, 28

Becker, Gustave, 196, 197

Becknell, William, 29

Bennett, E. J., 99

Bennett, I. W., 99

Bernavette, John, 42

Bond, Frank: affluence of, 133, 135, 137, 202; and attention to business, 148–49, 200–201, 202; and bank failures, 151–52; and Bond, Gusdorf, and McCarthy Company, 141; and Bond & Nohl Company, 143, 147, 148; and Bond-Gunderson Company, 146; and Bond-Sargent Company, 146; and Brown & Adams, 138, 139, 149, 150; and capital, 148, 175; and credit for customers, 91–92, 136–37, 150–51; death of, 152; and debt payments, 139, 150–51, 203; early life of, 133; and Ed Sargent, 100; employees of, 147, 151, 201–202, 254n27; and Espanola, 96, 132, 133, 136, 140, 142, 231n17; and feeder farms, 102; finances of, 252n3, 252n13, 254n35; and grazing fees, 145; incorporation of businesses

of, 143, 145; and land, 132, 145, 146; and Leandro Martinez, 147; letters of, 201, 254n32; and livestock, 201, 202; as a local merchant, 159; and managers, 142–43, 145, 147, 150; and Max Nordhaus, 149; mercantile empire of, 132–33, 143, 145–46, 147, 152, 202; and open-range grazing, 203; and *partidarios*, 135, 136, 201; and *partido* contracts, 139, 140, 143, 145, 202; and partnership with brother, 133, 135–36, 137, 140–45, 149–50, 201, 202; and role of patron, 136; and Servilleta facility, 142, 147, 152; and sheep industry, 131, 132–33, 135, 139, 140, 145, 146–47, 149, 150–52, 224; and silver as money, 94; and son, 134f; and Spanish-American people, 151, 152; wealth of, 201; wife of, 148; and wool, 96, 132–33, 135–36, 140, 143, 145, 148, 201

Bond, George W.: affluence of, 135, 202; and Bond, Gusdorf, and McCarthy Company, 141; and Bond & Nohl Company, 143; and Brown & Adams, 139, 149; and California, 145; and capital, 148; and credit for customers, 136–37, 150–51; and debt payments, 139, 150–51; empire of, 152; finances of, 252n3, 252n13; and Idaho, 145; incorporation of store of, 143; and land, 146; letter from brother of, 147; and livestock, 201, 202; and managers, 142–43; and mercantile establishment, 139–40; and *partidarios*, 135, 136; and *partido* contracts, 139, 140; and partnership with brother, 133, 135–36, 137, 140–45, 201; and sheep industry, 131, 132, 135, 136, 139, 140, 144, 145, 201; wealth of, 201; and wool, 135–36, 140, 144, 145

Bond & Wiest, 142, 150, 151

Bond brothers, 88, 92, 101, 131, 132, 133–50. *See also* Bond, Frank; Bond, George W.; sheep

Bond-Connell Sheep & Wool Co., 145–46

Bosque Redondo (Hweeldi), 8, 36, 54, 108, 219

Index 285

Bowie, Mary, 44

Britain, 50, 120, 149, 153–54, 156, 164. *See also* Stevens, Montague

Brooks, James F., 22

Cabeza de Baca, Fabiola, 128, 212, 214, 244n1, 249n6

Cabeza de Baca, Thomas, 6

California: and Anglo-Hispanic intermarriage, 235n6; and California-Oregon area, 75; cattle in, 38; and Donner Pass, 41; economy of, 94; food shortage in, 38–39, 42; and Gila River route, 45; and gold rush, 25, 38, 39, 40; and grazing fees, 215; and horses, 29, 39; livestock in, 29, 38, 39, 44; and Los Angeles, 39, 40, 41, 42, 43, 44; market of, 38–46; Merced River in, 59; Monterey in, 44; and real estate, 40; Sacramento in, 41, 42; San Diego in, 40; San Francisco in, 40, 42, 44–45; and sheep, 31, 36, 38, 39, 40–46, 59, 78, 99, 243n115; and sheep drives, 39, 40, 41–45, 59, 78, 80, 86, 235n7, 237n33, 237–238n39; and sheepmen, 75; and Solomon Luna's wife, 148; and trade, 25, 29, 39–46, 59; and woolen industry, 49; and wool production, 57t

Camino Real: and New Mexico, 9, 86; sheep drives on, 3, 12, 39, 46, 96; and trade, 18, 26, 38, 39, 46, 47, 86

Canada, 59, 72, 133, 202, 244n117

Carrejo, Earnesto, 5

Carson, Kit, 42, 43, 46, 53, 235n5

Catholicism, 27, 30

Catron, George, 198

Catron, Julia, 195, 199

Catron, Thomas: and Alliance Company of Dundee, Scotland, 188; and American Valley Company, 174, 178, 180, 181–84, 186, 187, 188, 190–91, 192, 194, 195–200, 203, 257–258n39; and Antonio Ortiz Grant, 249n72; and Atkinson buyout, 182, 185, 188; and banking, 175, 185, 187–88, 192, 195–98, 246n23; and bond sales, 194–95, 203;

as a businessman, 175, 178–80, 181, 182, 183, 184–85, 188, 195–98, 199, 200, 201, 202, 203; and cattle, 174, 178, 179, 182, 201, 203; and Charles H. Elmendorf, 197, 198, 199, 260n18, 260n19; death of, 263n50, 264n57; debts of, 203; dipping facility of, 251n89; early life of, 176; family of, 176, 195, 197, 198; and fencing, 251n89; and financial challenges, 258n2; finances of, 259n6, 260n19; and grant lands, 259n4; and Henry L. Warren, 179; and irrigation, 251n89; and labor problems, 202, 203; and land, 175, 182–83, 184, 185–86, 188–89, 196, 197, 199, 201, 203; and law practice, 175, 176, 178, 182, 197, 200; legal troubles of, 197; letters of, 175, 176, 178, 182, 195, 196, 197, 201, 259n6, 261n21; and livestock, 179, 196; and loan from Fidelity Trust Company, 196; and loan from Mrs. Perea, 196; and loans from banks, 196, 203; and local loans, 185; London connection of, 200; and open-range grazing, 203; partners of, 179, 183, 184–85, 187, 190, 191, 192, 194, 198, 202; and politics, 175, 176, 178, 180, 182, 183–84, 196, 200, 201; and Republican Party, 175, 258n1; as a Senator, 177f, 178, 200; and sheep industry, 131, 175, 182, 184–85, 200, 201, 224; and sheep ranches, 178–80, 189, 191–92, 196, 198, 199–200, 201, 203; and Solomon Luna, 192; in the US House of Representatives, 180; and US Supreme Court, 260n14; and Waco State Bank, 188; wealth of, 176, 203; and W. G. Walz, 198. *See also* American Valley Company

cattle industry, 79, 93, 95, 126, 127, 154–55, 174

Chacón, Governor Fernando de, 16, 49

Chase, M. M., 59

Chaves, Amado, 37, 117

Chaves, Felipe, 59, 87–88, 224

Chaves, J. Francisco (Jose Francisco), 36, 44, 87, 89f, 110–11, 236n13

Chaves, Manuel Antonio, 36, 37, 41, 117

286 INDEX

Chaves, Mariano, 19, 36
Chicago, Illinois, 224, 225
Christianity, 10–11, 12, 13, 15. *See also* Catholicism; church missions
church missions, 10–12, 38
Civil War: and Anglo immigrants, 120, 206; and antislavery forces, 85; and Confederate Army, 176; and cotton supply, 50, 52; and economic developments, 68; and expansion of woolen industry, 61, 62; and General Carleton's force, 236n22; and invasion of Confederates, 53; and mutton market, 97; and Native Americans' raids, 55; and New Mexico sheep, 74, 78, 79; onset of, 45, 51, 53; and peones as soldiers, 53; and post-Civil War period, 8, 54, 74, 79, 86, 93, 94, 124, 216–17; and railroads, 94; and southwestern slavery, 56; start of, 71; and technological developments, 68; and US Army forts, 93; veterans of, 250n83; and wool and woolen tariffs, 66; and wool production, 47, 50–51, 63, 88, 239n59
Clay, John, 137, 209
Clay, Robinson & Co., 137–38, 144, 184
Cleaveland, Agnes Morley, 7, 122, 127, 174, 216, 255n3
Collinson, John B., 185–87, 188
Colorado: and American Valley Company, 199; Antonito in, 141, 144, 145; Bennett Brothers of, 79, 99–100; and border with New Mexico, 27; Boulder in, 46; and coal mines, 218; Denver in, 46, 63, 95, 138, 144, 156, 194, 202, 230n6; discovery of gold in, 46; drought in, 168–69; economy of, 152; and feeder farms, 97, 99, 100, 224; and feeder ranchers, 138; Fort Collins in, 99–100, 101, 140; grass in, 72; and grazing fees, 215; and Hispanic New Mexicans, 78–79, 218; land in, 146, 211; Las Animas in, 95, 217; Livermore in, 79; livestock in, 97, 98; and mining, 74; Montrose in, 41; and New Mexico sheep, 78–79; and Old Spanish Trail, 237n35; and Pikes

Peak region, 46; and San Luis Valley, 132; and sheep breeding, 75, 76; and sheep drives, 41, 46, 59; and sheep markets, 46; and sheepmen, 75; sheep ranches in, 57; and small-scale growers, 216–17; and sugar beets, 98, 170, 217, 218; Trinidad in, 142, 144, 245n10; Walsenburg in, 99; and wool production, 57t, 243n110
Concha, Governor Fernando de la, 16
Connell, Walter, 145
Continental Trust Company, 188, 194
Coronado Expedition, 8–9, 231n16
cotton: after Civil War, 62; as cloth, 10; consumption of, 50, 51; and cotton industry, 239n58; and cotton products, 52; and foreign markets, 50; price of, 50; shortages of, 47; southern production of, 50, 57; and textile mills, 50, 52; and value of products, 51, 52f. *See also* agriculture
Court of Private Land Claims, 208

Davis, W. W. H., 47, 48, 49, 50, 239n53
Davison, John B., 59
Dick-Peddie, William, 105, 248n49
Dold, John, 87
Drake, Senator William A., 101
Duran y Chaves, Captain Fernando, 14, 19

Eddy, Charles, 129
Elkins, Stephen B., 176, 178, 184, 185, 187, 198. *See also* land grants
Elmendorf, Charles H., 181–82, 183, 184, 185, 187, 188. *See also* Catron, Thomas; ranches
Emory, Lieutenant W. H., 31, 32
encomienda system, 10–13, 231n20, 231n23
environment: and "Big Freeze" of 1886–1887, 182; changes in, 3, 82, 103–8; and desert scrubland, 104; and effects of overgrazing, 114, 209; and grasslands, 104–7, 210–11; and grazing, 20, 21, 33, 82, 103, 104–5, 106, 107–8; and human activity, 103, 107, 210–11; of New Mexico, 4, 33, 80, 82, 103–5, 106, 206,

210–11; and rangeland, 82, 103, 108, 167, 168, 210–11, 213; and range management, 213; and Sangre de Cristo Range, 105; and sheep, 167, 169; and vegetation, 248n49; and winter of 1899, 164. *See also* land

Escudero, Don Jose de, 83
Eulatel, Governor Juan de, 22

fencing, 124, 125–128, 163, 184, 205, 211. *See also* Catron, Thomas; land
Fergusson, Harvey, 110
Field, Neill B., 180
First National Bank of Santa Fe (FNBSF), 92, 140, 183, 192, 196, 197
Forest Reserve Act (1891), 214
Fort Laramie, Wyoming, 42, 74

Gallegos, J. D., 90
Garcia y Ortiz, Eusebio, 92
Garrett, A. D., 113
Giddings, George, 58–59
Gilfillan, Archer B., 6
Gonzales, J. Manuel, 112
Gordon, Clarence W., 58, 244n6
grass: availability of, 97; and buffalo grass (genus Buchloe), 72; and desert grassland, 104; as a food source, 72–73, 97, 247n33; and grama grass (genus Bouteloua), 33, 72, 104, 109, 221; and grazing, 33, 72, 97, 101, 104, 105; and juniper savanna, 226–27; lack of, 32, 33; and livestock, 72, 104, 105, 108–9; in New Mexico, 104–5; and 100th meridian, 72; studies of, 213; and S. U. range, 161; in Texas, 72; and water, 33, 72, 164, 210; and western grasses, 72–73
Great Plains-Rocky Mountain region, 26, 29, 78, 80, 97
Greenough, John, 119
Gregg, Josiah, 19, 48, 49, 72
Gregg Bros., 87
Gregory, Herbert, 109
Gross, Kelly & Co., 150, 192, 196, 197, 246n23
Grubbs, Frank, 133, 252n3

Gusdorf, Alexander, 141
Gusdorf, Gerson, 141
Gutierrez, Don Clemente, 16
G. W. Bond & Bro., 133, 135–36, 140–41, 143, 146–47

Hagerman, James, 129
Hallowell, Jones & Donald, 150
Harvard Medical School, 154
Hatcher, John L., 42
Homestead Act of 1862, 121, 250n83
homesteaders, 10f, 101, 115, 120, 123, 129. *See also* agriculture; land
Hughs, J. T., 32
Hunning, Franz, 110

Ilfeld, Charles: brothers of, 141; capital of, 87; and competition with Frank Bond, 150; and feeding enterprises, 102; finances of, 246n19; and future profits, 139; and grazing land, 146; as a local merchant, 159; and Max Nordhaus, 90, 141, 149; and *partidarios*, 88, 90; and *partido* contracts, 88, 90; and role of patron, 136; sheep herd of, 88, 245n13; and sheep industry, 224; and shipping wool, 95, 96; and small-scale growers, 244n6

Jaramillo, Cleofas, 38
Jaramillo, Jose, 45t
Jaramillo, Venceslao, 38, 92

Kansas, 9, 72, 74, 76, 78, 80. *See also* wool
Kansas City, Missouri, 35
Kearney, Colonel Stephen Watts, 24, 30, 31, 33, 103, 108, 237n38
Kelly, Harry W., 112, 150

labor: and Anglo Americans, 116; availability of, 73, 83, 85, 170–72, 202; and captive Native slaves, 13–14, 15, 22, 28, 31, 56, 130, 231n22, 234n46; cost of, 163, 192; and field work, 14; and Frank Bond, 147, 201–2; and *genizaros*, 15, 83, 232n28; and herders, 258n45; and Hispanic

288 INDEX

labor, 170–72, 217, 257–58n39; and labor problems, 189–90, 203, 255n1; and lumber industry, 218; and managers, 129–130, 146–147, 201–202; and *mestizos*, 15, 232n28; and mill workers, 65; and mining, 217, 218; and *obrajes* (workshops), 22; and open-range grazing, 74, 127, 170; and *partidarios*, 20, 83, 84, 85, 90, 109, 127, 136, 200; and *partido* contracts, 83–84, 85, 88, 90, 136, 202, 244n2; and *partido* system, 22, 83–85, 136; and *pastores*, 6, 7, 110; and patrones, 6–7, 13, 15, 19, 28, 43, 83, 84, 85, 86, 109–10, 136, 172, 232n29, 266n30; and peasant labor, 11; and peonage system, 13–14, 22, 31, 56, 84, 85, 130, 225; and peones, 5, 6–7, 13–14, 27, 28, 56, 73, 83, 84, 172, 200; and Pueblo labor, 10–11, 13, 22, 231n22; and railroads, 71, 95, 217, 218; reorganization of, 205; and repartimiento system, 12–13, 231n23; and seasonal employment, 217, 218; and sharecropping, 27, 83; and sheep dipping, 111; and sheep herders, 22, 43, 46, 73, 83, 130, 202; and sheep industry, 124, 169–72, 218; and slave labor, 11; and sugar beet industry, 170, 218; and urban workers, 69, 225; and wages, 43, 46, 73, 130, 170, 184, 189, 217, 218; and the West, 75, 217–18; and wool, 48. *See also* encomienda system; Navajo people; sheepmen

land: allocation of, 14; and American Valley, 182, 183, 189; and arable land, 31; and arroyos, 33, 106–8, 227, 248n54; as an asset, 176; and Bond brothers, 146, 201; and capital, 120; cattle on, 209; and Chaves family, 117; and common lands, 70, 249–250n73; and community grants, 250n76; and compensation for military service, 14; competition for, 205, 206–207, 210, 211–212; and conservation movement, 214–215; degradation of, 20, 21, 23, 32, 37, 51, 64, 101, 106, 107, 108–9, 114, 115–16, 126, 205, 206, 209, 215, 219, 221–22, 265n18, 266n30; and Desert Land Act, 120; and desert

scrubland, 104, 105; and disappearance of frontier, 204; and effects of overgrazing, 219, 226–27; erosion of, 106, 107–8, 210–11, 214, 219; and farming, 205; and farmland, 22, 23, 69, 100; fencing of, 213, 215–16, 221, 251n90, 251n93; and free lands, 64, 76, 101; of the government, 75, 88, 119–21, 205, 214–15, 223; and grass, 98, 99, 101, 103–5, 106, 107, 119, 126; and grasslands, 226; and grazing allotments, 225; and grazing fees, 215, 216, 217; and grazing resources, 67–68, 70, 71, 72, 79, 88, 92, 94, 97, 103, 104–5, 108, 109, 116–17, 119, 120, 122, 145, 146, 182–83, 201, 206, 207–10, 212, 214, 215, 216, 221, 225, 265n22; and grazing rights, 145; and Great Plains–Rocky Mountain region, 67–68, 94; and herd space, 73, 126, 210, 215; and homesteads, 69, 70, 120, 121, 122, 123–24, 154, 178, 182, 205, 207–212, 214, 215, 225, 265n21; and irrigation, 98, 107, 121, 122, 126, 163, 167, 169, 208, 213; and juniper savanna, 104, 105–6, 107; and land laws, 207, 208, 210, 264n9; and land tenure, 30, 117, 119; and land titles, 70, 117, 120, 121, 123, 207, 208, 214; and land wars, 242n95; leases for, 92, 114, 115; and livestock, 69, 71–72, 105–8, 216; and Lorenzo Labadie, 36; and lumber mills, 173; and Mexican citizenship, 27; and Mexican sovereignty, 206; modernization of, 205–6; and mortgages, 155–56, 158, 160, 181, 196, 199, 203; and national forests of the West, 215; and Native Americans, 13, 53–54, 55, 71–72, 108–9, 120, 124, 206; and natural resources, 214–5; in Nebraska, 181; in New Mexico, 70, 71, 76, 103, 104–5, 146, 181, 182–83, 196; and open-range grazing, 20, 25, 76, 103, 205, 207–8; overgrazing of, 209; and ownership, 116–19, 120, 121–24, 146, 178, 179, 181, 183, 184, 207, 212, 214, 225, 235n4, 236n14, 242n95; and pastureland, 67–68, 69, 72; and Pino family, 36; and Plains-Mesa grasslands,

104; and *pobladores* (settlers), 31, 207; and Preemption Act of 1841, 121, 122; price of, 68, 69, 70, 71, 73, 75, 124, 207; and private grants, 249n72; and private land, 88, 205–6, 223; and property taxes, 117; and public domain, 20, 70, 101, 119, 122, 123–24, 126–27, 129, 160, 205, 206, 208, 209, 214, 242n95, 249–250n73, 259n5, 264–265n12; and public land, 37, 114, 119–21, 123, 126, 145, 178, 200, 206, 207–8, 214, 250n83, 264n10; and ranches, 74, 86; and rangeland, 212; and *rico* families, 20, 36, 37, 86, 117; and right of occupation, 220; scarcity of, 38, 101–2, 205; security of, 52; and sheep feeding, 101–2; and sheep herds, 209–10; and Solomon Luna, 120; and Spanish Civil Law, 117; and Spanish colonial period, 204, 206; and Spanish-Mexican grants, 264–65n12; and Spanish occupancy custom, 70; stealing of, 72; and sugar beet industry, 98; taxation of, 120, 210, 218; and timber resources, 214; use of, 190–91, 205–6, 209–10, 214; and water, 105–6, 107, 121, 122, 128–29, 178, 182, 201, 205, 208, 211, 227, 264n9; and wells, 205, 264n9; and western land, 71–73, 75, 182–83, 203, 205–14, 227; and western ranching industry, 72; and western Socorro County, 155, 215; and windmills, 205; and wool production, 48; and Wyoming, 79. *See also* agriculture; Court of Private Land Claims; fencing; land grants; National Forest Reserves

land grants: and American sovereignty, 27; Anglo American acquisition of, 117, 119; and Anton Chico Grant, 196, 263n50; and Antonio Ortiz Grant, 196, 249n72; and Bartolome Fernandes Grant, 36; and Beaubien-Miranda Land Grant, 27, 235n4; and Bond brothers, 253n26; and Bosque del Apache Grant, 185–86, 188–89, 199, 264n57; and community grants, 15, 20, 70, 117, 234n43; 266n30; and "deed of trust," 261n24;

herd size, 101; and Hispanic land, 266n30; and horses and mules, 28; and Maxwell Land Grant, 27–28, 92, 117, 236n24; and Mora Grant, 196, 197–98, 263n50; in New Mexico, 234n43; and Ojo del Espiritu Grant, 37; and open-range grazing, 206; and ownership, 206, 250n76, 263n50; and Pablo Montoya Grant, 117, 250n76, 250n78, 250n81; *partido* system on, 28; and populated areas, 20, 28; and Preston Beck Grant, 146, 253n26; and private grants, 15, 20, 27, 117, 234n43, 250n76; and public domain, 208; and ranches, 86, 146; recipients of, 14, 20, 27, 28; and *ricos*, 20, 110, 116, 117; sales of, 110; and San Clemente Land Grant, 6, 37; and San Miguel del Bado Grant, 249n73; and settlement, 232n27; and sheep, 145, 249–250n73, 250n76; and sheep raising, 20, 27–28, 117; size of, 20, 27–28; in southern Colorado, 234n43; and Spanish-Mexican grants, 176, 207, 234n43, 250n75, 250n80; and Spanish-Mexican system, 70, 117, 119; and the state, 20–21, 234n43; and Stephen Elkins, 249n72; and territorial period, 20

Leavenworth, E. S., 144

Lee, Harry F., 112, 113

Letcher, Adolph, 149

Lewis and Clark, 26

Lincoln, President Abraham, 45, 238n44, 258n1

Lovelace, Roe, 120, 209, 250n81, 251n91

Lummis, Charles F., 3, 84

Luna, Antonio Jose, 41, 238n41

Luna, Jesus, 44

Luna, Juan, 5–6

Luna, Rafael, 41

Luna, Solomon, 37, 60, 66, 112, 113, 115, 193f. *See also* Catron, Thomas; sheep

MacArthur, Archibald, 141, 142

Majors, Alexander, 67, 68

Manifest Destiny, 119

290 INDEX

Marcy, William L., 32
Maxwell, Lucian B., 27, 28, 35, 42, 43, 46, 236n24. See also mercantile capitalism
McCarthy, Justin H., 141
McKenna, US Attorney General, 157
McKinley, President William, 157, 159, 238n44
Mendizábal, Governor López de, 12
mercantile capitalism: and Anglo merchants, 86, 88, 132, 152; and Anglo sheepmen, 131, 132; and Bond company, 132–33, 135, 140, 141; and Bond enterprises, 148, 152; and capitalization, 81, 139, 140, 141, 152, 205; and Charles Ilfeld Company, 87, 90, 96, 141; and Chaves family, 87–88; and dealers, 138, 139; development of, 96; and German-Jewish immigrants, 87; and Hispanic merchants, 35, 87–88, 152; and industrial capitalism, 245n10; and international crop data, 91; and Lucian B. Maxwell, 92, 235n5, 246n23; and market volatility, 148, 149; in New Mexico, 24, 31, 35, 47, 82, 83–91; and Santa Fe trade, 29–30, 35; and Santa Fe Trail, 85, 87; and sheep, 31, 35, 85, 139; and sutlers, 35; and wool, 31, 35, 47, 51, 85, 86–88, 139. See also Bond brothers
Mercure, Henry, 42
Mexico: and buffalo grass (genus Buchloe), 72; Chihuahua in, 15–16, 17, 18, 21, 26, 29, 30, 36, 40–41, 43, 233n34, 245n11; and Coahuila, 16; and desert scrubland, 104; and Durango, 16, 19, 30, 40, 233n36; exportation of sheep and wool to, 15–17, 19, 30, 40, 46, 233n36; government of, 18–19, 20, 21–22, 24, 30, 234n43; independence of, 18, 24, 25, 234n1; and livestock, 14, 18; markets in, 3, 12, 16, 17, 18, 19, 24; Mexico City in, 16, 18; as New Spain, 16; Parral in, 12; population of, 234n42; and sheep drives, 232n29, 233n41, 243n113; sheep in, 40; silver and gold from, 16, 29; and silver miners, 16; Sonora in, 16, 42; and trade caravans, 26

Miles, General Nelson, 154
Miranda, Guadalupe, 27
Mississippi River, 35, 69, 75, 76, 93, 242n90
Missouri: and American Valley Company, 200; and cost of sheep production, 76; Independence in, 238n42; Kansas City in, 35, 49, 58, 63, 95, 97, 99, 176, 185, 192, 194, 195, 196, 198; Lexington in, 198; and Old Spanish Trail, 237n35; and Santa Fe Trail, 29, 176; and sheep drives, 74, 95; St. Louis in, 30, 36, 40, 41, 49, 87, 99, 195; University of, 176; and woolen industry, 51; and wool industry, 48–49, 87, 88
Missouri River, 35, 67, 225, 235n10
Mitchell, Governor Robert B., 56
Montana, 67, 78, 79, 80, 115, 169. See also sheep; wool
Moore, J. A., 75
Mora Ceballos, Governor Francisco de la, 12
Morley, Ray, 174, 215
Morrison, John V., 189, 190
mountain men, 5, 26, 27, 42

National Forest Reserves, 114–15, 168, 205, 214–16, 217
Native Americans: ancestral hunting grounds of, 71, 124; and Apaches, 15, 22, 23, 32, 41, 53, 107, 154; and buffalos, 71; ceremonies of, 13; children of, 14; and Christianity, 10–11; and Comanches, 23, 53; and cotton weaving, 24; forced marches of, 54; hunting and gathering of, 23, 32; and Mary Chischillie, 6; and Navajos, 4–5, 6, 8, 13, 14, 15, 18, 22, 24, 32, 52–55, 107, 108–9, 146, 219–23, 266n37; and nomadic tribes, 15, 18, 24, 31, 32, 34, 45, 51, 53, 71, 72, 124, 234n46; and peonage, 56; and Plains Indian trade, 29; and Pueblos, 10–11, 13, 17, 22, 23–24, 32, 231n16, 232n32; raiding parties of, 5–6, 7, 9, 13, 18, 21, 22, 31, 32, 34, 36, 44, 45, 51–53, 54, 55, 60, 71, 84, 119, 206, 234n46, 238n39; and the

Index 291

Reconquest, 13; and removal of from land, 71–72; and reservations, 71, 93, 108, 146, 219; and sheep, 8, 13, 18, 22, 23–24, 32, 34, 52–53, 54, 55, 56, 108; and sheep shearing, 171–72; and slaves, 5, 13, 15, 27, 56; and trans-Mississippi West, 71; and US occupying force, 34; and Utes, 15, 22, 32, 40, 41, 42, 54; and warfare, 34, 84; and women, 6, 14, 32; and Yuma people, 41. *See also* Navajo people; Pueblo Revolt (1680)

Navajo people: and Anglo merchants, 223; and cattle, 32, 219; and the *churro*, 4–5; deaths of, 54; and detribalization, 15; family groups of, 8, 54, 55, 219, 220–21; and federal stock reduction program, 219–22; and goats, 53, 54, 55, 219, 220, 221; and horses, 54, 219, 266n37; imprisonment of, 8, 54, 108; lands of, 13, 53–54, 55, 108–9, 219–22; and livestock, 55, 108, 219–22; and the Long Walk, 54; movement of homes of, 8; and Navajo Reservation, 6, 8, 54, 108, 109, 146, 219, 220–21; and peonage system, 14; population of, 219; and Pueblos, 13; raiding parties of, 54, 55, 107; and relocation to Fort Sumner, 54; and sheep herds, 6, 8, 24, 32, 45, 52–53, 54, 55, 107, 108, 219, 220, 221, 222; and sheep husbandry, 13; and stock reduction program, 266n37; in the territorial period, 55; tribal council of, 221; as ward of US government, 55; and women, 8, 14, 54, 55, 222, 230n14; and wool weaving, 13, 14, 22, 55, 222–23

Nebraska, 76, 78, 80, 96, 99, 132. *See also* sheep

New Mexico: and Abiquiu, 237n35; and Albuquerque, 12, 23, 34, 36, 42, 62, 100, 101, 110, 113, 114, 132, 141, 145, 152, 159, 166, 174, 196, 197, 233n37, 245n10; and American education, 30, 236n13; and American markets, 31, 34–35, 38–46; Americans' arrival in, 25–34, 35; and American sovereignty, 21, 25, 30–31, 34; and American Valley Company,

199–200; and Anglo immigrants, 27–28, 34, 35, 53, 60, 109, 120, 133, 154, 155, 163, 182, 204–7, 226; annexation of, 6, 19, 20, 27, 30, 31, 32, 34, 35, 36, 38, 47, 49, 52, 53, 60, 70, 85, 87, 103, 106, 117, 206, 207, 224, 225, 235n5, 236n13, 236n14, 237n38; and Armijo family, 29, 37; and Bernalillo, 14; and Bernalillo County, 34, 37, 44, 45t, 53, 84; and Bond enterprises, 148, 152; and buffalo, 10, 247n37; Catron County in, 5; cattle in, 3, 7, 9, 10, 11f, 14, 27, 28, 32, 93, 95, 96, 107, 129, 151, 163, 171, 182, 204–5, 206, 212, 231n17, 233n37, 238n39, 246n24, 246n26; Cebolleta in, 34; Ceja-Llano region of, 212, 214, 265n18; and census of 1757, 15, 232n30; changes in, 199, 205–6, 212, 224; and Chaves family, 29; and *churros*, 4–5, 11f, 76; class consolidation in, 19, 22; climate of, 4, 5, 6, 9, 20, 23, 33, 60, 64, 97, 98–99, 105, 106–7, 108, 109, 128, 161, 164, 169, 172, 179, 182, 224, 227, 241n83, 246n26; Colfax County in, 59, 127, 212; and colonists' economy, 234n46; and conflicts over land, 211; constitution of, 37; and Cuba, 107, 108; and Cuervo, 141, 142, 150, 212; Datil in, 6, 122, 127, 258n45; Department of Agriculture of, 11f, 77f; economy of, 16, 17–18, 26, 28, 29, 30, 31, 34–35, 38, 47, 49, 58, 64, 77–78, 85, 87, 88, 102–3, 116, 130, 133, 152, 199, 207, 216–17, 218, 223–24, 227; in the eighteenth century, 83; and El Cerrito village, 249n73; and El Paso, 15; Encino in, 145; and Espanola, 135, 136, 143, 145, 147, 151, 231n17, 247n28; and exportation of sheep, 78, 80–81, 96, 113; and exportation of wool, 47, 96; and foreign markets, 26, 29, 30; and French Canadians, 26, 27; and fur trade, 26, 28, 49, 235n5; Galisteo in, 32–33, 39; Gallup in, 109; *genizaro* class in, 13, 15; goats in, 3, 7, 15, 18, 36; government of, 22, 36, 62, 64, 110, 212, 225; and grazing land, 67, 128–29, 175, 199, 212; and Great Plains, 265n18; and growers'

292   INDEX

peonage, 17; and Guadalupe County, 128, 146; Hispanic population in, 19–20, 34–36, 53, 110–11; Hispanic settlements in, 32; and homestead legislation, 225; and horses, 9, 22, 32–33, 207, 232n30, 233n34, 233n37; and imported goods, 233n34; and industrialization, 225; intermarriage of elites in, 14–15, 27, 28; and irrigation, 64, 102; and Jornada del Muerto, 16; and La Joya de Sevilleta, 16; Las Cruces in, 102; Los Lunas in, 41, 172; and Las Vegas, 23, 32, 34, 40, 62, 87, 88, 90, 92, 96, 101, 117, 141, 246n27; and "lease law," 114–15; and livestock, 8–12, 14, 15, 16, 17, 18, 20, 22, 24, 25–26, 28, 32, 33, 34, 36, 37–40, 41, 46, 53, 59, 71, 83, 86, 87, 92, 96, 107, 128, 136, 160, 204–5, 213, 225, 227, 231n17, 231n21, 232n29, 232n30, 233n37; living conditions in, 16, 150; and lumbering, 225; and Luna village, 37; Magdelena in, 60, 122, 161, 163, 164, 192, 255n5; and mercantile establishments, 245n10; and Mexican Indians, 231n17; and Mexican sovereignty, 3, 19, 25, 27, 46, 52, 204–5; and Miguel Antonio Otero Jr., 238n44; military occupation of, 30, 34–35; and mining, 225, 227; and mixed-race mestizos, 15; and Mora, 23, 212; and mutton, 25, 39, 76; and national defense, 227; and national forest reserves, 225; and New Mexico Sheep Sanitary Board, 37, 112, 113, 114; northeastern part of, 58; and Old Spanish Trail, 39, 40, 237n35; and open-range grazing, 204–5, 227; and Pecos River, 54; and Perea family, 29; and pobladores, 28, 30, 31, 32; and pobres (poor people), 17–18, 46; and popular elections, 30; population of, 10f, 12, 15, 16, 22, 23, 34, 53, 206, 208, 225–26, 231n17, 234n43; and public domain, 123, 124, 208; Pueblo population in, 232n32; Pueblo settlements in, 32; and Puerco Valley, 107–8; Puerto de Luna in, 36, 59; Quemado in, 178; Reconquest of, 12, 117, 232n27; Reserve in, 154; rico families

of, 14, 19, 22, 29, 30, 35, 36–38, 232n29, 233n36; rico-pobre (rich-poor) divide in, 46, 239n51; and Rio Abajo, 11, 12, 15, 16, 18, 42, 44, 231n21; and Rio Arriba, 12, 15, 231n21; and Rio Arriba County, 34; Rio Chama in, 9; and Rio Grande, 33, 36, 37, 52, 104, 171, 189, 231n21; Rio Grande Valley of, 9, 11, 16, 22, 107, 206, 247n33; and Rio Pecos, 33, 36; and Rio Puerco, 37, 107, 108, 256n20; and Rio Tularosa, 160; and Rocky Mountain–Great Plains region, 95; and Roswell, 112, 152; and Sandoval County, 37; and San Luis Valley, 136; and San Miguel County, 146, 212, 251n93; San Miguel in, 23, 34, 36, 88, 128; Santa Ana County in, 34, 53; and Santa Cruz, 12, 15, 23, 233n37; and Santa Fe County, 34; Santa Fe in, 11, 12, 15, 22, 23, 26–27, 28, 32, 34, 36, 37, 40, 42, 43, 55, 87, 117, 135, 151–52, 176, 189, 231n21, 233n37, 245n11, 246n24; and Santa Fe trade, 28–30, 31, 35, 36, 42, 94–95, 235n8, 237n26; and Santa Rosa, 130, 141; and Santo Domingo Pueblo, 33; scientific research in, 227; sheep and wool merchants in, 150, 224–25; and sheep drives, 78, 95; sheep in, 3–4, 14, 15, 16, 17, 18, 20–24, 26, 31, 34, 35–46, 50, 51–55, 58–59, 61, 62, 75–81, 90–91, 96, 111–14, 163, 225, 227, 231n16, 231n17, 232n34, 233n37; and small-scale growers, 216–18, 227; society of, 13, 17–18, 19, 28, 82, 84, 94, 109–11, 128, 227, 232n28, 233n36, 235n5; and Socorro, 34, 157, 245n10; and Socorro County, 153, 155, 170, 178, 185–86, 197, 255n1, 255n3; and Spanish army, 14, 26; and Spanish civil law, 236n14; and Spanish colonial period, 8–18, 227, 234n1, 237n27; Spanish conquistadores in, 8–9; and Spanish Cortez, 36; and Spanish-Mexican period, 5, 204; Spanish population of, 232n30; Spanish settlement in, 231n17; and Spanish sovereignty, 3, 4, 26, 52, 219; and the Spiegelbergs, 141; and statehood, 37, 85–86, 115, 145, 199,

200, 225; and St. Augustine Plains, 37; and Taos County, 34; Taos in, 23, 26, 27, 32, 104, 141, 145, 235n5, 245n10; and territorial era, 3, 4, 14, 28, 31, 36, 38, 39, 46, 47, 55–56, 58, 60, 61, 62, 64, 73–74, 76, 82, 85–86, 91, 93, 94, 97, 110, 112, 115, 133, 140, 145, 176, 199, 205–6, 208, 223, 224, 225, 227, 258n1; Texas cattlemen in, 206; and textiles and hides, 16, 232n34, 233n34; and trade caravans, 15, 16–17, 24, 231n21, 232n34; and trade with California, 39–46; and trade with Mexico, 15–19, 24, 29, 30, 38, 39, 44, 231n22, 232n34, 237n33; and Tucson, 33; and the twentieth century, 226, 227; Union forces in, 53–54; and University of New Mexico, 252n3; and Valencia, 34; and Valencia County, 36, 37, 44, 45t; vegetation of, 103–5, 106, 107, 226–27; Wagon Mound in, 90, 101, 139, 140, 141, 142, 143, 144; wells in, 128–29, 251n98, 264n9; and wool production, 57, 57t; and Yrizarri family, 29. See also Bond, Frank; sheep industry; wool

New York: and American Valley Company, 200; and banking, 40, 145, 191, 223; Buffalo in, 185; and Charles H. Elmendorf, 189, 194, 198; and Hudson River, 58; and Leon Arnold & Co., 87; and New York City, 86, 87, 149, 155, 159, 187, 191, 194, 195, 198, 237n33; and wool, 50

Ohio River, 35
Oñate, Don Juan de, 9
Oregon, 226
Otero, Judge Antonio Jose, 43
Otero, Miguel Antonio, Jr., 41, 62, 64, 92–93, 110, 122, 236n13. See also New Mexico
Otero, Sellar & Co., 92

Palen, R. J., 197
Paltenghe, Manuel, 141, 142
Patterson, John D., 182
Pattie, James O., 5

Peck, Lieutenant W. G., 32
Pena, Abe, 8
Peralta, Governor Pedro de, 22
Perea, Colonel Franciso, 36
Perea, Don Jose Leandro, 37
Perea, Francisco, 43, 44, 236n13, 237n33, 238n44
Perea, Joaquin, 45t
Perea, Jose Leandro, 57–58
Pike, Lieutenant Zebulon Montgomery, 26, 232n34
Pike Expedition, 225
Pino, Facundo, 36
Pino, Miguel, 36
Pino, Nicolas, 36, 43
Pino, Pedro Bautista, 36, 43, 253n26
Platte River, 99, 100, 102, 218
pobladores (settlers): and churro flocks, 4; debts of, 13; and land, 28, 30–32, 207, 209; and Maxwell Land Grant, 28; and Mexican livestock, 14
Porter, H. M., 127
Potter, James Brown, 119
Prager, W.S., 112
Prince, Governor L. Bradford, 63
Pueblo Revolt (1680), 10, 12, 13, 17, 20, 117

railroads: arrival of, 10f, 12, 29, 50, 62, 63, 71, 82, 87, 95, 96, 133, 141, 146, 218; and Atchison, Topeka and Santa Fe Railway (AT&SF), 62, 94, 95, 217, 246n27; and barbed wire, 128; and capital, 94; and Chicago, Rock Island, and Pacific Railroad, 141; and Colorado, 95, 217, 247n28; and Cuervo, 253n16; and Denver and Rio Grande Western Railroad (D&RGW), 95, 96, 133, 135–136, 247n28; and eastern markets, 208; and freight rates, 114; and grant lands, 120, 124; and Hispanic labor, 170; and homesteaders, 208; and Kansas, 94, 95; in the Midwest, 68, 208; in New Mexico, 63, 64, 82, 91, 94–96, 158, 160, 208; and sheep industry, 79, 94–96, 142, 147, 161, 211; and shipping materials, 125; and Southern Pacific Railroad, 94;

294 INDEX

and trade, 47, 49–50; and transportation, 68, 78, 94–96, 98, 128, 208; and
the West, 94, 94–96; and wool industry,
49–50, 63, 94
ranches: and American Valley Company,
184, 190–191; and American Valley
Company ranch, 251n89; and Anglo
sheepmen, 131, 157–59; and Baca
ranches, 6, 173; and barbed wire, 125,
126, 127, 251n94; and Becker, Blackwell
& Co., 191; and Bell Ranch, 117, 119,
127, 129, 249n72, 265n14; and Blain
ranches, 161; and Bond brothers, 146;
and capitalization, 81, 82, 152, 203;
and cattle-ranching, 7, 93, 126, 135,
154–155, 178, 201, 246n24, 265n14; and
Charles H. Elmendorf, 189, 190, 191,
192; and commercial lending, 175; and
estancias (working livestock ranches),
24; and feeding ranches, 144, 146; and
Garland Ranch, 167; and Gorras Blancas,
128; and Guadalupe County, 64; and
Guy Spears, 258n45; and homesteads,
257n24; and Horse Springs, 166, 167;
and Horse Springs Ranch, 253n16; and
irrigation, 129, 184; and Jack Culley,
129; and John Chisum's ranch area,
129; and labor problems, 189–190, 191;
land of, 120, 122–23, 126–29, 161; and
livestock, 74, 78, 129, 179; and managers, 135; and mortgages, 203; murder
near, 178, 179; in northern Colorado, 57;
in northern Wyoming, 57; and open-
range ranching, 57, 74, 122–23, 128, 178,
205; and ranchers, 35, 47, 70, 175, 205;
and Reserve, New Mexico, 154; and San
Miguel Ranch, 37; and sheep ranches,
21, 30, 36, 37, 38, 56, 57, 64, 70, 74, 78, 81,
86, 92, 99, 116, 124, 128–29, 152, 153, 156,
161, 164, 165–67, 169, 171–73, 178, 184,
189–91, 192, 203, 250n80, 255n3; and
Spur Ranch, 163, 165, 167, 257n24; and
Steven Dorsey, 247n41; and S.U. Cattle
Company, 160; and S.U. Ranch, 156, 160,
167; in the trans-Mississippi West, 26,
176; and Wilson Waddingham, 129. See

also American Valley Company; land
Raynolds, Jefferson W., 64, 122
repartimiento system, 12–13
Rocky Mountains, 26, 51, 57, 60, 67–68, 72.
See also sheep industry
Roosevelt, President Theodore, 163, 214–
15, 255n3
Rosas, Governor Luis de, 22
Russell, Majors, and Waddell, 67

San Miguel College, 37
San Miguel National Bank of Las Vegas, 93
scab, 6, 111, 112, 164, 166, 213
Schmidt, John Justus, 90, 139
Scotland, 243n103
Sena, Abe, 5, 6
sheep: and American market economy,
24, 31, 39, 40, 41–46, 63–64, 75–78, 109,
148, 149, 176; and Anglo Americans,
39, 76–77, 109, 218–219; annual earnings for, 77f; and Armijo family, 19, 41;
behavior of, 6; and Bond brothers, 136,
137, 147, 152, 201, 252n3; and Boston,
63–64; breeding of, 37, 74, 98–99, 227;
and bucks, 190; and Chaves family,
19, 36–37, 233n41; and church funding, 24; and churros, 4–5, 11f, 25, 26,
42, 44–45, 46, 51, 58, 59, 60–61, 62, 63,
67, 68, 74, 78–79, 80, 101, 117, 159, 162,
163; and churro seed stock, 74, 79; and
churro wool and fleece, 4–5, 61, 79, 159;
clothing from, 4, 9, 22, 24, 47; and
Cochiti Pueblo, 14; and Colorado, 79, 80,
99–101; and common "Mexican" sheep,
163; cost of, 243n109; and Cotswold
rams from Canada, 59; diet of, 4, 5, 8;
diseases of, 6, 60, 111, 112, 113, 114, 125,
136, 164, 166; in the East, 73, 74; and
economy, 16; and effects of overgrazing, 109; and ewes, 4, 14, 16, 43, 45t, 59,
60, 61, 63, 74, 76, 79, 80, 83, 84, 99, 101,
130, 139, 158, 159, 161, 164, 190, 252n100;
and expansion of Hispanic homeland,
22–23, 78–79; exportation of, 12, 15–17,
26, 30, 45–46, 47, 78, 96; feeding of, 82,
92, 97–102, 137–38, 143, 144, 165–69,

201, 242n93, 247–248n42, 247n32, 247n33, 248n47; as a food source, 3, 4, 9, 22, 23, 38–39, 43, 46, 47, 54, 56, 62, 63, 68, 74, 83, 230n14, 231n16, 237n36; and Frank Bond, 145–46; and Galisteo–Pecos River area, 9; and *genizaros*, 20; and grazing, 8, 10, 20, 27, 37, 53, 62, 97, 114, 142, 145, 146, 155, 158, 163, 168, 212, 215; and growers' organizations, 82, 111–15; and herding, 3, 4, 5–8, 9, 14, 15, 23, 27, 32, 36, 39; and Hispanic growers, 218–19, 244n6; and Idaho, 78, 99; and Illinois, 43, 76; and Indiana, 76; and Kansas, 96, 99, 100, 242n93; and Kentucky, 59; and lambs, 6, 8, 37, 40, 63, 69, 76, 83, 97, 98, 99, 100, 101, 103, 124–25, 126, 130, 138, 143, 144, 152, 159, 160, 163, 164, 168–69, 171, 172, 173, 176, 184, 192, 202, 227, 252n100; large flocks of, 106, 107, 129; marketing of, 38, 44, 58, 82, 97, 98, 138–39; and meat market, 69, 80, 95, 97, 101, 224; and Merino-*churro* crosses, 62; and Merino sheep, 58–61, 62, 158, 161, 163, 239n54, 241n81; milk of, 9, 164; and mission herds, 11, 12, 14, 15, 23, 24, 38; and mixed-race *mestizos*, 15; and Montana, 80, 96, 226; and mutton, 4, 10, 16, 23, 39, 43, 51, 56, 62, 63, 64, 67, 69, 76, 80, 97, 101, 103, 155, 165, 176, 202, 238n39; and Native Americans' raids, 22, 41, 45, 51–53; and Navajos' herds, 55; and Nebraska, 74, 78, 100, 144, 242n93; and Nevada, 41, 74, 78, 138; and New Mexico growers, 39, 43–44, 51, 56, 57–58, 63, 66–67, 73, 74; and Ohio, 43, 59, 75, 184, 244n117; and "Old Roberts," 40; and Omaha, 63; and open-range grazing, 115–16, 117, 125, 170, 176, 199, 203, 223; and Ortiz family, 19; and Otero family, 19, 37, 233n41; and ownership, 230n14; and *partidarios*, 6–7, 19, 20; and *partido* contracts, 16, 37; and Pennsylvania, 59; and peones, 20; and Perea family, 19, 37, 235n7; and Philadelphia, 63–64; and Pino family, 19; population of, 10, 11f,

15, 18, 45, 51, 58, 64, 76, 78, 79, 103, 108, 146, 209, 225–26, 239–40n59, 241n81, 243n114, 267n2; and post–Civil War period, 39, 73, 78–81; predators of, 6, 60, 96, 159, 213; price of, 6, 16, 19, 26, 29, 40, 41, 42, 43–44, 45, 46, 59, 63, 64, 74, 75, 76, 80, 93, 157–60, 165, 172, 241n84; production of, 74, 75–76, 81, 86, 88, 91, 98, 103, 117, 202, 203, 205, 213, 227; and Pueblo herds, 13; raising of, 6, 8, 11, 15, 18, 55, 60, 63, 67–68, 76, 82, 83, 84–85, 101, 165, 169, 182, 202, 204–5, 213, 223, 227, 230n14; and rams, 59, 60, 61, 63, 74, 79, 80, 124, 158, 161; and Reserve, New Mexico, 154; and *rico* families, 15, 17, 19, 36–38, 47, 86; sales of, 163, 173; and Sandoval family, 19; selective breeding of, 58–62, 80, 117, 124, 239n55; and Sevilla area, 9; shearing of, 37, 83, 92, 96, 124, 126, 130, 158, 159, 160, 166–67, 171, 222; and sheep dipping, 37, 111–12, 113, 125, 142, 159, 161, 164, 166, 167, 171, 205, 225, 261n21; and sheep drives, 3, 4, 18, 19, 25, 26, 29, 40, 41–45, 46, 74, 78, 80, 96, 185, 232n29, 232n33, 233n41, 237–238n39; and sheep husbandry, 61; and sheep thief, 230n6; shelter for, 73, 166; and Shropshire rams, 161; slaughter of, 74, 92, 201; and Solomon Luna, 148, 161, 166, 172, 173, 178, 224, 236n13, 238n41; and Spanish herds, 13; and stock losses, 18, 52–53, 59, 63, 96, 159, 161, 164, 169, 171, 182, 185, 190, 191, 192, 194, 252n100; and S. U. Ranch, 157, 159–60; and tallow, 9; and Texas, 59, 76, 78, 80, 164, 184, 185; transportation of, 62, 78, 82, 86, 95–96, 98, 99, 147; and Utah, 41, 74, 76, 78; and Vermont, 59, 244n117; and water, 20, 105, 109; in the West, 71–78; and western wool industry, 78; and wethers, 45t, 59, 63, 76, 83, 159, 184, 192; and Wisconsin, 76, 100; and Wyoming, 76, 78, 79–80, 96, 217, 226. *See also* scab; wool

sheep industry: and American growers, 24, 25–26, 64–65, 66, 67, 69, 73, 109,

296 INDEX

138–39; and American Valley Company, 199–200; and Anglo Americans, 245n6; and Anglo leadership, 64, 86; and banking, 91–93, 174, 200, 202, 224, 225; capitalization of, 113, 116, 130–31, 133, 179; capital requirements for, 115–16, 138, 165–67, 174, 176, 202, 255n1; and Chaves family, 36, 37; and Civil War period, 50, 85–86; commercialization of, 3, 55, 75; in the East, 55, 69, 75; and economic developments, 75, 86; and feeder farms, 96–103; and foreign markets, 149; foundation of, 3; and government policies, 21–22, 24, 55, 101, 113–14, 115; and Great Plains–Rocky Mountain region, 75, 77, 80–81; and Gross, Kelly, 100; growth of, 19, 21, 24, 30, 31–32, 50, 76, 77–81, 84, 90–92, 96, 103, 124, 206; and Hispanic growers, 216–18; and Hispanic suppliers, 139; importance of merchants to, 91–92; and industrialization, 130–31; and land distribution, 20–22, 121–24; as largest industry in New Mexico, 227; and Louis F. Nohl, 143; and Mexican period, 18–22, 30, 32; in the Midwest, 69; modernization of, 24, 176; and Moulton-Ilfeld Company, 100; and Native Americans, 21, 32, 55; and natural resources, 115, 168, 169, 205; and Nebraska, 200; and New Mexico's economy, 49, 102–3, 140, 148, 200, 223–24; and New Mexico sheep, 80, 117, 169, 225; news of, 149–50; and Northeastern states, 200; and *partido* system, 59; and patrones, 15, 19; and Perea family, 40; and post–Civil War period, 49, 50, 56, 81, 91; profitability of, 115, 117, 124, 129, 130, 139, 147, 148–149, 165, 192, 198, 225; and railroads, 95–96; regulation of, 112–13, 115; and *rico* families, 15, 19, 36–38; risks of, 60, 63, 64–65, 91, 96, 138, 148–49, 153, 165, 168, 169, 201, 203, 255n1; and Rocky Mountain–Great Plains region, 78, 80, 97, 182, 206, 209, 226; and Santa Fe trade, 86; and Santa Fe Trail, 28–29, 94–95, 133; and

sheep drives, 12, 19, 39, 40–41, 80, 95, 96; and small-scale growers, 244–45n6; and Southwest's economy, 130; and Spanish period, 30, 32; and territorial period, 5, 14, 30; and "The Great Die-Up," 182; and transportation, 55, 94–96; and University of New Mexico, 255n1; in the West, 7, 31, 38, 64–65, 68, 74–81, 94, 115–16; and western Dakota Territory, 80. *See also* sheepmen

sheepmen: and Anglo Americans, 35, 40, 58, 59, 70, 79, 80, 84–85, 116, 131; and Anglo stockmen, 235n7; and Armijo family, 37, 41, 44, 84, 239n51; and Baca family, 239n51; and "Big Freeze" of 1886-1887, 79; and capitalization, 77; and Daniel Troy, 61; and descendants of Capt. Duran y Chaves, 14, 19; families of, 7, 19, 23, 32, 36, 37–38, 44, 57–58; and feeder farms, 98, 99; and Gila River route, 41, 42; and government taxes, 18–19; and grazing, 55, 71, 125, 215–216; and *guias* (permits), 19, 215; and Hispanic growers, 85, 86, 182, 237n31; and Hispanic herders, 5–8, 25, 36, 37, 39, 41, 42, 43, 70, 71, 73, 80, 85, 107, 123, 136, 158, 163, 170–71, 206, 230n6, 255n1; and Hispanic ranchers, 3, 37, 44, 46, 117, 163, 173; and Hubble family, 237n31; and John and Thomas Cosgriff, 217; in Kansas, 80; and labor problems, 170–73; and lambing, 258n42; and large *churro* flocks, 79, 200; and livestock, 125–126; loans to, 92–93; and Luna family, 44, 45t, 239n51; and Native Americans' raids, 18, 22, 41, 44, 51–53, 54; in New Mexico, 18, 19, 22–23, 35–38, 39, 40–46, 51, 53, 56, 58–59, 62–63, 75, 76, 78; from Ohio Valley, 75; and open-range grazing, 3, 5, 20, 62–63; organizations of, 111–15, 225; and Otero family, 37, 41, 44, 45t, 64, 239n51; and ownership, 44, 45t, 46, 84, 85, 88; and *partidarios*, 6–7, 22, 83–84, 85; and Perea family, 37, 44, 45t, 57–58, 239n51; and Pino family, 43, 239n51; and *ricos*, 110,

116, 214; and Romero family, 237*n31*; and Santa Fe trade, 36; and "Santiago" (James Lawrence) Hubbell, 44, 45*t*; and settlement in villages, 23; and sheep breeding, 58–62, 78, 80, 98, 99; and sheep drives, 12, 18, 19, 41–45, 46, 59, 78, 80, 88, 95, 98; and smaller land tracts, 213, 214; and speculation, 38, 39, 41, 44; and Toribio Romero, 45*t*; and *vaqueros* (mounted overseers), 7; and wells, 124; and the West, 63, 70–71, 74, 78, 79; and wool, 51, 63; and Yrisarris, 237*n31. See also* labor; Patterson, John D.

Sherman, General William T., 97

silver mines, 12, 16, 74

Slaughter, William B., 178, 179, 184

slavery: abolitionists' opposition to, 31, 55, 56, 85; and captive Native slaves, 240*n67*; and The Master-Servant Act of 1851, 56; and Native Americans, 13–14, 15, 27, 31, 56, 130, 225; and New Mexico, 85–86; and peones, 56, 225; and Peon Law of 1867, 56; and *poblador* families, 13; regulation of, 55–56, 225; and slave hunting, 54; and slave owners, 56; and slaves, 40, 56, 231*n17*; and southwestern slavery, 56, 85–86; and US Constitution's 13th Amendment, 56, 85. *See also* Civil War; labor

Spain: and *churros*, 4; government of, 234*n43*, 236*n22*; Malaga in, 195; Mexican independence from, 18, 24, 25; and Mexican livestock, 14; and New Mexico, 3, 4, 14, 17; Sevilla area of, 9; soldiers of, 236*n22*

Spanish-American War, 154, 163

Springer, Frank, 127

Staab, Abraham, 92, 140

Stevens, Montague: and attention to business, 200–201; and cattle, 154–55, 157, 158, 160–61, 201, 202, 256*n8*; and Dan Gatlin, 154, 155, 163, 174; death of, 257*n27*; debts of, 203; dipping facility of, 111–12, 159, 166, 173, 253*n16*; education of, 153–54; employees of, 169–72, 173, 190, 202, 203, 258*n43*; family of, 202;

flocks of, 161–64, 166, 167, 168, 257*n23*; and funds from England, 166, 173, 202, 255*n5*; and grazing permits, 215; and Helen Gordon Dill, 155, 159, 163–64, 169, 174, 255*n5*; and Horse Springs Ranch, 166, 253*n16*, 257*n27*; and Jacob H. Wood, 159, 160, 163; and Judge Hamilton, 156, 157; and land, 122, 155–57, 160, 161, 162, 168, 169, 173, 201; and Leonard Wood, 159, 160, 161, 163, 164, 166, 167, 169, 171, 172, 202; letters of, 153, 157, 164, 167, 169, 170, 173, 174, 201, 257*n24*; and livestock, 173; and Mogollon Mountains, 154; and open-range grazing, 203; parents of, 153; and sheep industry, 131, 160–74, 201, 224; and sheep ranches, 152, 155, 157–59, 160, 161, 162, 165–67, 168, 169, 171–74, 178, 255*n3*; and Shropshire rams, 60; and S.U. Ranch, 156, 157, 158–59, 256*n8*; wealth of, 120, 153, 175, 202; and western Socorro County, 244–45*n6*; and wool, 164, 166–67

Stoll, Judge C. H., 199

Stoneroad, George W., 59

Sultemeier, Peggy, 130

Swan Land and Cattle Company, 79

tariffs: woolen tariff, 65–66, 241n87; wool tariff, 65–66, 114, 149, 157, 194, 225, 240*n62*, 241*n87*

Taylor, H. M., 213

Tisdall, Arthur J., 129

Treaty of Guadalupe-Hidalgo, 31

Troy, Daniel, 116

Turley, Jesse B., 41

Turner, Frederick Jackson, 204

United States: and American Southwest, 31; and Apache wars, 154; Army of, 21, 30, 31, 32–33, 34, 35, 45, 50–51, 53–54, 55, 56, 57, 71, 93, 94, 103, 119, 154, 225, 230*n6*; and Army of the West, 24, 30; and buffalo removal, 71–72; cattle in, 67–68, 77f, 79, 80, 99, 154, 155, 156–58; and census reports, 70, 77f, 78, 234*n42*, 240*n60*, 265*n12*; Congress of, 207, 214,

238n44; Constitution of, 204; cotton shortages in, 47, 50, 52; currency in, 244n1; and demographics, 205; Department of Agriculture of, 53, 112, 114, 213, 215, 227; and Department of the Interior, 214; disappearance of frontier in, 204–5; discovery of, 204; economy of, 24, 31, 47, 64, 67, 102–3, 223–24; and expert Carman, 61; and federal laws, 65, 114–15, 123; financial community of, 175; and foreign imports, 58, 65; government of, 30, 31–32, 34, 55, 65, 66, 67, 68, 85, 91, 108, 109, 114–15, 121, 124, 207, 213, 214–16, 220, 221, 225, 266n37; and Great Plains, 60, 67, 68, 75; and industrialization, 62, 68–69, 128, 205, 225, 226; and Leonard Wood's military career, 163; and manufactured goods, 235n10; markets in, 25, 38–46, 47–48, 91; North Dakota in, 215; Pacific Coast of, 75; and Panic of 1853, 44, 65; and Panic of 1893, 66, 98, 100, 135, 139, 241n84; and Panic of 1907, 151; and *partido* system, 84; and post–Civil War period, 47, 66–67; and public domain, 70, 117, 119, 206; and railroads, 47, 68; settlement in, 22–23, 68–71; and South Dakota, 6; Supreme Court of, 215, 260n14; and tariffs, 65; and territorial era, 10, 12; and trade with New Mexico, 29, 30; transportation problem in, 49–50; and treatment of Navajos, 54–55; urban population of, 97; and value of cotton and wool, 52f; Washington, DC, in, 26, 31, 37, 55, 66, 114, 115, 117, 157, 178, 183, 184, 200; western migration in, 70–71, 75; and West's economic history, 151; and wool industry, 149. *See also* California; Civil War; Manifest Destiny; New Mexico; US census reports
United States–Mexico War, 38, 40, 49, 259n5
US census reports, 10f, 11f, 45, 48, 51, 52. *See also* United States
Utah, 226, 237n35

Vargas, Don Diego de, 12, 19
Vigil, Francisco Estevan, 39

Waddingham, Wilson, 117, 129, 188, 196, 265n14
Warren Livestock Company, 79
Warshauer, Fred, 139, 141, 144, 148
Warshauer-McClure Sheep Company, 144
Webb, James Josiah, 49
White, Joseph, 40–41
Wiest, Andy, 141, 142, 150, 212
Wilcox, E. V., 60, 115, 207–8
windmills, 124, 128–129
Wood, Leonard, 153, 154, 155, 156, 157, 158. *See also* Stevens, Montague; United States
wool: and American market economy, 24, 25, 31, 35, 47, 48–50, 51, 56–57, 61, 62, 65, 66, 74, 76, 101, 124–25, 138–39, 149, 176, 216–17, 226; and American Valley Company, 190, 194; and Anglo merchants, 39, 164; annual earnings for, 77f; and Arizona, 57t; and Australia, 149; and blankets and rugs, 4, 5, 17, 51, 55, 83, 222, 232n34; and Bond brothers, 136, 137, 139, 140, 147, 148, 202, 244n6; and Boston, Massachusetts, 137, 202; and brokers, 159; and Brown & Adams, 137, 138, 139; buying of, 90–91, 137, 138, 143, 145, 150; and *churro* wool, 4–5, 35, 47, 59, 62, 74, 222; classifications of, 241n88; and clothing, 4, 9, 24, 50–51, 83, 231n22; and Colorado sheepmen, 100; confiscation of, 92; and dealers, 201; and eastern mills, 25, 29, 35, 51, 62, 86, 94, 224; and *efectos del pais* (woolen goods), 29, 39, 48; exportation of, 15, 17, 96; and foreign imports, 241n85; and Frank Bond, 146, 201; and goods to be sold, 22, 35, 42, 47–51, 52, 57, 83, 223; and Gross, Blackwell & Co., 96; and Hispanic merchants, 88; and Idaho, 57t; 226; and imported wool, 47, 50, 57, 64, 65, 66, 67; and Kansas, 88; and landed Hispanic families, 57–58; marketing of, 86, 159; and Montana, 57t, 226; and

Index 299

national markets, 227; and National Wool Growers Association, 114, 115; and Navajo women, 230n14; and New Mexico wool, 67, 76, 86, 135–36, 159, 226; and New Mexico Wool Growers Association, 37, 66, 245n6; and northern textile mills, 50–51, 52, 62, 64, 137, 224; and Oregon, 57t; and *partido* system, 83, 84, 135; and Pennsylvania, 224; price of, 49, 51, 57, 63–64, 66, 69, 75, 77f, 91, 155, 157–158, 159, 165, 172, 192, 241n84; production of, 4, 5, 47, 48, 48f, 49, 50–51, 57, 57t, 58, 60, 63, 64, 66, 67, 68, 74, 75, 76, 79, 81, 126, 135, 152, 161, 163, 191–92, 202, 203, 205, 226, 227, 242n90, 267n3; profitability of, 76; and railroads, 95, 135–136; and ranchers, 62; and *rico* families, 35, 36, 37; sales of, 150, 159–160, 190, 192, 194; and Santa Fe Trail, 35, 36, 46, 49, 51, 62; and selective breeding, 37, 58, 59–60, 61, 62, 63, 80, 135, 226; and shearing, 130, 166–67; shedding of, 111; and territorial period, 67; and trade routes, 35, 36, 47–49; transportation of, 166–67; and Utah, 57t; and value of products, 51, 52f;

weaving of, 4, 5, 13, 22, 55, 222–23; and western wool, 56–58, 65, 67, 94, 114, 149, 226; and woolen industry, 25, 65, 239n58; and woolen tariff, 241n87; and wool industry, 47–51, 65–66, 149, 160, 239n59; and wool tariff, 65–67, 114, 149, 157, 194, 225, 240n69; and Wyoming, 57t, 226. *See also* Bond, Frank; Bond, George W.

wool industry: and Bond brothers, 147, 148, 149, 150, 152; and commission houses, 149; and foreign markets, 149; growth of, 96, 226; and mercantilists' operations, 86–88, 148, 149; and New Mexico, 88, 96, 226; profitability of, 147; and Santa Fe trade, 86; and US wool tariff, 65–67; and western wool industry, 46, 65, 75, 226; and woolen tariff, 65–66

Wooton, E. O., 109

World War I, 265n13, 267n2

World War II, 5

Wootton, Richens Lacy (Uncle Dick), 41, 42, 46

Wyoming, 57t, 78, 79–80, 99, 154, 164. *See also* sheep; wool